Shojo Beat

My love STORY!!

Story
KAZUNE
KAWAHARA

Art
ARUKO

7

My love STORY!!

7

CONTENTS

STORY Thus Far...

Takeo Goda, a first-year high school student, is a hot-blooded guy who is 6'6" tall and weighs 265 pounds. Boys look up to him, but the girls he falls in love with all end up liking his handsome best friend, Makoto Sunakawa! But all that changes when Takeo saves Rinko Yamato from a groper on the train, and she becomes his girlfriend. Girls other than Yamato begin to notice Takeo's charms, but Takeo only has eyes for Yamato. And now the two have finally shared their first kiss!

On Valentine's Day, Takeo is overjoyed to receive his first-ever chocolate given out of love. Sunakawa, on the other hand, has always received chocolate from all kinds of girls—and every year he gets chocolate from a girl who never reveals her name...

Since his baby sister's birth, Takeo's senses have grown even keener. When he detects an unfamiliar presence following him and Sunakawa, he tracks down its source and finds himself face-to-face with the girl who's been anonymously giving Sunakawa chocolate for so many years...!!

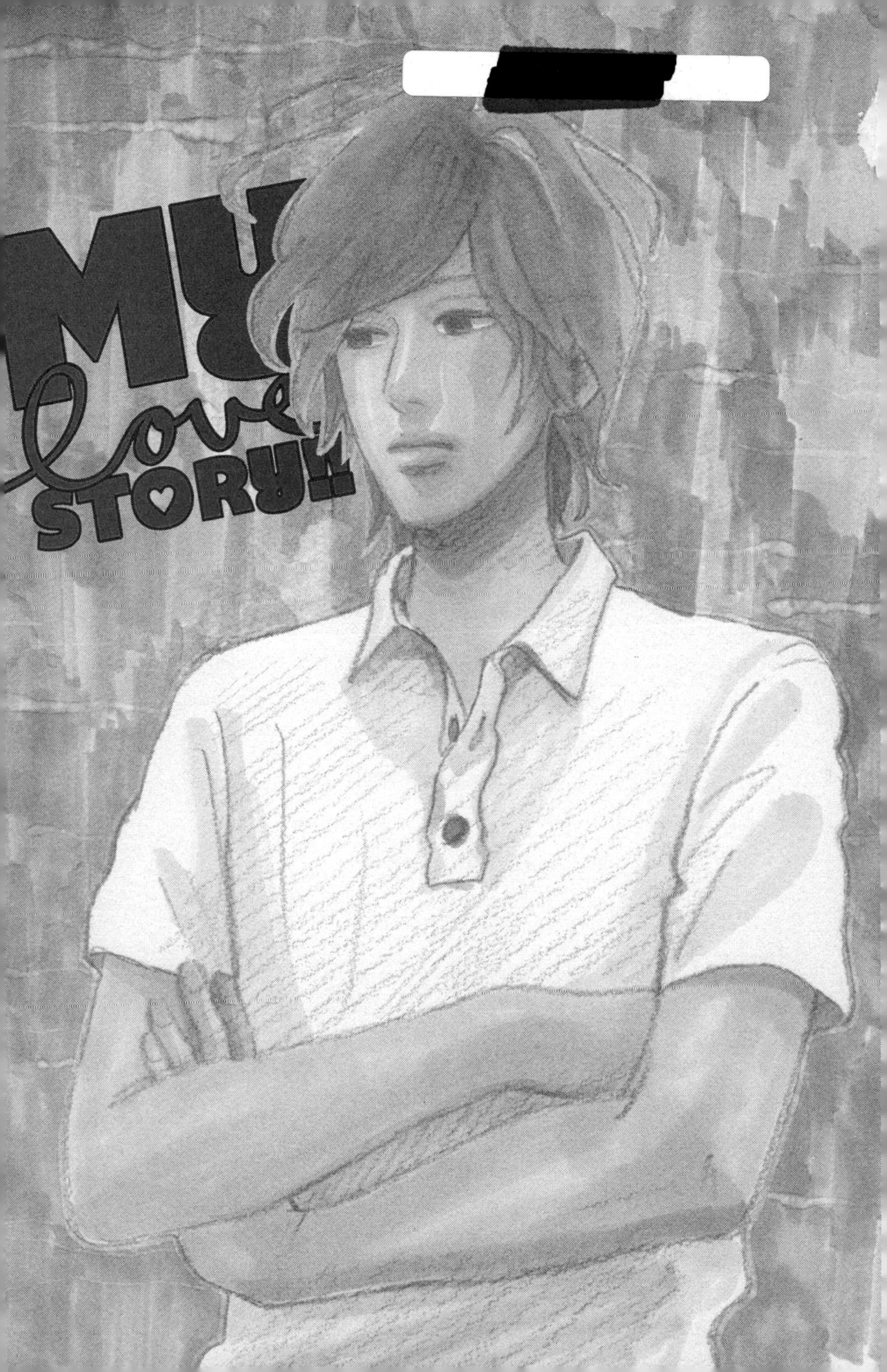
[redacted]
MY love STORY!!

IT'S VOLUME 7!!

THANK YOU SO MUCH!

I'd like to thank all my readers, Kawahara Sensei... ♡

...and my editor!

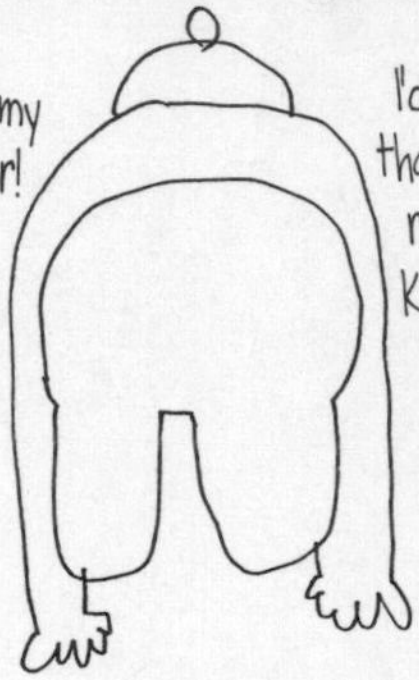

It feels like volume 1 was just yesterday, but we're already on volume 7! Things move so quickly... And so much has happened to Takeo and his friends!

I chewed so much gum that my tooth filling came off—or more accurately, the cap came off.

I chew tons of gum when I'm working on manga pages. I've got a pack-a-day (or more) habit! So when I'm working on manga, it makes my jaw hurt so badly that it feels like it's about to break. And yet I just can't make myself stop.

A thing my kid (who's in preschool) just told me:

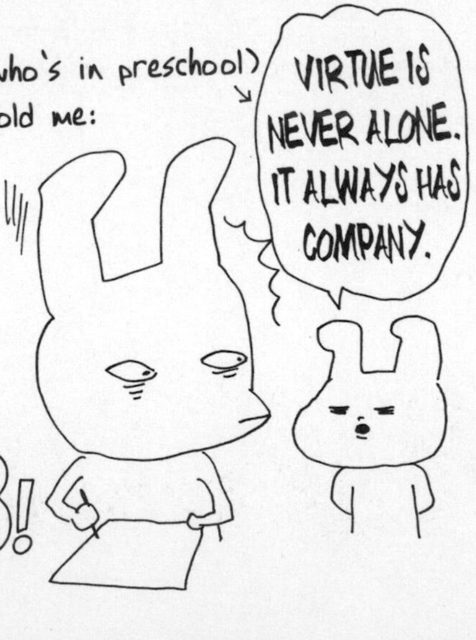
VIRTUE IS NEVER ALONE. IT ALWAYS HAS COMPANY.

That really freaked me out.

I HOPE WE'LL SEE YOU AGAIN IN **VOLUME 8!**

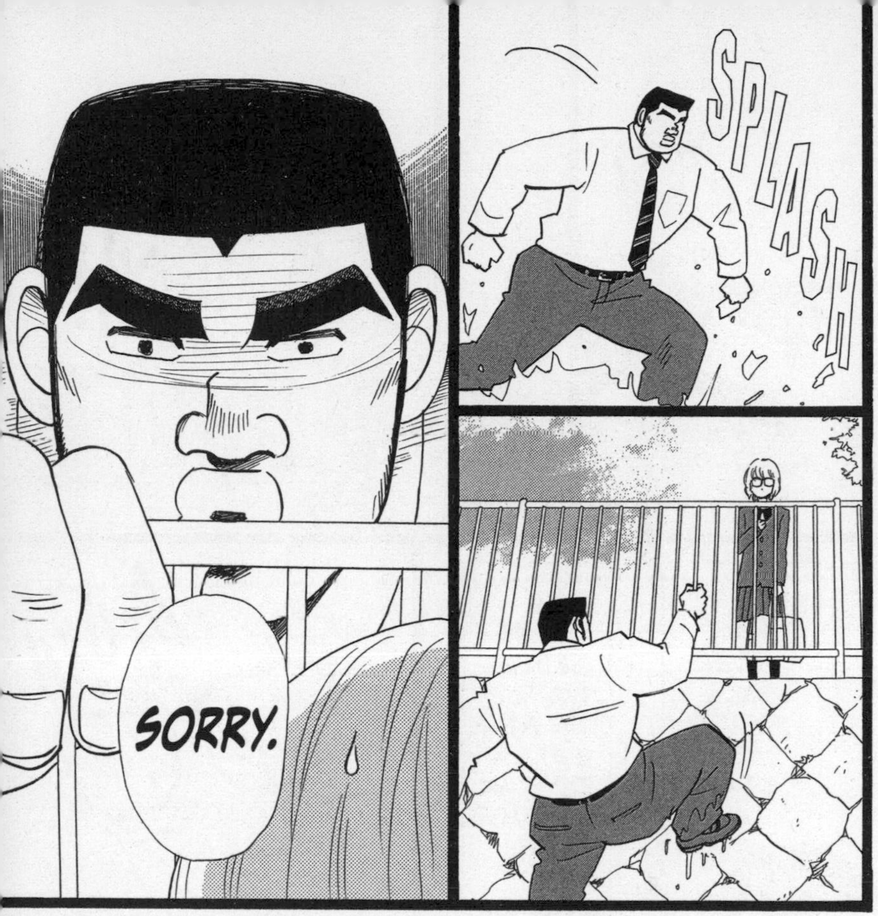
SPLASH
SORRY.

MY love STORY!!

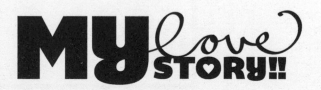

I MISUNDERSTOOD THE SITUATION.
AND... I READ YOUR LETTER.
Makoto Sunakaw
I don't need anything in return. Please like me back.
BLUSH
...HAS BEEN WRITING THE SAME LETTER TO SUNA ALL THIS TIME...
...AND NEVER EVEN SIGNED HER NAME.
THIS GIRL ...
SORRY FOR RUINING IT.

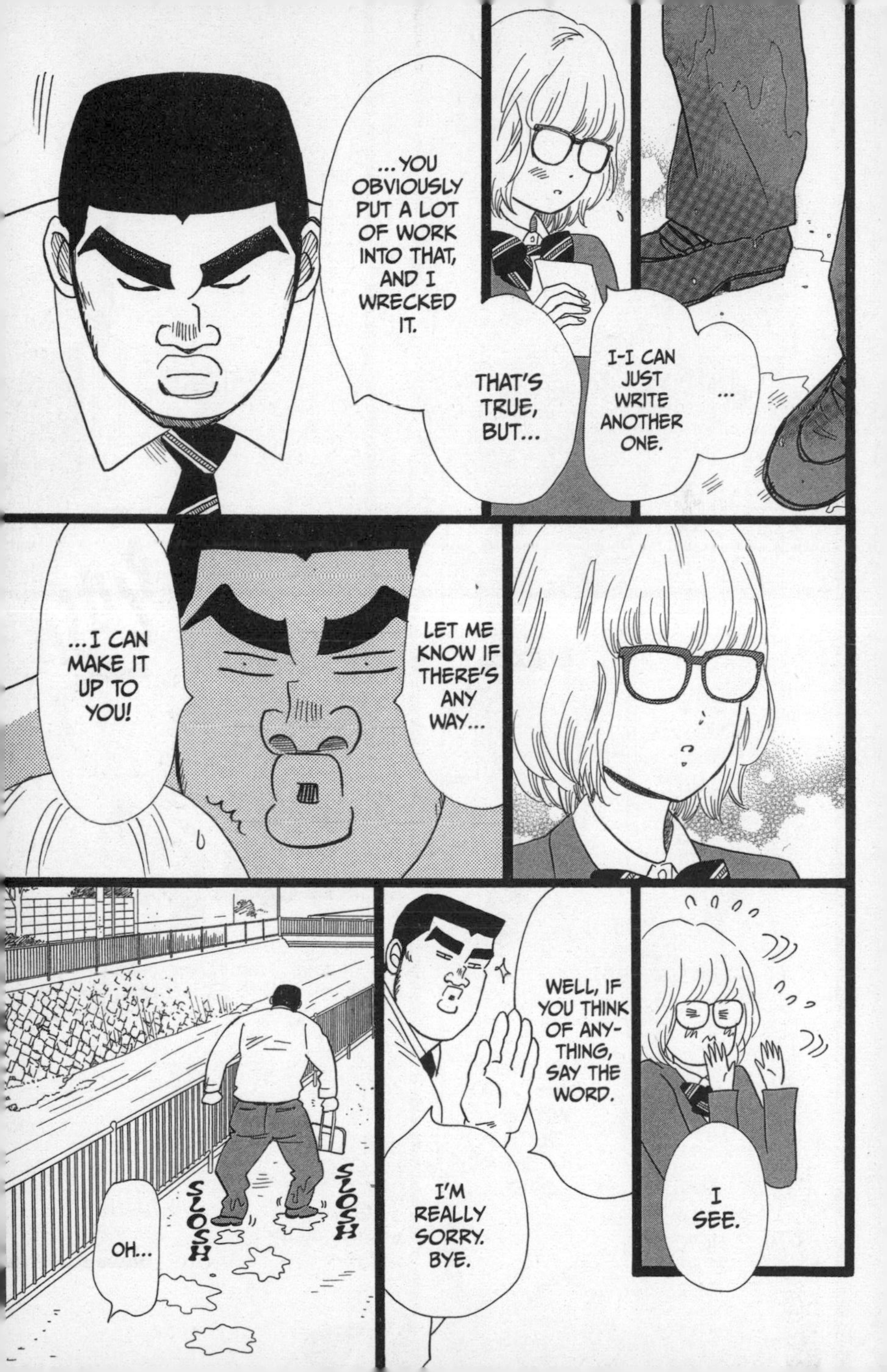
I-I CAN JUST WRITE ANOTHER ONE.
...
THAT'S TRUE, BUT...
...YOU OBVIOUSLY PUT A LOT OF WORK INTO THAT, AND I WRECKED IT.
LET ME KNOW IF THERE'S ANY WAY...
...I CAN MAKE IT UP TO YOU!
I SEE.
WELL, IF YOU THINK OF ANY-THING, SAY THE WORD.
I'M REALLY SORRY. BYE.
SLOSH
SLOSH
OH...

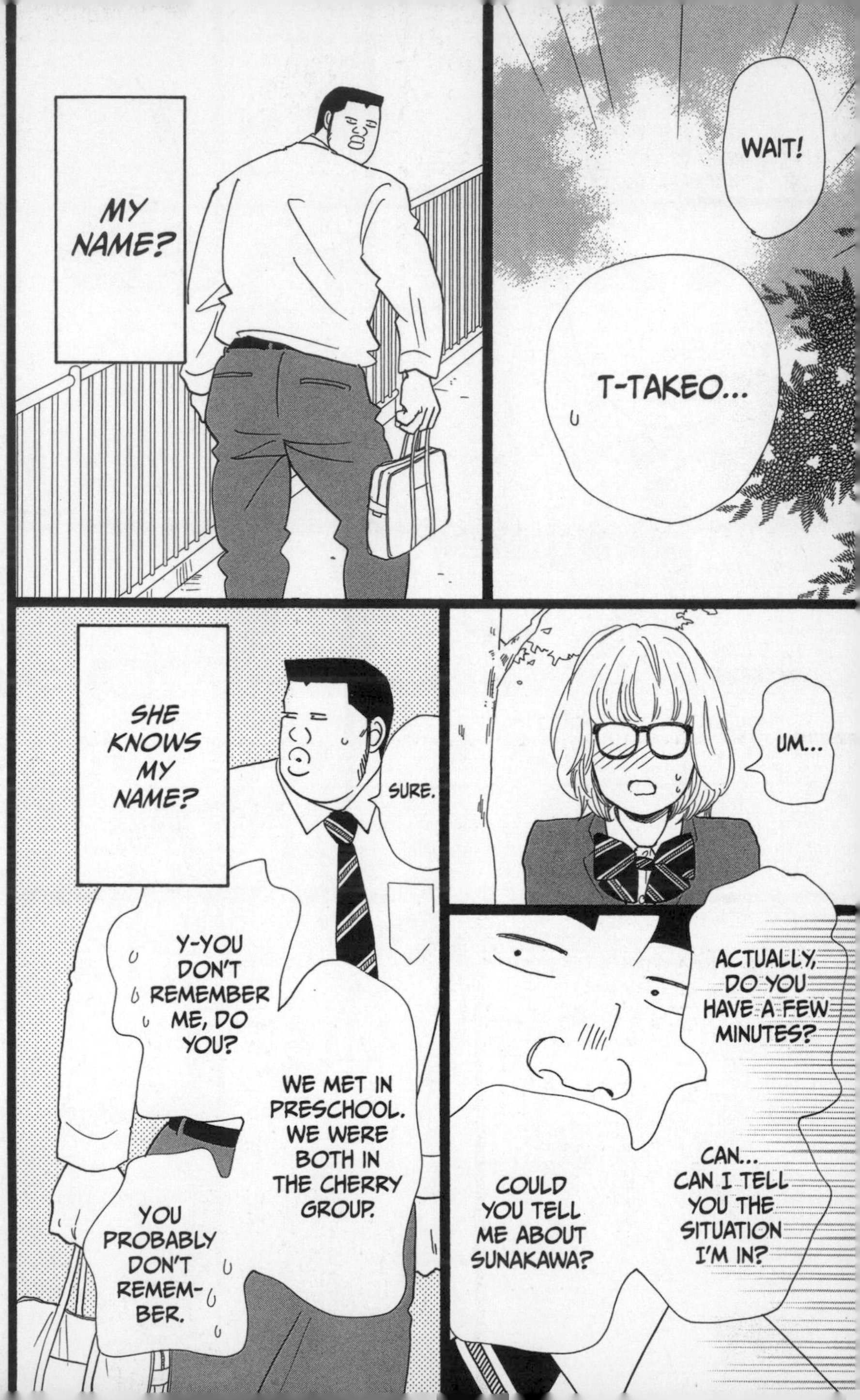
WAIT!
T-TAKEO...
MY NAME?
UM...
ACTUALLY, DO YOU HAVE A FEW MINUTES?
CAN... CAN I TELL YOU THE SITUATION I'M IN?
COULD YOU TELL ME ABOUT SUNAKAWA?
SHE KNOWS MY NAME?
SURE.
Y-YOU DON'T REMEMBER ME, DO YOU?
WE MET IN PRESCHOOL. WE WERE BOTH IN THE CHERRY GROUP.
YOU PROBABLY DON'T REMEM-BER.

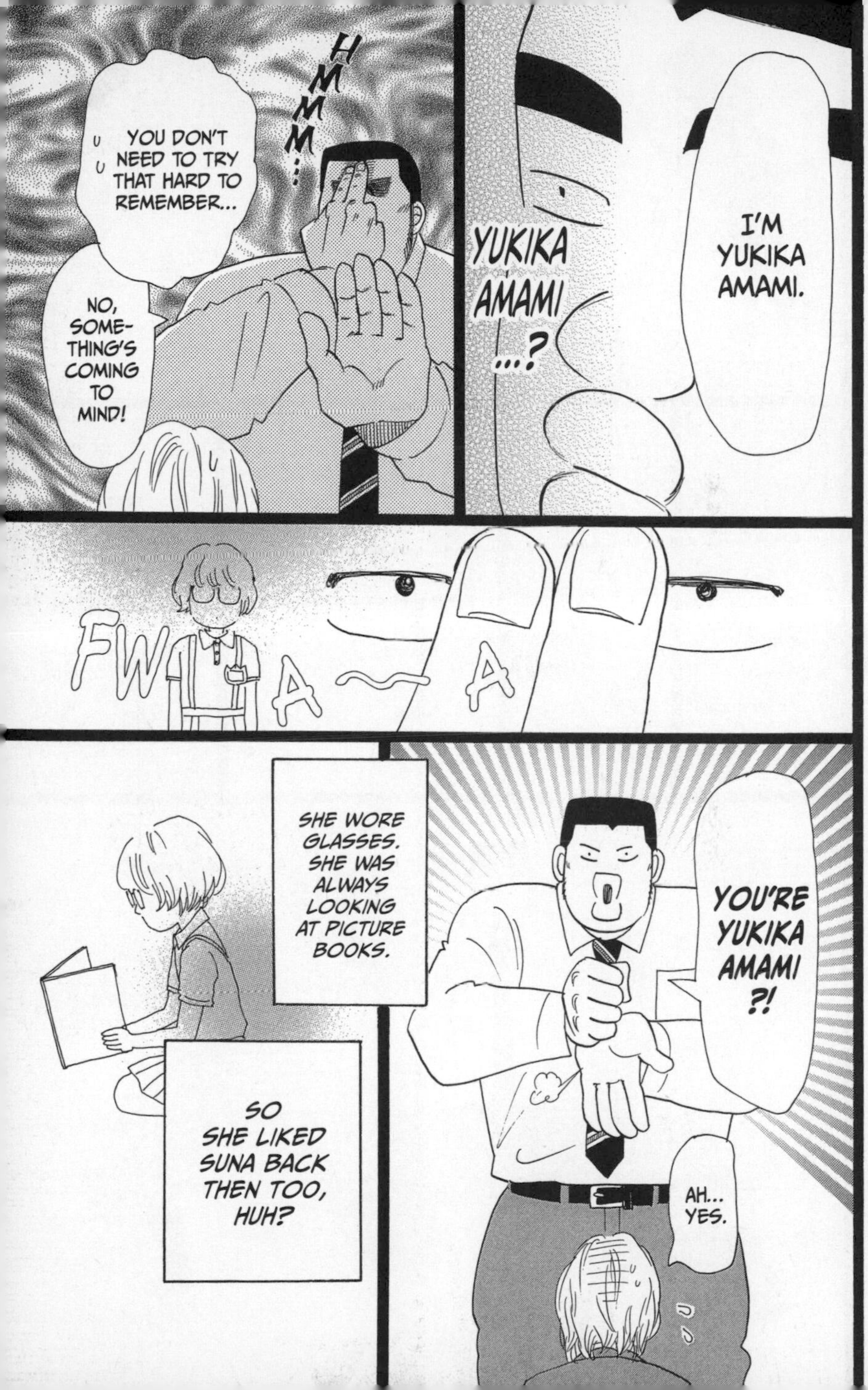
I'M YUKIKA AMAMI.
YUKIKA AMAMI ...?
HMMM...
YOU DON'T NEED TO TRY THAT HARD TO REMEMBER...
NO, SOMETHING'S COMING TO MIND!
FWA~A
YOU'RE YUKIKA AMAMI?!
AH... YES.
SHE WORE GLASSES. SHE WAS ALWAYS LOOKING AT PICTURE BOOKS.
SO SHE LIKED SUNA BACK THEN TOO, HUH?

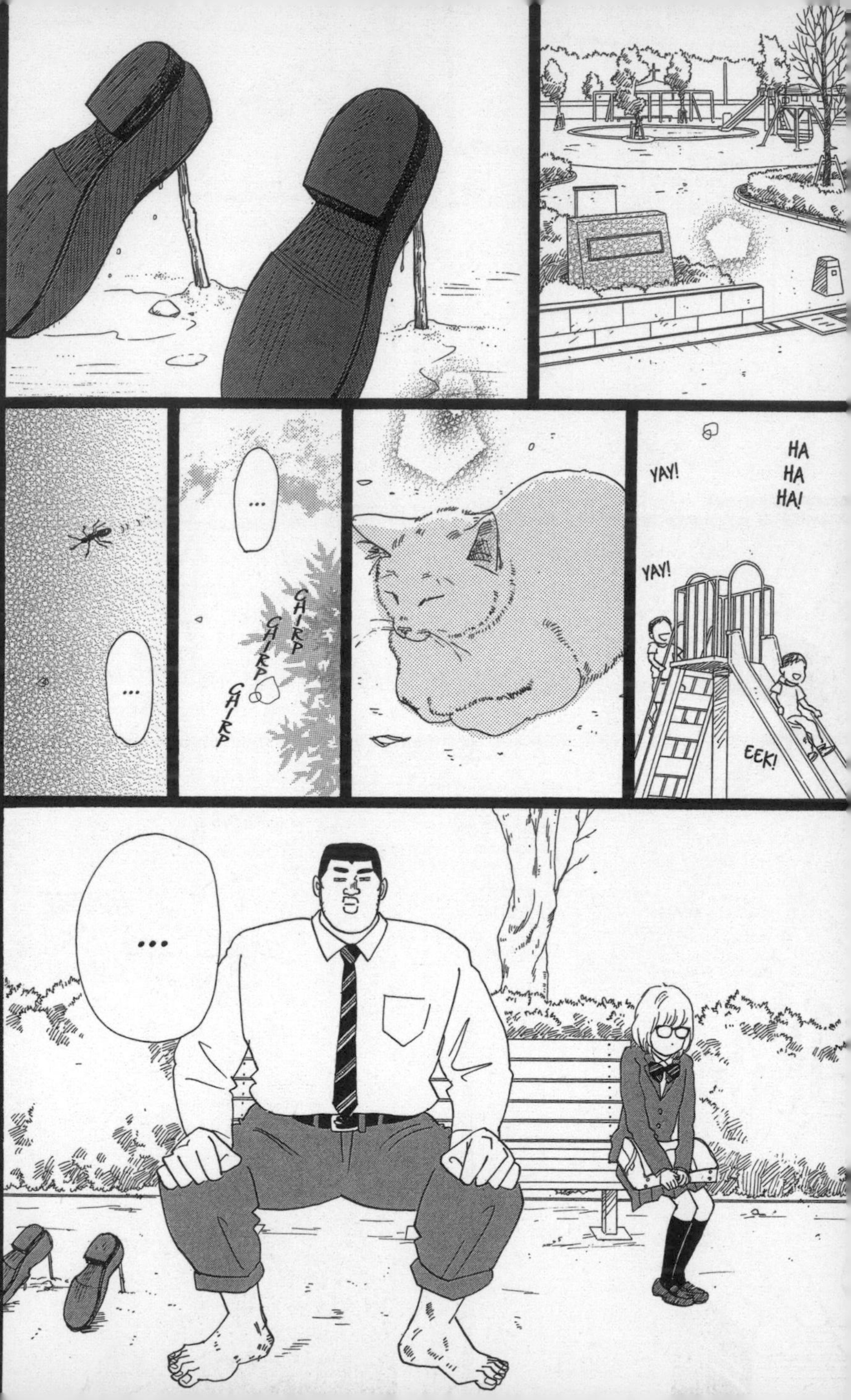
HA HA HA!
YAY!
YAY!
EEK!
...
CHIRP CHIRP
CHIRP CHIRP
...
...

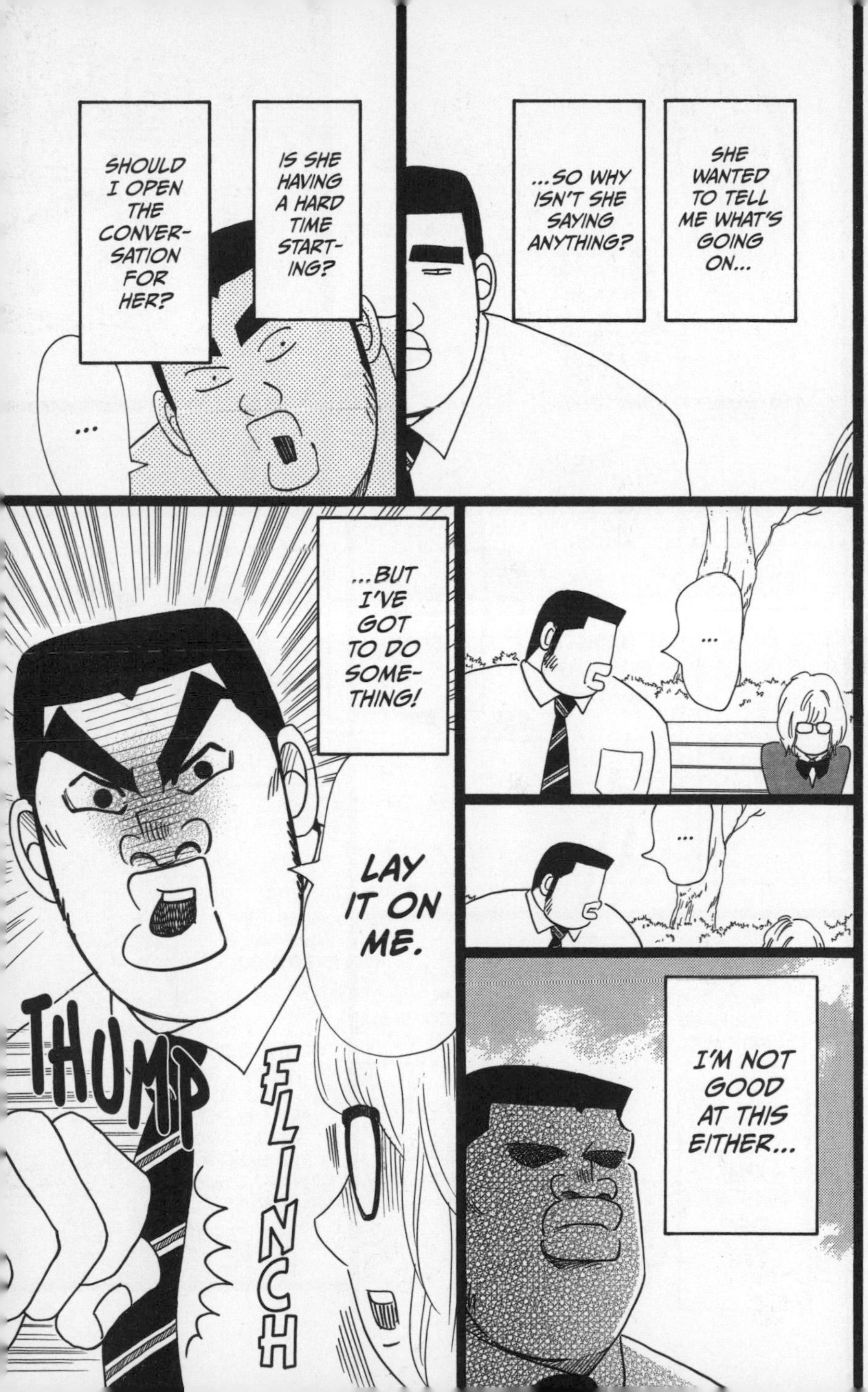
SHE WANTED TO TELL ME WHAT'S GOING ON...
...SO WHY ISN'T SHE SAYING ANYTHING?
IS SHE HAVING A HARD TIME STARTING?
SHOULD I OPEN THE CONVERSATION FOR HER?
...
...
...
I'M NOT GOOD AT THIS EITHER...
...BUT I'VE GOT TO DO SOMETHING!
LAY IT ON ME.
THUMP
FLINCH

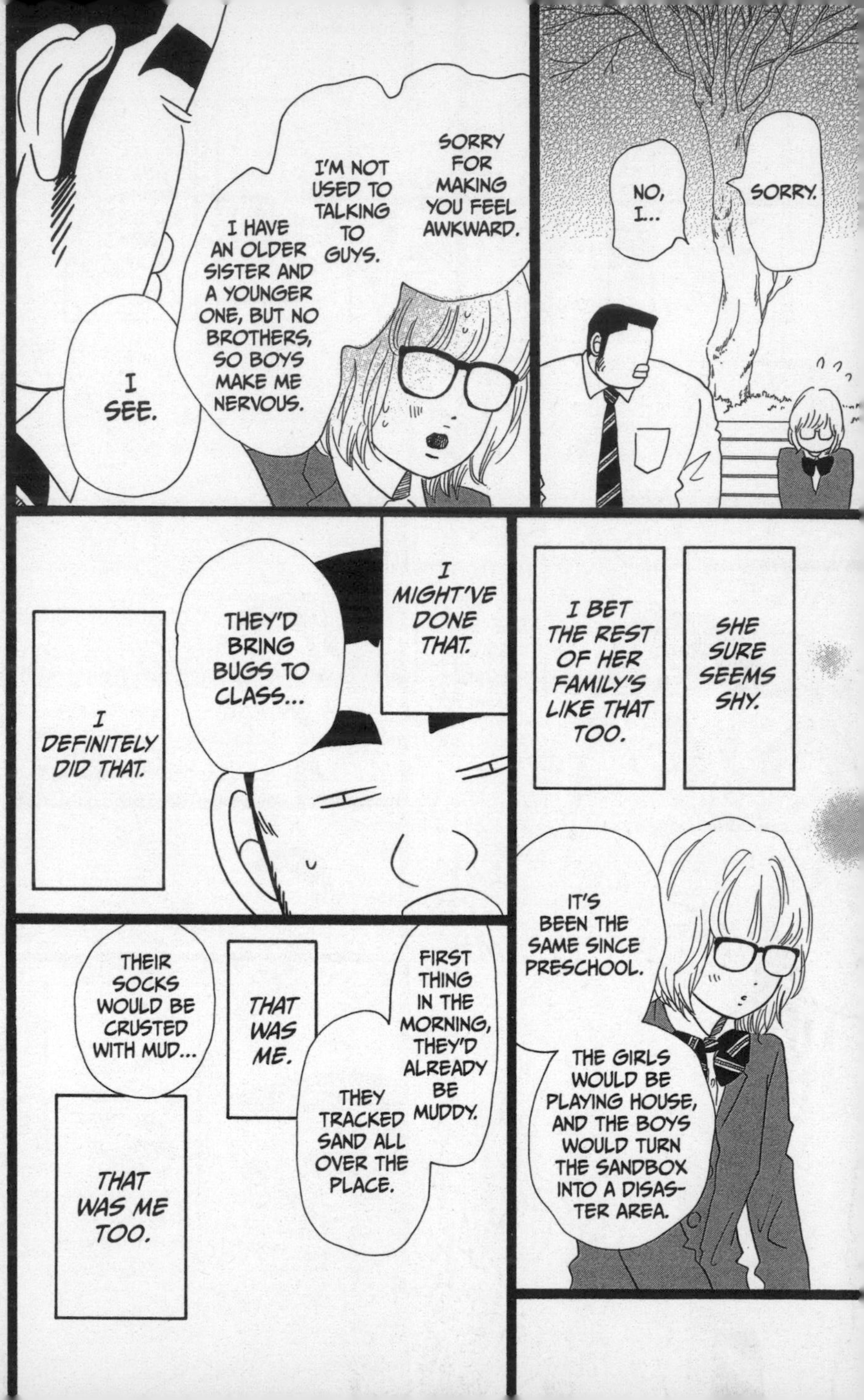
SORRY.
NO, I...
SORRY FOR MAKING YOU FEEL AWKWARD.
I'M NOT USED TO TALKING TO GUYS.
I HAVE AN OLDER SISTER AND A YOUNGER ONE, BUT NO BROTHERS, SO BOYS MAKE ME NERVOUS.
I SEE.
SHE SURE SEEMS SHY.
I BET THE REST OF HER FAMILY'S LIKE THAT TOO.
IT'S BEEN THE SAME SINCE PRESCHOOL.
THE GIRLS WOULD BE PLAYING HOUSE, AND THE BOYS WOULD TURN THE SANDBOX INTO A DISASTER AREA.
THEY'D BRING BUGS TO CLASS...
I MIGHT'VE DONE THAT.
I DEFINITELY DID THAT.
FIRST THING IN THE MORNING, THEY'D ALREADY BE MUDDY.
THEY TRACKED SAND ALL OVER THE PLACE.
THAT WAS ME.
THEIR SOCKS WOULD BE CRUSTED WITH MUD...
THAT WAS ME TOO.

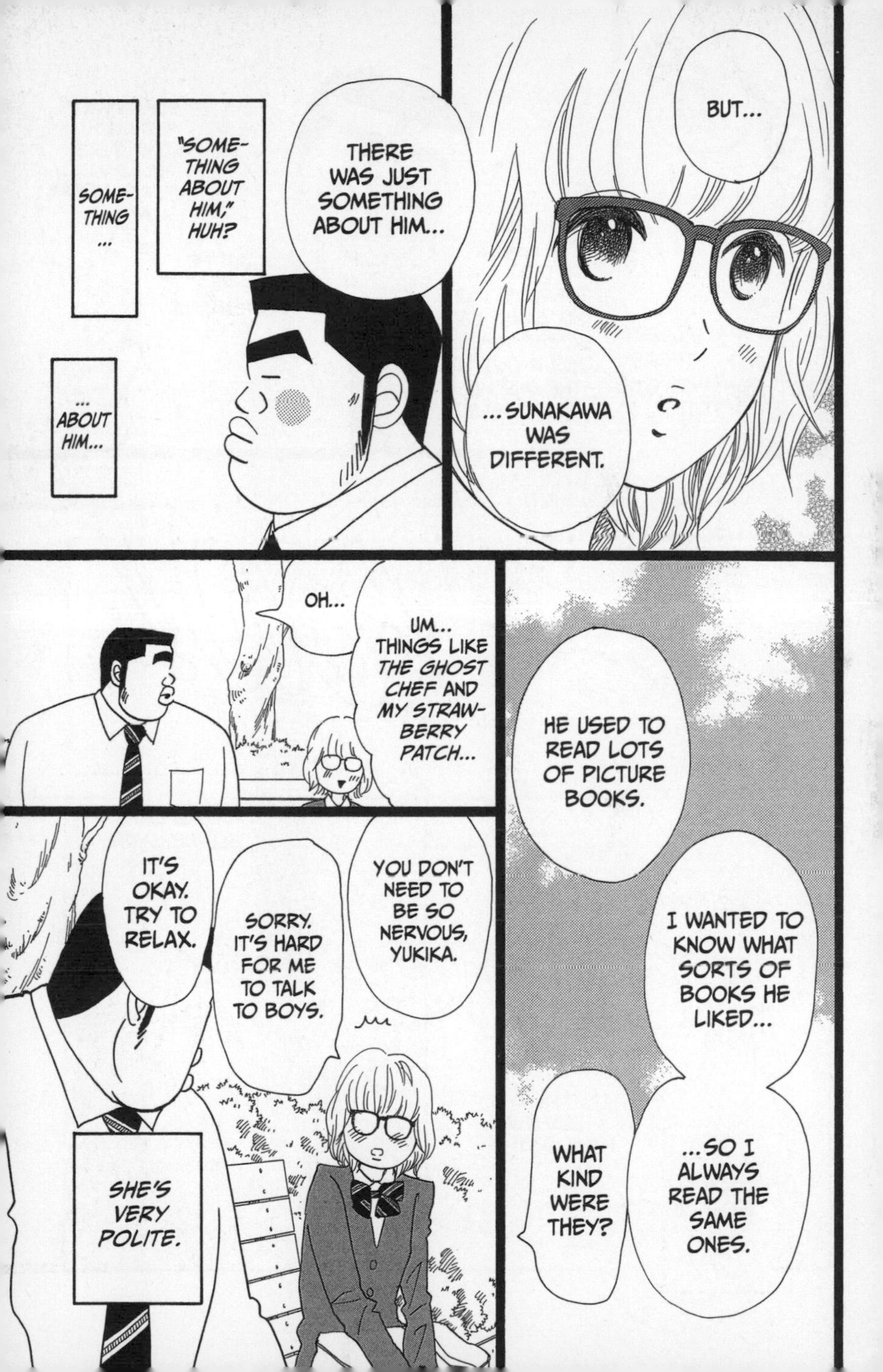
BUT...
...SUNAKAWA WAS DIFFERENT.
THERE WAS JUST SOMETHING ABOUT HIM...
"SOMETHING ABOUT HIM," HUH?
SOMETHING...
...ABOUT HIM...
HE USED TO READ LOTS OF PICTURE BOOKS.
I WANTED TO KNOW WHAT SORTS OF BOOKS HE LIKED...
...SO I ALWAYS READ THE SAME ONES.
WHAT KIND WERE THEY?
UM... THINGS LIKE *THE GHOST CHEF* AND *MY STRAWBERRY PATCH*...
OH...
YOU DON'T NEED TO BE SO NERVOUS, YUKIKA.
SORRY. IT'S HARD FOR ME TO TALK TO BOYS.
IT'S OKAY. TRY TO RELAX.
SHE'S VERY POLITE.

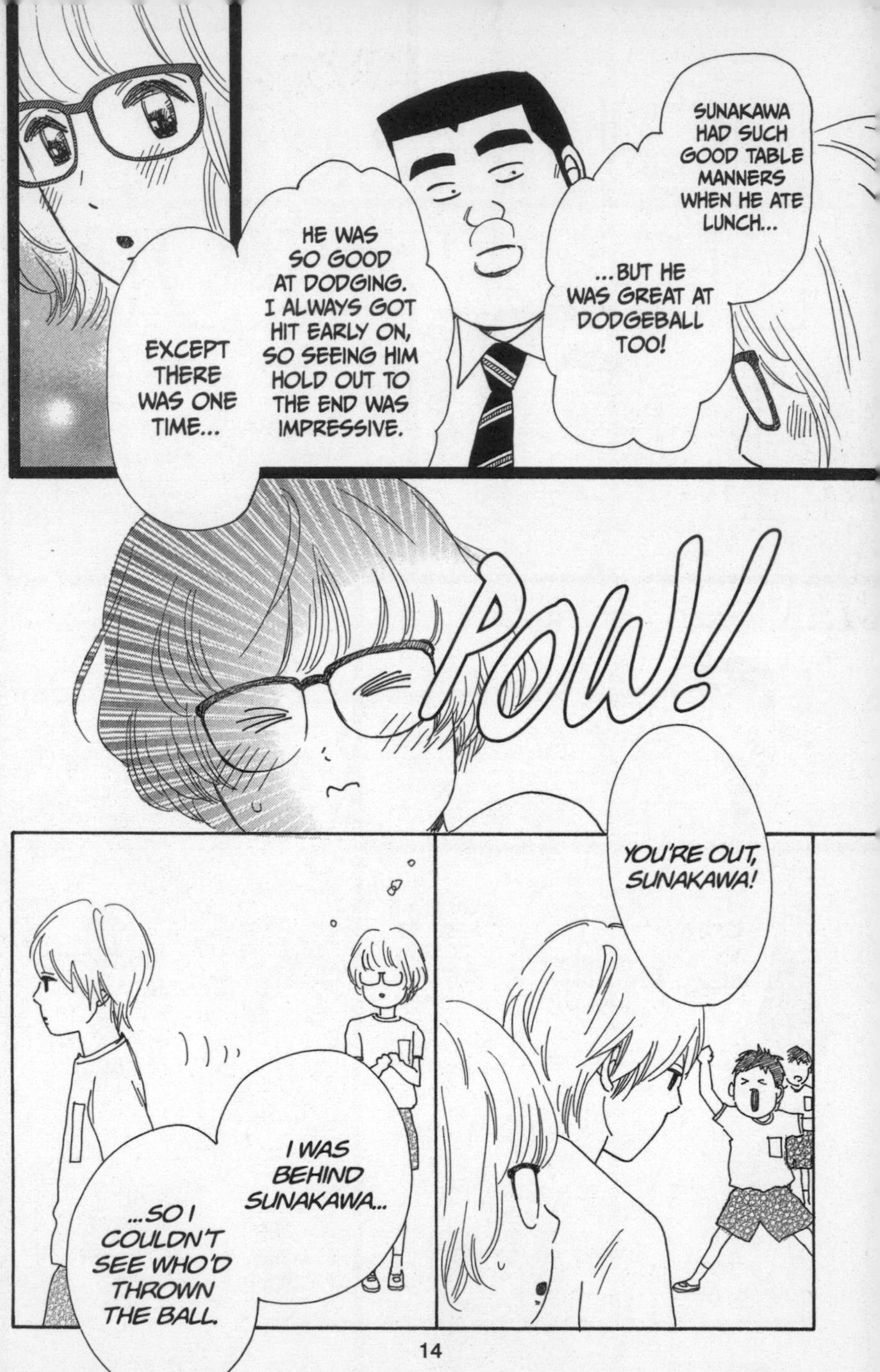
SUNAKAWA HAD SUCH GOOD TABLE MANNERS WHEN HE ATE LUNCH...
...BUT HE WAS GREAT AT DODGEBALL TOO!
HE WAS SO GOOD AT DODGING. I ALWAYS GOT HIT EARLY ON, SO SEEING HIM HOLD OUT TO THE END WAS IMPRESSIVE.
EXCEPT THERE WAS ONE TIME...
POW!
YOU'RE OUT, SUNAKAWA!
I WAS BEHIND SUNAKAWA...
...SO I COULDN'T SEE WHO'D THROWN THE BALL.

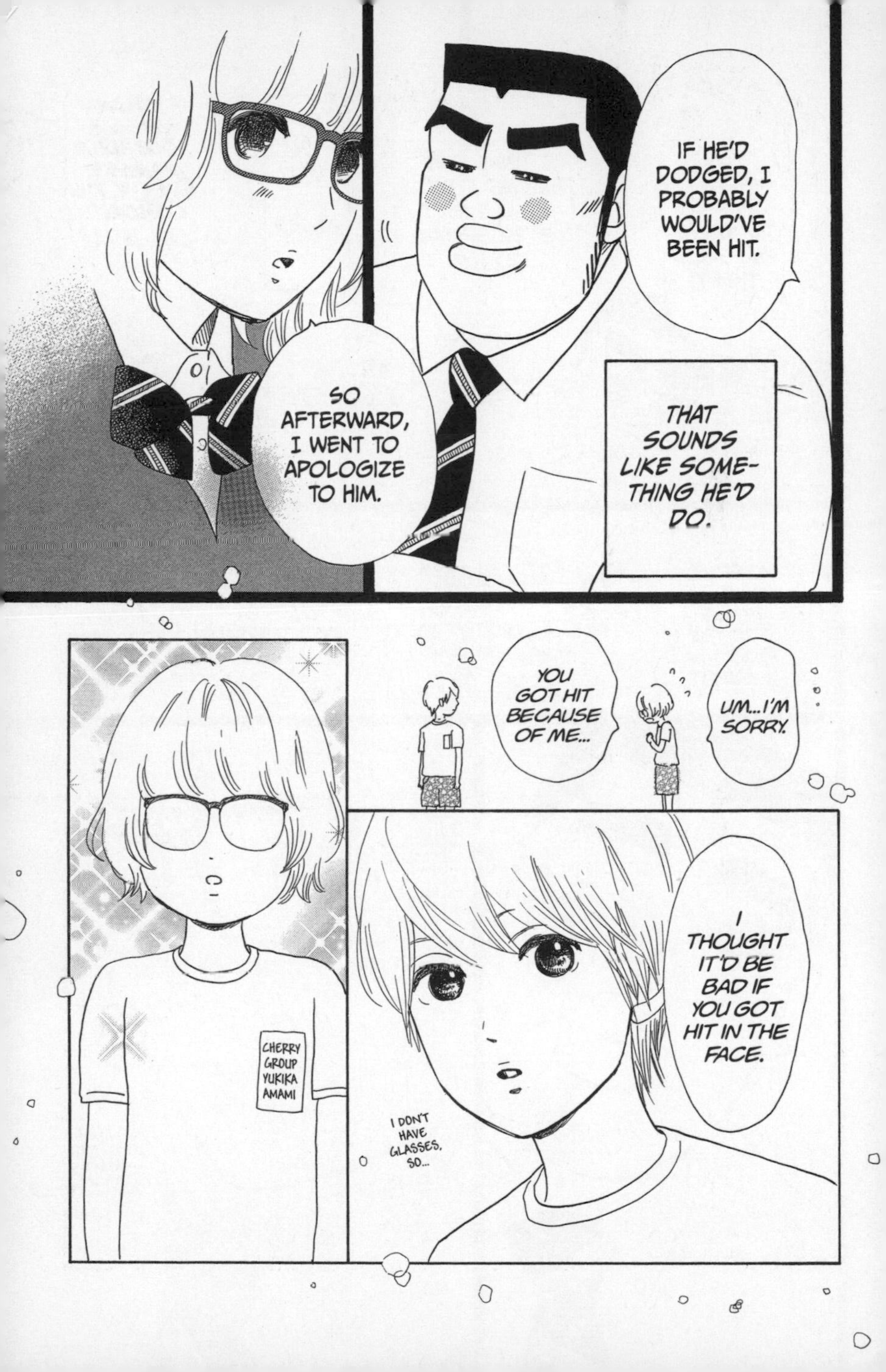
IF HE'D DODGED, I PROBABLY WOULD'VE BEEN HIT.
THAT SOUNDS LIKE SOME-THING HE'D DO.
SO AFTERWARD, I WENT TO APOLOGIZE TO HIM.
UM...I'M SORRY.
YOU GOT HIT BECAUSE OF ME...
I THOUGHT IT'D BE BAD IF YOU GOT HIT IN THE FACE.
I DON'T HAVE GLASSES, SO...
CHERRY GROUP YUKIKA AMAMI

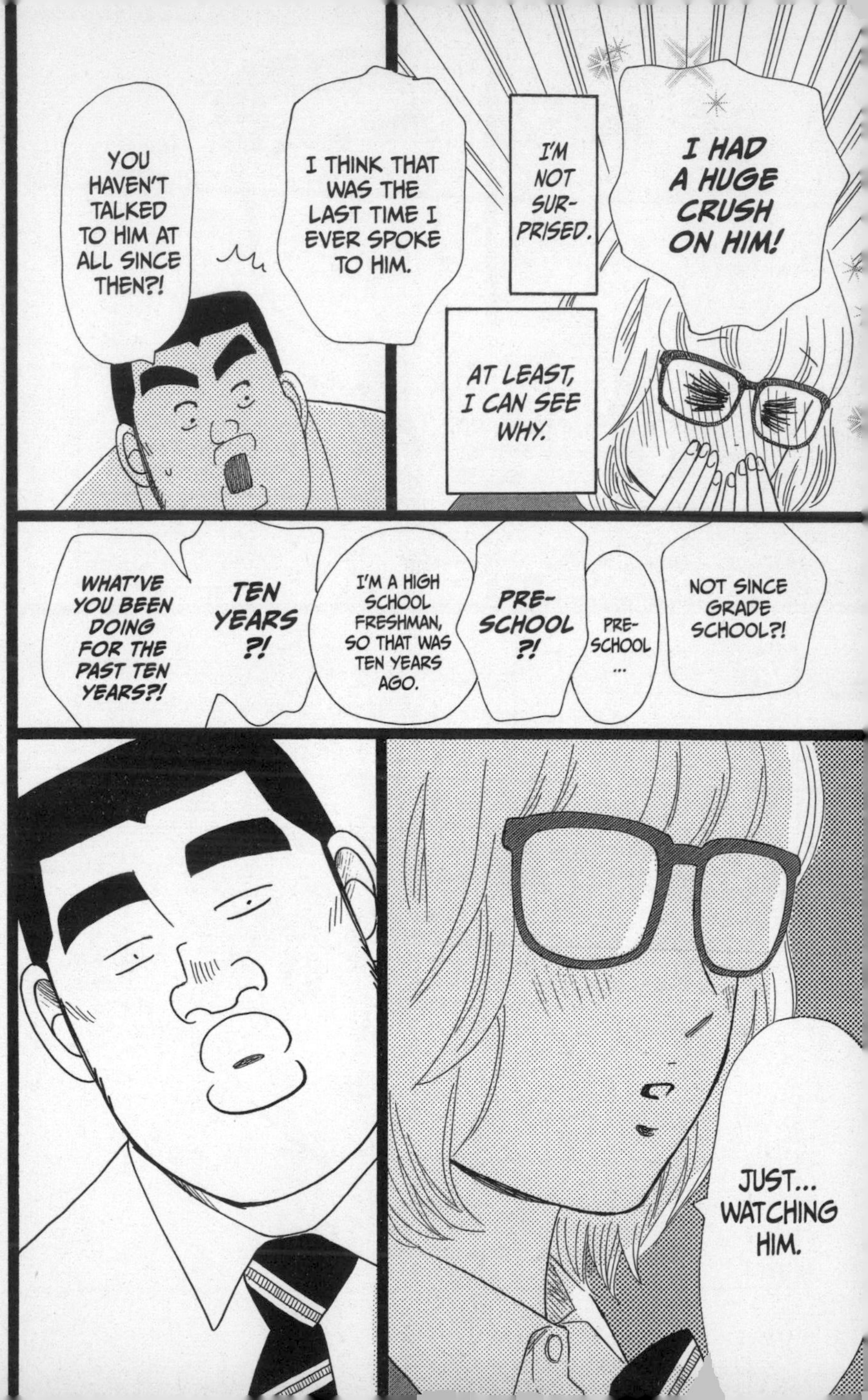
I HAD A HUGE CRUSH ON HIM!
I'M NOT SURPRISED.
AT LEAST, I CAN SEE WHY.
I THINK THAT WAS THE LAST TIME I EVER SPOKE TO HIM.
YOU HAVEN'T TALKED TO HIM AT ALL SINCE THEN?!
NOT SINCE GRADE SCHOOL?!
PRE-SCHOOL...
PRE-SCHOOL?!
I'M A HIGH SCHOOL FRESHMAN, SO THAT WAS TEN YEARS AGO.
TEN YEARS?!
WHAT'VE YOU BEEN DOING FOR THE PAST TEN YEARS?!
JUST... WATCHING HIM.

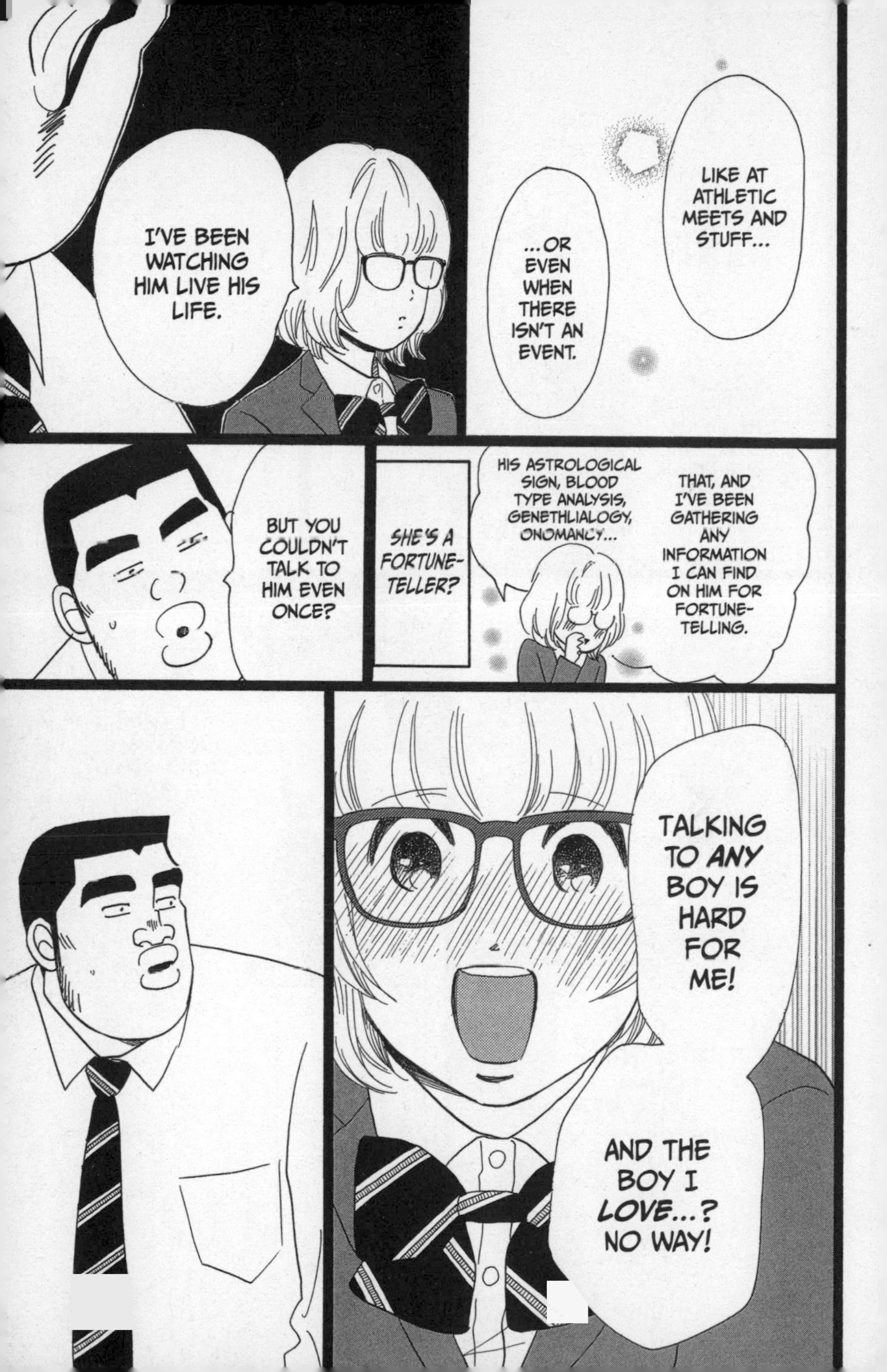
LIKE AT ATHLETIC MEETS AND STUFF...
...OR EVEN WHEN THERE ISN'T AN EVENT.
I'VE BEEN WATCHING HIM LIVE HIS LIFE.
THAT, AND I'VE BEEN GATHERING ANY INFORMATION I CAN FIND ON HIM FOR FORTUNE-TELLING.
HIS ASTROLOGICAL SIGN, BLOOD TYPE ANALYSIS, GENETHLIALOGY, ONOMANCY...
SHE'S A FORTUNE-TELLER?
BUT YOU COULDN'T TALK TO HIM EVEN ONCE?
TALKING TO *ANY* BOY IS HARD FOR ME!
AND THE BOY I *LOVE*...? NO WAY!

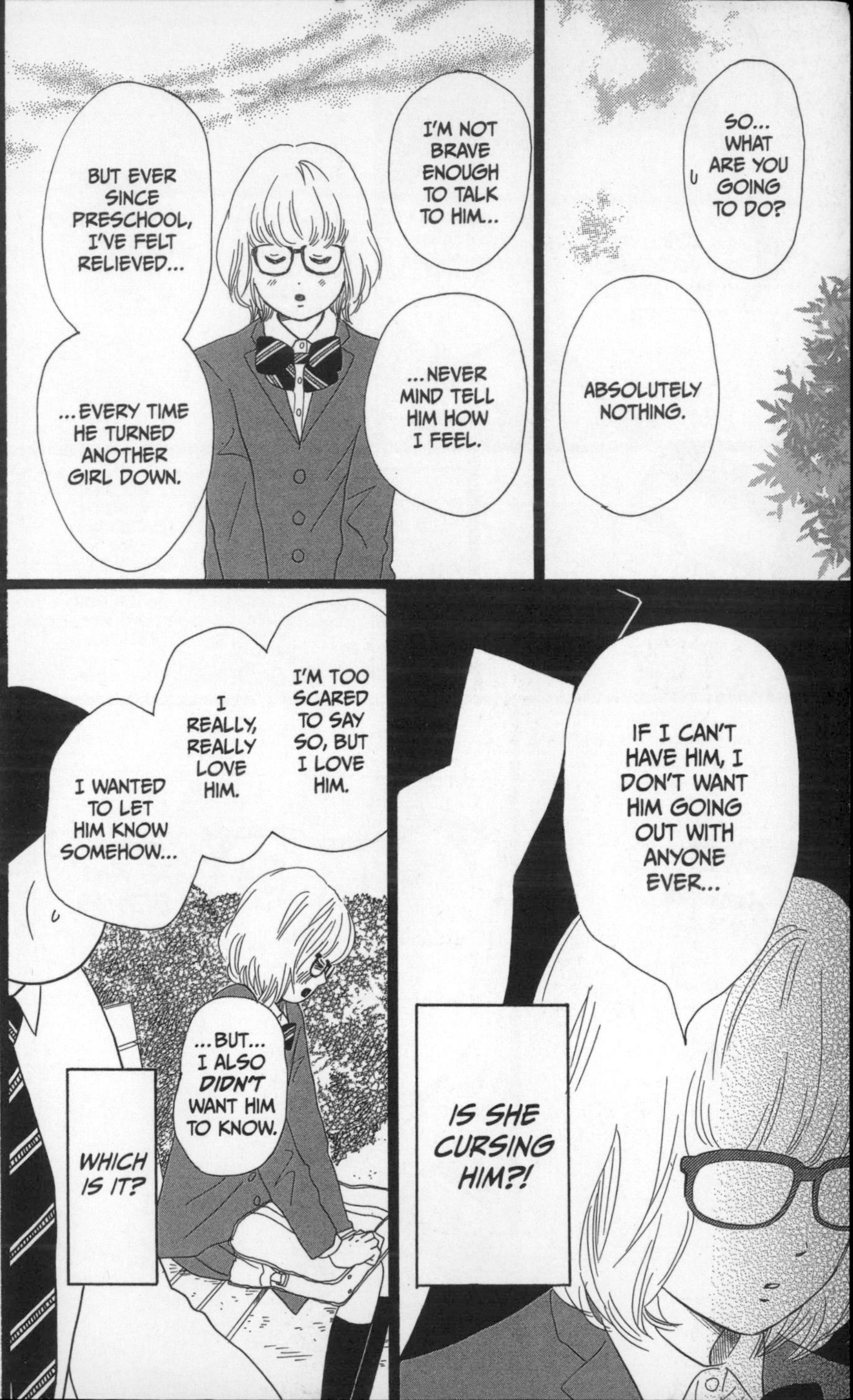

SO... WHAT ARE YOU GOING TO DO?
ABSOLUTELY NOTHING.
I'M NOT BRAVE ENOUGH TO TALK TO HIM...
...NEVER MIND TELL HIM HOW I FEEL.
BUT EVER SINCE PRESCHOOL, I'VE FELT RELIEVED...
...EVERY TIME HE TURNED ANOTHER GIRL DOWN.
IF I CAN'T HAVE HIM, I DON'T WANT HIM GOING OUT WITH ANYONE EVER...
IS SHE CURSING HIM?!
I'M TOO SCARED TO SAY SO, BUT I LOVE HIM.
I REALLY, REALLY LOVE HIM.
I WANTED TO LET HIM KNOW SOMEHOW...
...BUT... I ALSO *DIDN'T* WANT HIM TO KNOW.
WHICH IS IT?

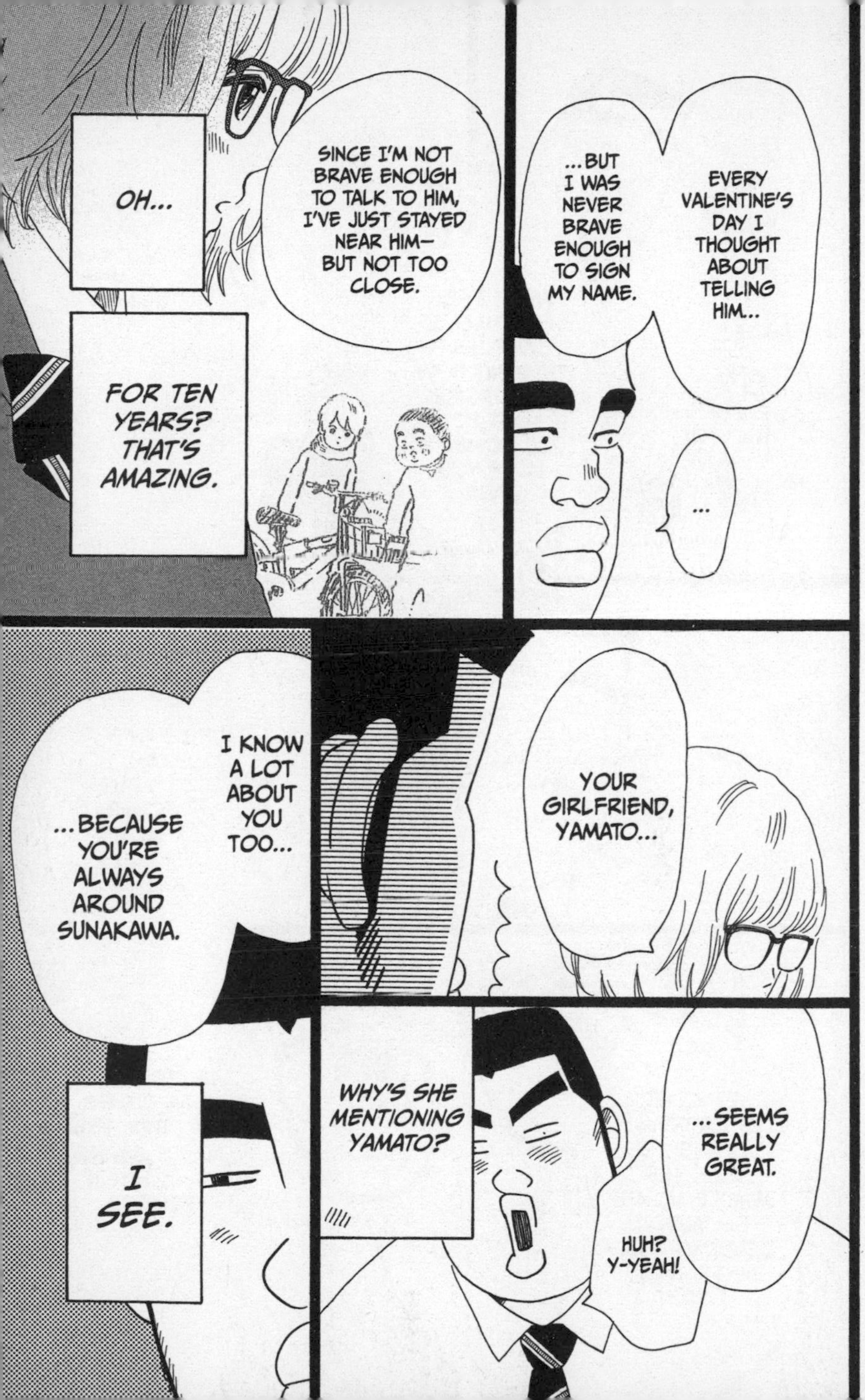
EVERY VALENTINE'S DAY I THOUGHT ABOUT TELLING HIM...
...BUT I WAS NEVER BRAVE ENOUGH TO SIGN MY NAME.
...
SINCE I'M NOT BRAVE ENOUGH TO TALK TO HIM, I'VE JUST STAYED NEAR HIM—BUT NOT TOO CLOSE.
OH...
FOR TEN YEARS? THAT'S AMAZING.
YOUR GIRLFRIEND, YAMATO...
...SEEMS REALLY GREAT.
HUH? Y-YEAH!
WHY'S SHE MENTIONING YAMATO?
I KNOW A LOT ABOUT YOU TOO...
...BECAUSE YOU'RE ALWAYS AROUND SUNAKAWA.
I SEE.

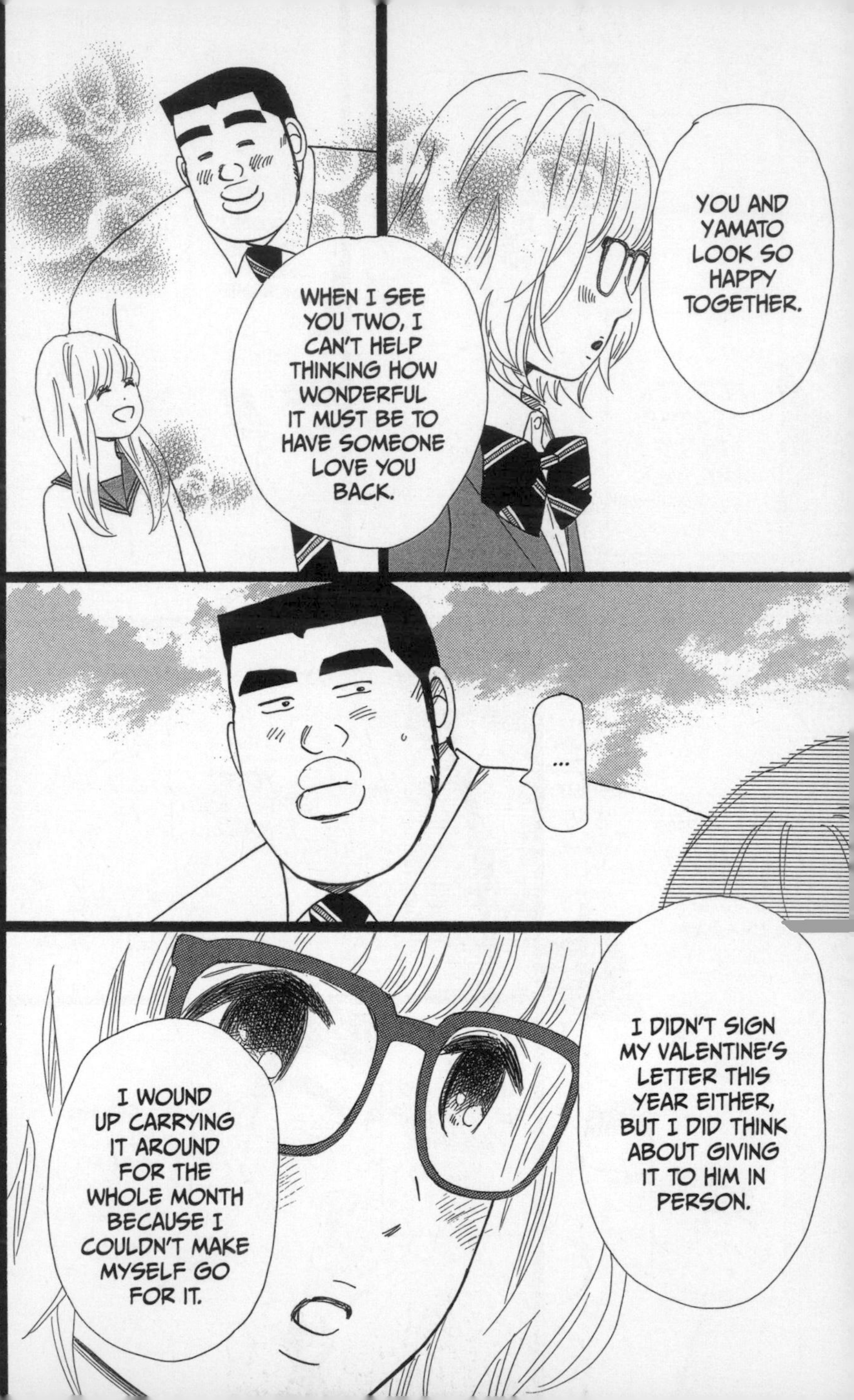
YOU AND YAMATO LOOK SO HAPPY TOGETHER.
WHEN I SEE YOU TWO, I CAN'T HELP THINKING HOW WONDERFUL IT MUST BE TO HAVE SOMEONE LOVE YOU BACK.
...
I DIDN'T SIGN MY VALENTINE'S LETTER THIS YEAR EITHER, BUT I DID THINK ABOUT GIVING IT TO HIM IN PERSON.
I WOUND UP CARRYING IT AROUND FOR THE WHOLE MONTH BECAUSE I COULDN'T MAKE MYSELF GO FOR IT.

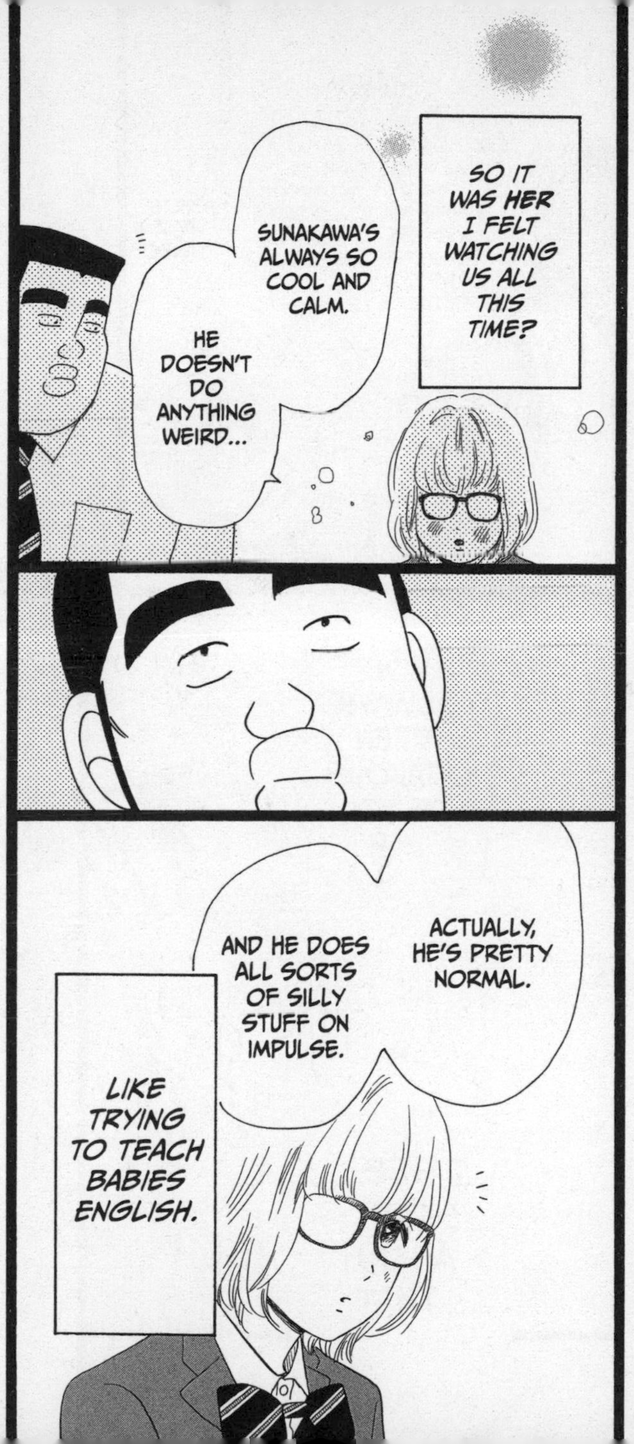
SO IT WAS HER I FELT WATCHING US ALL THIS TIME?
SUNAKAWA'S ALWAYS SO COOL AND CALM.
HE DOESN'T DO ANYTHING WEIRD...
ACTUALLY, HE'S PRETTY NORMAL.
AND HE DOES ALL SORTS OF SILLY STUFF ON IMPULSE.
LIKE TRYING TO TEACH BABIES ENGLISH.

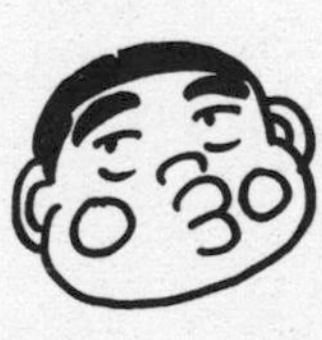

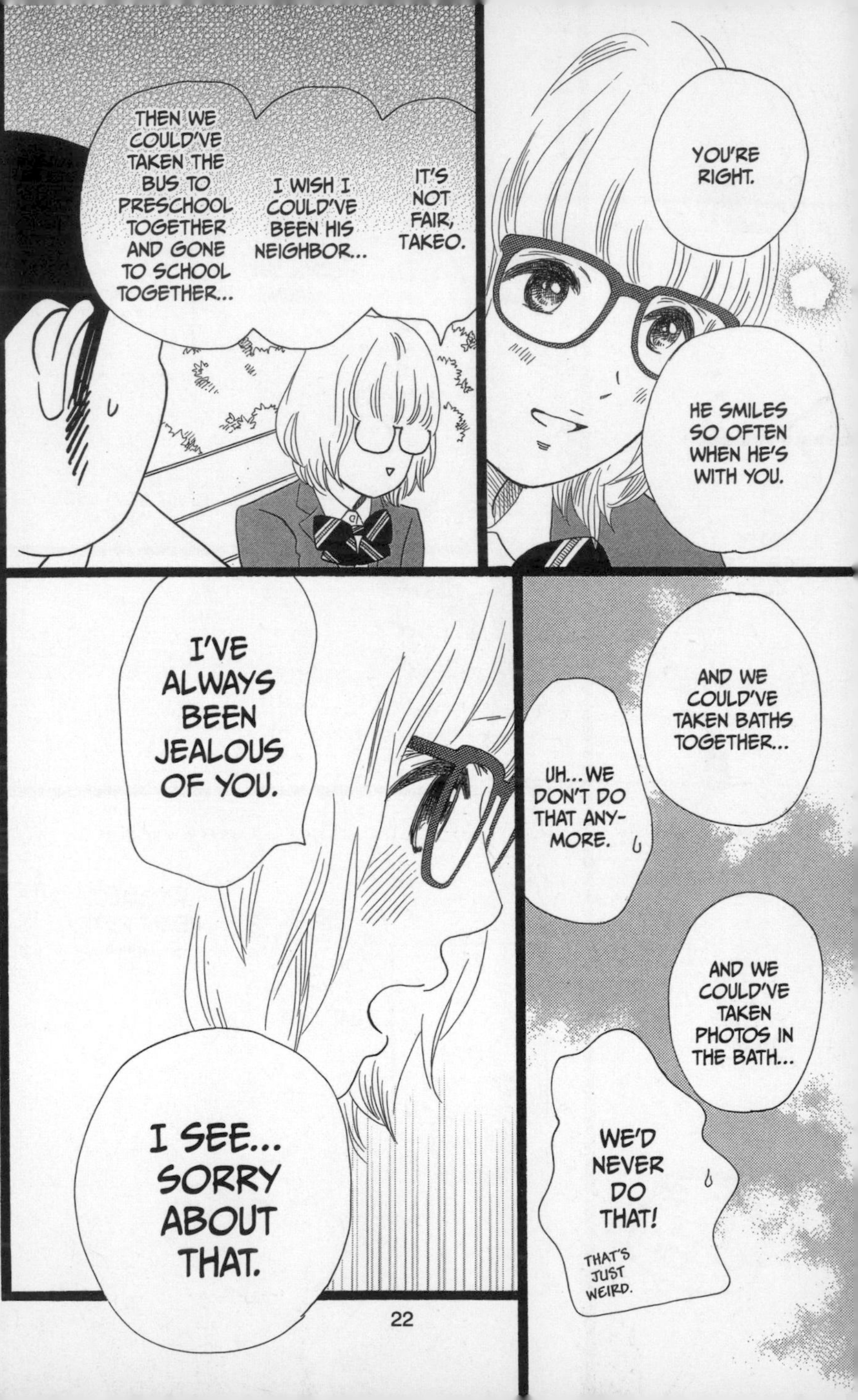
YOU'RE RIGHT.
HE SMILES SO OFTEN WHEN HE'S WITH YOU.
IT'S NOT FAIR, TAKEO.
I WISH I COULD'VE BEEN HIS NEIGHBOR...
THEN WE COULD'VE TAKEN THE BUS TO PRESCHOOL TOGETHER AND GONE TO SCHOOL TOGETHER...
AND WE COULD'VE TAKEN BATHS TOGETHER...
UH...WE DON'T DO THAT ANY-MORE.
AND WE COULD'VE TAKEN PHOTOS IN THE BATH...
WE'D NEVER DO THAT!
THAT'S JUST WEIRD.
I'VE ALWAYS BEEN JEALOUS OF YOU.
I SEE... SORRY ABOUT THAT.

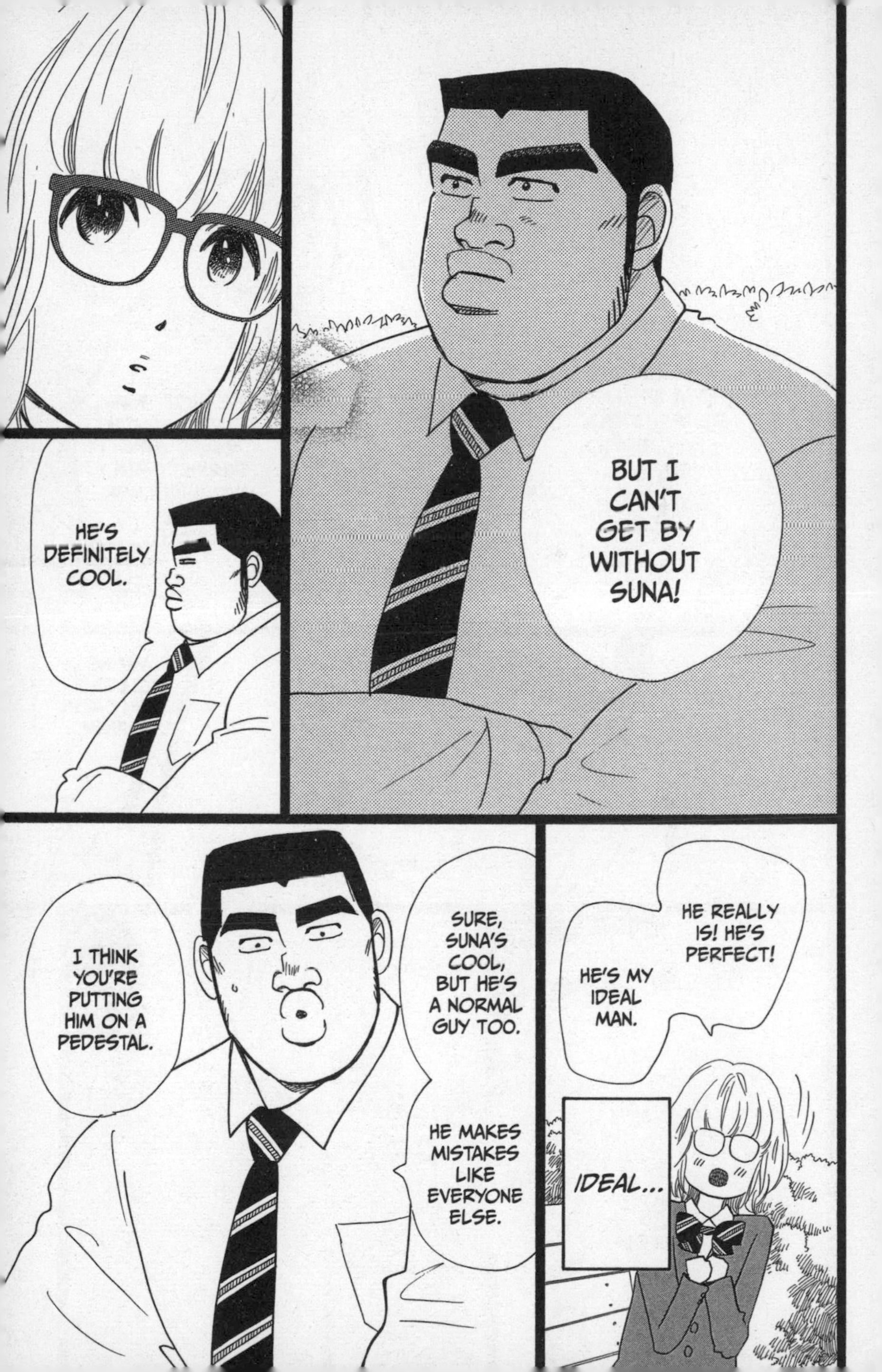
BUT I CAN'T GET BY WITHOUT SUNA!
HE'S DEFINITELY COOL.
HE REALLY IS! HE'S PERFECT!
HE'S MY IDEAL MAN.
IDEAL...
SURE, SUNA'S COOL, BUT HE'S A NORMAL GUY TOO.
HE MAKES MISTAKES LIKE EVERYONE ELSE.
I THINK YOU'RE PUTTING HIM ON A PEDESTAL.

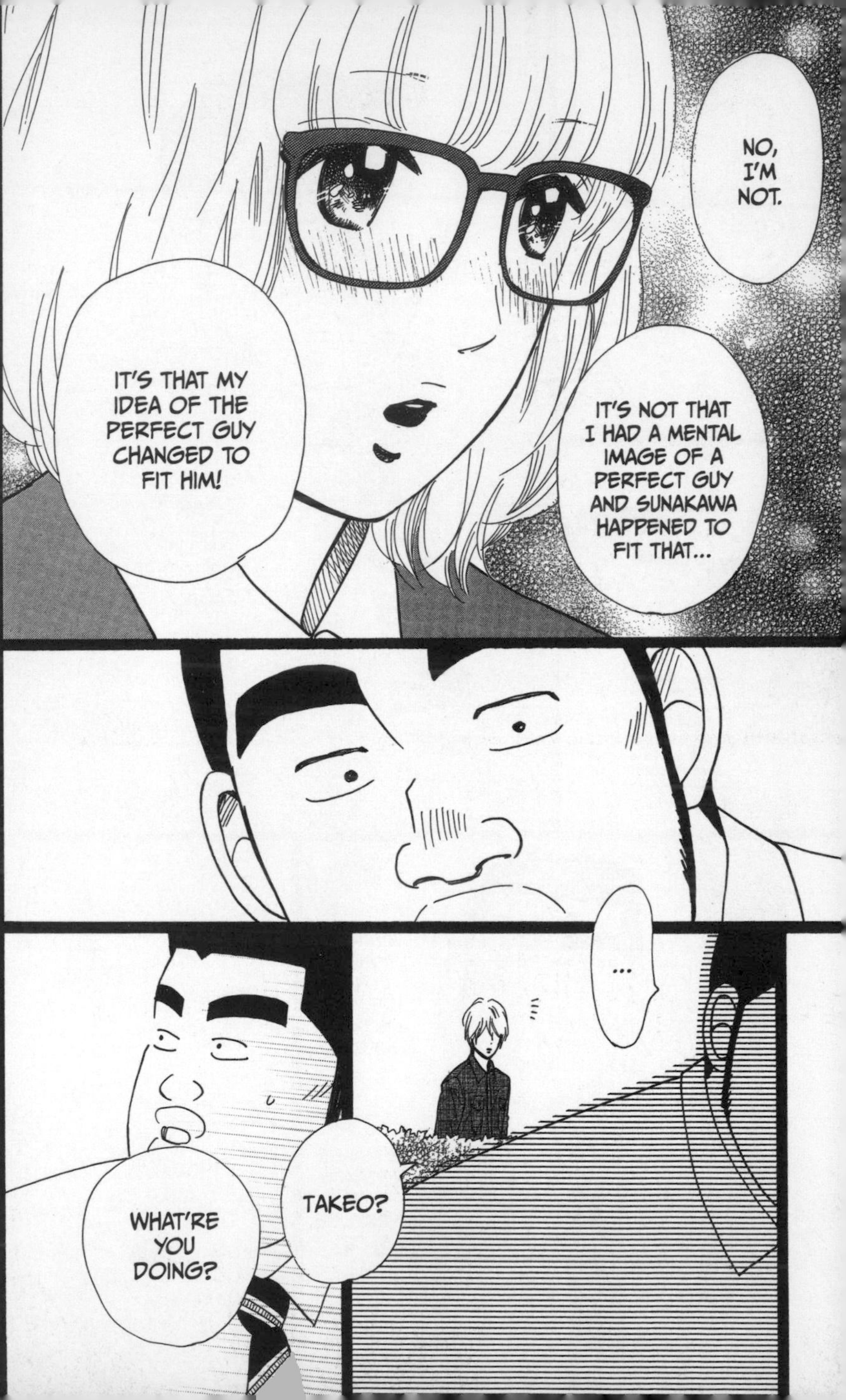
NO, I'M NOT.
IT'S NOT THAT I HAD A MENTAL IMAGE OF A PERFECT GUY AND SUNAKAWA HAPPENED TO FIT THAT...
IT'S THAT MY IDEA OF THE PERFECT GUY CHANGED TO FIT HIM!
...
TAKEO?
WHAT'RE YOU DOING?

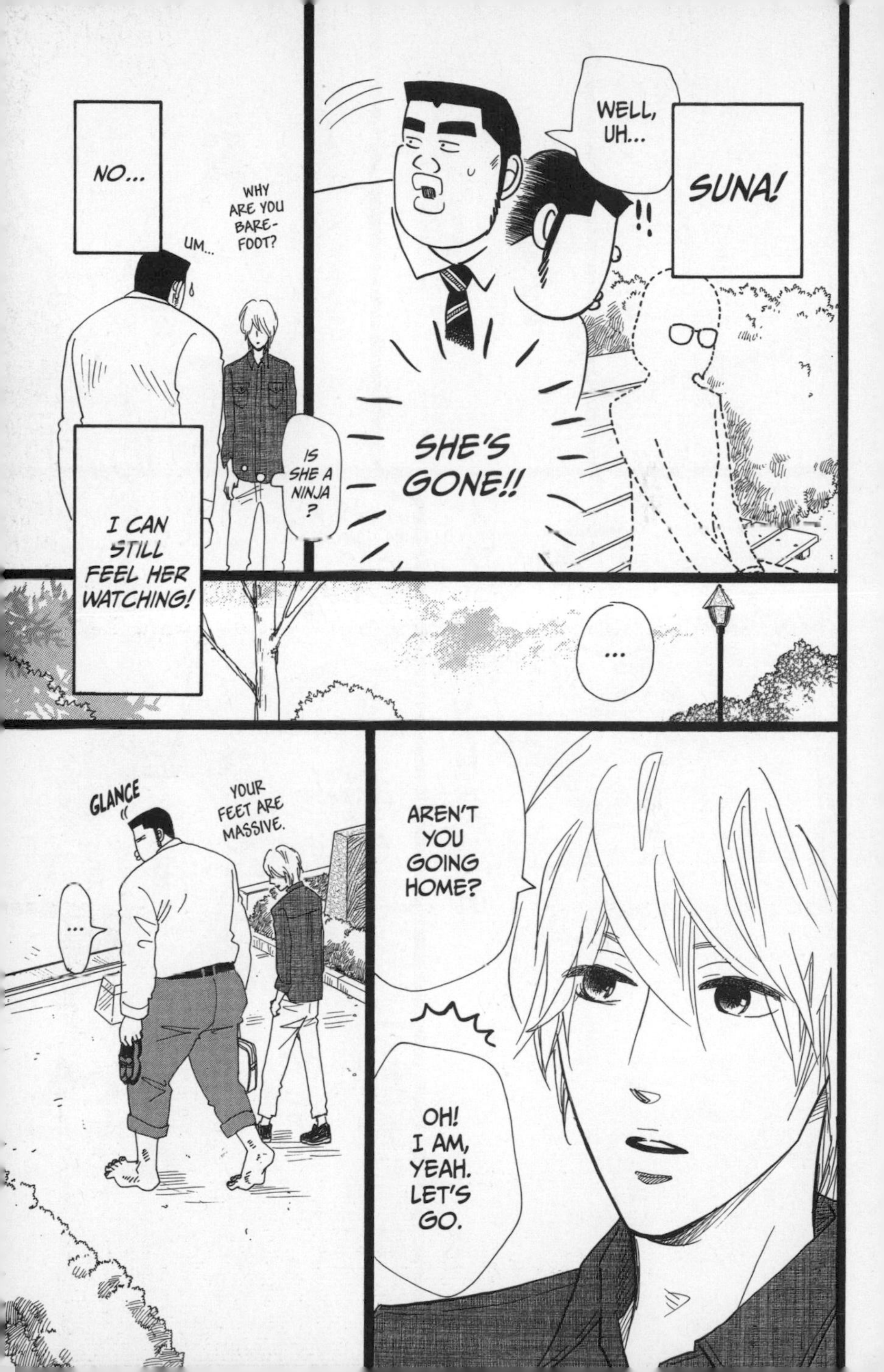
WELL, UH...
SUNA!
!!
SHE'S GONE!!
NO...
WHY ARE YOU BARE-FOOT?
UM...
IS SHE A NINJA?
I CAN STILL FEEL HER WATCHING!
...
AREN'T YOU GOING HOME?
OH! I AM, YEAH. LET'S GO.
YOUR FEET ARE MASSIVE.
GLANCE
...

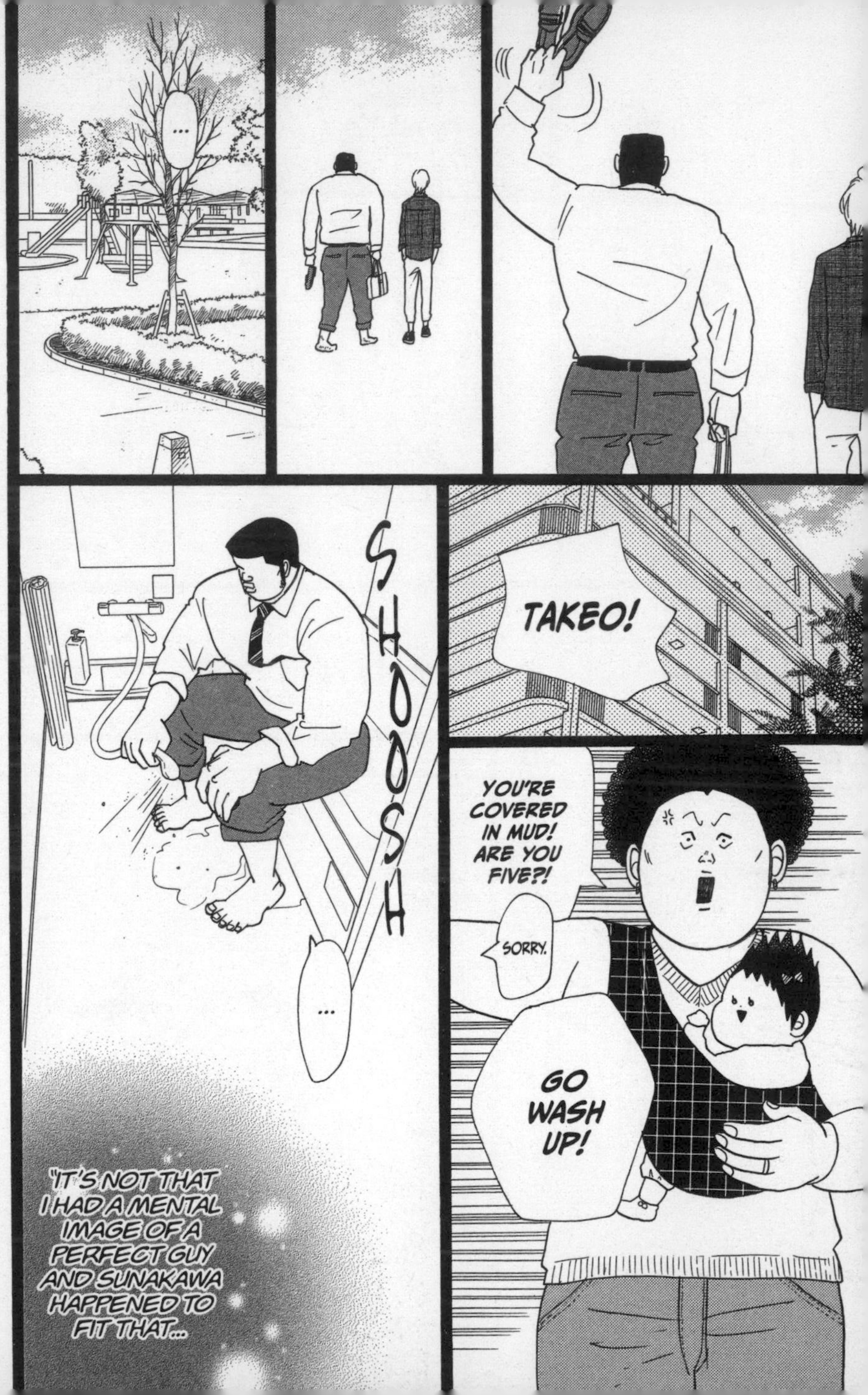
...
TAKEO!
YOU'RE COVERED IN MUD! ARE YOU FIVE?!
SORRY.
GO WASH UP!
SHOOSH
...
"IT'S NOT THAT I HAD A MENTAL IMAGE OF A PERFECT GUY AND SUNAKAWA HAPPENED TO FIT THAT...

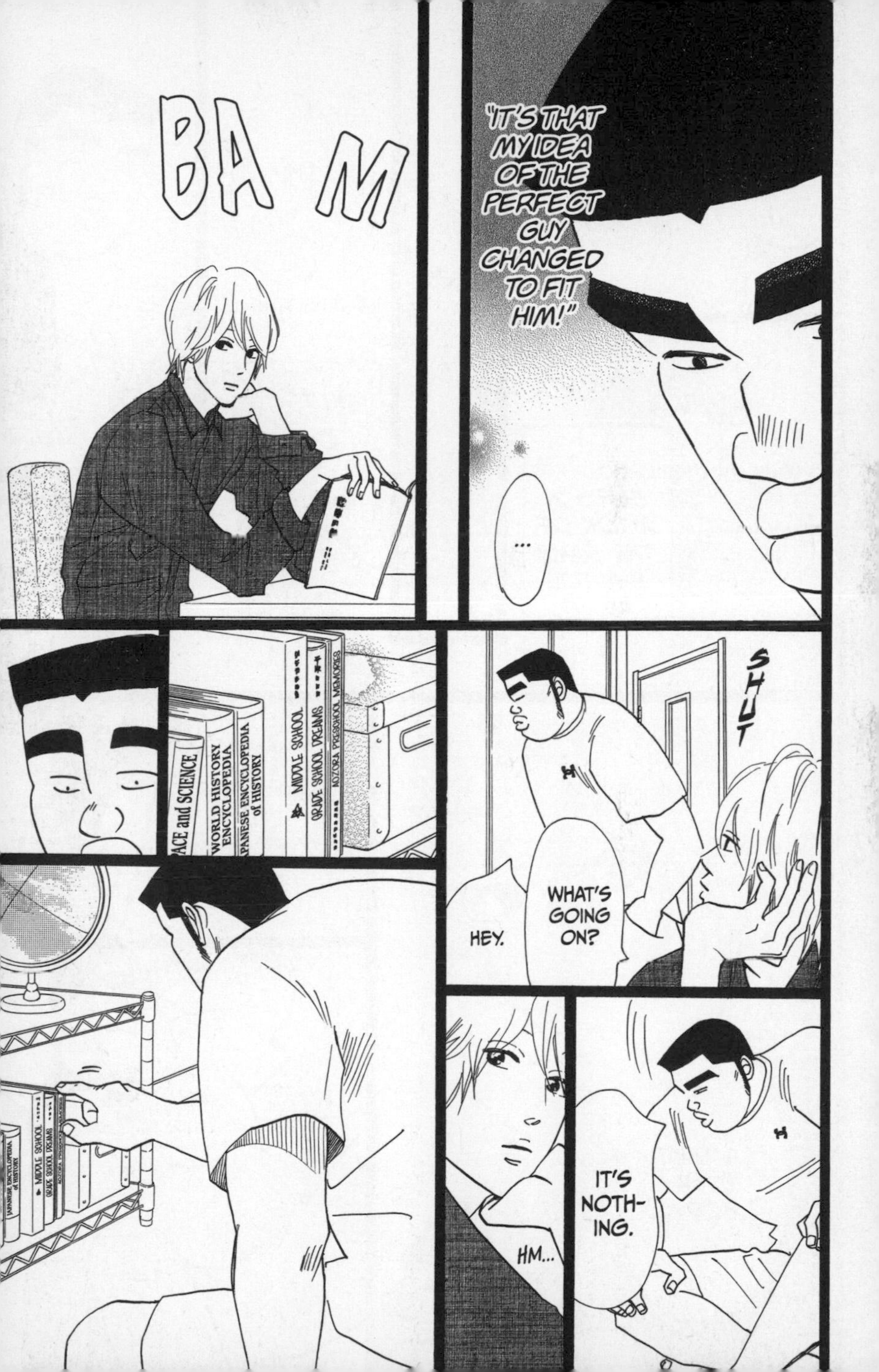
"IT'S THAT MY IDEA OF THE PERFECT GUY CHANGED TO FIT HIM!"
...
BAM
SHUT
WHAT'S GOING ON?
HEY.
IT'S NOTHING.
HM...
ACE and SCIENCE
WORLD HISTORY ENCYCLOPEDIA
JAPANESE ENCYCLOPEDIA of HISTORY
MIDDLE SCHOOL
GRADE SCHOOL DREAMS
AOZORA PRESCHOOL MEMORIES

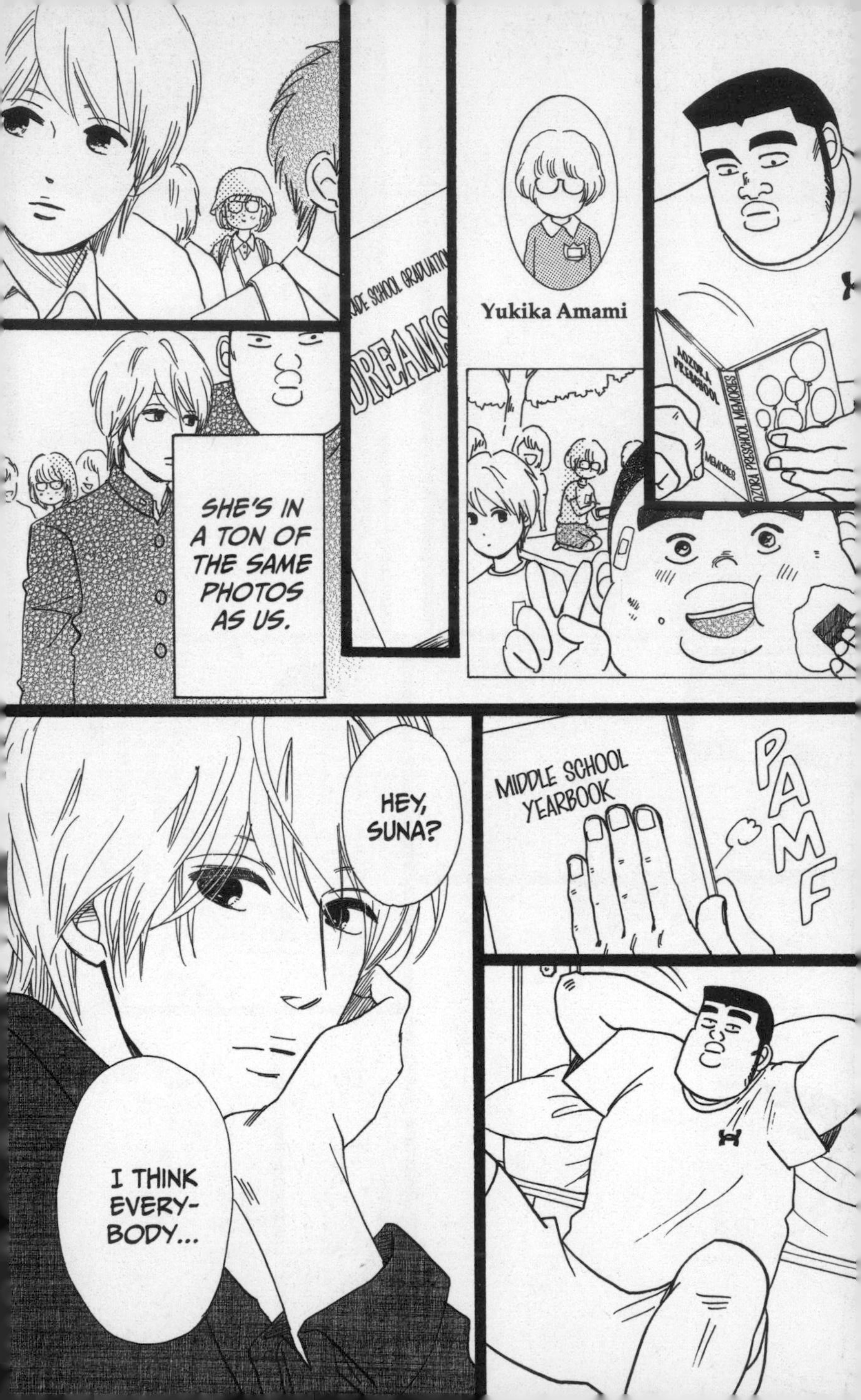
PRESCHOOL
OZORA PRESCHOOL MEMORIES
MEMORIES
Yukika Amami
DREAMS
SHE'S IN A TON OF THE SAME PHOTOS AS US.
MIDDLE SCHOOL YEARBOOK
PAMF
HEY, SUNA?
I THINK EVERY-BODY...

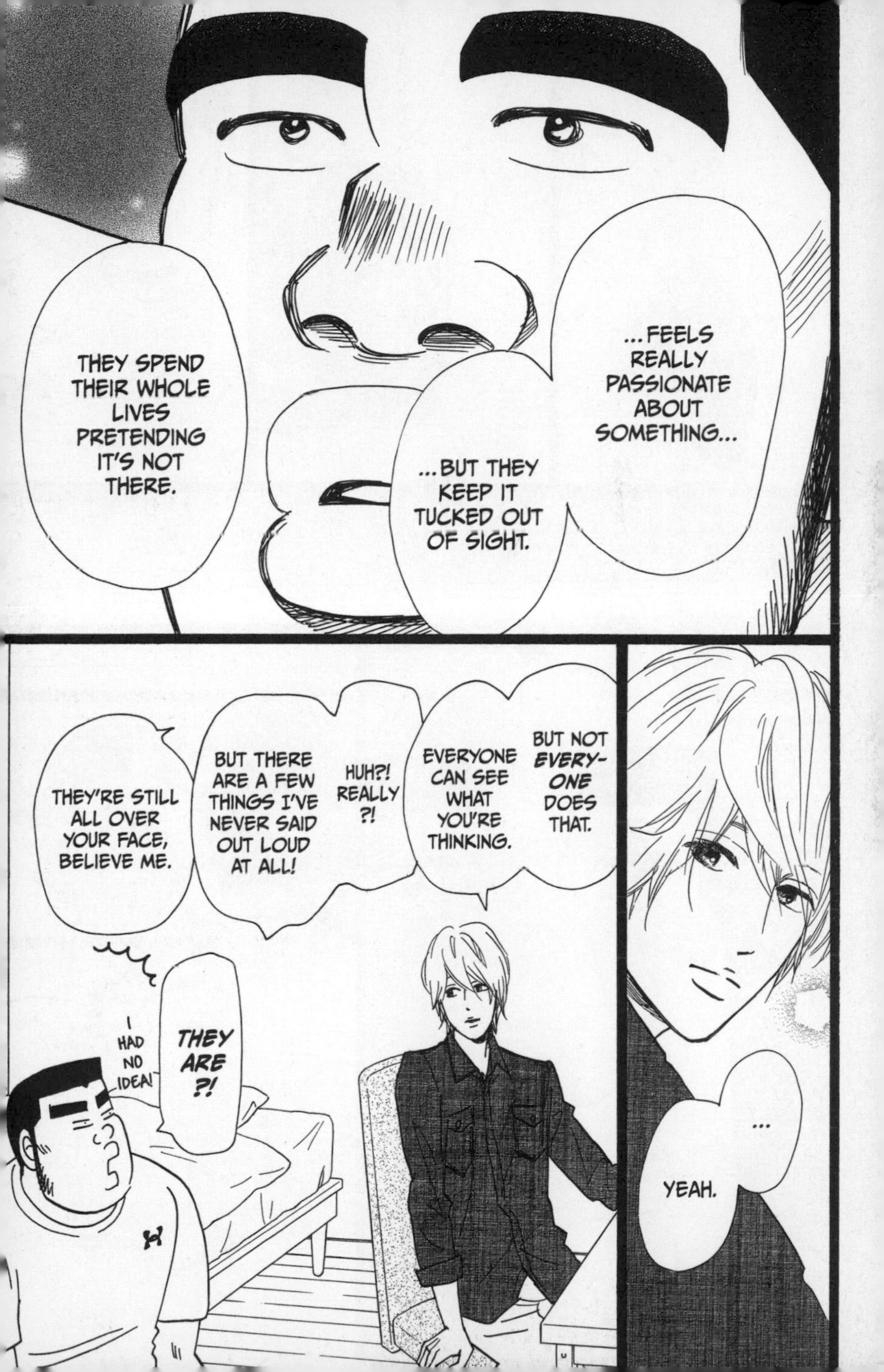
...FEELS REALLY PASSIONATE ABOUT SOMETHING...
...BUT THEY KEEP IT TUCKED OUT OF SIGHT.
THEY SPEND THEIR WHOLE LIVES PRETENDING IT'S NOT THERE.
...
YEAH.
BUT NOT *EVERYONE* DOES THAT.
EVERYONE CAN SEE WHAT YOU'RE THINKING.
HUH?! REALLY?!
BUT THERE ARE A FEW THINGS I'VE NEVER SAID OUT LOUD AT ALL!
THEY'RE STILL ALL OVER YOUR FACE, BELIEVE ME.
THEY ARE?!
I HAD NO IDEA!

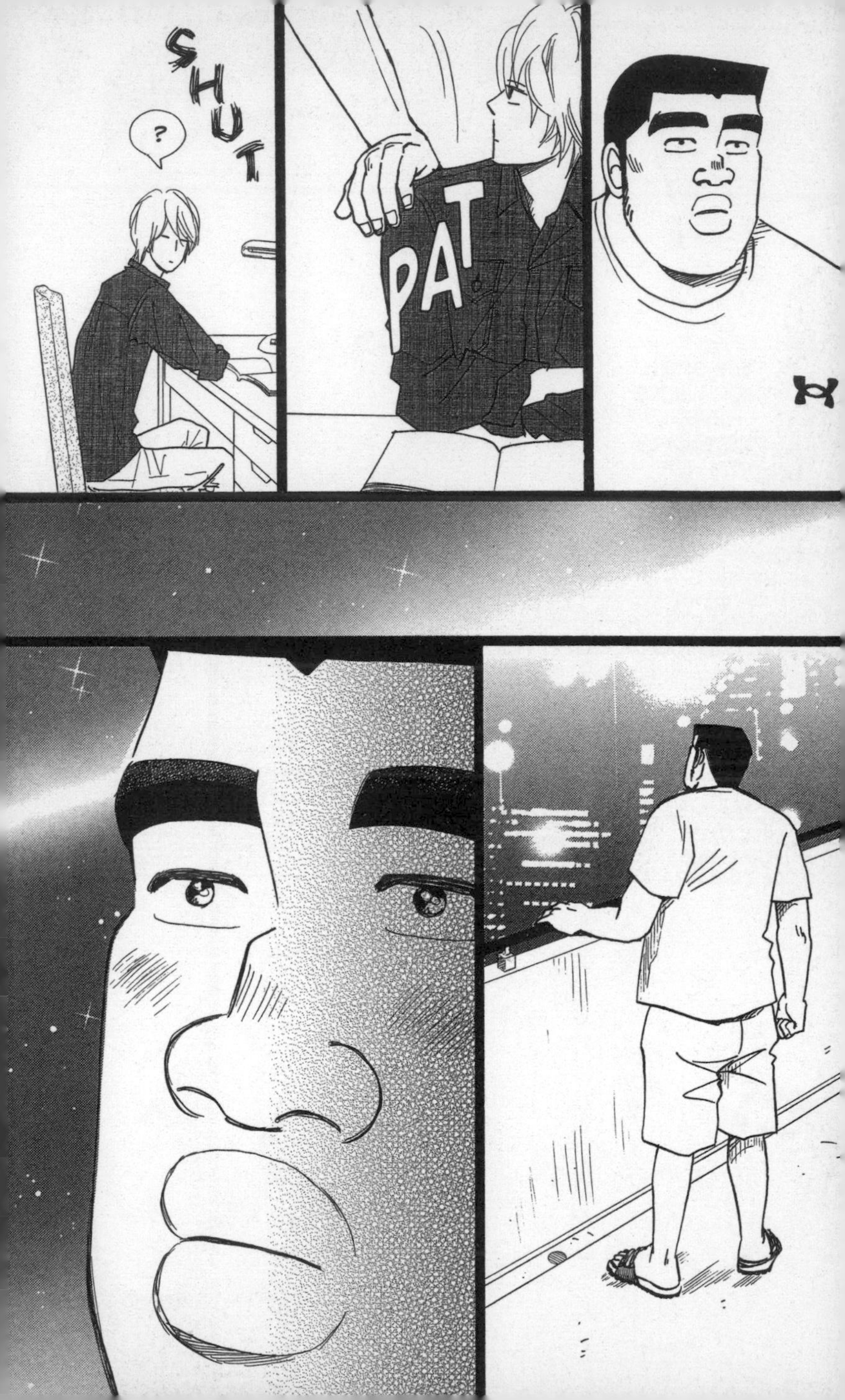
PAT
SHUT
?

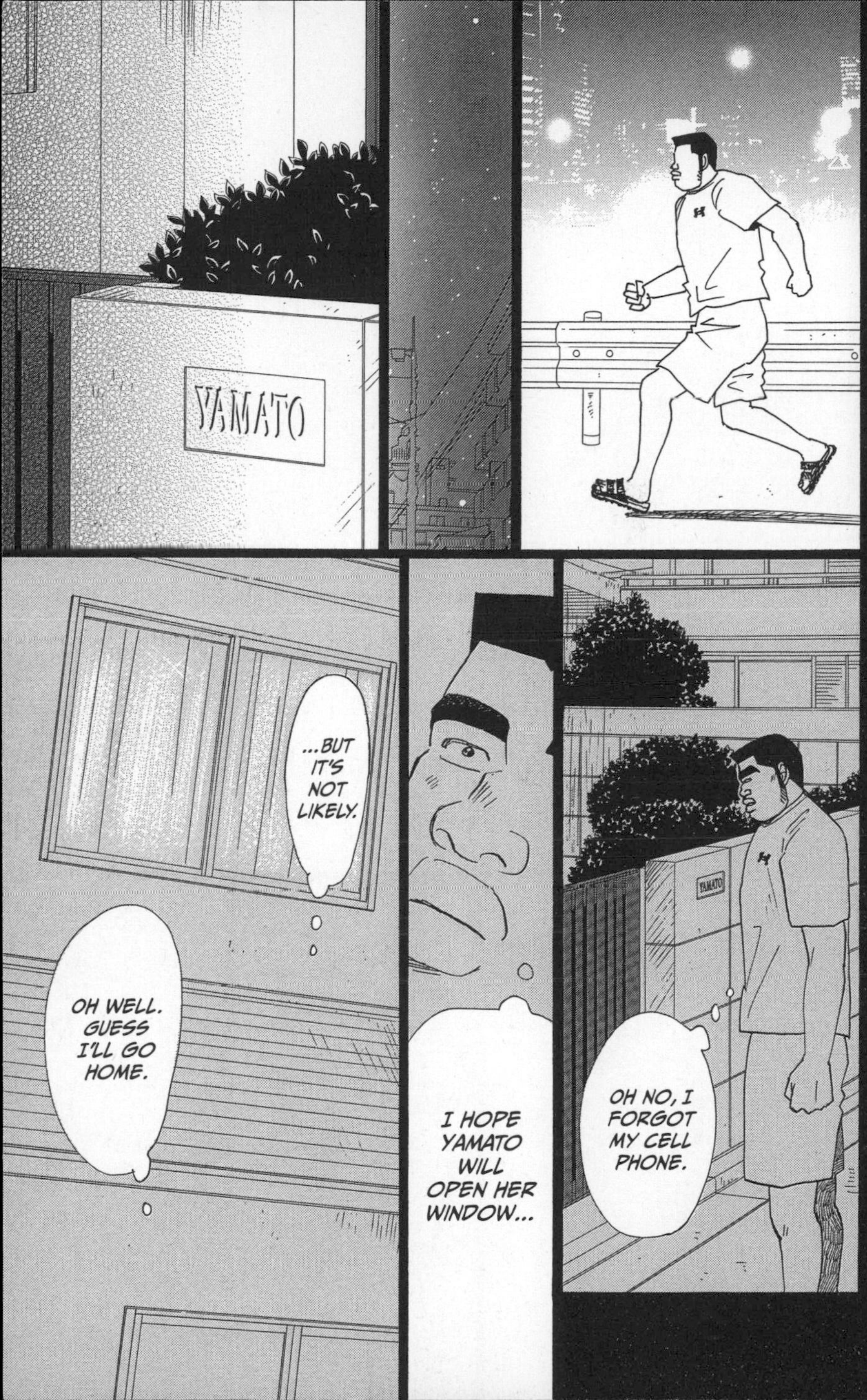
YAMATO
YAMATO
OH NO, I FORGOT MY CELL PHONE.
I HOPE YAMATO WILL OPEN HER WINDOW...
...BUT IT'S NOT LIKELY.
OH WELL. GUESS I'LL GO HOME.

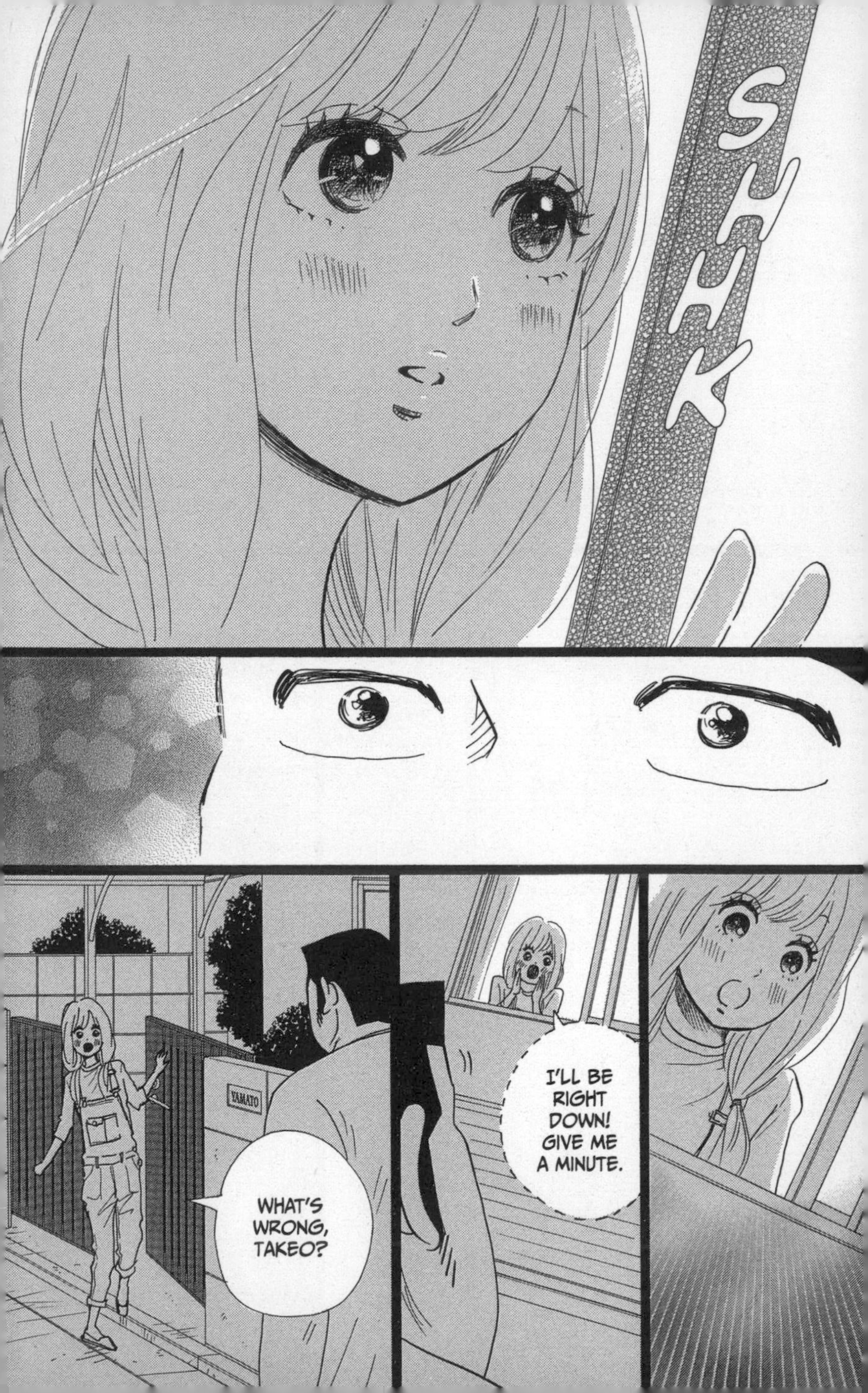
SHHK
I'LL BE RIGHT DOWN! GIVE ME A MINUTE.
YAMATO
WHAT'S WRONG, TAKEO?

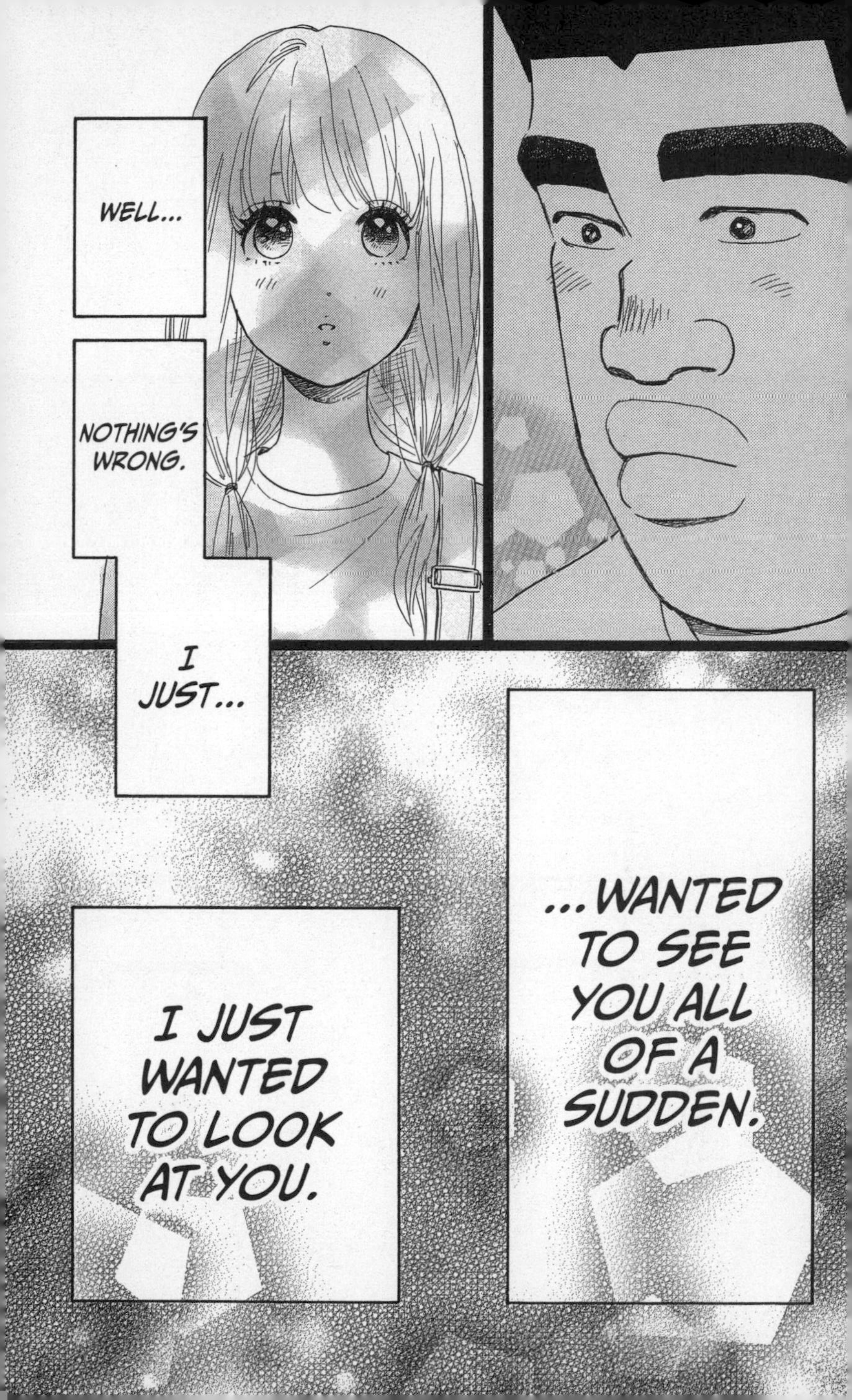
WELL...
NOTHING'S WRONG.
I JUST...
...WANTED TO SEE YOU ALL OF A SUDDEN.
I JUST WANTED TO LOOK AT YOU.

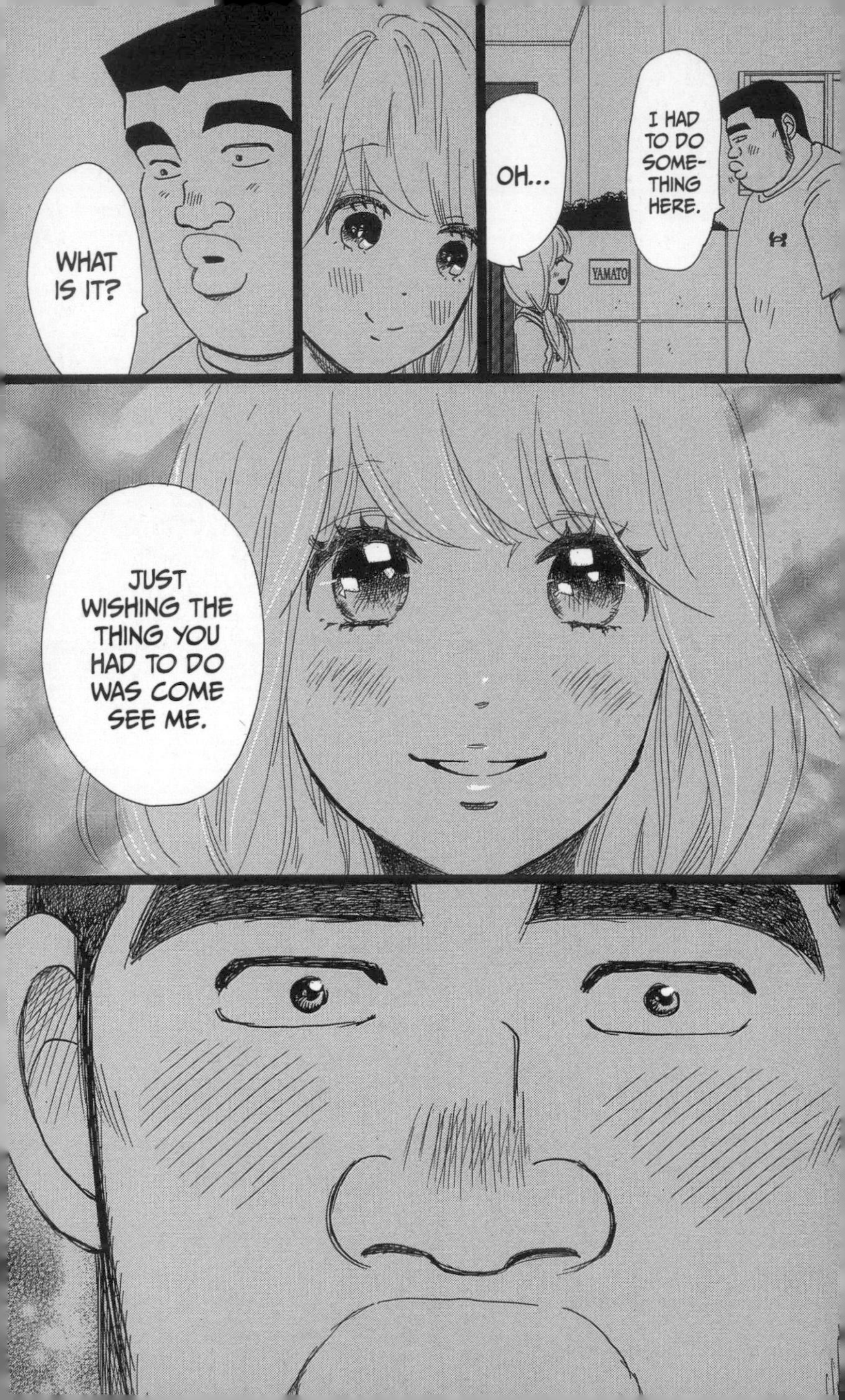
I HAD TO DO SOME-THING HERE.
OH...
YAMATO
WHAT IS IT?
JUST WISHING THE THING YOU HAD TO DO WAS COME SEE ME.

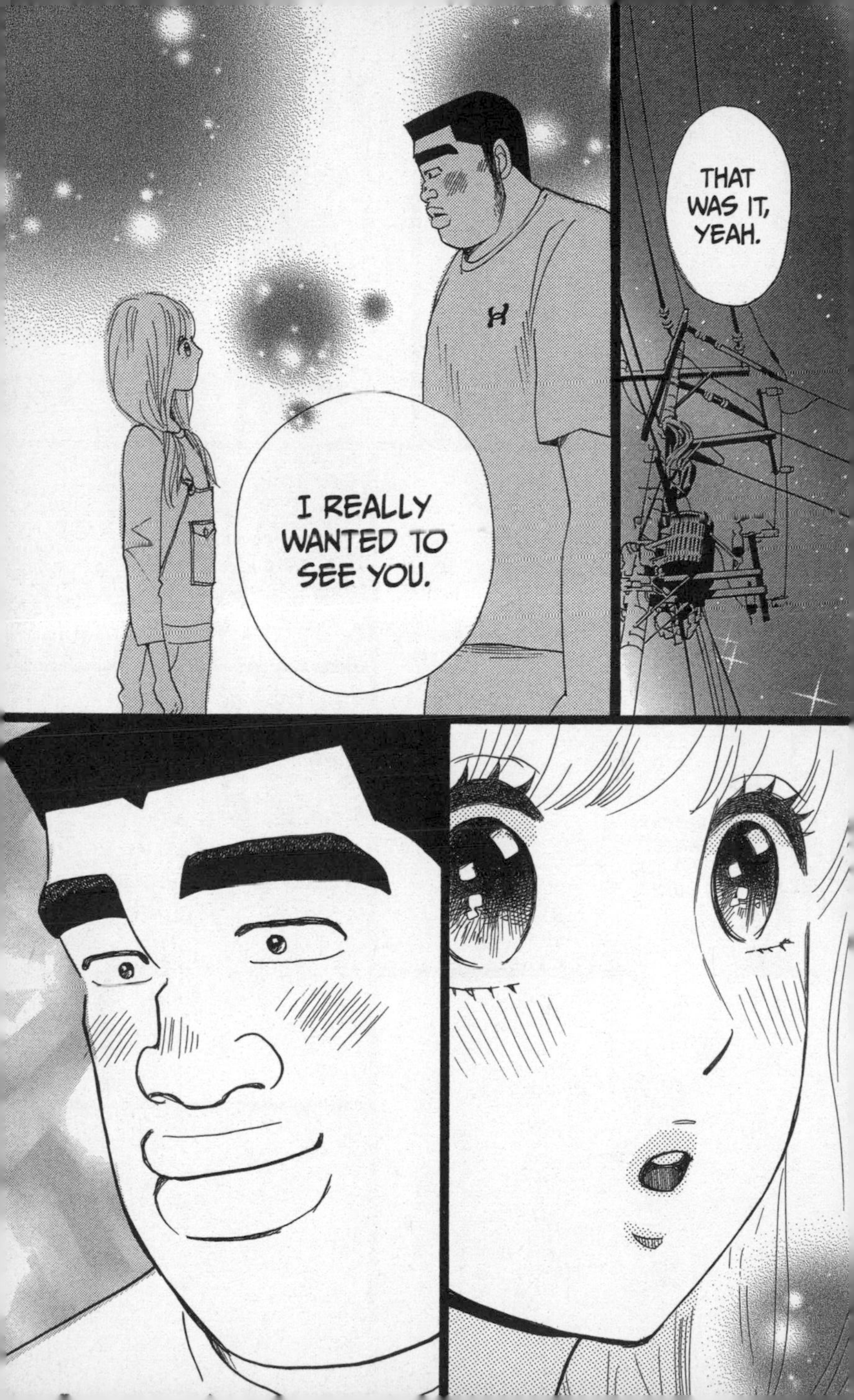
THAT WAS IT, YEAH.
I REALLY WANTED TO SEE YOU.

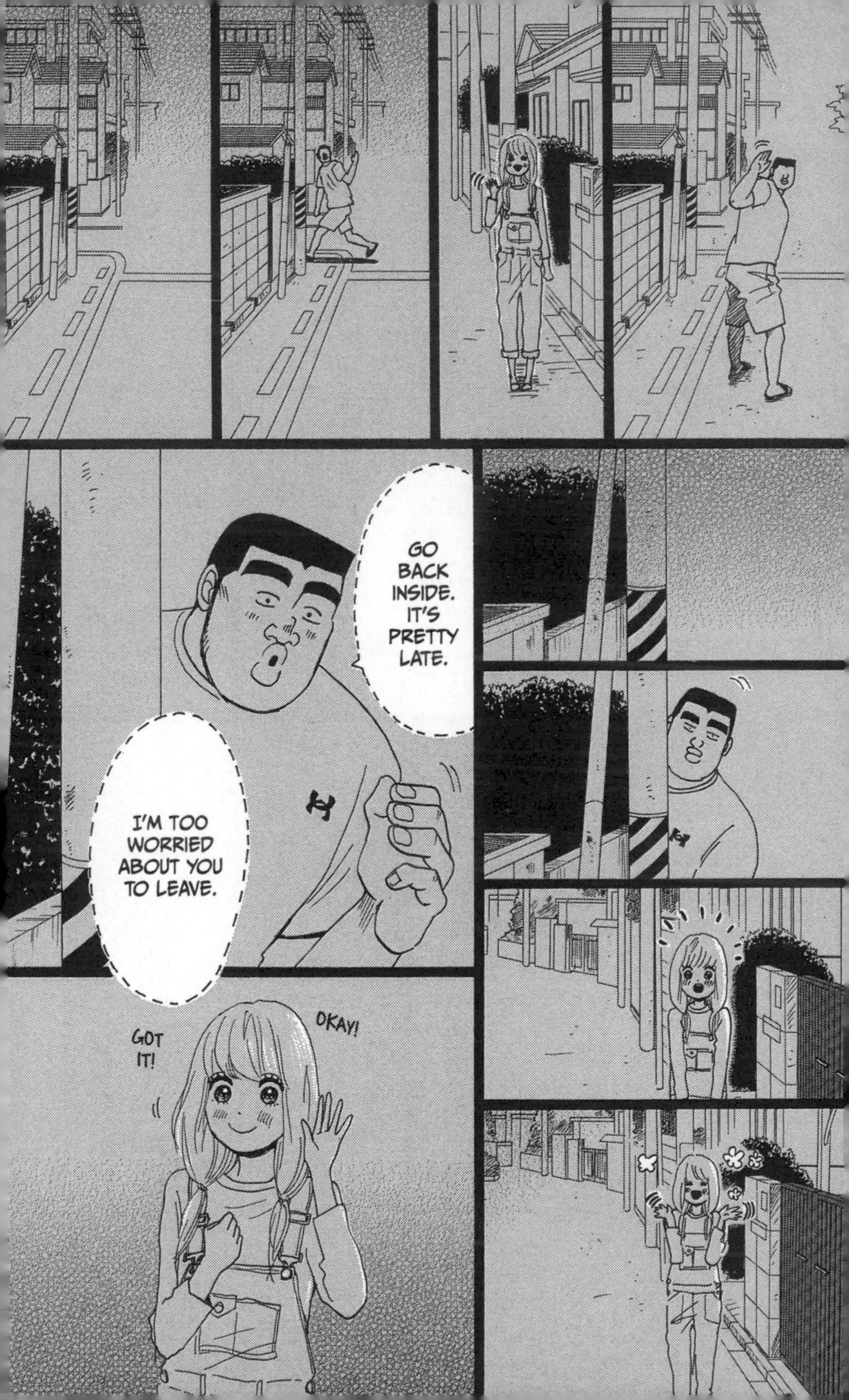
GO BACK INSIDE. IT'S PRETTY LATE.
I'M TOO WORRIED ABOUT YOU TO LEAVE.
OKAY!
GOT IT!

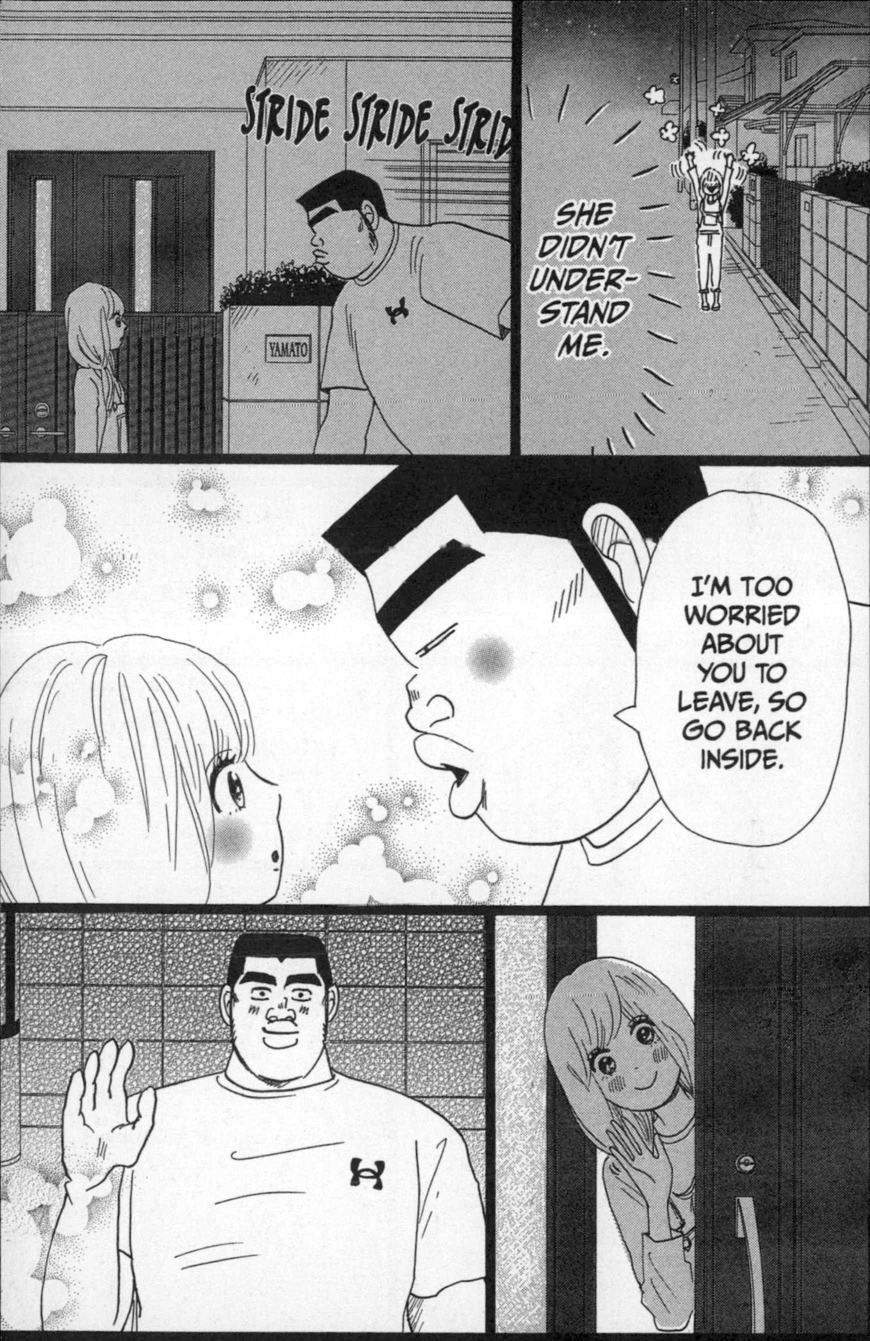
SHE DIDN'T UNDER-STAND ME.
STRIDE STRIDE STRID
YAMATO
I'M TOO WORRIED ABOUT YOU TO LEAVE, SO GO BACK INSIDE.

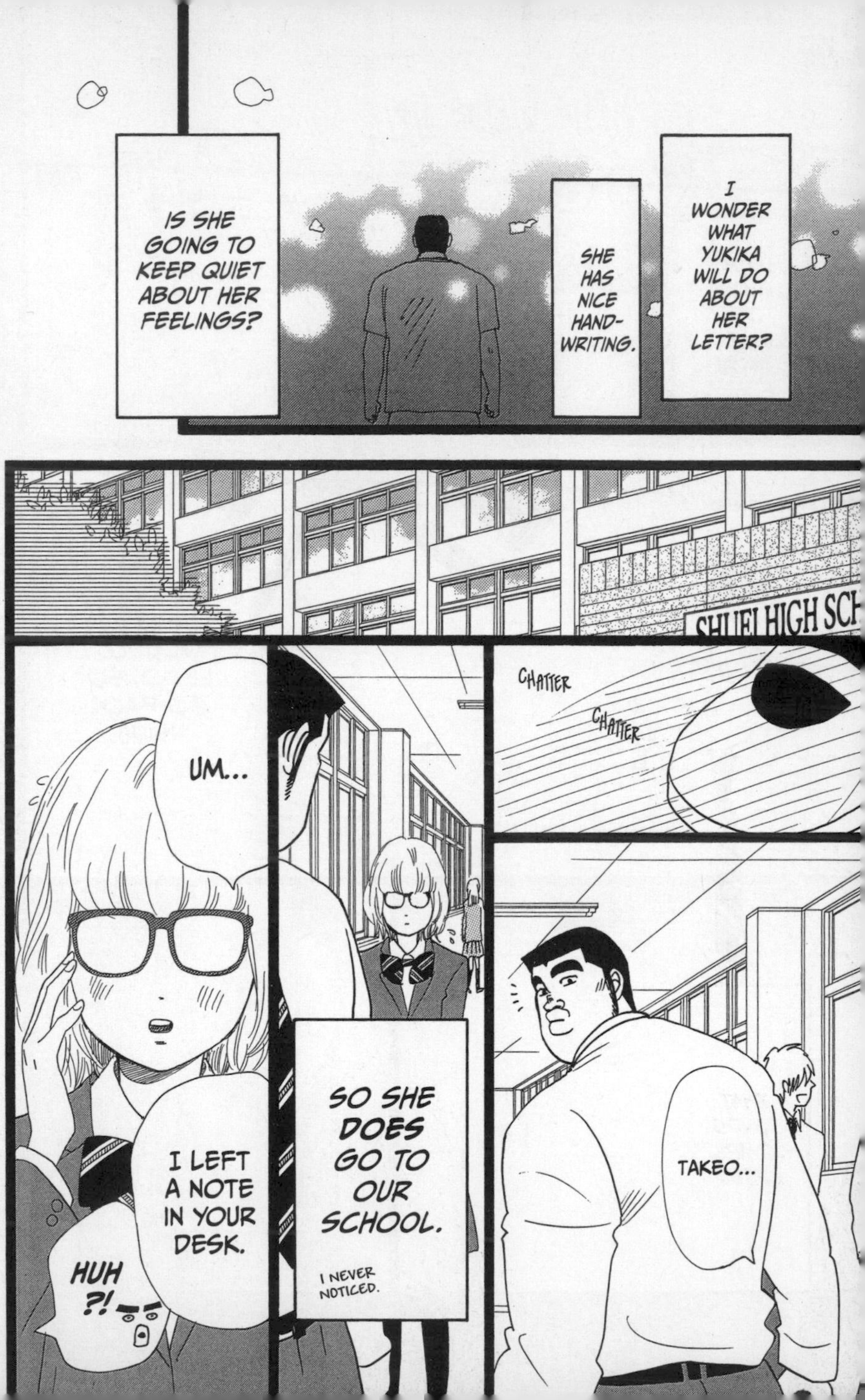
I WONDER WHAT YUKIKA WILL DO ABOUT HER LETTER?
SHE HAS NICE HAND-WRITING.
IS SHE GOING TO KEEP QUIET ABOUT HER FEELINGS?
SHUEI HIGH SCH
CHATTER
CHATTER
TAKEO...
SO SHE DOES GO TO OUR SCHOOL.
I NEVER NOTICED.
UM...
I LEFT A NOTE IN YOUR DESK.
HUH ?!

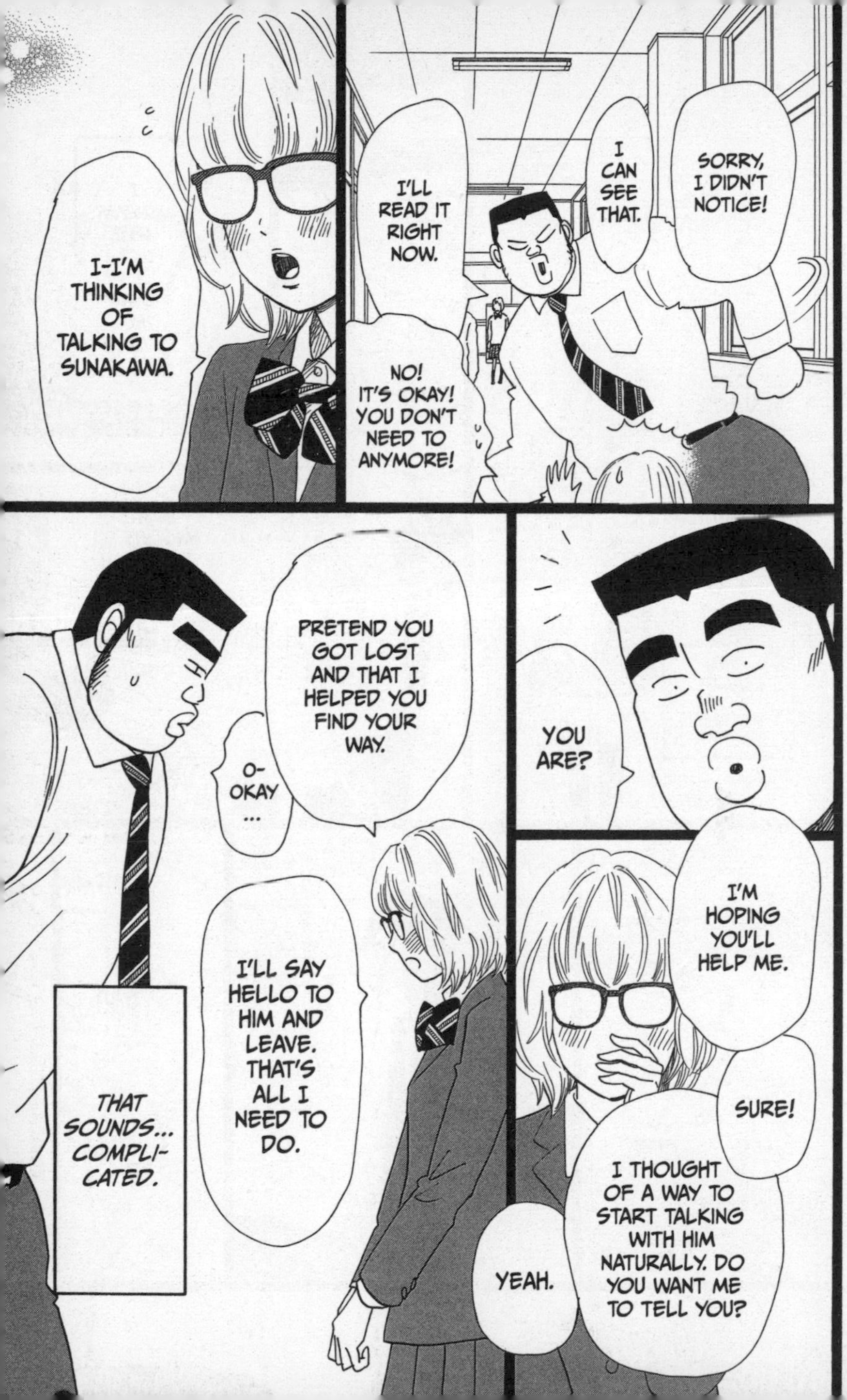
SORRY, I DIDN'T NOTICE!
I CAN SEE THAT.
I'LL READ IT RIGHT NOW.
NO! IT'S OKAY! YOU DON'T NEED TO ANYMORE!
I-I'M THINKING OF TALKING TO SUNAKAWA.
YOU ARE?
I'M HOPING YOU'LL HELP ME.
SURE!
I THOUGHT OF A WAY TO START TALKING WITH HIM NATURALLY. DO YOU WANT ME TO TELL YOU?
YEAH.
PRETEND YOU GOT LOST AND THAT I HELPED YOU FIND YOUR WAY.
O-OKAY...
I'LL SAY HELLO TO HIM AND LEAVE. THAT'S ALL I NEED TO DO.
THAT SOUNDS... COMPLICATED.

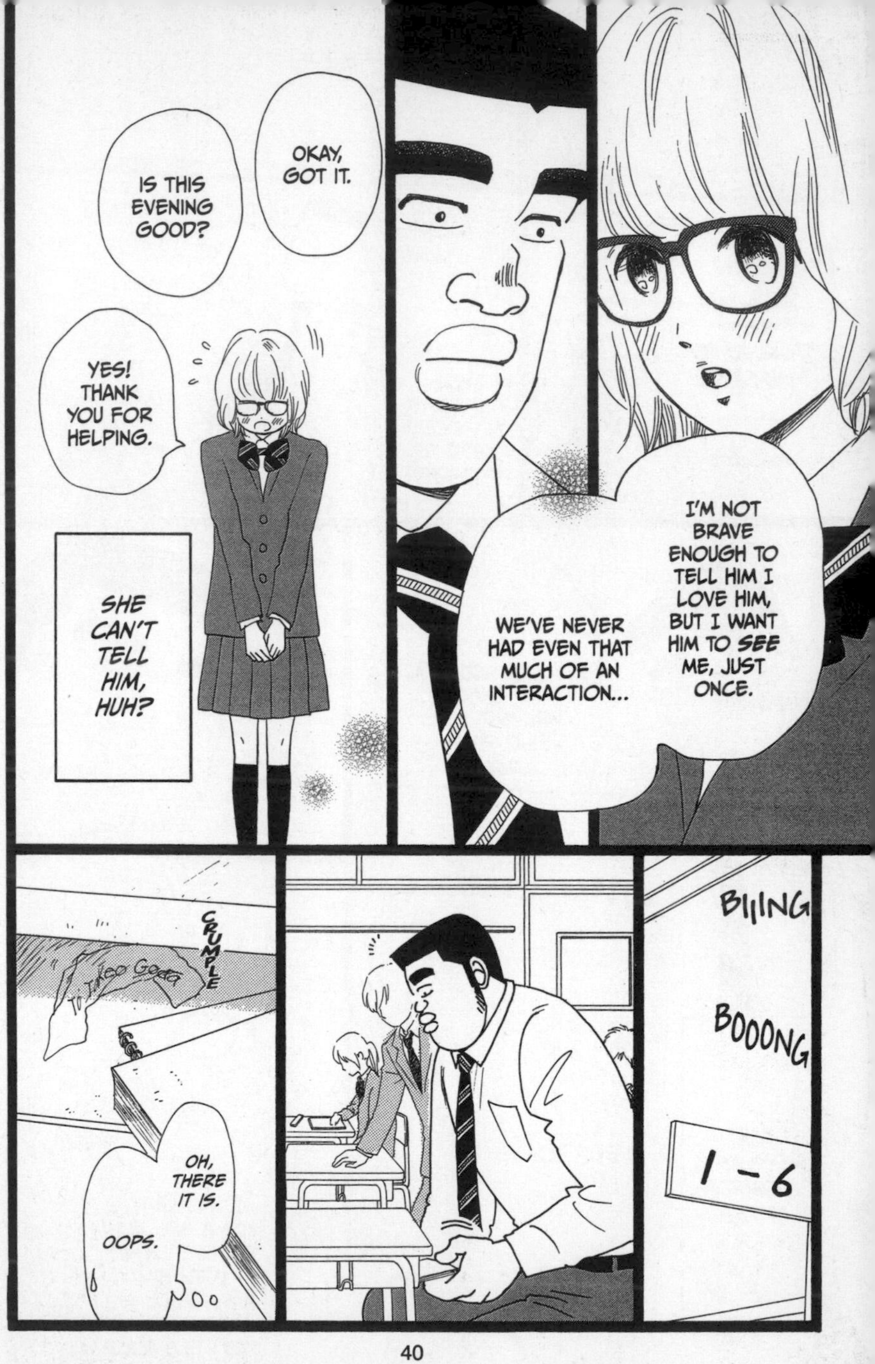
I'M NOT BRAVE ENOUGH TO TELL HIM I LOVE HIM, BUT I WANT HIM TO *SEE* ME, JUST ONCE.
WE'VE NEVER HAD EVEN THAT MUCH OF AN INTERACTION...
OKAY, GOT IT.
IS THIS EVENING GOOD?
YES! THANK YOU FOR HELPING.
SHE CAN'T TELL HIM, HUH?
BIIING
BOOONG
1-6
CRUMPLE
To Takeo Goda
OH, THERE IT IS.
OOPS.

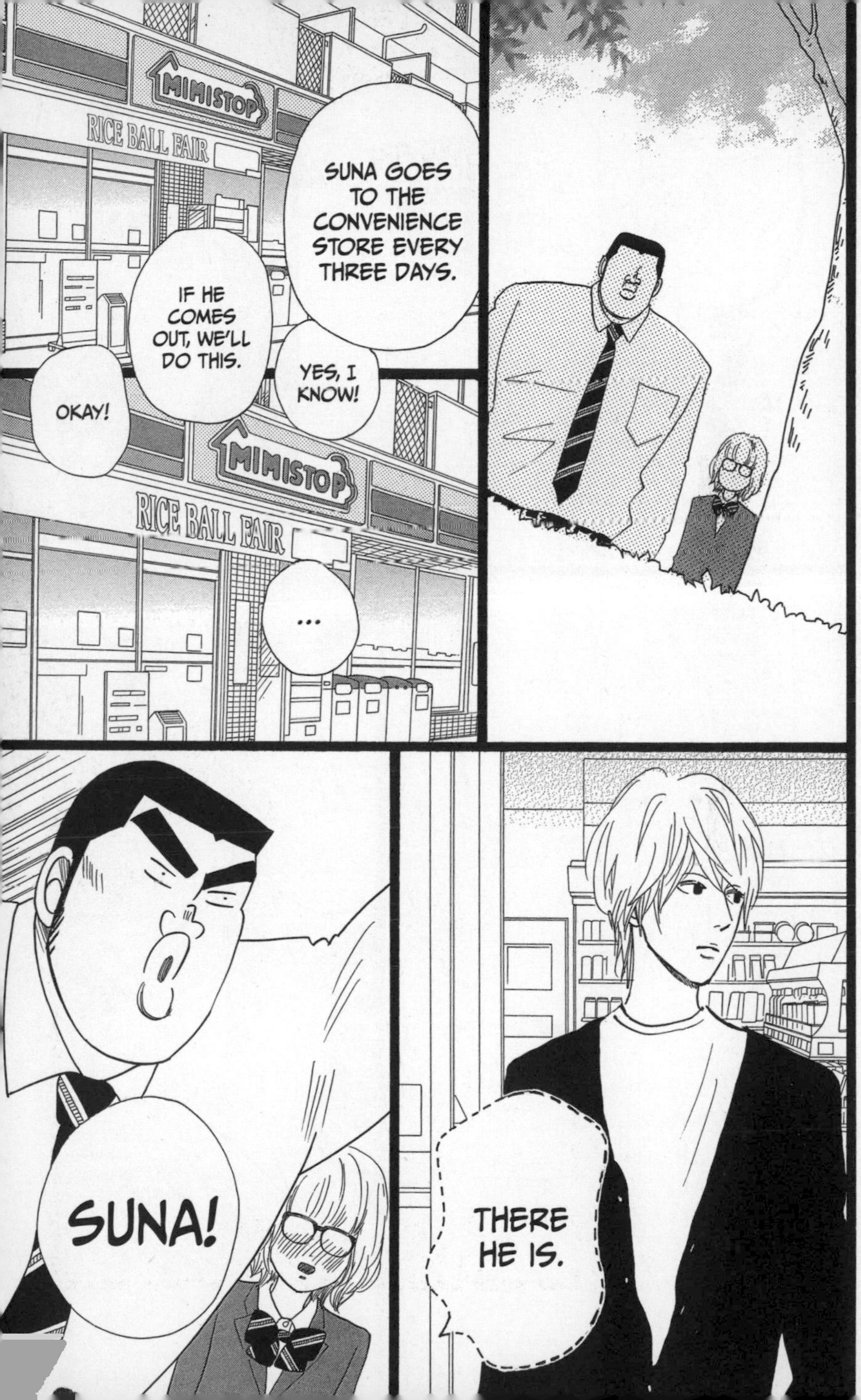

RICE BALL FAIR
MIMISTOP
SUNA GOES TO THE CONVENIENCE STORE EVERY THREE DAYS.
IF HE COMES OUT, WE'LL DO THIS.
YES, I KNOW!
OKAY!
...
THERE HE IS.
SUNA!

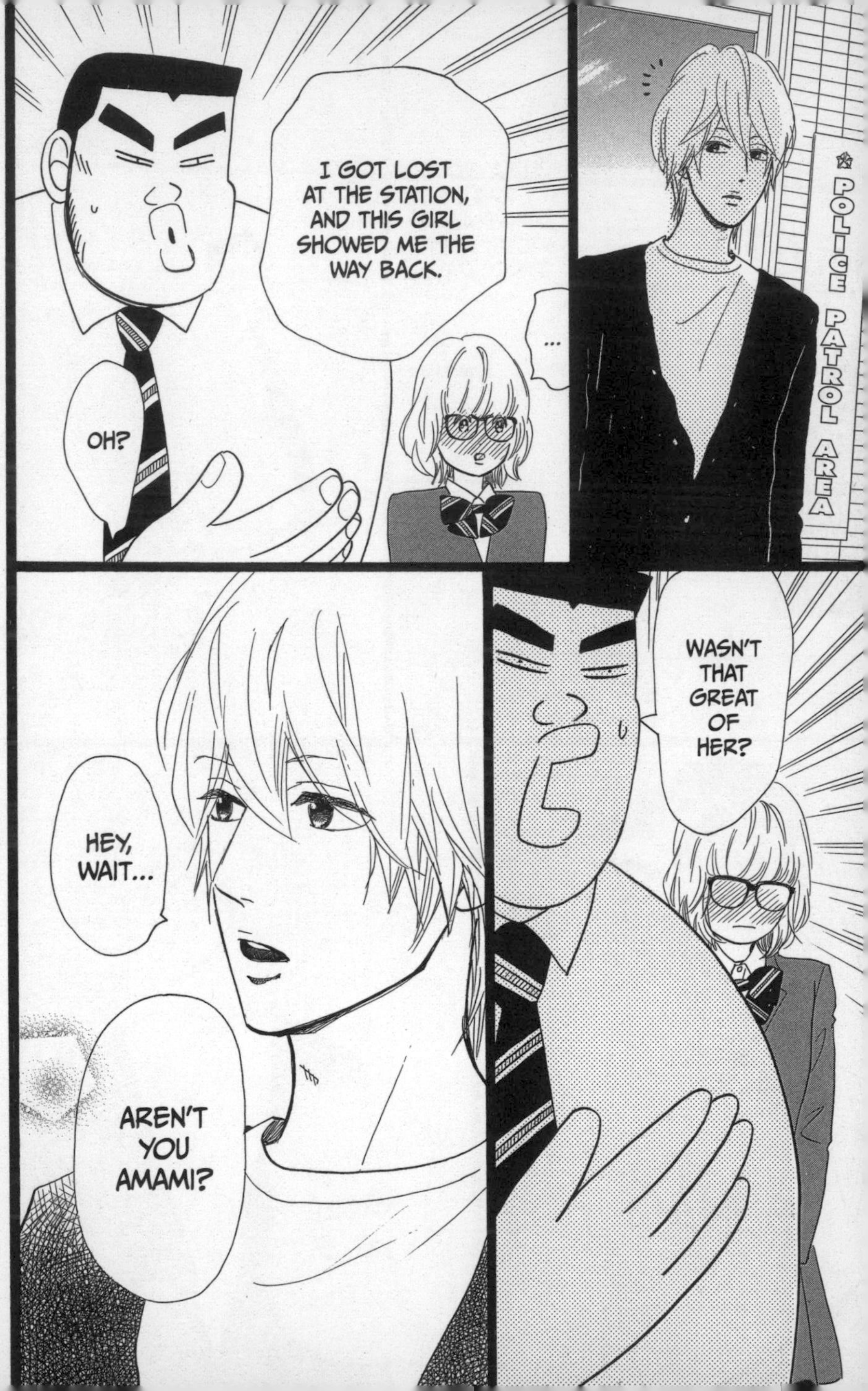
POLICE PATROL AREA
I GOT LOST AT THE STATION, AND THIS GIRL SHOWED ME THE WAY BACK.
...
OH?
WASN'T THAT GREAT OF HER?
HEY, WAIT...
AREN'T YOU AMAMI?

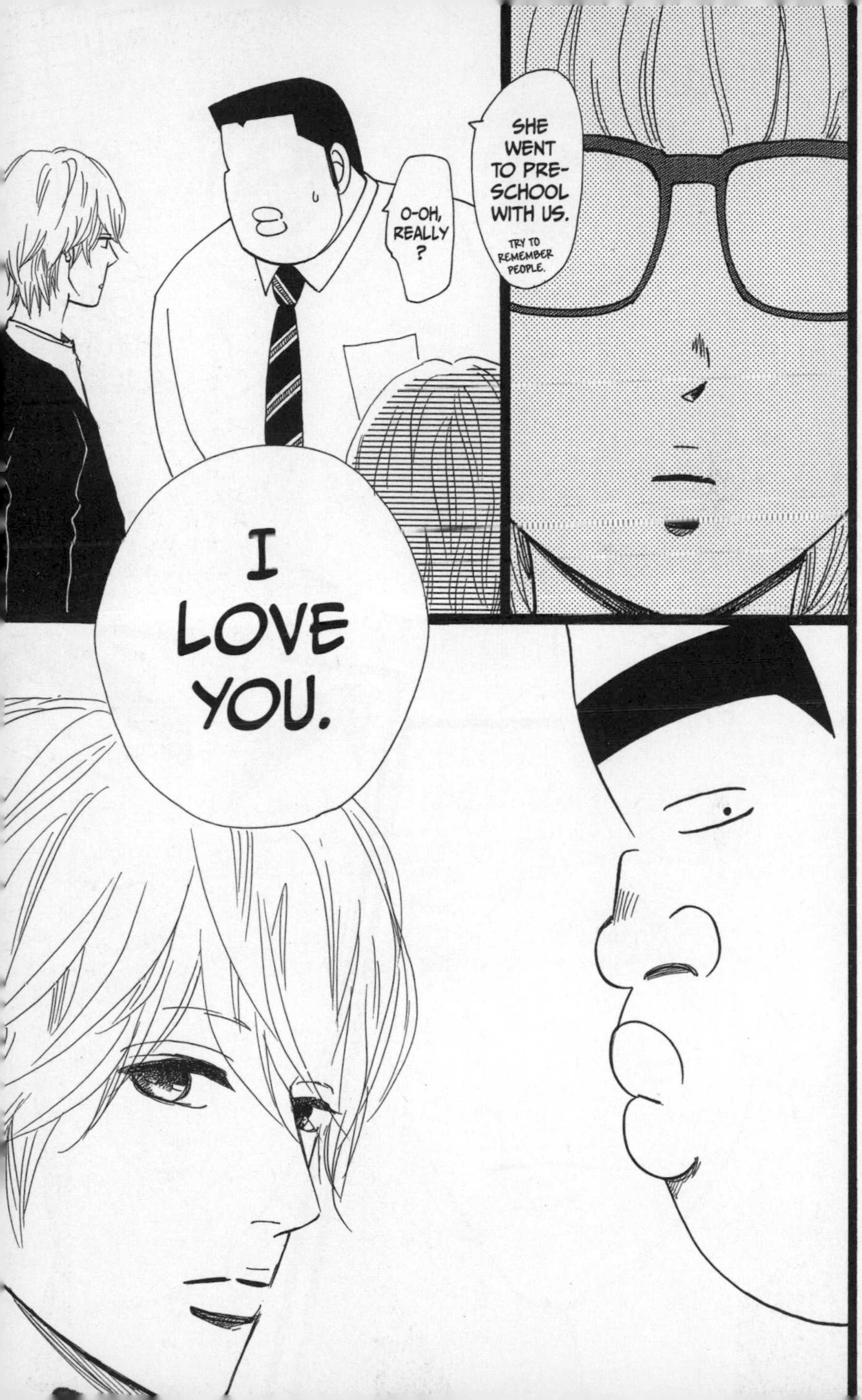
SHE WENT TO PRE-SCHOOL WITH US.
TRY TO REMEMBER PEOPLE.
O-OH, REALLY?
I LOVE YOU.

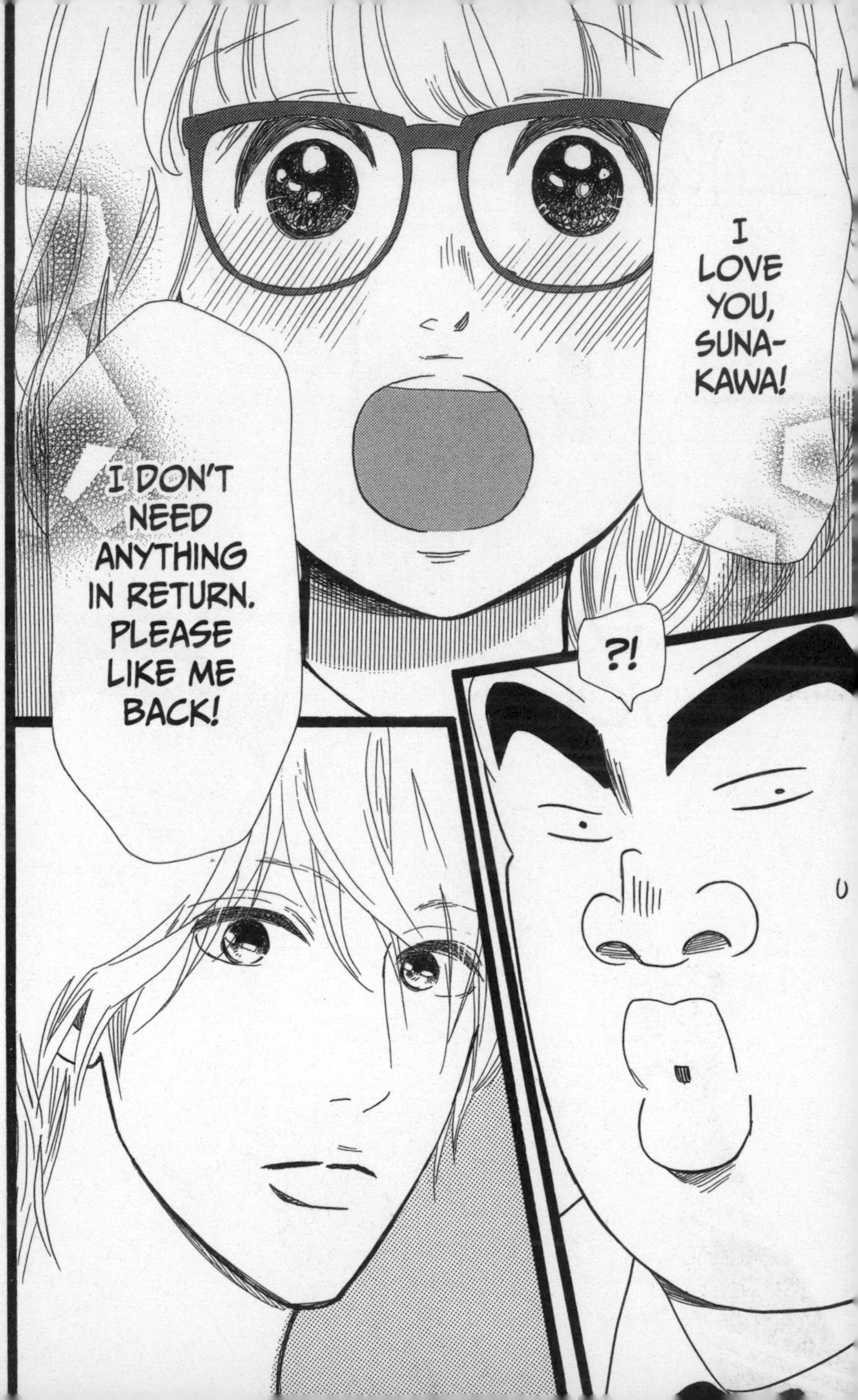
I LOVE YOU, SUNA-KAWA!
I DON'T NEED ANYTHING IN RETURN. PLEASE LIKE ME BACK!
?!

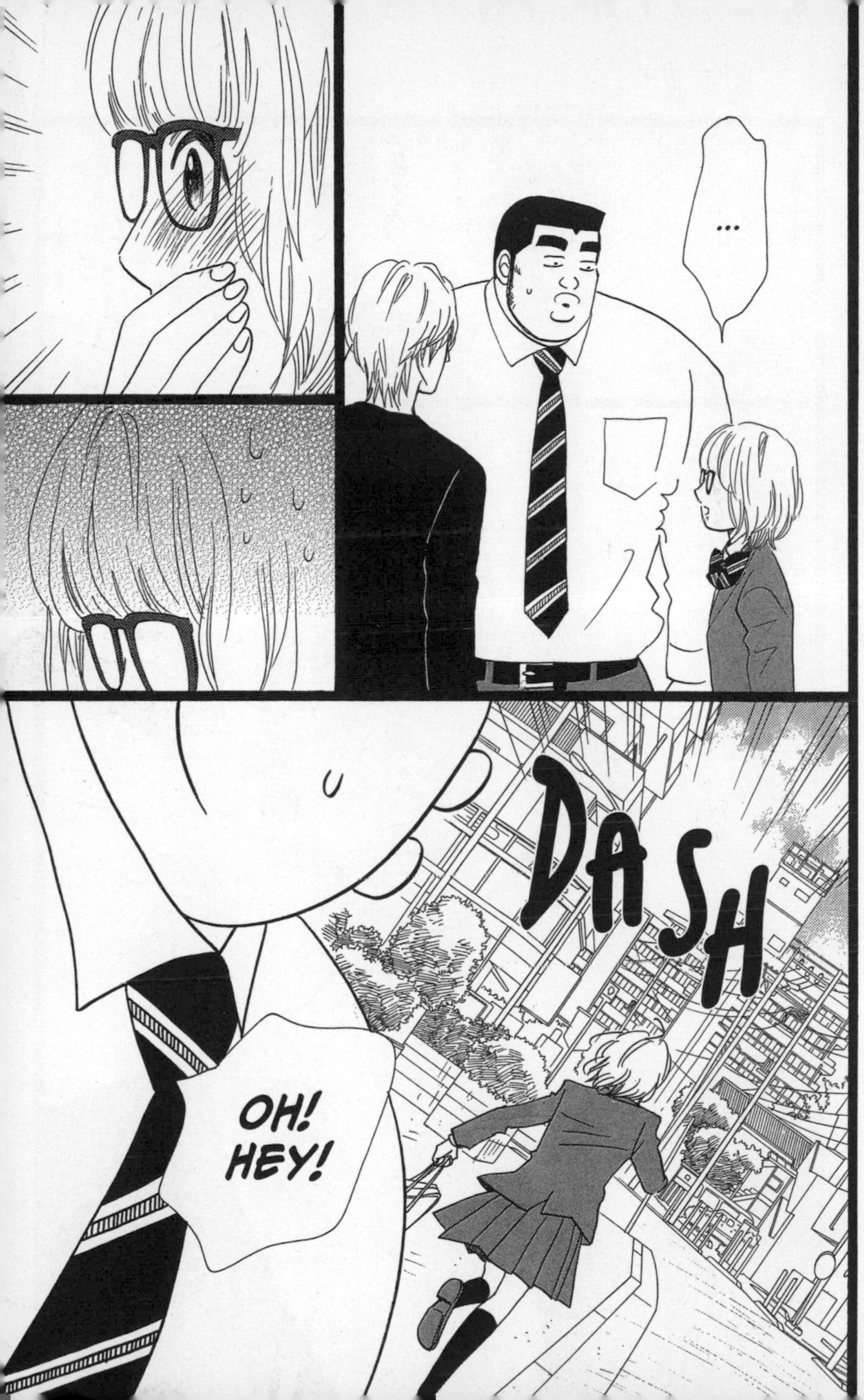
...
DASH
OH! HEY!

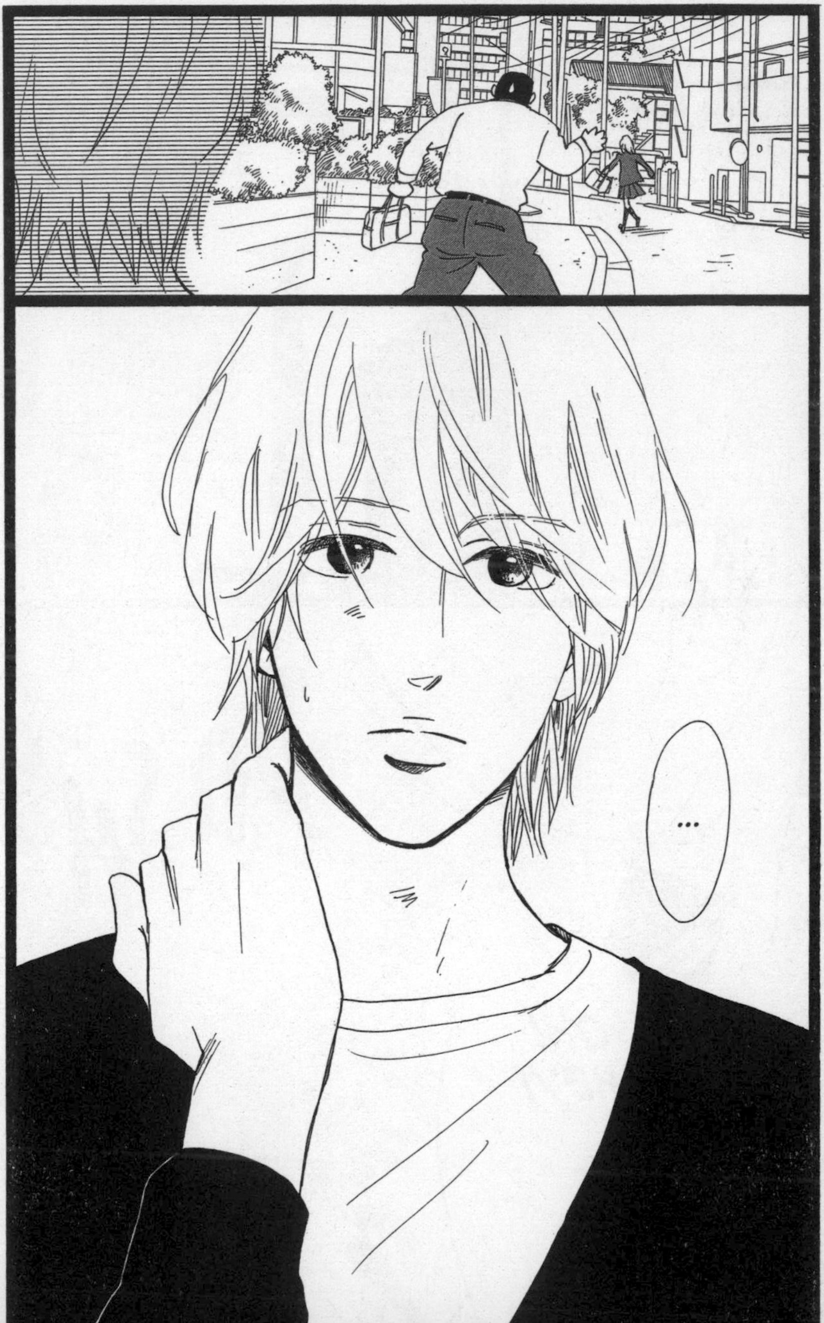
...

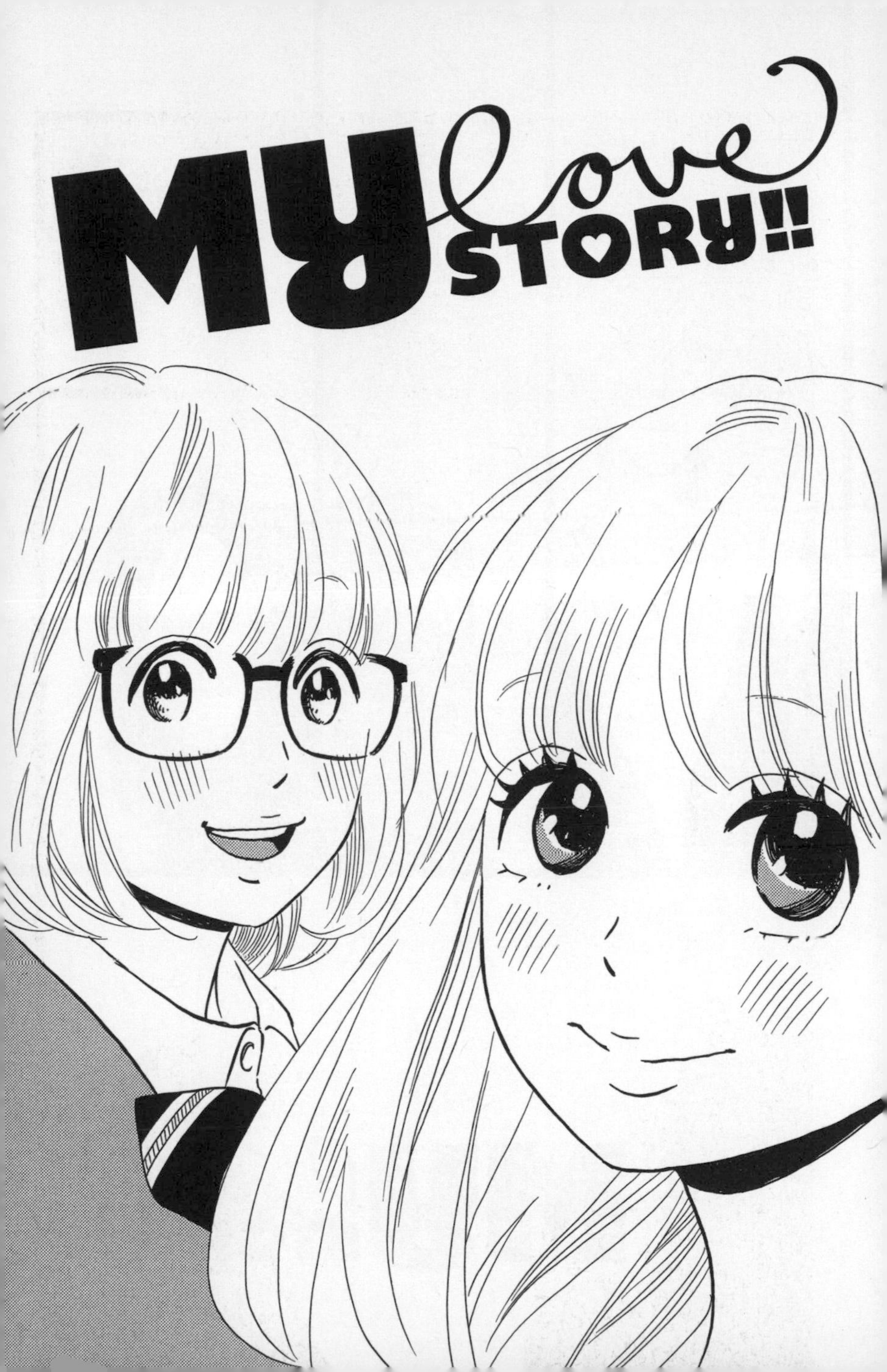
MY love STORY!!

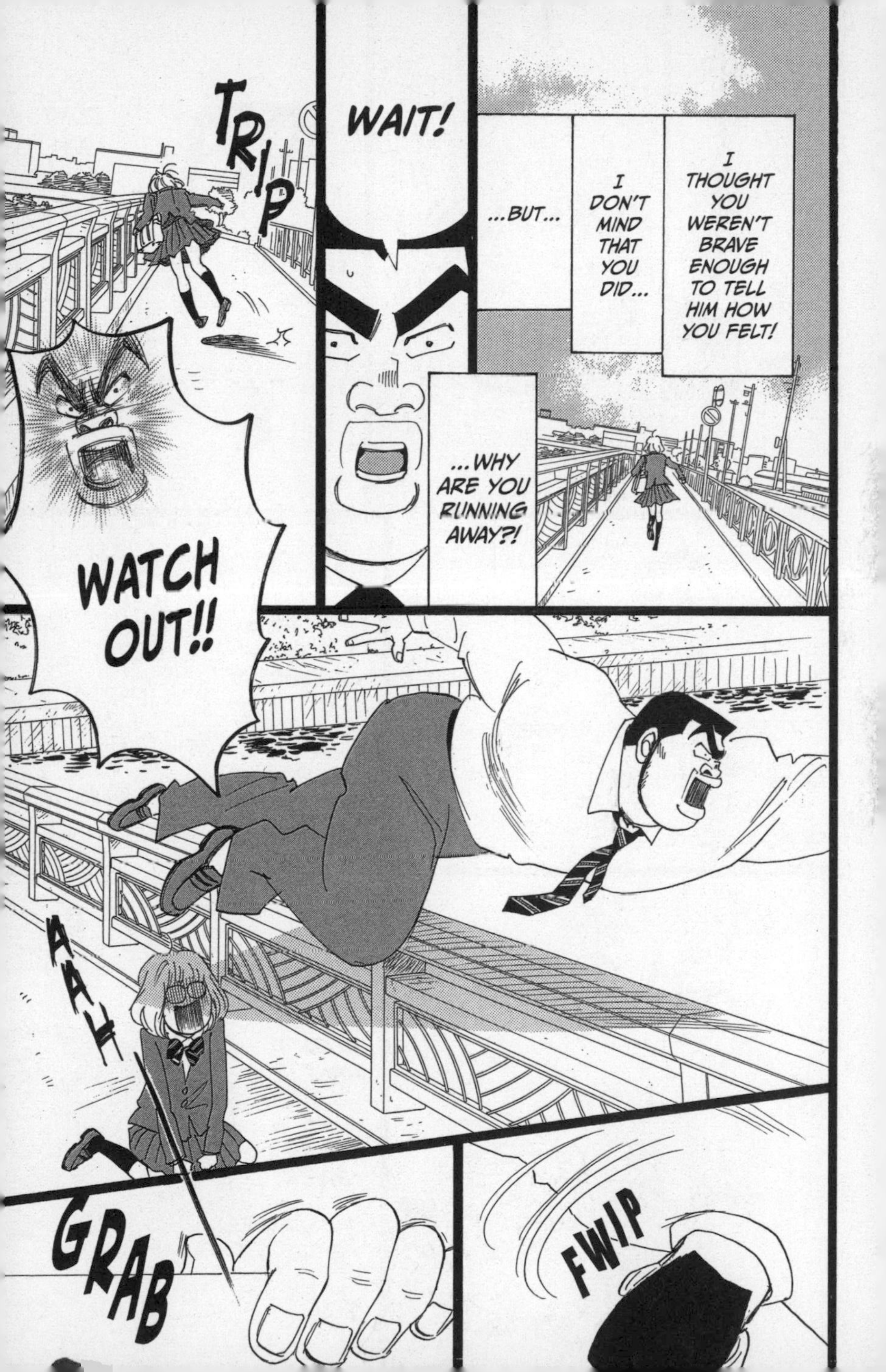
I THOUGHT YOU WEREN'T BRAVE ENOUGH TO TELL HIM HOW YOU FELT!
I DON'T MIND THAT YOU DID...
...BUT...
...WHY ARE YOU RUNNING AWAY?!
WAIT!
TRIP
WATCH OUT!!
AAAH
FWIP
GRAB

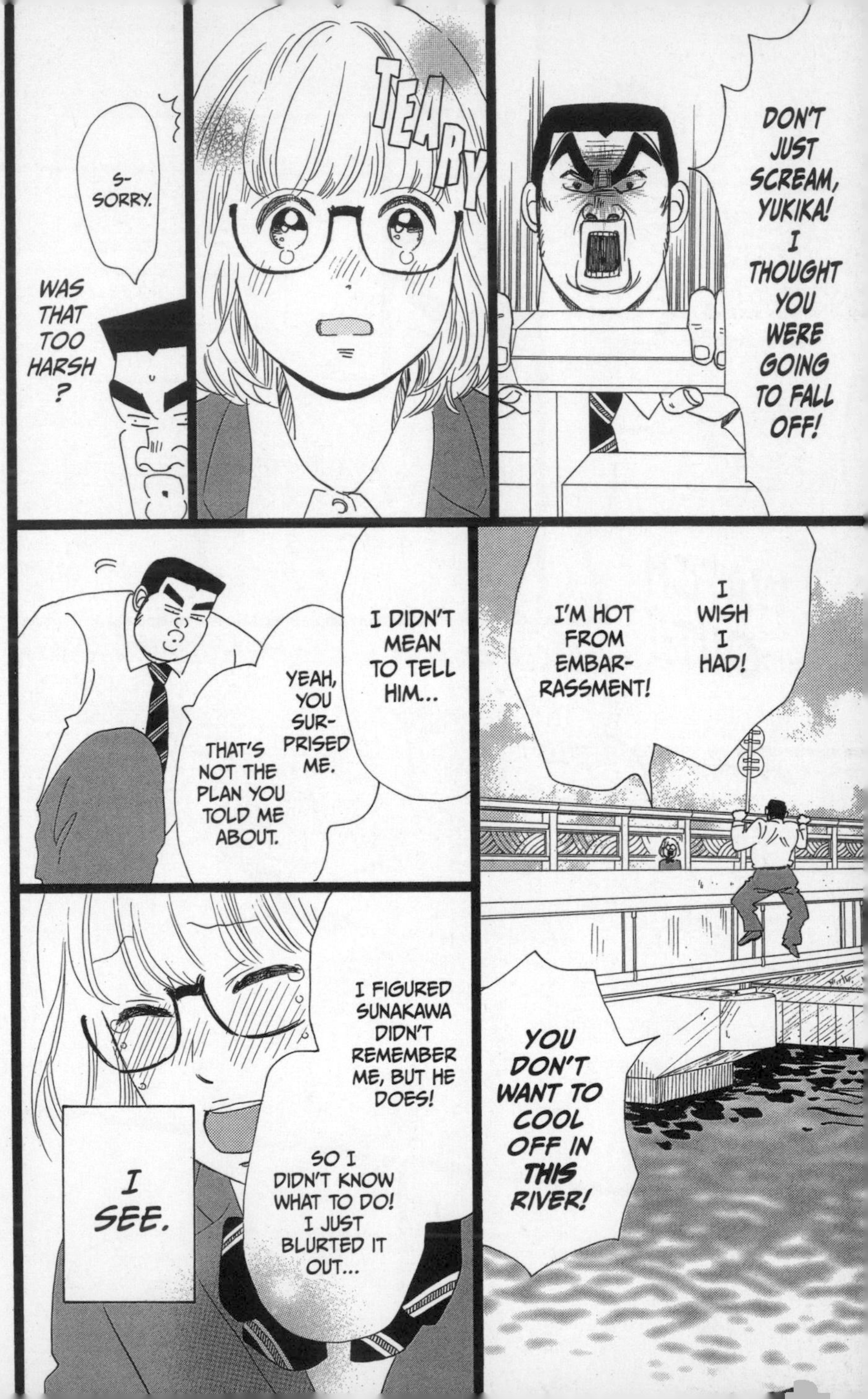
DON'T JUST SCREAM, YUKIKA! I THOUGHT YOU WERE GOING TO FALL OFF!
TEARY
S-SORRY.
WAS THAT TOO HARSH?
I WISH I HAD!
I'M HOT FROM EMBARRASSMENT!
YOU DON'T WANT TO COOL OFF IN THIS RIVER!
I DIDN'T MEAN TO TELL HIM...
YEAH, YOU SURPRISED ME.
THAT'S NOT THE PLAN YOU TOLD ME ABOUT.
I FIGURED SUNAKAWA DIDN'T REMEMBER ME, BUT HE DOES!
SO I DIDN'T KNOW WHAT TO DO! I JUST BLURTED IT OUT...
I SEE.

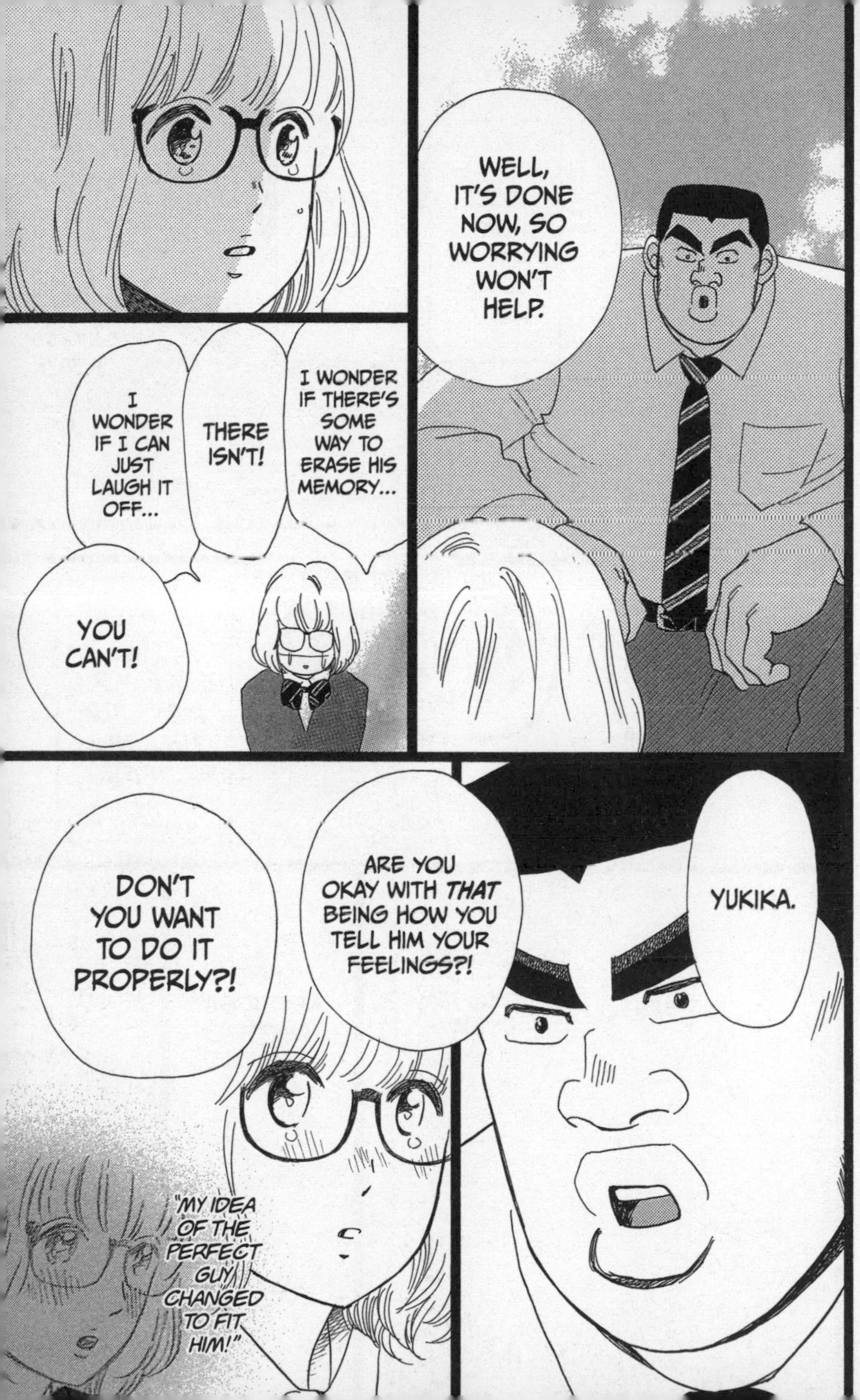
WELL, IT'S DONE NOW, SO WORRYING WON'T HELP.
I WONDER IF THERE'S SOME WAY TO ERASE HIS MEMORY...
THERE ISN'T!
I WONDER IF I CAN JUST LAUGH IT OFF...
YOU CAN'T!
YUKIKA.
ARE YOU OKAY WITH *THAT* BEING HOW YOU TELL HIM YOUR FEELINGS?!
DON'T YOU WANT TO DO IT PROPERLY?!
"MY IDEA OF THE PERFECT GUY CHANGED TO FIT HIM!"

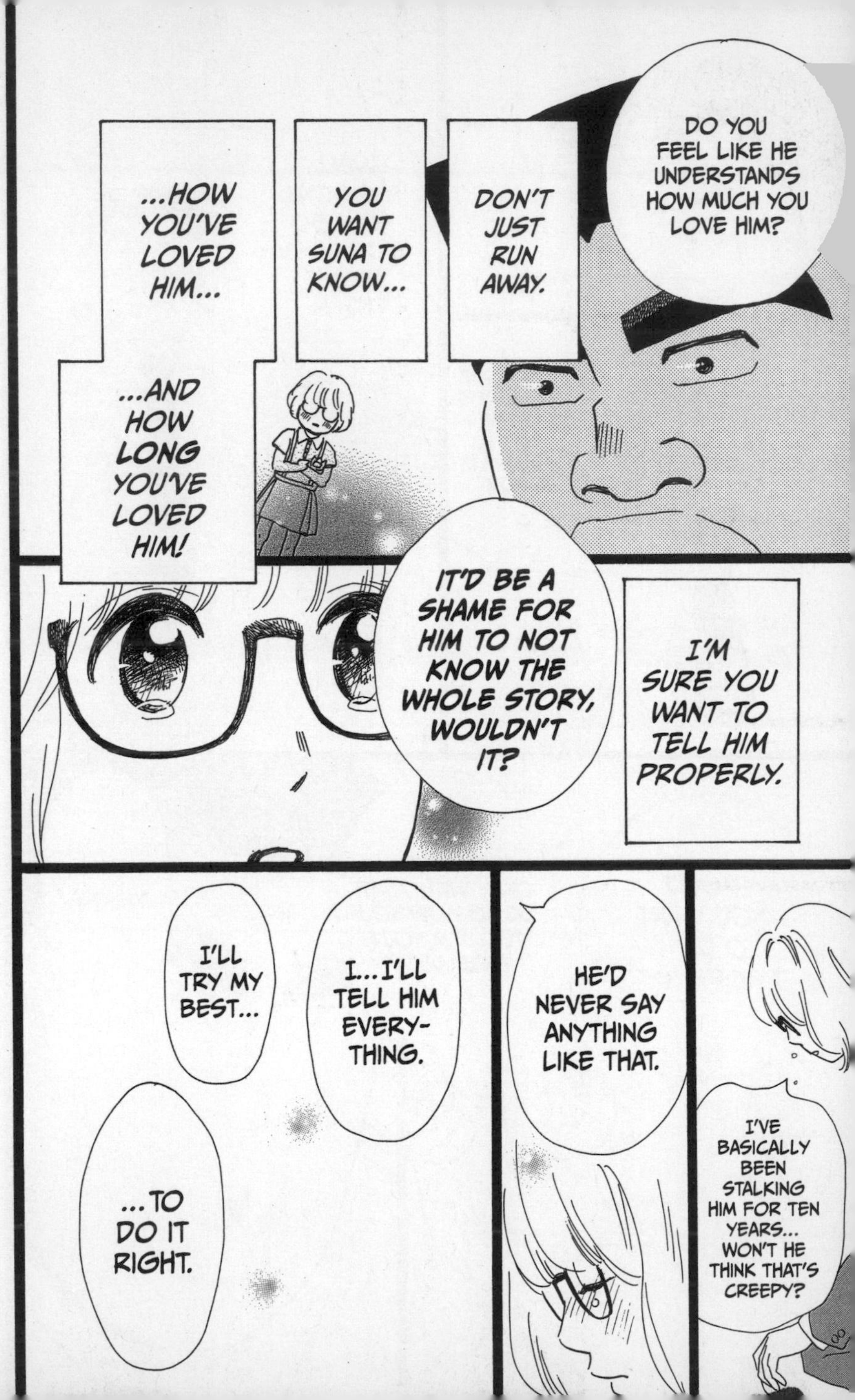

DO YOU FEEL LIKE HE UNDERSTANDS HOW MUCH YOU LOVE HIM?
DON'T JUST RUN AWAY.
YOU WANT SUNA TO KNOW...
...HOW YOU'VE LOVED HIM...
...AND HOW LONG YOU'VE LOVED HIM!
I'M SURE YOU WANT TO TELL HIM PROPERLY.
IT'D BE A SHAME FOR HIM TO NOT KNOW THE WHOLE STORY, WOULDN'T IT?
I'VE BASICALLY BEEN STALKING HIM FOR TEN YEARS... WON'T HE THINK THAT'S CREEPY?
HE'D NEVER SAY ANYTHING LIKE THAT.
I...I'LL TELL HIM EVERYTHING.
I'LL TRY MY BEST...
...TO DO IT RIGHT.

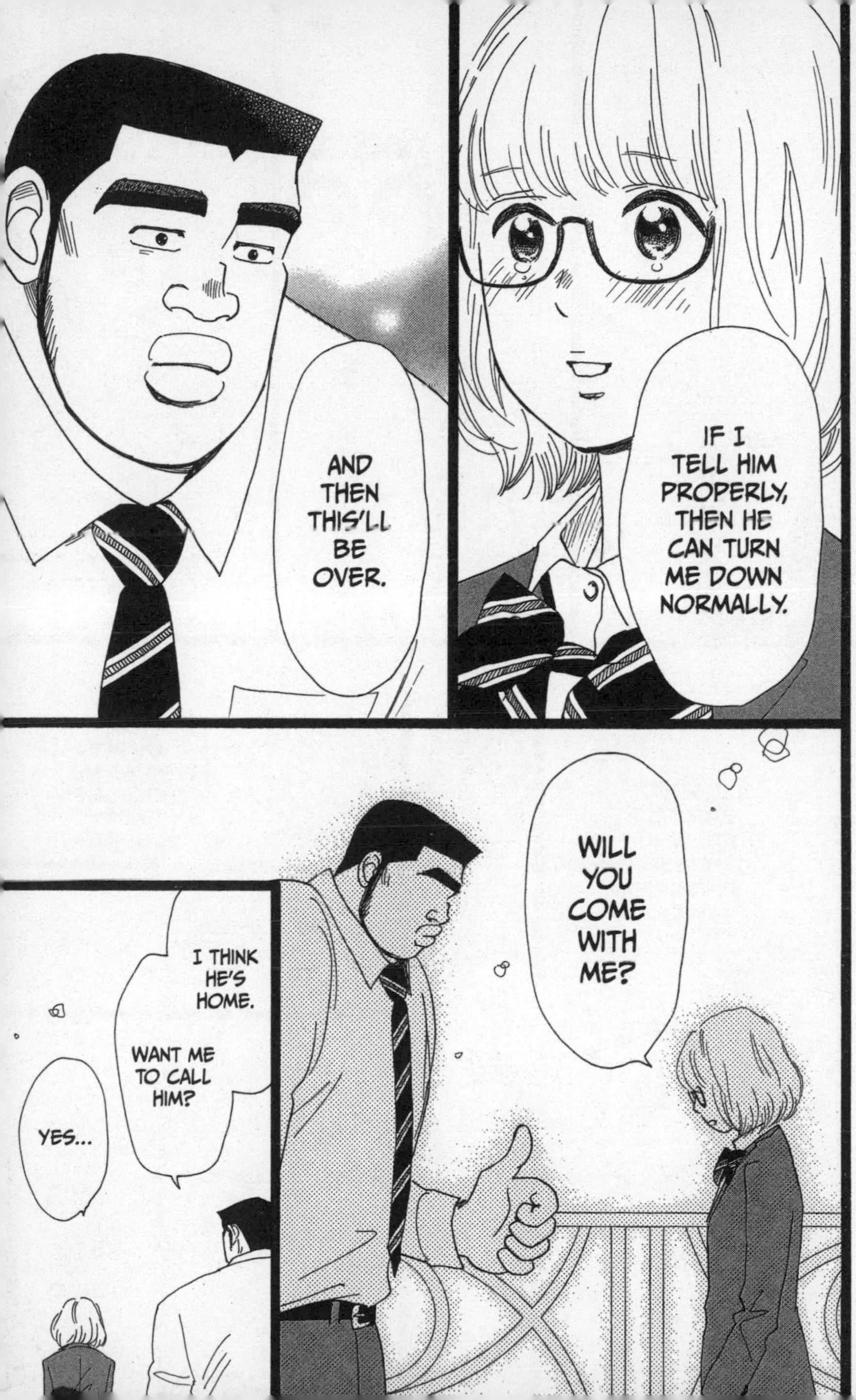
IF I TELL HIM PROPERLY, THEN HE CAN TURN ME DOWN NORMALLY.
AND THEN THIS'LL BE OVER.
WILL YOU COME WITH ME?
I THINK HE'S HOME.
WANT ME TO CALL HIM?
YES...

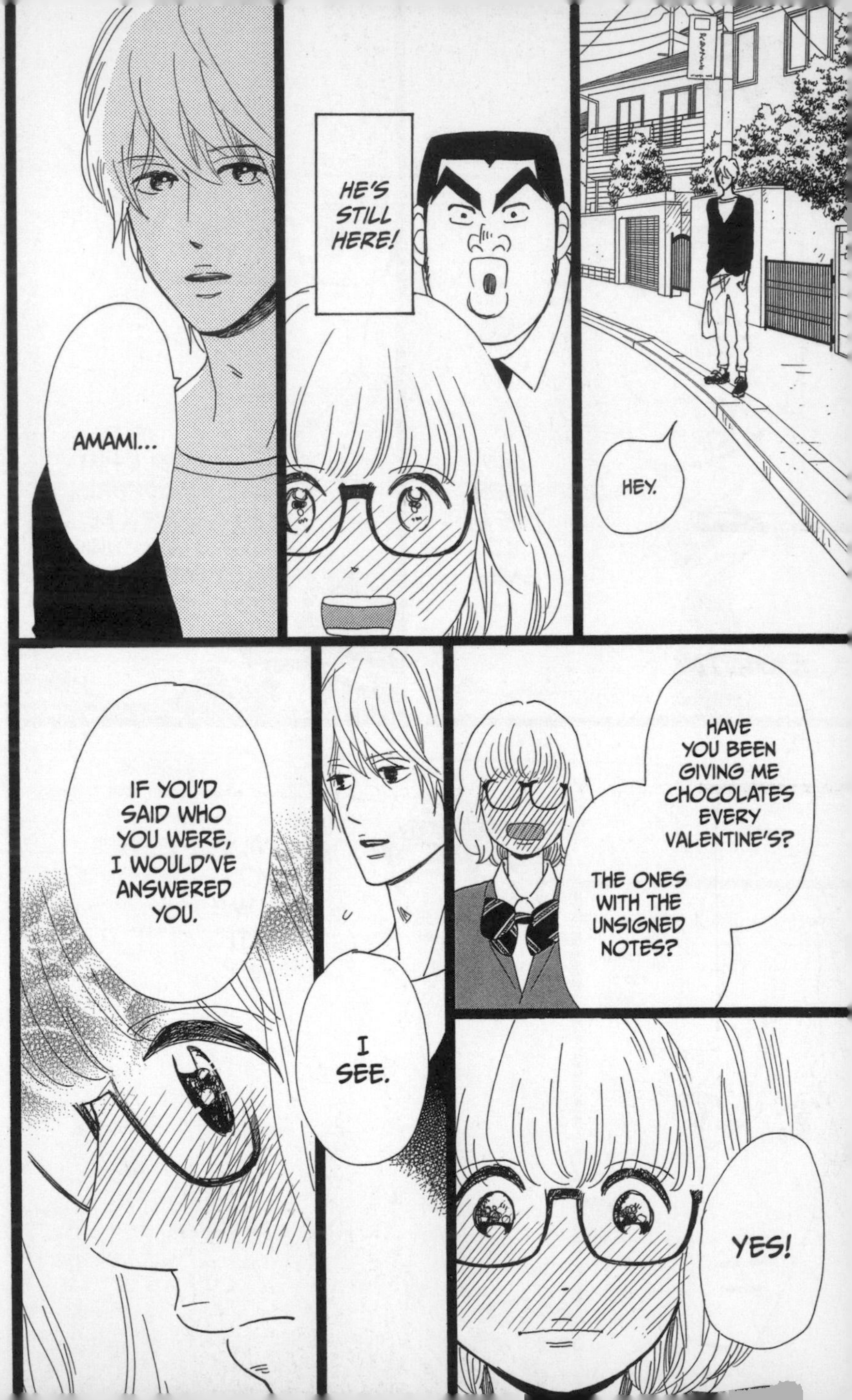
HEY.
HE'S STILL HERE!
AMAMI...
HAVE YOU BEEN GIVING ME CHOCOLATES EVERY VALENTINE'S?
THE ONES WITH THE UNSIGNED NOTES?
YES!
I SEE.
IF YOU'D SAID WHO YOU WERE, I WOULD'VE ANSWERED YOU.

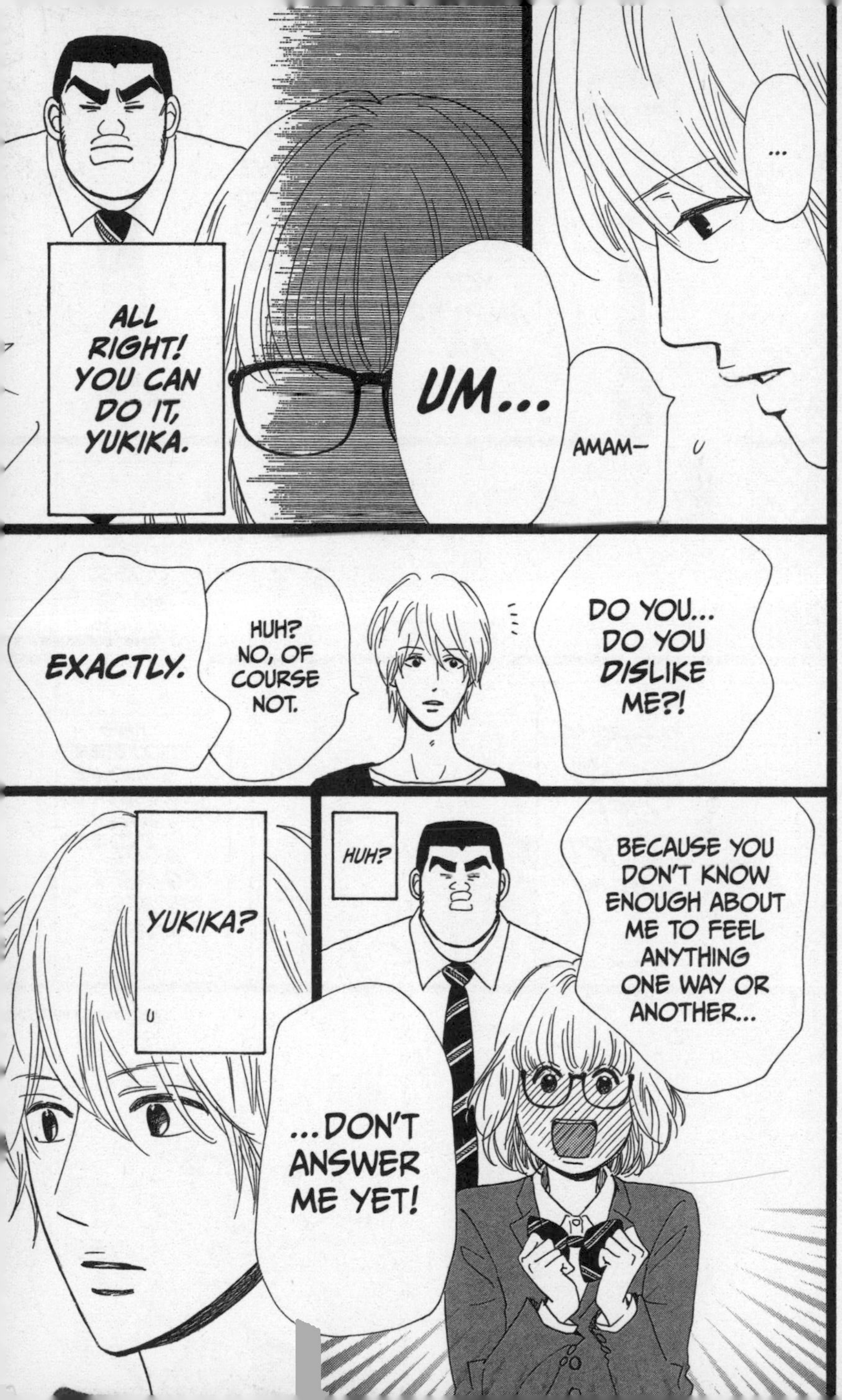
...
AMAM—
UM...
ALL RIGHT! YOU CAN DO IT, YUKIKA.
DO YOU... DO YOU DISLIKE ME?!
HUH? NO, OF COURSE NOT.
EXACTLY.
BECAUSE YOU DON'T KNOW ENOUGH ABOUT ME TO FEEL ANYTHING ONE WAY OR ANOTHER...
HUH?
...DON'T ANSWER ME YET!
YUKIKA?

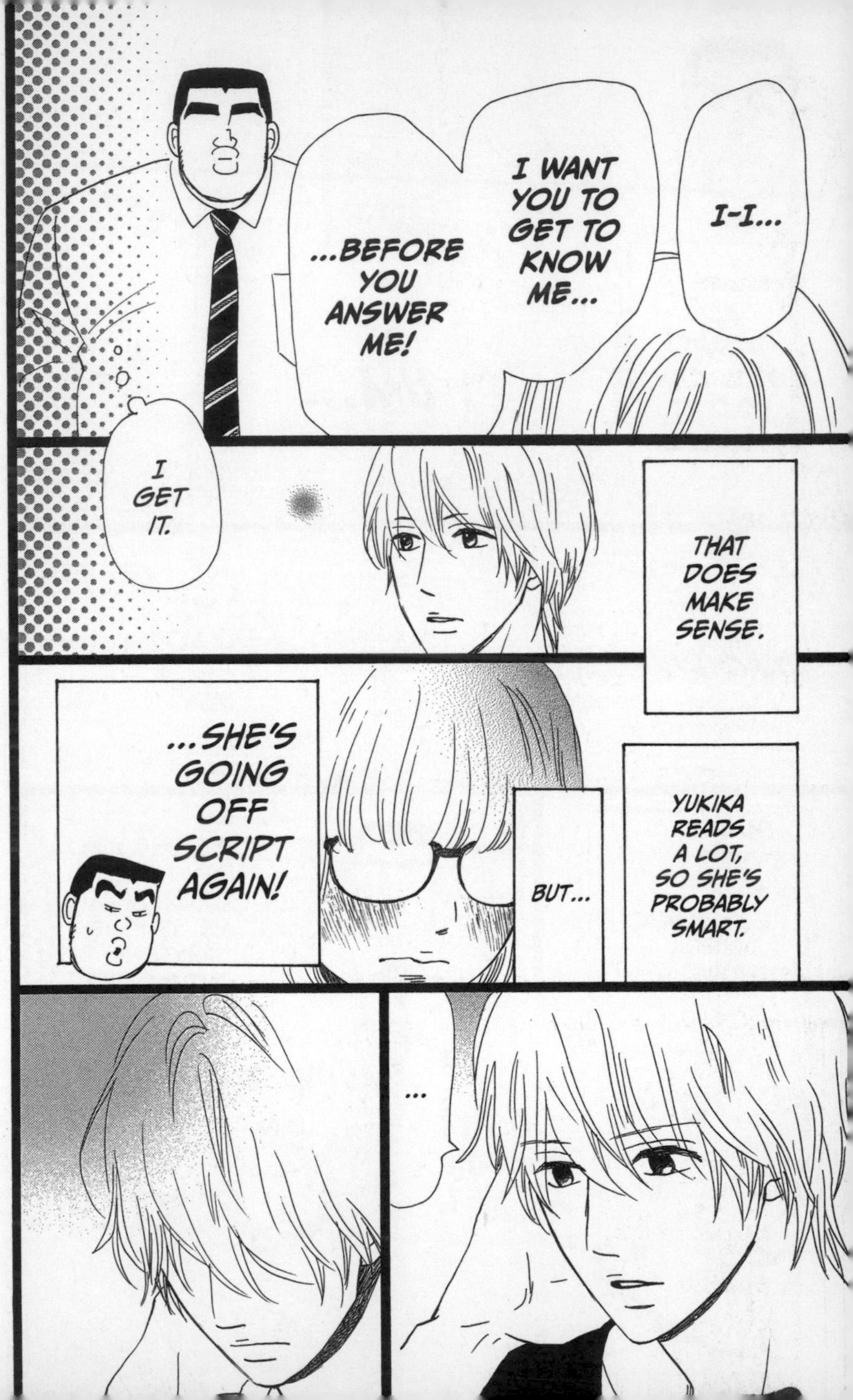
I-I...
I WANT YOU TO GET TO KNOW ME...
...BEFORE YOU ANSWER ME!
I GET IT.
THAT DOES MAKE SENSE.
YUKIKA READS A LOT, SO SHE'S PROBABLY SMART.
BUT...
...SHE'S GOING OFF SCRIPT AGAIN!
...

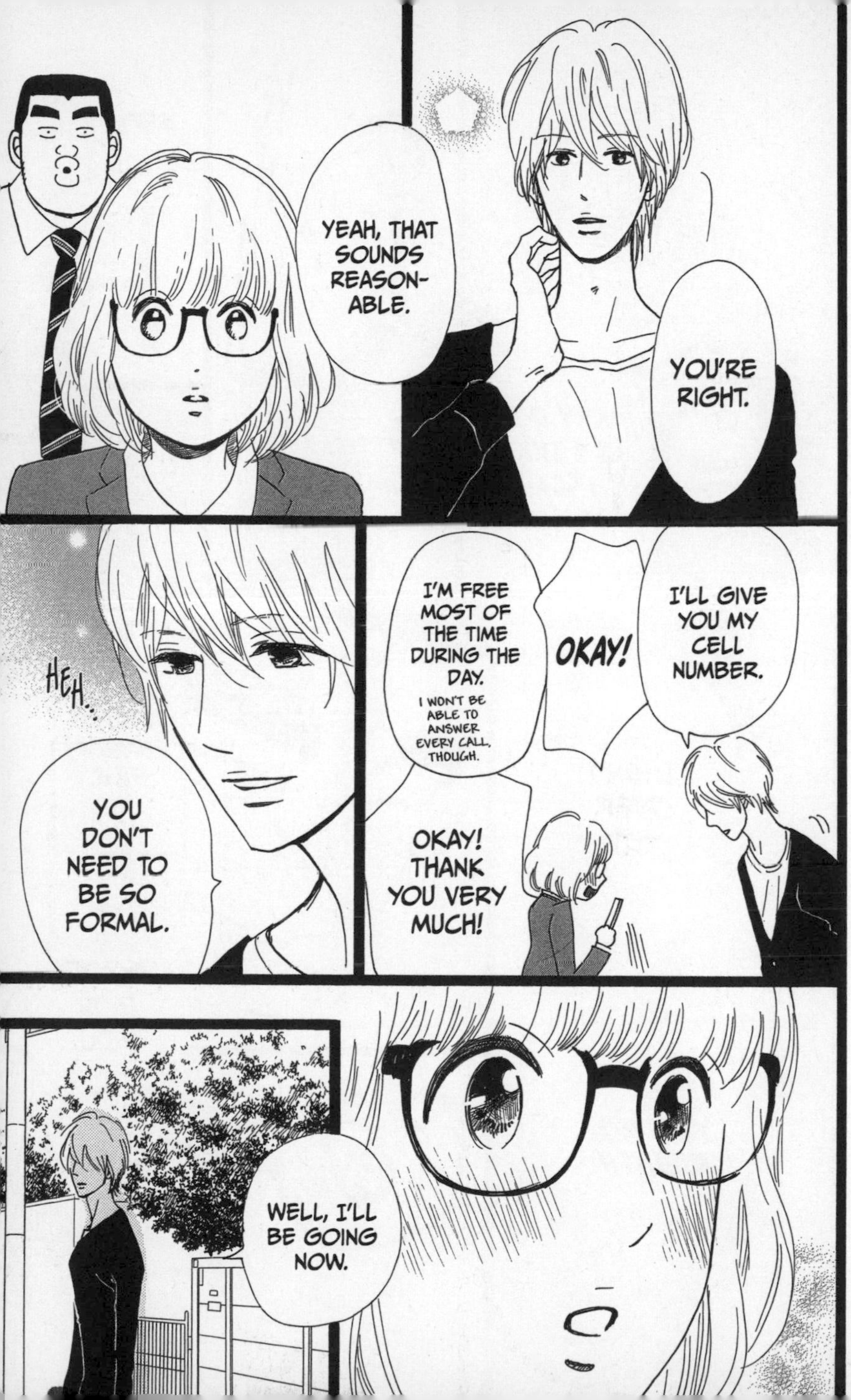
YEAH, THAT SOUNDS REASON-ABLE.
YOU'RE RIGHT.
I'LL GIVE YOU MY CELL NUMBER.
OKAY!
I'M FREE MOST OF THE TIME DURING THE DAY.
I WON'T BE ABLE TO ANSWER EVERY CALL, THOUGH.
OKAY! THANK YOU VERY MUCH!
HEH...
YOU DON'T NEED TO BE SO FORMAL.
WELL, I'LL BE GOING NOW.

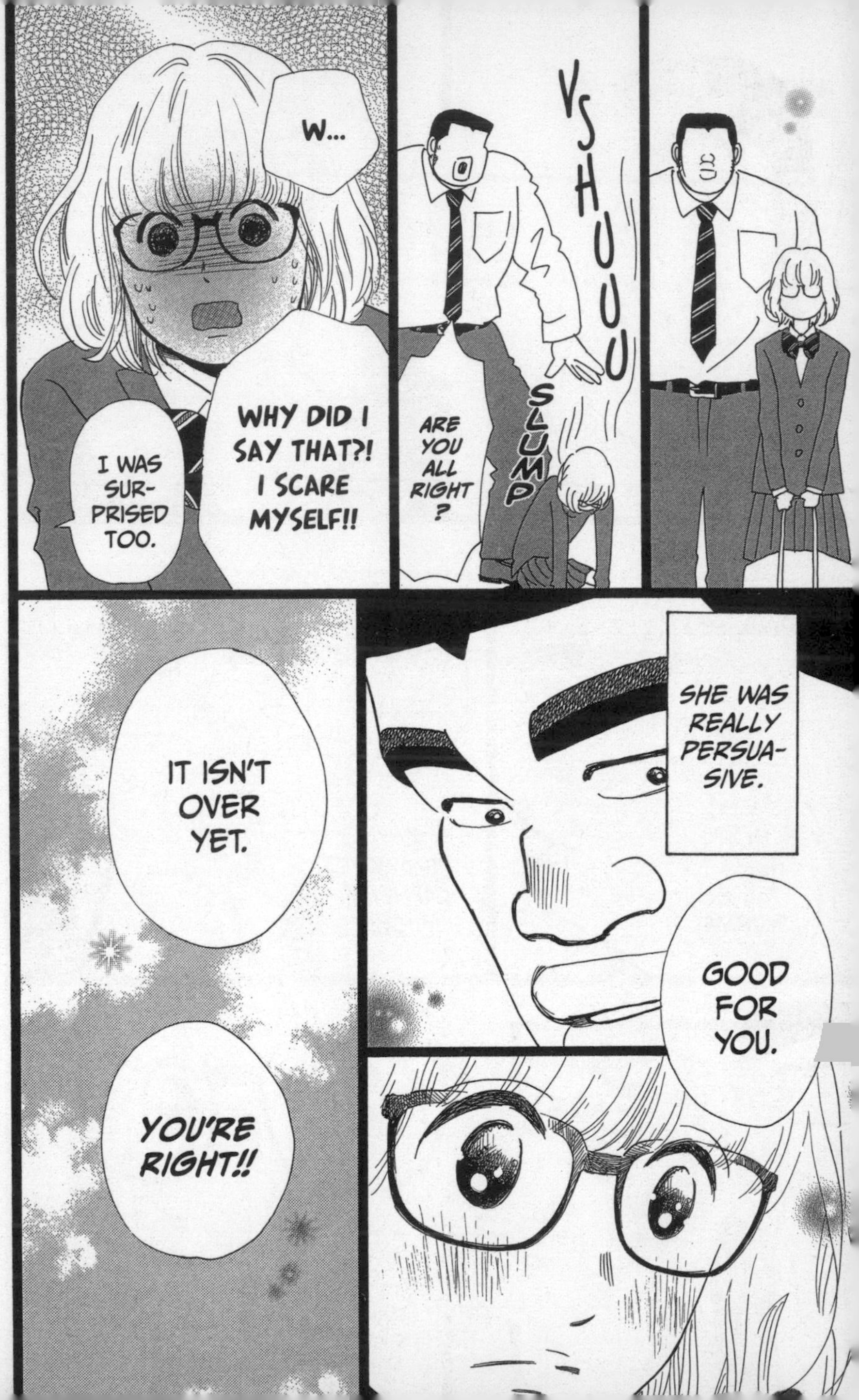
VSHUUUU
SLUMP
ARE YOU ALL RIGHT?
W...
WHY DID I SAY THAT?! I SCARE MYSELF!!
I WAS SURPRISED TOO.
SHE WAS REALLY PERSUA-SIVE.
GOOD FOR YOU.
IT ISN'T OVER YET.
YOU'RE RIGHT!!

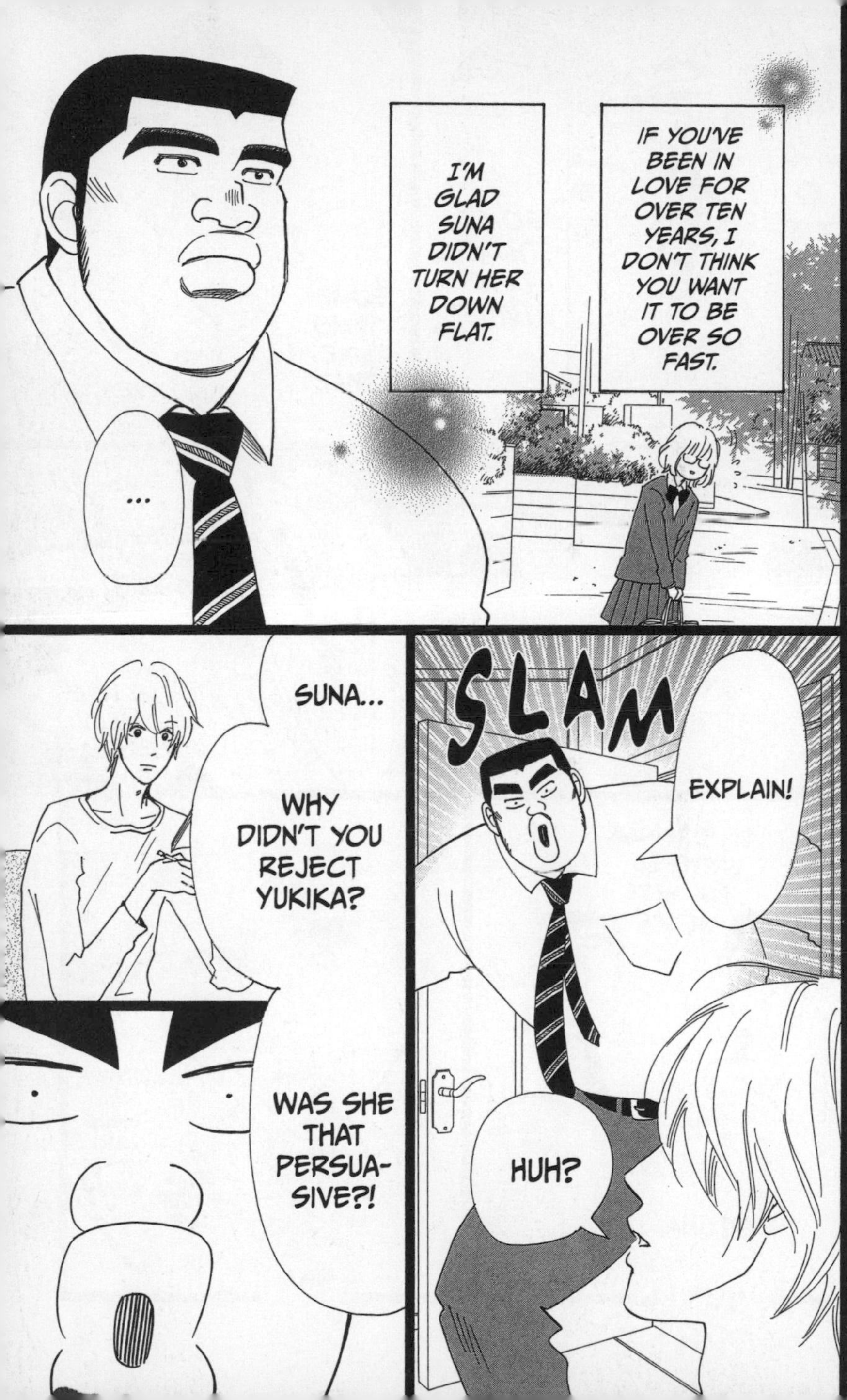
IF YOU'VE BEEN IN LOVE FOR OVER TEN YEARS, I DON'T THINK YOU WANT IT TO BE OVER SO FAST.
I'M GLAD SUNA DIDN'T TURN HER DOWN FLAT.
...
SLAM
EXPLAIN!
HUH?
SUNA...
WHY DIDN'T YOU REJECT YUKIKA?
WAS SHE THAT PERSUA-SIVE?!

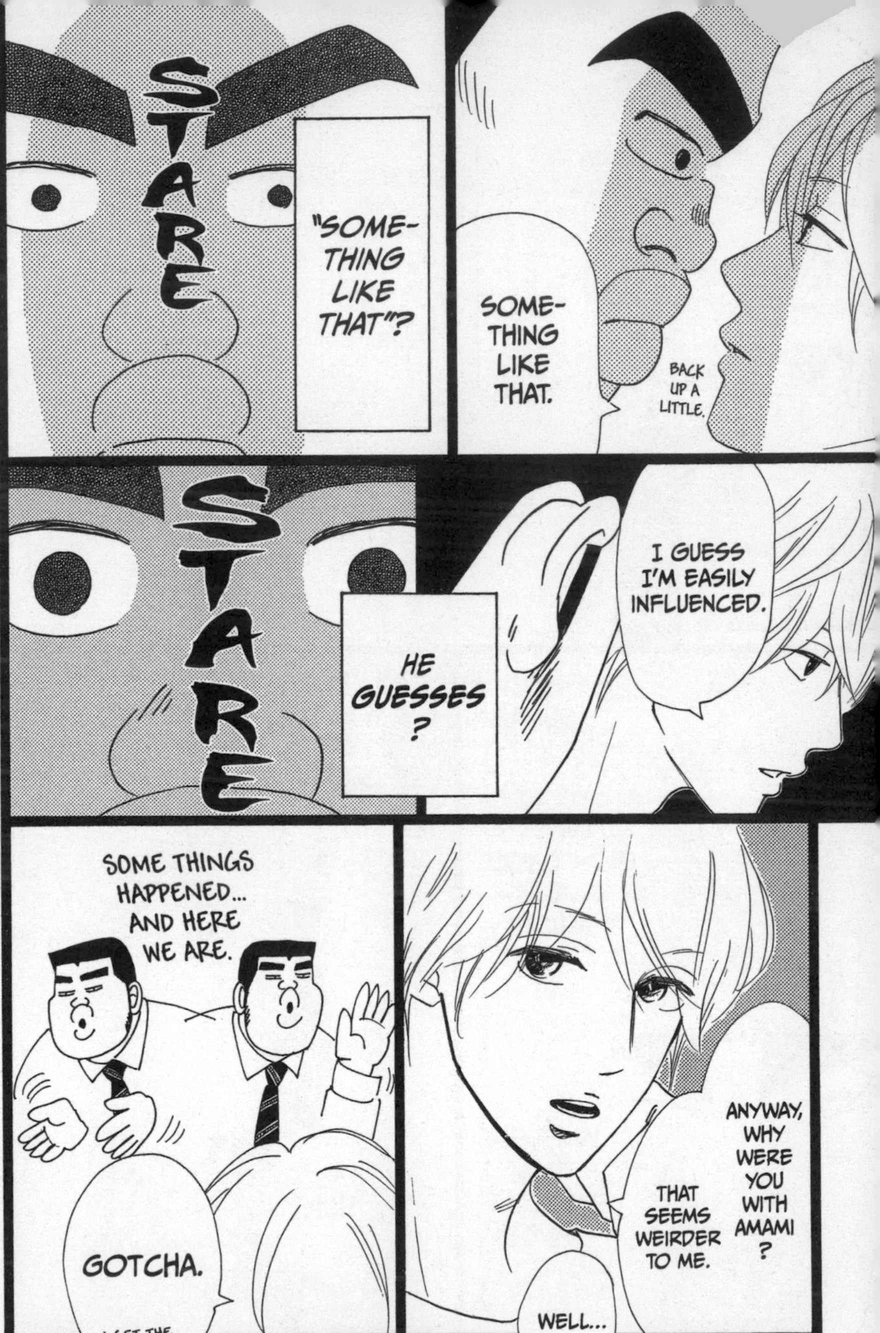
SOME-THING LIKE THAT.
BACK UP A LITTLE.
STARE
"SOME-THING LIKE THAT"?
I GUESS I'M EASILY INFLUENCED.
STARE
HE GUESSES?
ANYWAY, WHY WERE YOU WITH AMAMI?
THAT SEEMS WEIRDER TO ME.
WELL...
SOME THINGS HAPPENED... AND HERE WE ARE.
GOTCHA.
I GET THE DRIFT.

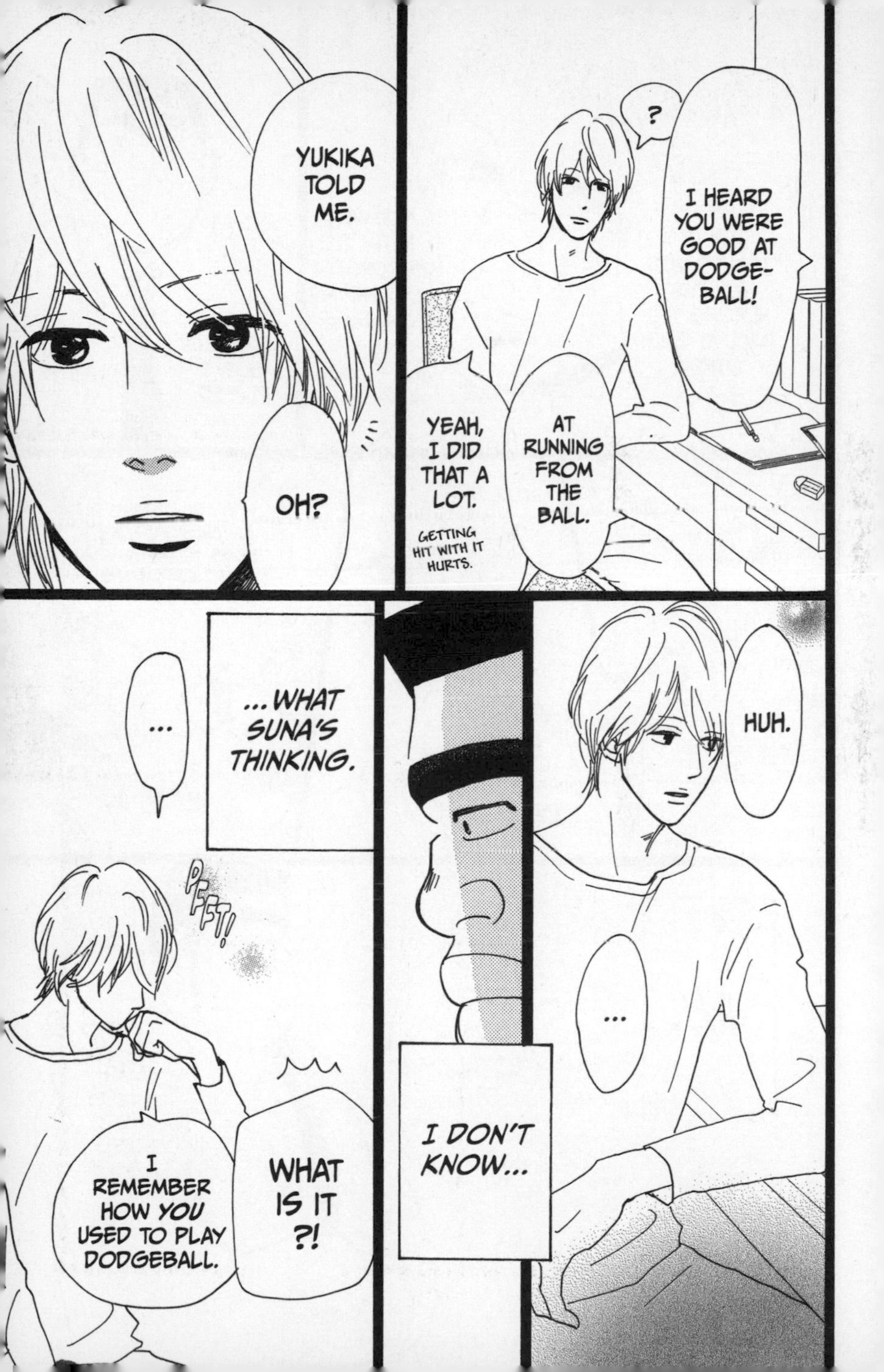
?
I HEARD YOU WERE GOOD AT DODGE-BALL!
AT RUNNING FROM THE BALL.
YEAH, I DID THAT A LOT.
GETTING HIT WITH IT HURTS.
YUKIKA TOLD ME.
OH?
HUH.
...
I DON'T KNOW...
...WHAT SUNA'S THINKING.
...
PFFT!
WHAT IS IT ?!
I REMEMBER HOW *YOU* USED TO PLAY DODGEBALL.

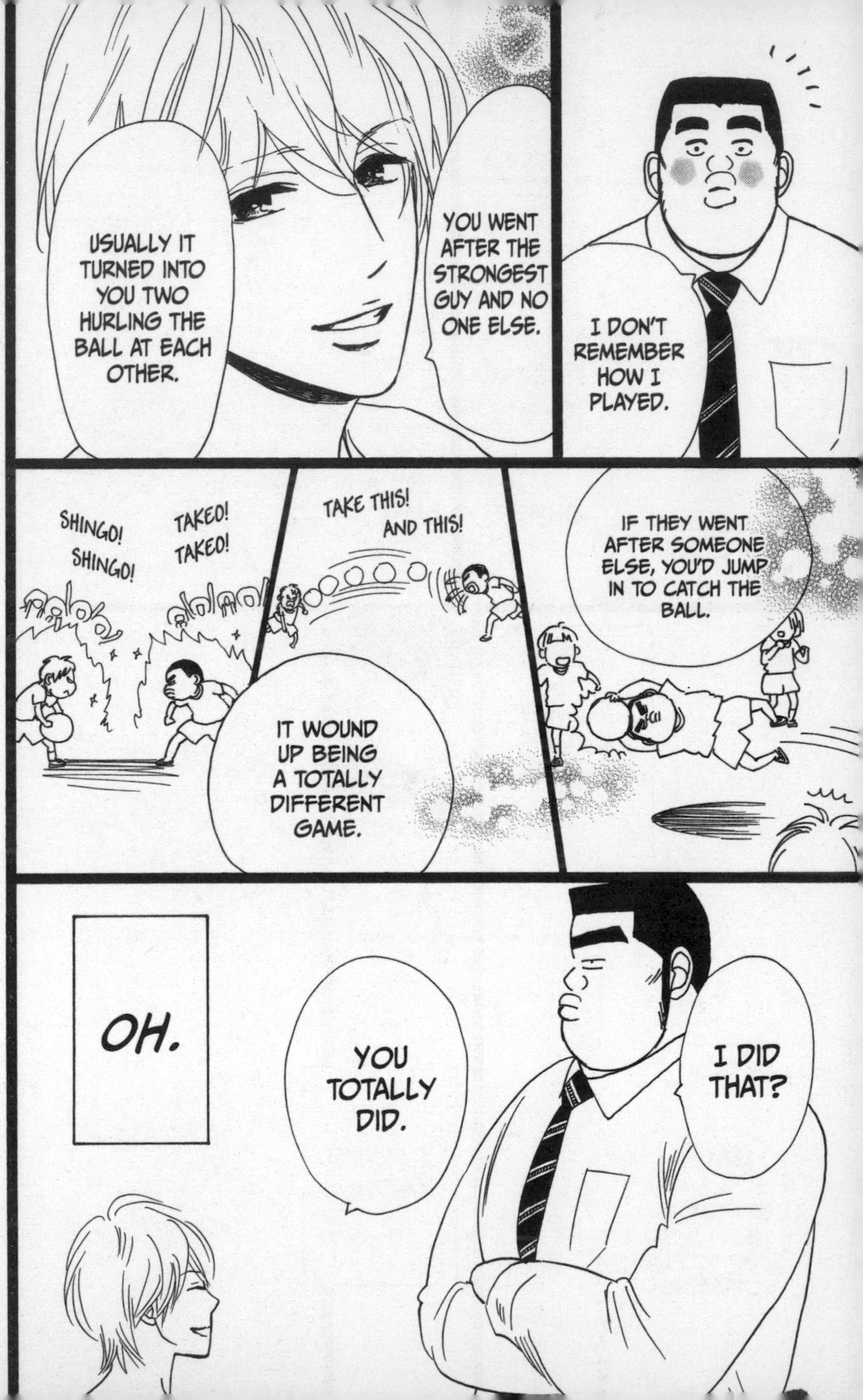
I DON'T REMEMBER HOW I PLAYED.
YOU WENT AFTER THE STRONGEST GUY AND NO ONE ELSE.
USUALLY IT TURNED INTO YOU TWO HURLING THE BALL AT EACH OTHER.
IF THEY WENT AFTER SOMEONE ELSE, YOU'D JUMP IN TO CATCH THE BALL.
TAKE THIS!
AND THIS!
IT WOUND UP BEING A TOTALLY DIFFERENT GAME.
TAKEO! TAKEO!
SHINGO! SHINGO!
I DID THAT?
YOU TOTALLY DID.
OH.

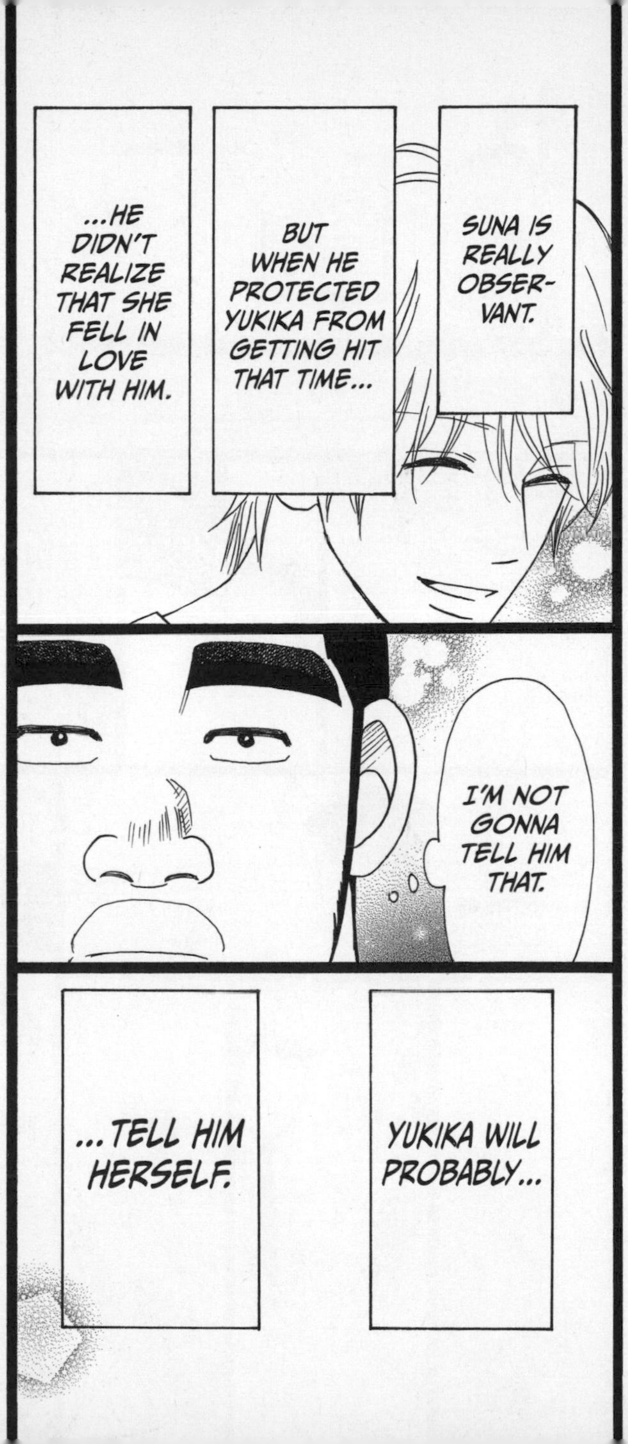
SUNA IS REALLY OBSERVANT.
BUT WHEN HE PROTECTED YUKIKA FROM GETTING HIT THAT TIME...
...HE DIDN'T REALIZE THAT SHE FELL IN LOVE WITH HIM.
I'M NOT GONNA TELL HIM THAT.
YUKIKA WILL PROBABLY...
...TELL HIM HERSELF.
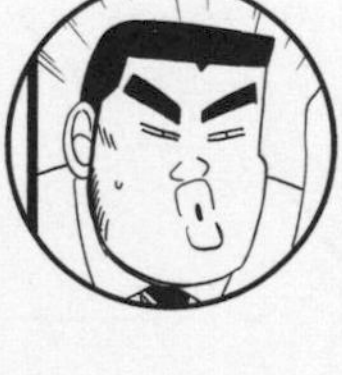

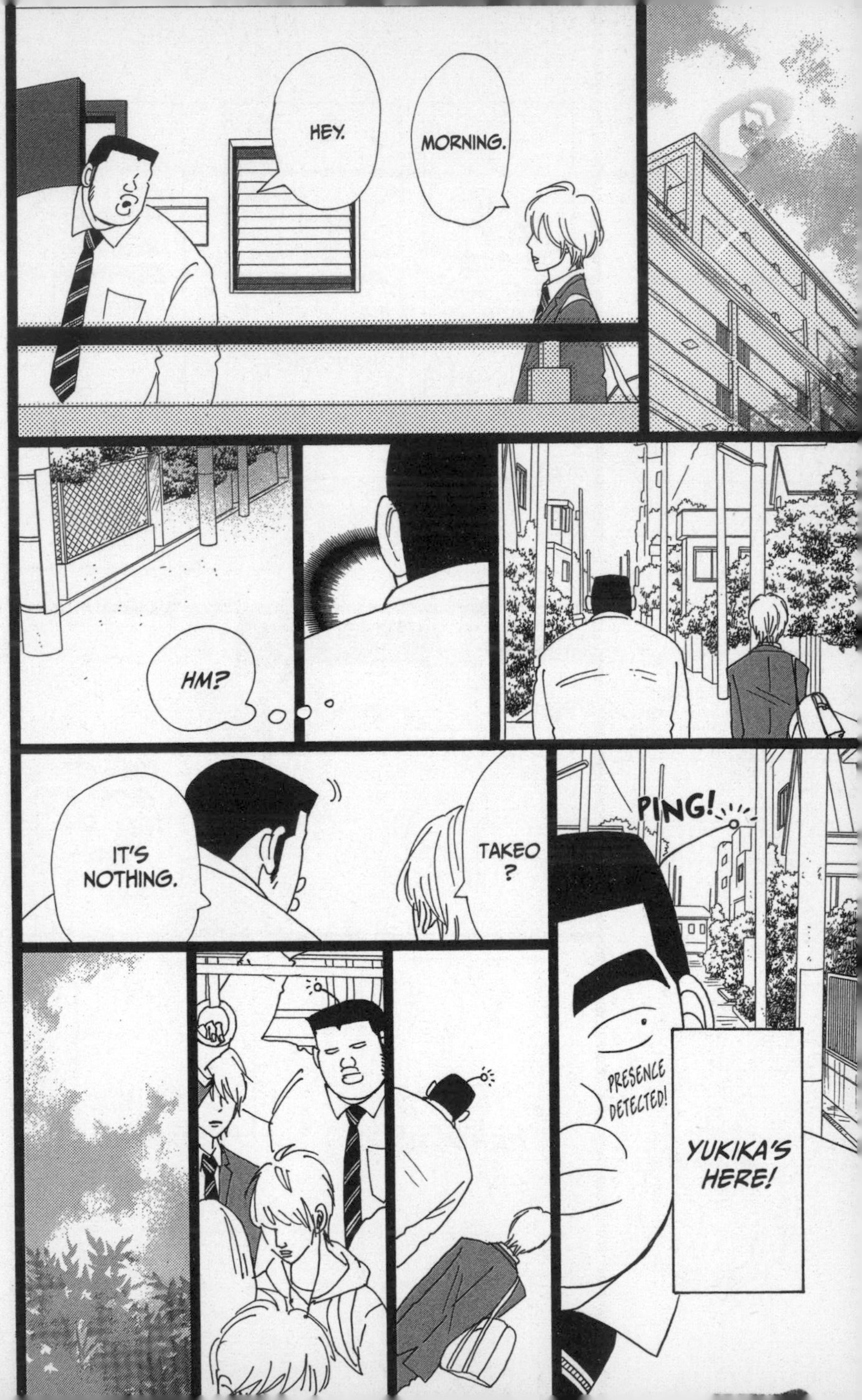
MORNING.
HEY.
HM?
PING!
YUKIKA'S HERE!
PRESENCE DETECTED!
TAKEO ?
IT'S NOTHING.

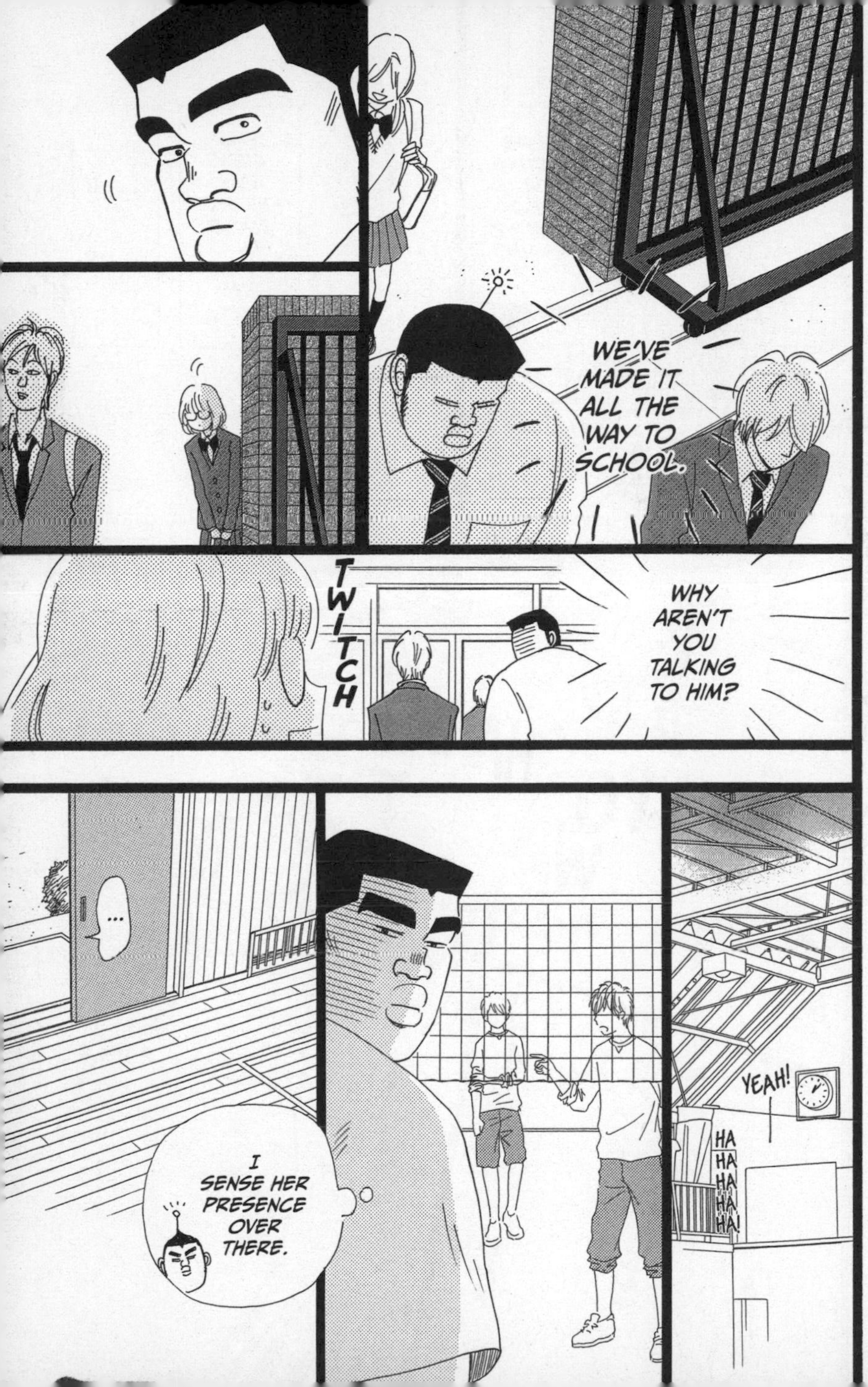
WE'VE MADE IT ALL THE WAY TO SCHOOL.
TWITCH
WHY AREN'T YOU TALKING TO HIM?
...
YEAH!
HA HA HA HA HA!
I SENSE HER PRESENCE OVER THERE.

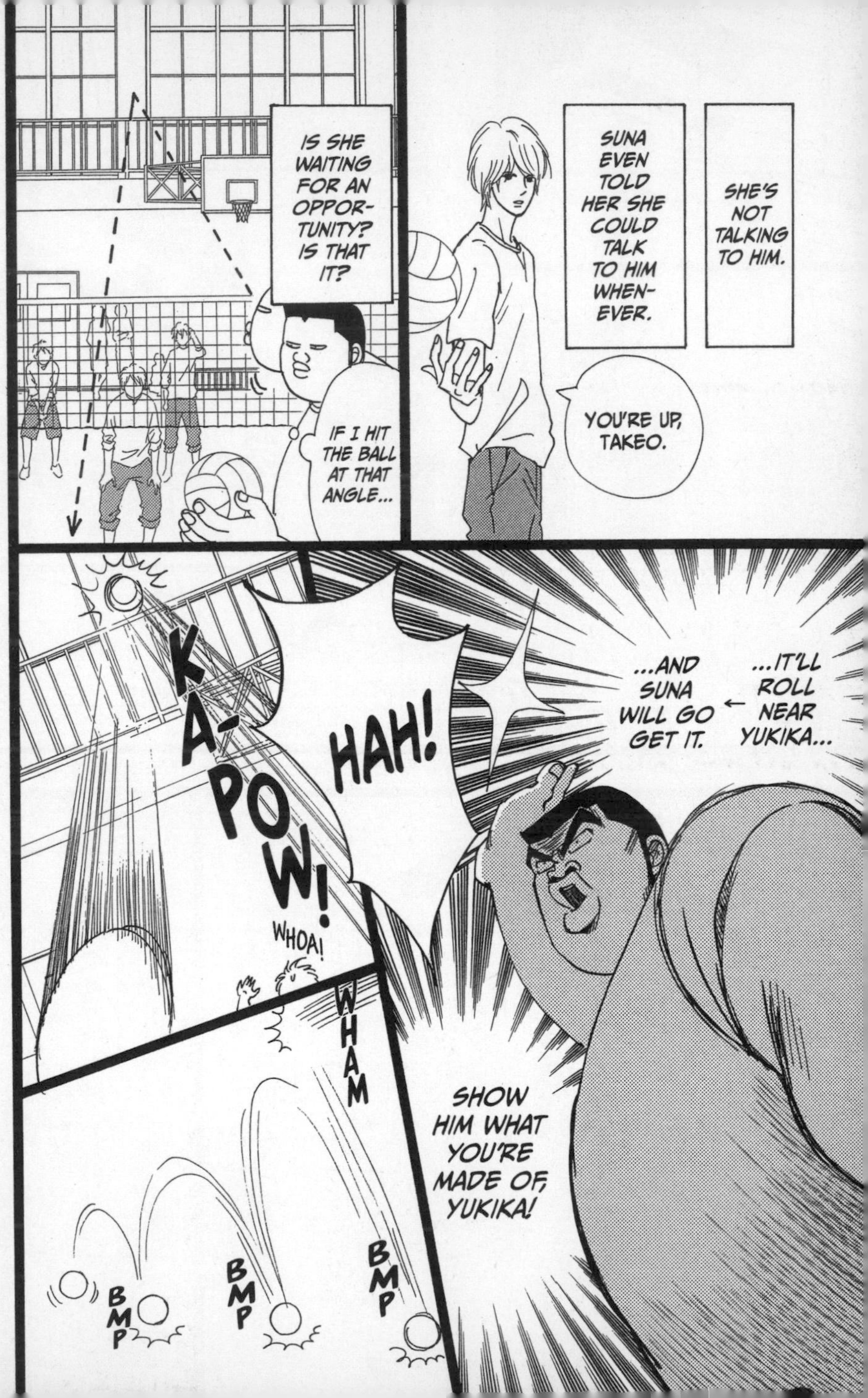
SHE'S NOT TALKING TO HIM.
SUNA EVEN TOLD HER SHE COULD TALK TO HIM WHENEVER.
YOU'RE UP, TAKEO.
IS SHE WAITING FOR AN OPPORTUNITY? IS THAT IT?
IF I HIT THE BALL AT THAT ANGLE...
...IT'LL ROLL NEAR YUKIKA...
...AND SUNA WILL GO GET IT.
HAH!
KA-POW!
WHOA!
SHOW HIM WHAT YOU'RE MADE OF, YUKIKA!
WHAM
BMP
BMP
BMP

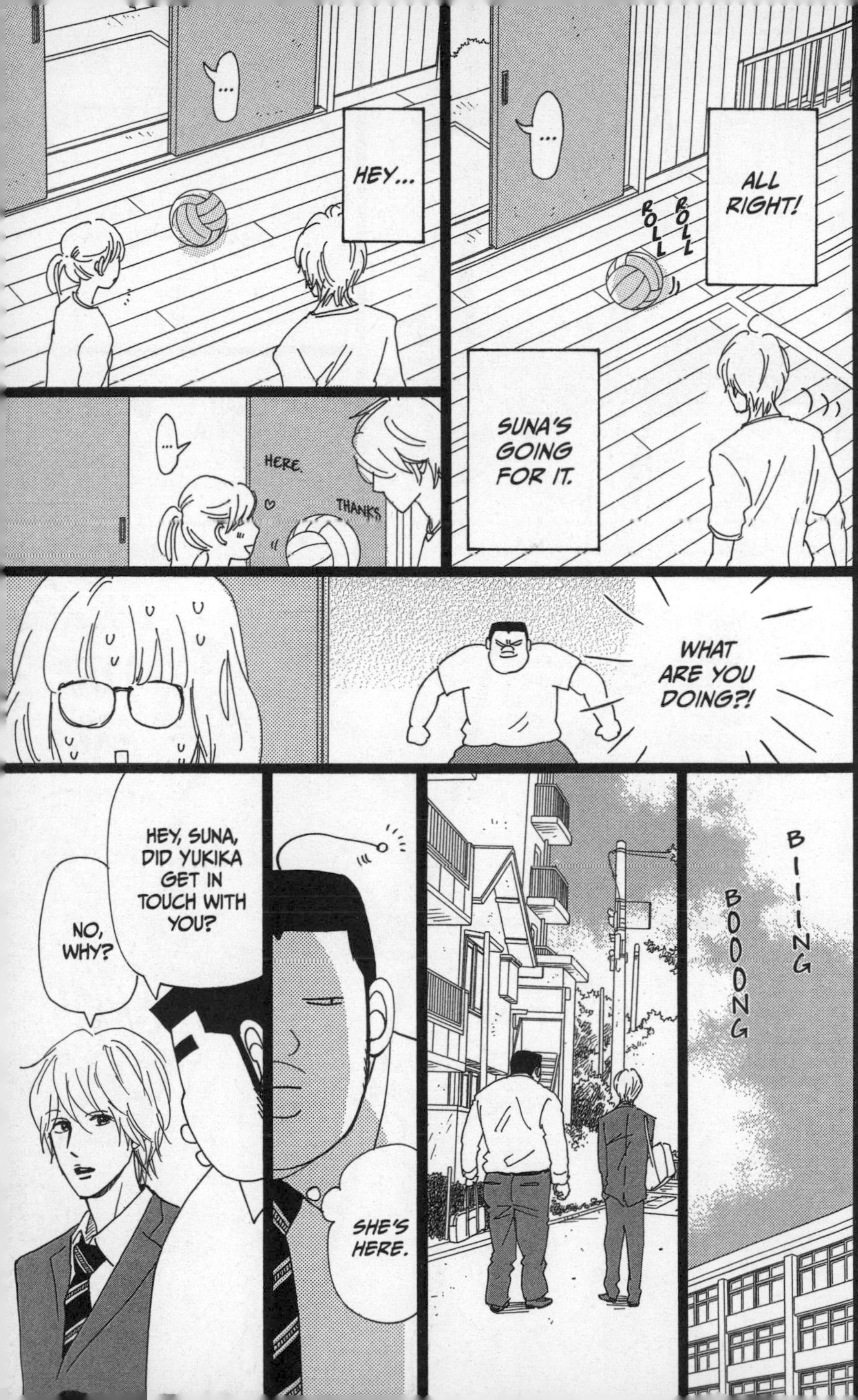
...
ALL RIGHT!
ROLL ROLL
SUNA'S GOING FOR IT.
...
HEY...
...
HERE.
THANKS
WHAT ARE YOU DOING?!
BIIING BOOONG
SHE'S HERE.
HEY, SUNA, DID YUKIKA GET IN TOUCH WITH YOU?
NO, WHY?

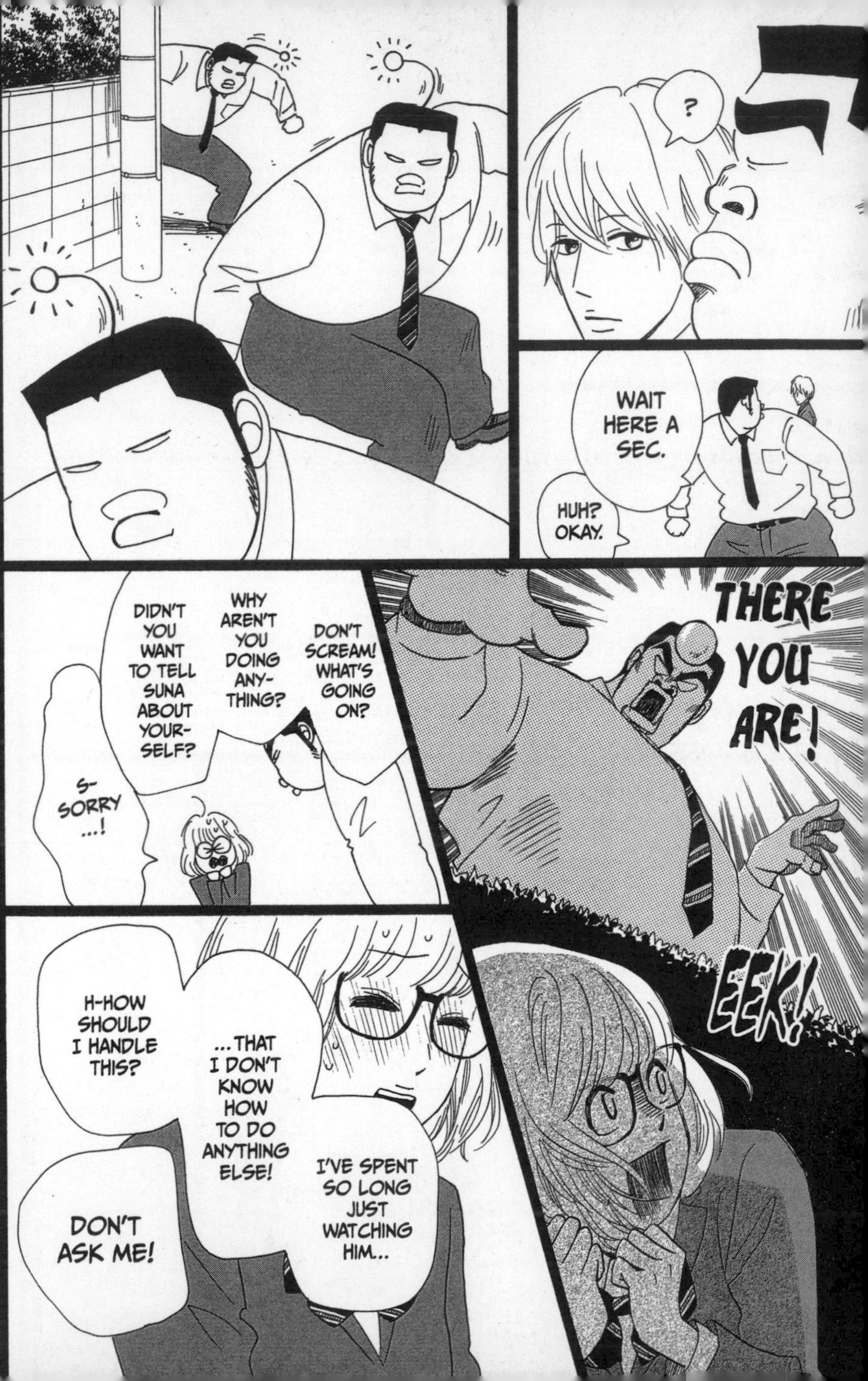
?
WAIT HERE A SEC.
HUH? OKAY.
THERE YOU ARE!
EEK!
DON'T SCREAM! WHAT'S GOING ON?
WHY AREN'T YOU DOING ANYTHING?
DIDN'T YOU WANT TO TELL SUNA ABOUT YOURSELF?
S-SORRY ...!
I'VE SPENT SO LONG JUST WATCHING HIM...
...THAT I DON'T KNOW HOW TO DO ANYTHING ELSE!
H-HOW SHOULD I HANDLE THIS?
DON'T ASK ME!

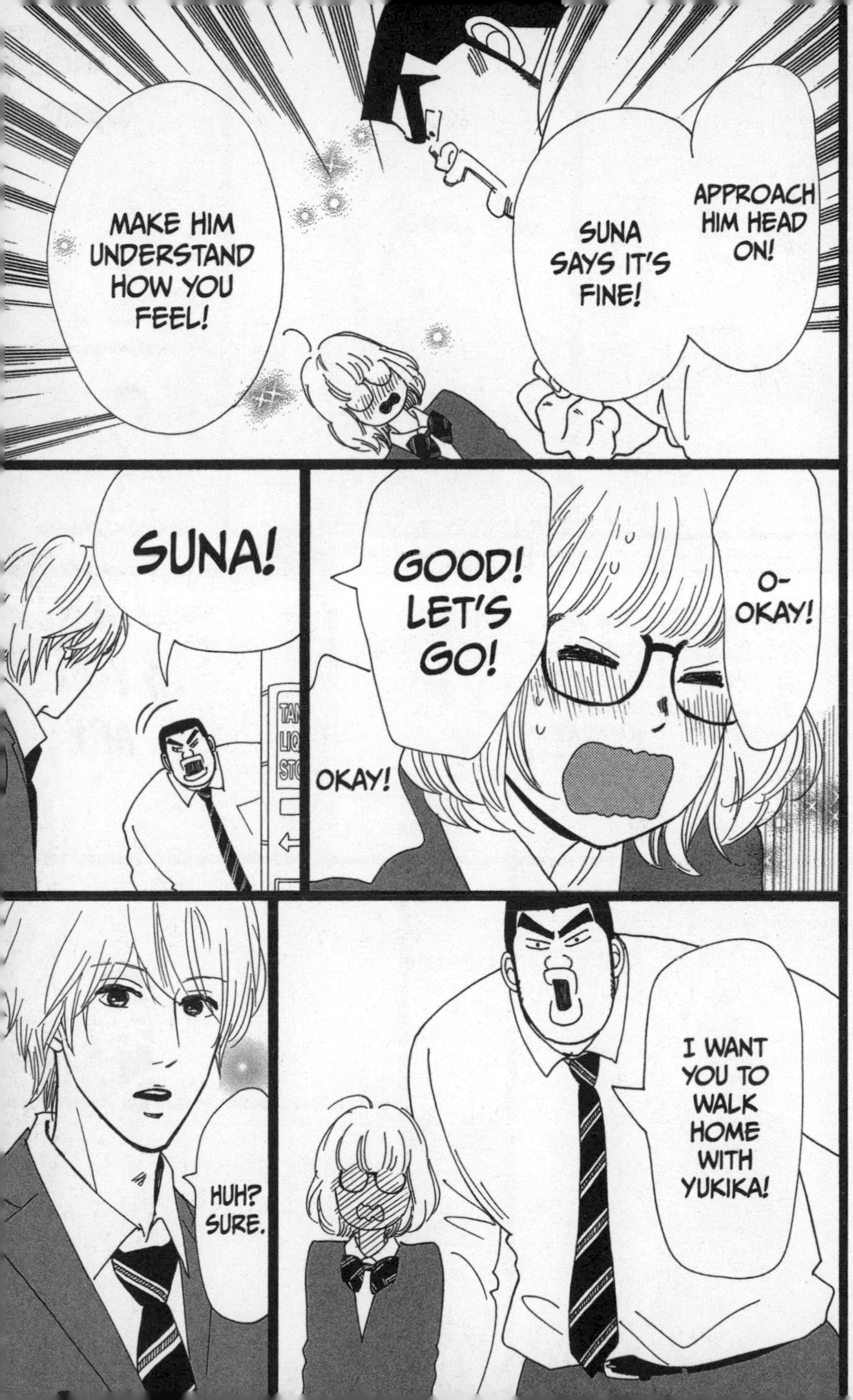
APPROACH HIM HEAD ON!
SUNA SAYS IT'S FINE!
MAKE HIM UNDERSTAND HOW YOU FEEL!
O-OKAY!
GOOD! LET'S GO!
OKAY!
SUNA!
I WANT YOU TO WALK HOME WITH YUKIKA!
HUH? SURE.

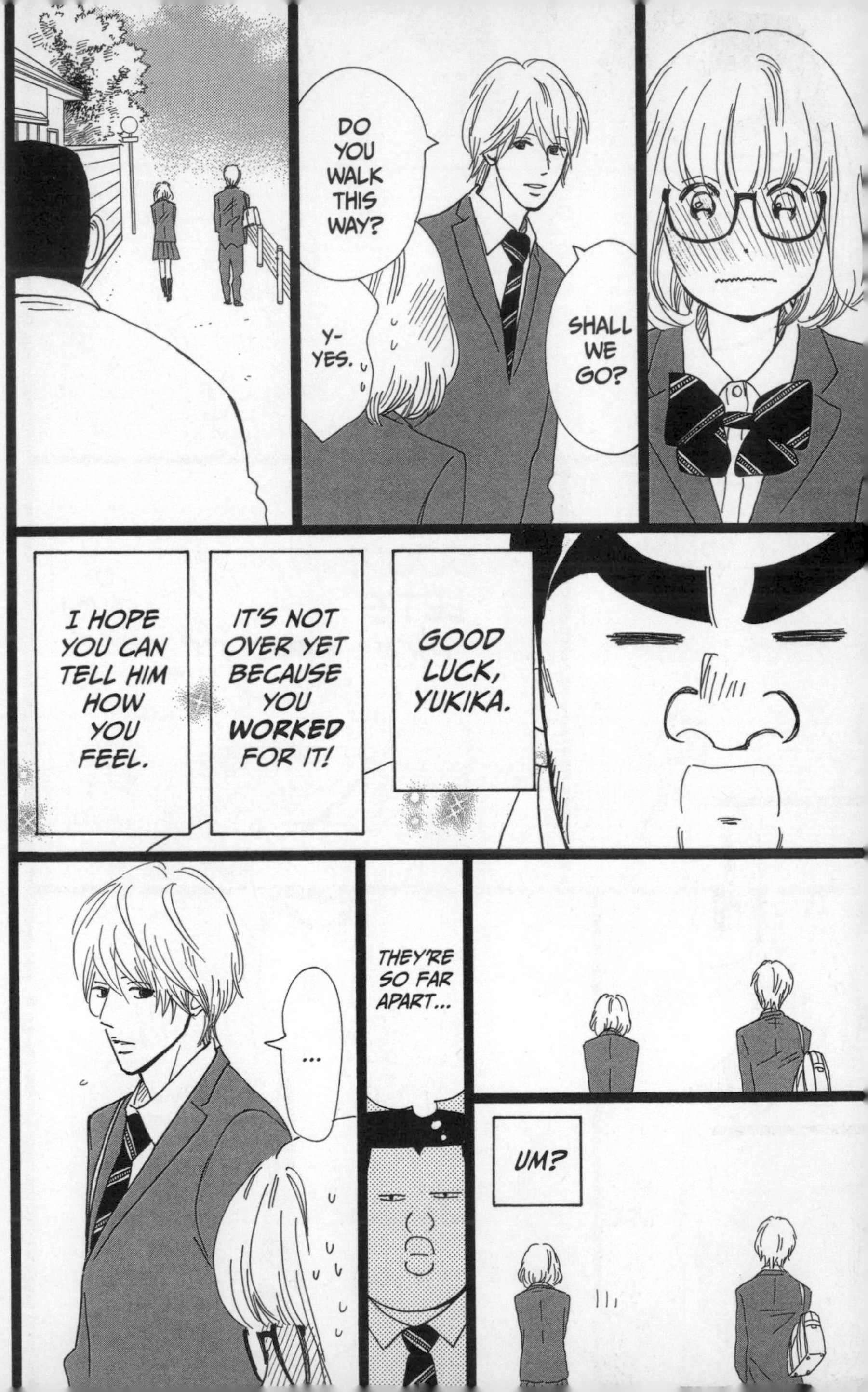
DO YOU WALK THIS WAY?
Y-YES.
SHALL WE GO?
GOOD LUCK, YUKIKA.
IT'S NOT OVER YET BECAUSE YOU WORKED FOR IT!
I HOPE YOU CAN TELL HIM HOW YOU FEEL.
UM?
THEY'RE SO FAR APART...
...

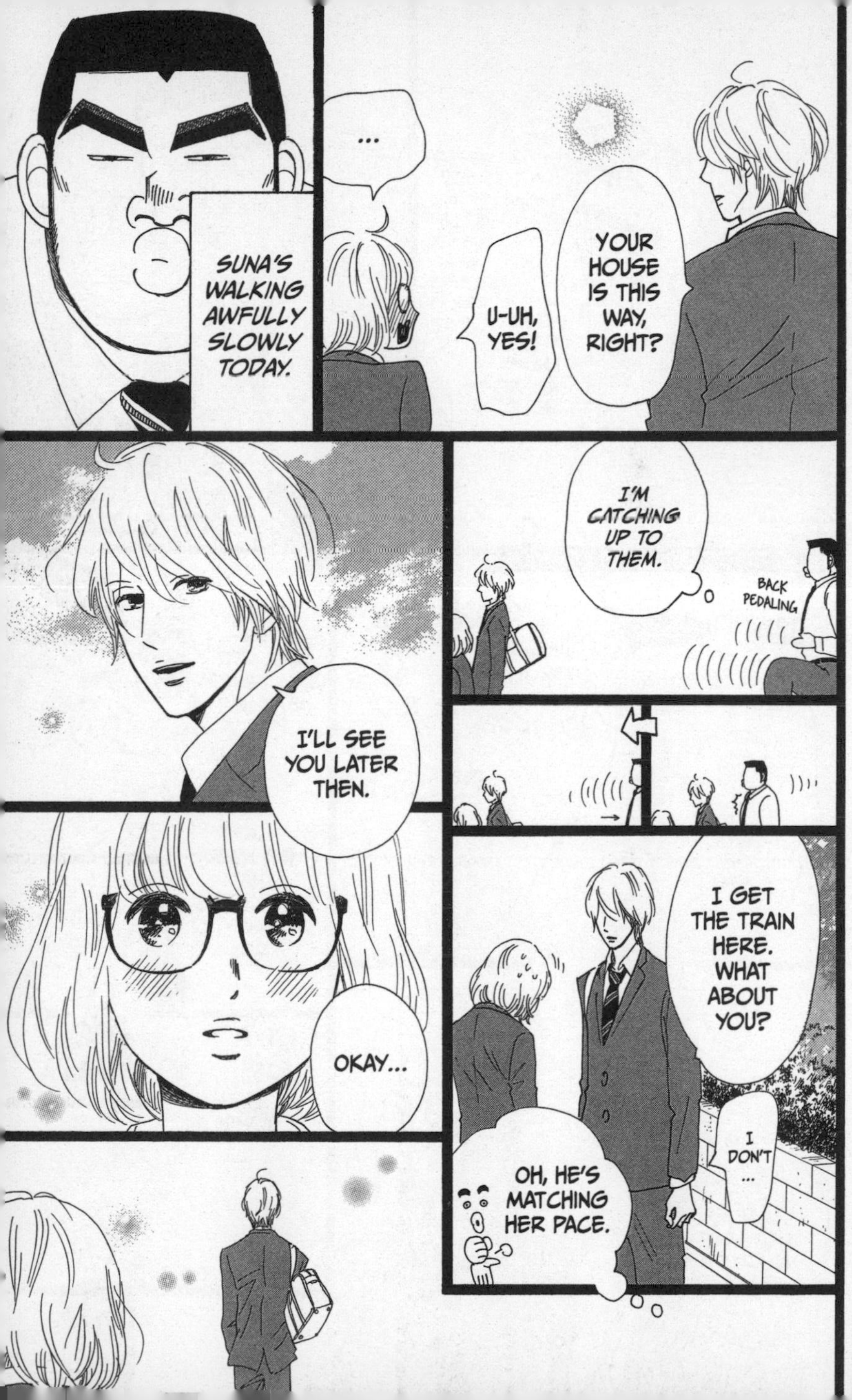
YOUR HOUSE IS THIS WAY, RIGHT?
U-UH, YES!
...
SUNA'S WALKING AWFULLY SLOWLY TODAY.
I'M CATCHING UP TO THEM.
BACK PEDALING
I GET THE TRAIN HERE. WHAT ABOUT YOU?
I DON'T ...
OH, HE'S MATCHING HER PACE.
I'LL SEE YOU LATER THEN.
OKAY...

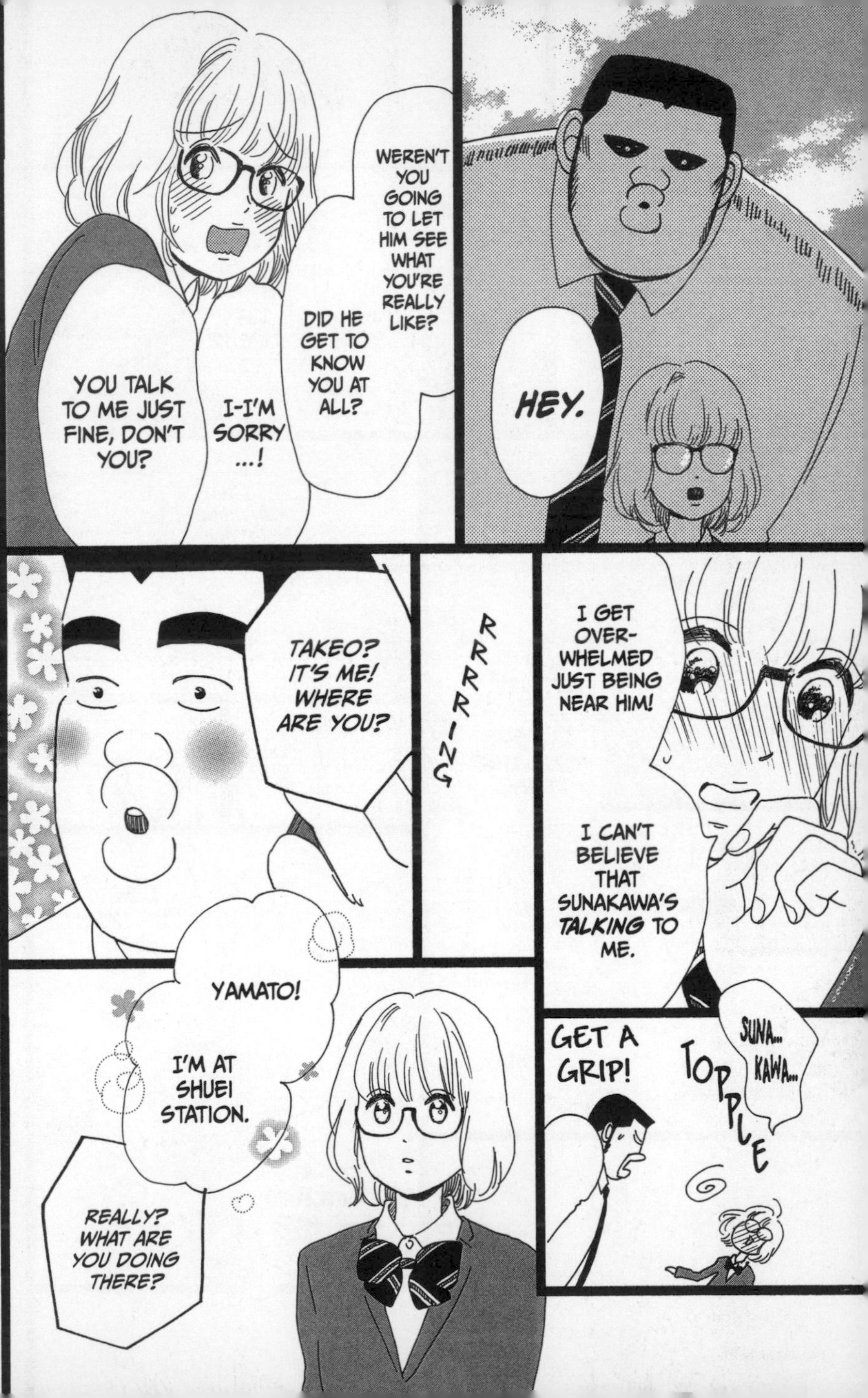
HEY.
WEREN'T YOU GOING TO LET HIM SEE WHAT YOU'RE REALLY LIKE?
DID HE GET TO KNOW YOU AT ALL?
I-I'M SORRY ...!
YOU TALK TO ME JUST FINE, DON'T YOU?
I GET OVER-WHELMED JUST BEING NEAR HIM!
I CAN'T BELIEVE THAT SUNAKAWA'S *TALKING* TO ME.
RRRRING
TAKEO? IT'S ME! WHERE ARE YOU?
SUNA... KAWA...
TOPPLE
GET A GRIP!
YAMATO!
I'M AT SHUEI STATION.
REALLY? WHAT ARE YOU DOING THERE?

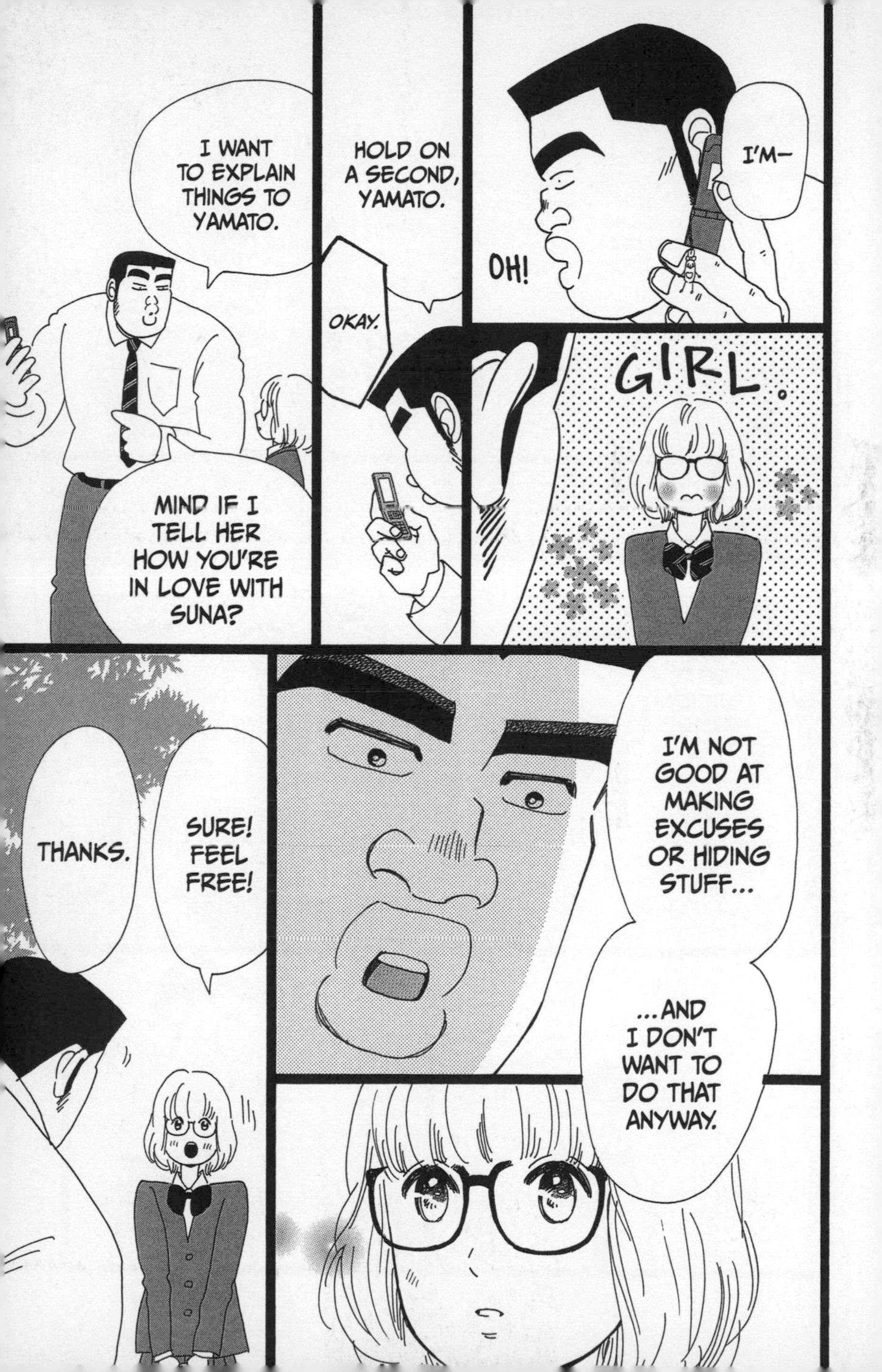
I'M—
OH!
GIRL.
HOLD ON A SECOND, YAMATO.
OKAY.
I WANT TO EXPLAIN THINGS TO YAMATO.
MIND IF I TELL HER HOW YOU'RE IN LOVE WITH SUNA?
I'M NOT GOOD AT MAKING EXCUSES OR HIDING STUFF...
...AND I DON'T WANT TO DO THAT ANYWAY.
SURE! FEEL FREE!
THANKS.

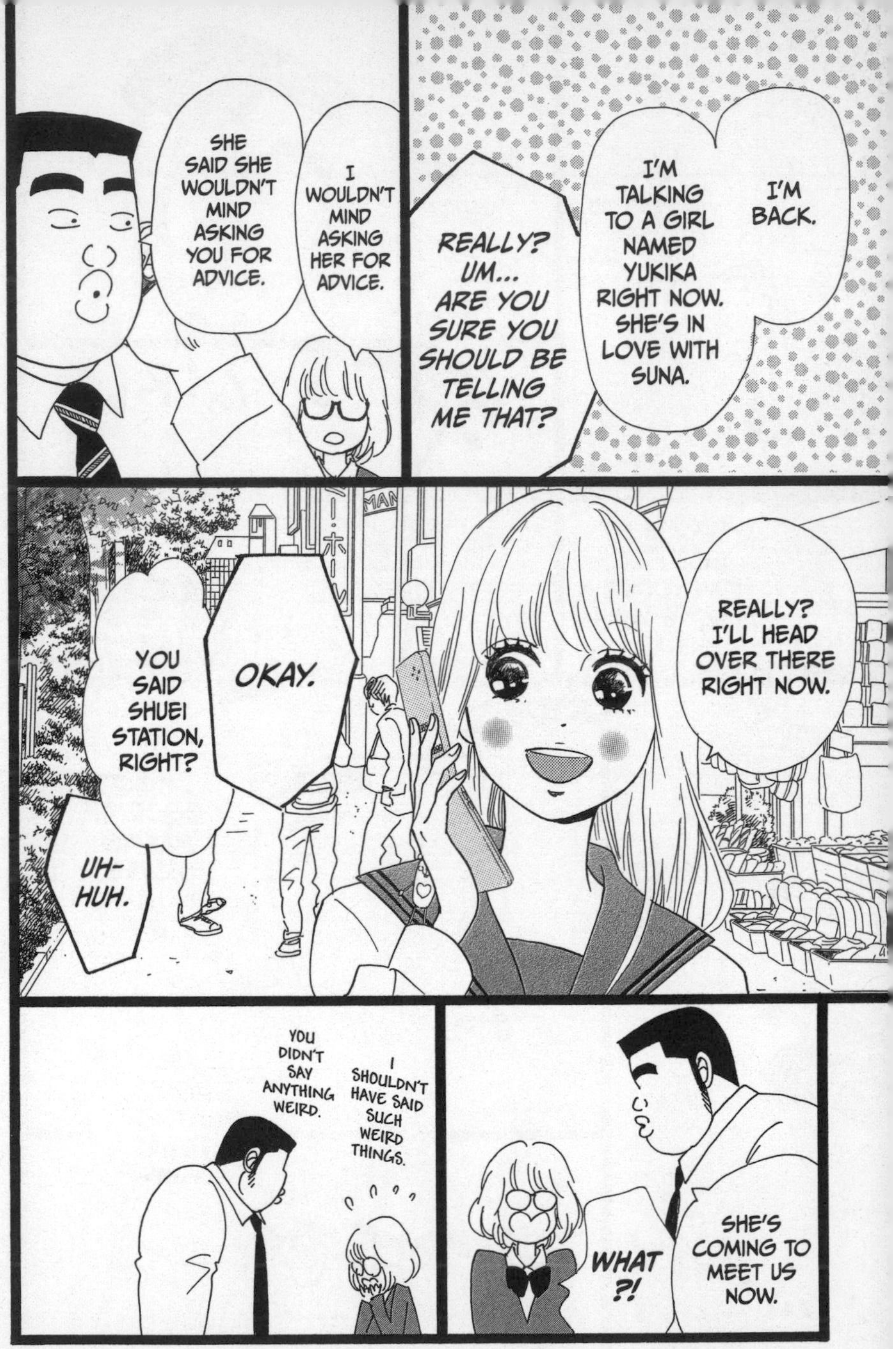
I'M BACK.
I'M TALKING TO A GIRL NAMED YUKIKA RIGHT NOW. SHE'S IN LOVE WITH SUNA.
REALLY? UM... ARE YOU SURE YOU SHOULD BE TELLING ME THAT?
I WOULDN'T MIND ASKING HER FOR ADVICE.
SHE SAID SHE WOULDN'T MIND ASKING YOU FOR ADVICE.
REALLY? I'LL HEAD OVER THERE RIGHT NOW.
OKAY.
YOU SAID SHUEI STATION, RIGHT?
UH-HUH.
SHE'S COMING TO MEET US NOW.
WHAT?!
I SHOULDN'T HAVE SAID SUCH WEIRD THINGS.
YOU DIDN'T SAY ANYTHING WEIRD.

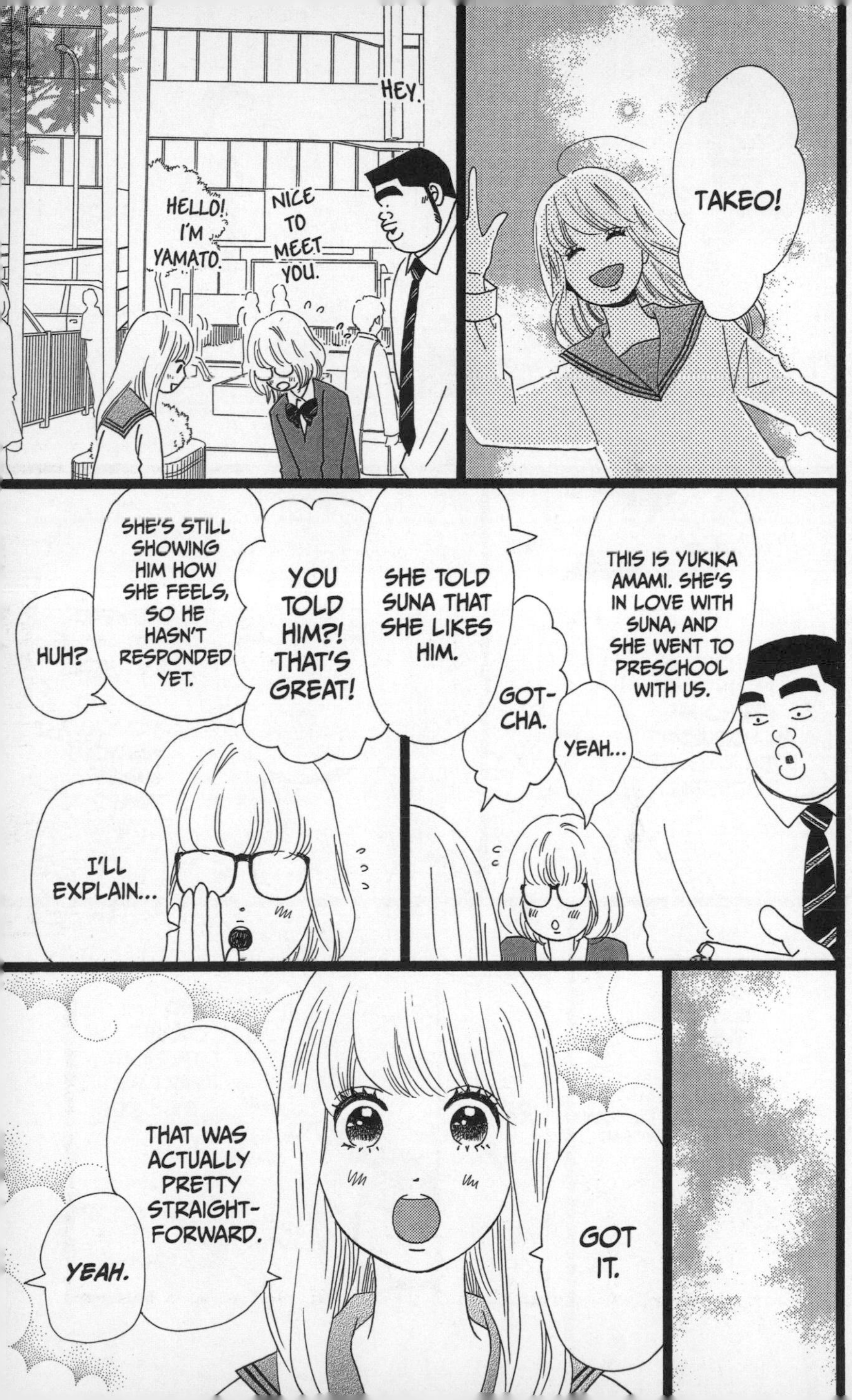
TAKEO!
HEY.
NICE TO MEET YOU.
HELLO! I'M YAMATO.
THIS IS YUKIKA AMAMI. SHE'S IN LOVE WITH SUNA, AND SHE WENT TO PRESCHOOL WITH US.
GOT-CHA.
YEAH...
SHE TOLD SUNA THAT SHE LIKES HIM.
YOU TOLD HIM?! THAT'S GREAT!
SHE'S STILL SHOWING HIM HOW SHE FEELS, SO HE HASN'T RESPONDED YET.
HUH?
I'LL EXPLAIN...
GOT IT.
THAT WAS ACTUALLY PRETTY STRAIGHT-FORWARD.
YEAH.

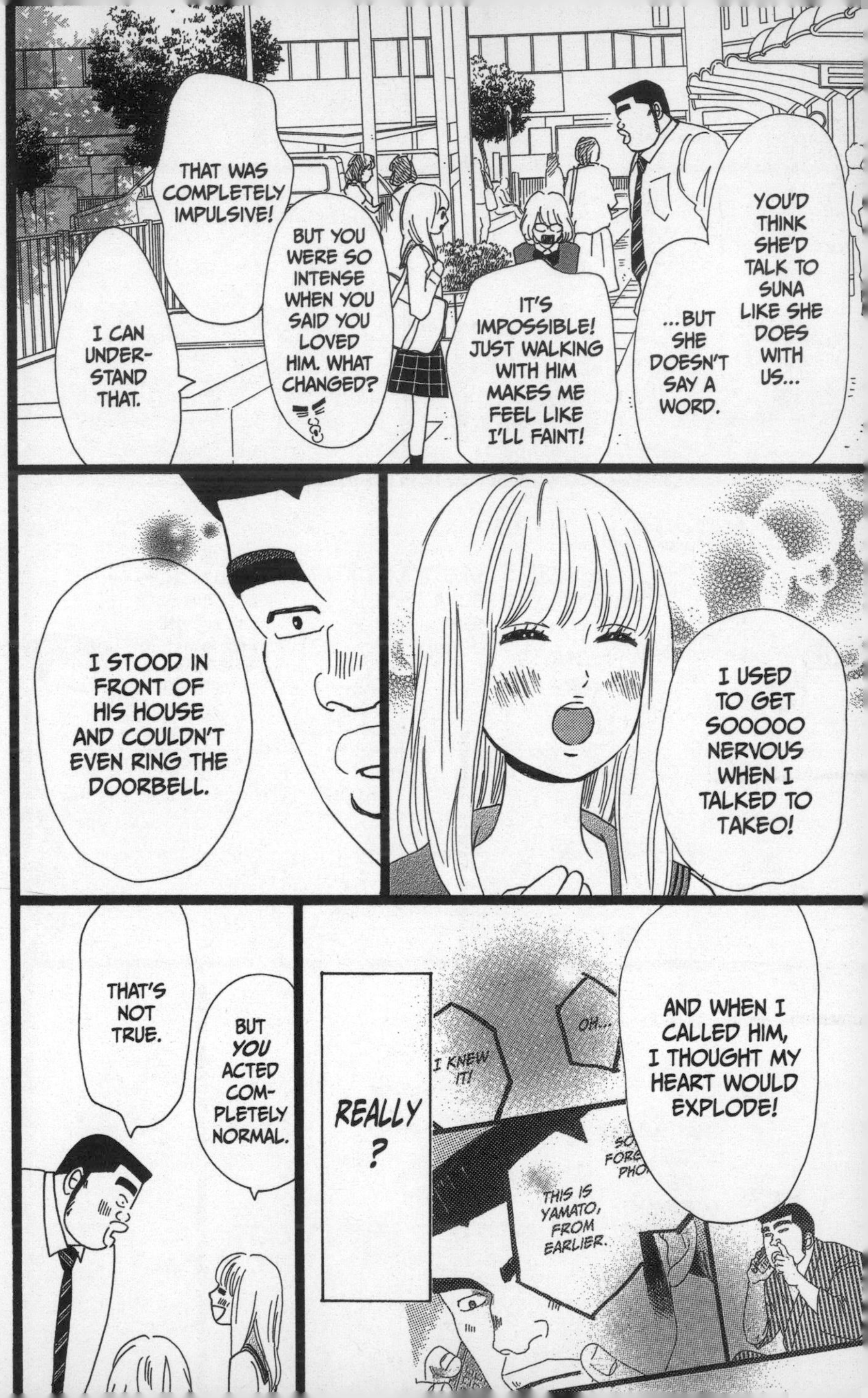
YOU'D THINK SHE'D TALK TO SUNA LIKE SHE DOES WITH US...
...BUT SHE DOESN'T SAY A WORD.
IT'S IMPOSSIBLE! JUST WALKING WITH HIM MAKES ME FEEL LIKE I'LL FAINT!
BUT YOU WERE SO INTENSE WHEN YOU SAID YOU LOVED HIM. WHAT CHANGED?
THAT WAS COMPLETELY IMPULSIVE!
I CAN UNDER-STAND THAT.
I USED TO GET SOOOOO NERVOUS WHEN I TALKED TO TAKEO!
I STOOD IN FRONT OF HIS HOUSE AND COULDN'T EVEN RING THE DOORBELL.
AND WHEN I CALLED HIM, I THOUGHT MY HEART WOULD EXPLODE!
OH...
I KNEW IT!
THIS IS YAMATO, FROM EARLIER.
REALLY?
BUT YOU ACTED COM-PLETELY NORMAL.
THAT'S NOT TRUE.

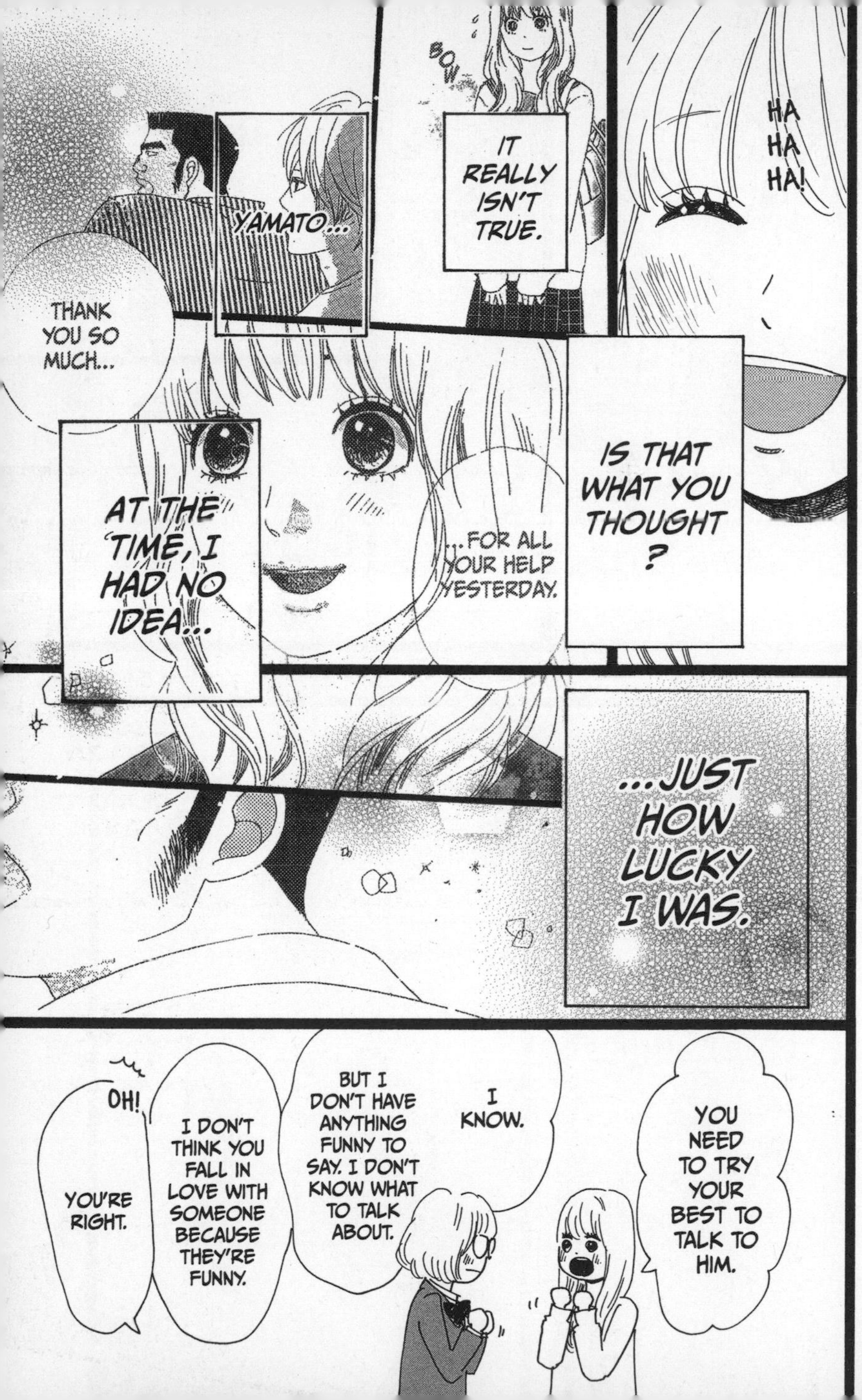
HA HA HA!
BON
IT REALLY ISN'T TRUE.
YAMATO...
IS THAT WHAT YOU THOUGHT?
THANK YOU SO MUCH...
...FOR ALL YOUR HELP YESTERDAY.
AT THE TIME, I HAD NO IDEA...
...JUST HOW LUCKY I WAS.
YOU NEED TO TRY YOUR BEST TO TALK TO HIM.
I KNOW.
BUT I DON'T HAVE ANYTHING FUNNY TO SAY. I DON'T KNOW WHAT TO TALK ABOUT.
I DON'T THINK YOU FALL IN LOVE WITH SOMEONE BECAUSE THEY'RE FUNNY.
OH! YOU'RE RIGHT.

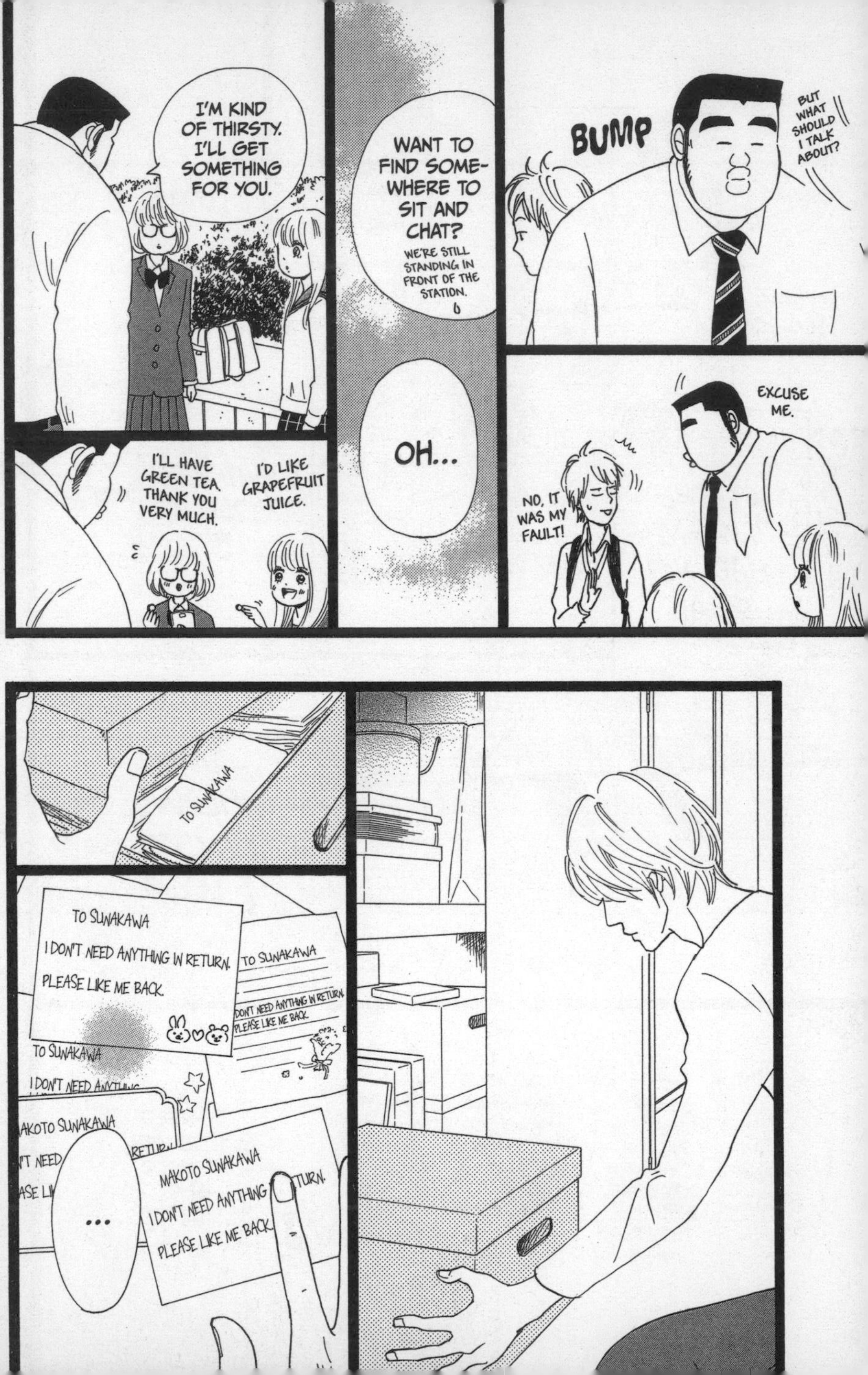

BUMP
BUT WHAT SHOULD I TALK ABOUT?
EXCUSE ME.
NO, IT WAS MY FAULT!
WANT TO FIND SOME-WHERE TO SIT AND CHAT?
WE'RE STILL STANDING IN FRONT OF THE STATION.
OH...
I'M KIND OF THIRSTY. I'LL GET SOMETHING FOR YOU.
I'D LIKE GRAPEFRUIT JUICE.
I'LL HAVE GREEN TEA. THANK YOU VERY MUCH.
TO SUNAKAWA
TO SUNAKAWA
I DON'T NEED ANYTHING IN RETURN.
PLEASE LIKE ME BACK.
TO SUNAKAWA
I DON'T NEED ANYTHING IN RETURN.
PLEASE LIKE ME BACK.
TO SUNAKAWA
I DON'T NEED ANYTHING
AKOTO SUNAKAWA
'T NEED
RETURN
ASE LI
MAKOTO SUNAKAWA
I DON'T NEED ANYTHING
TURN.
PLEASE LIKE ME BACK.
...

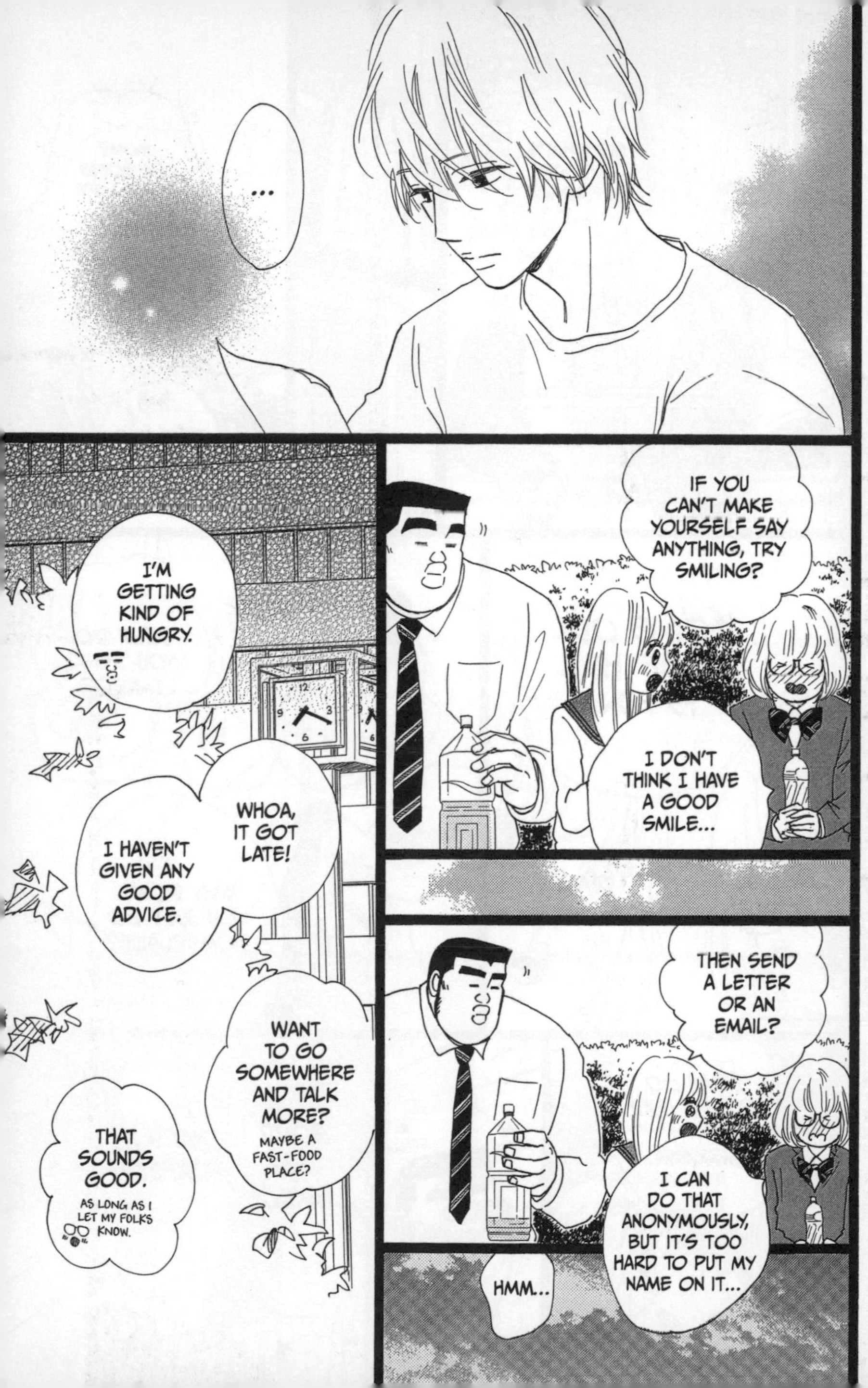
...
IF YOU CAN'T MAKE YOURSELF SAY ANYTHING, TRY SMILING?
I DON'T THINK I HAVE A GOOD SMILE...
THEN SEND A LETTER OR AN EMAIL?
I CAN DO THAT ANONYMOUSLY, BUT IT'S TOO HARD TO PUT MY NAME ON IT...
HMM...
I'M GETTING KIND OF HUNGRY.
WHOA, IT GOT LATE!
I HAVEN'T GIVEN ANY GOOD ADVICE.
WANT TO GO SOMEWHERE AND TALK MORE?
MAYBE A FAST-FOOD PLACE?
THAT SOUNDS GOOD.
AS LONG AS I LET MY FOLKS KNOW.

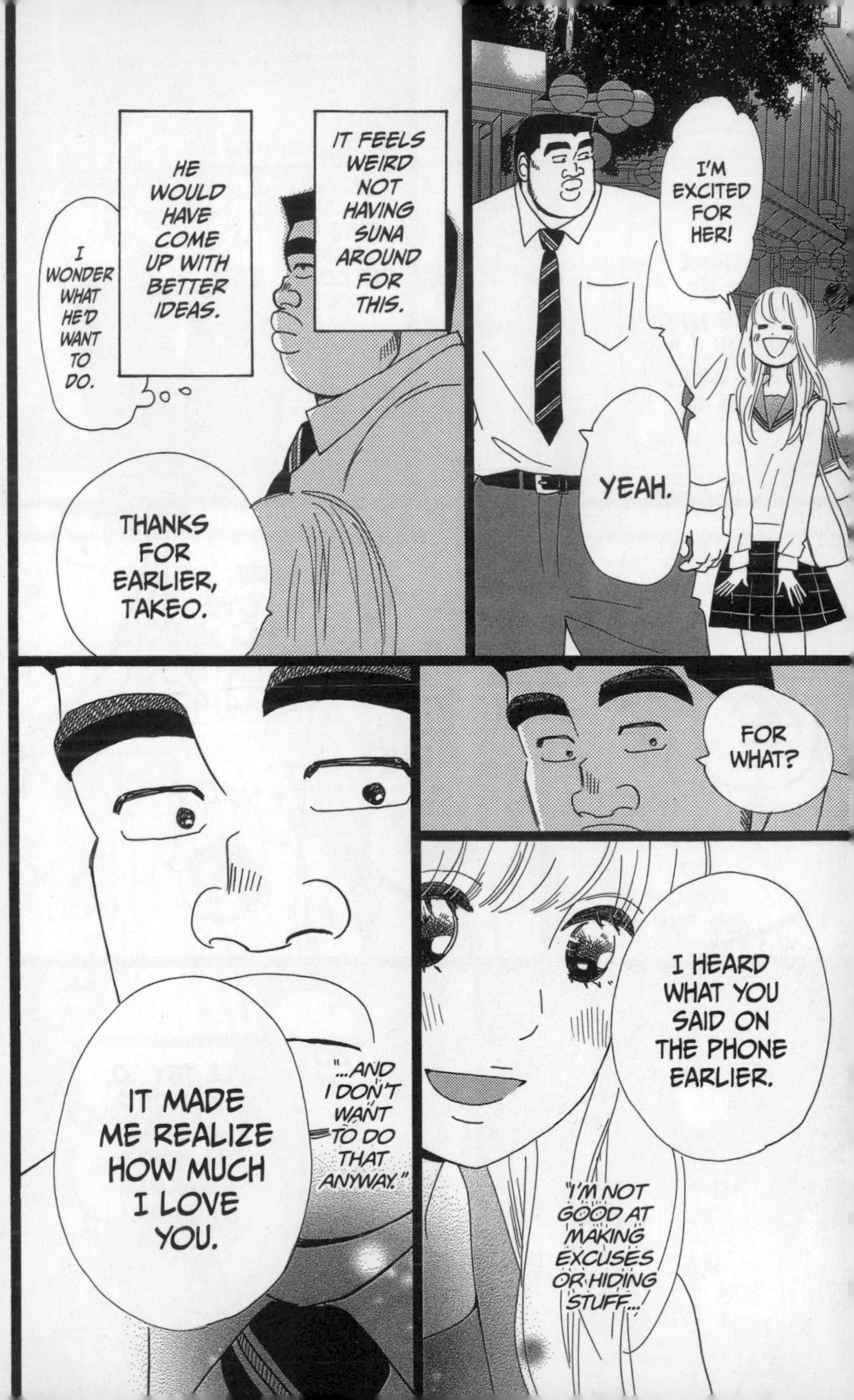
I'M EXCITED FOR HER!
YEAH.
IT FEELS WEIRD NOT HAVING SUNA AROUND FOR THIS.
HE WOULD HAVE COME UP WITH BETTER IDEAS.
I WONDER WHAT HE'D WANT TO DO.
THANKS FOR EARLIER, TAKEO.
FOR WHAT?
I HEARD WHAT YOU SAID ON THE PHONE EARLIER.
"I'M NOT GOOD AT MAKING EXCUSES OR HIDING STUFF...
"...AND I DON'T WANT TO DO THAT ANYWAY."
IT MADE ME REALIZE HOW MUCH I LOVE YOU.

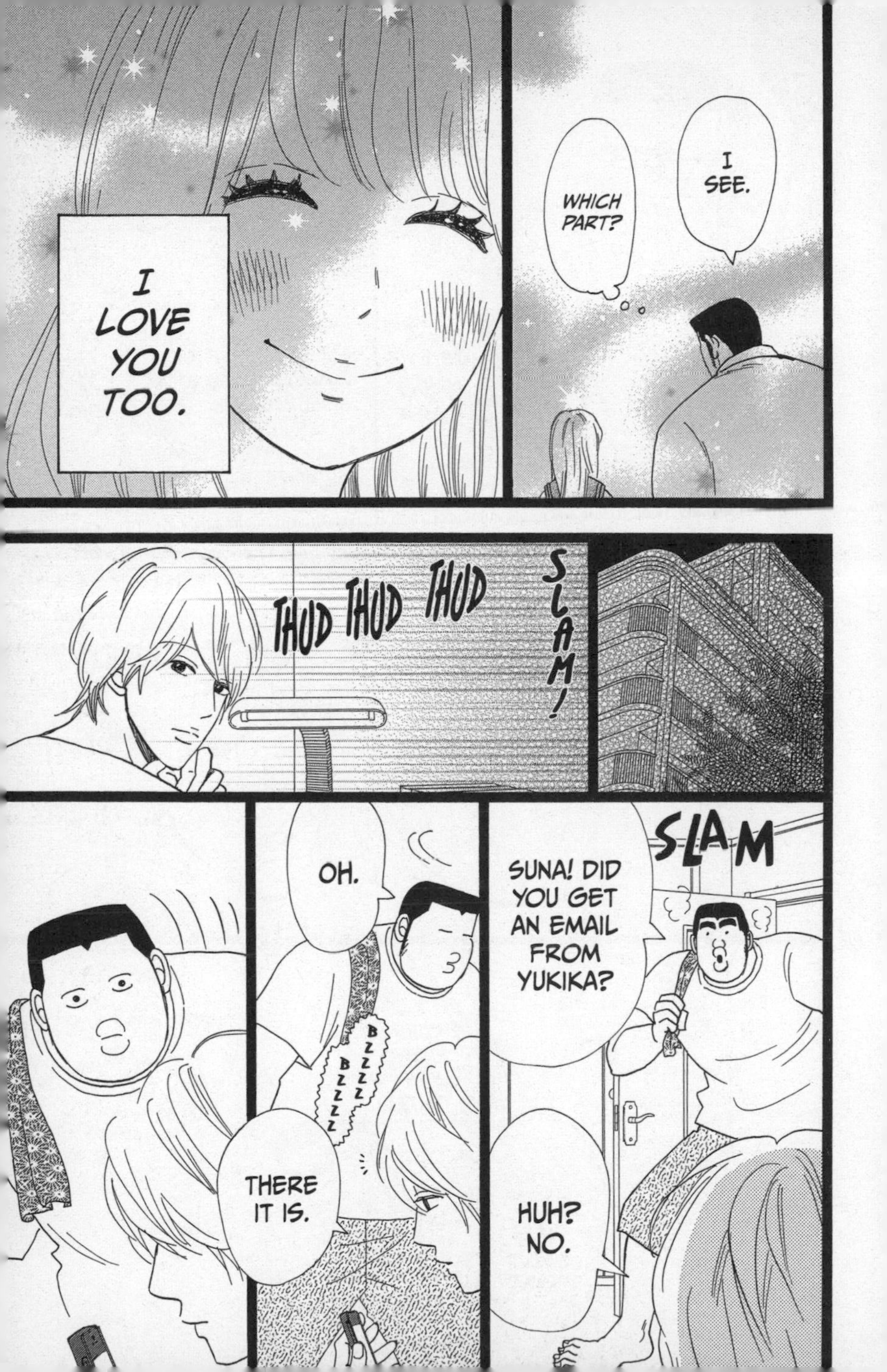
I SEE.
WHICH PART?
I LOVE YOU TOO.
SLAM!
THUD THUD THUD
SLAM
SUNA! DID YOU GET AN EMAIL FROM YUKIKA?
HUH? NO.
OH.
BZZZZ BZZZZ
THERE IT IS.

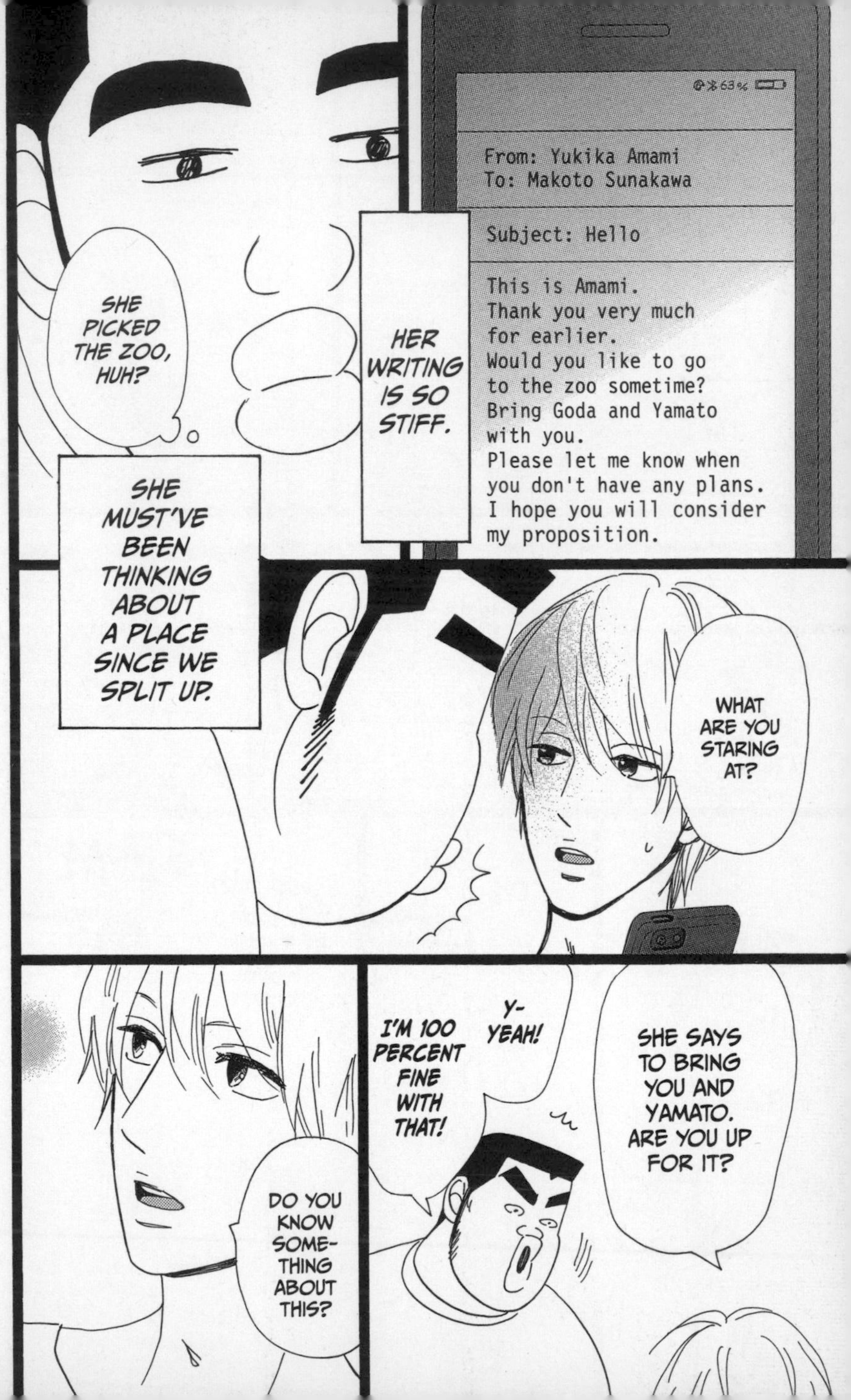

63%
From: Yukika Amami
To: Makoto Sunakawa
Subject: Hello
This is Amami. Thank you very much for earlier. Would you like to go to the zoo sometime? Bring Goda and Yamato with you. Please let me know when you don't have any plans. I hope you will consider my proposition.
HER WRITING IS SO STIFF.
SHE PICKED THE ZOO, HUH?
SHE MUST'VE BEEN THINKING ABOUT A PLACE SINCE WE SPLIT UP.
WHAT ARE YOU STARING AT?
SHE SAYS TO BRING YOU AND YAMATO. ARE YOU UP FOR IT?
Y-YEAH!
I'M 100 PERCENT FINE WITH THAT!
DO YOU KNOW SOMETHING ABOUT THIS?

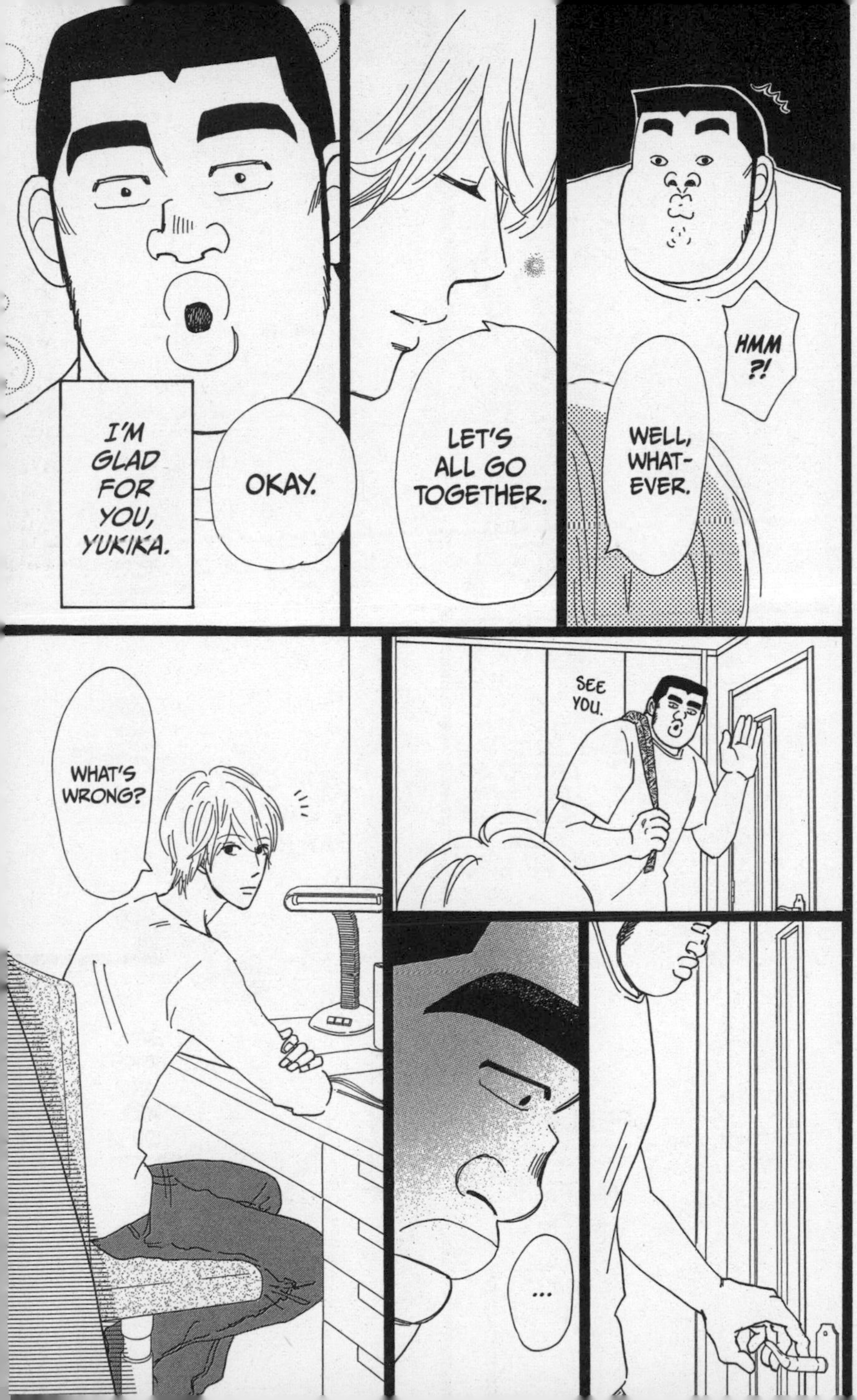
HMM?!
WELL, WHAT-EVER.
LET'S ALL GO TOGETHER.
OKAY.
I'M GLAD FOR YOU, YUKIKA.
SEE YOU.
...
WHAT'S WRONG?

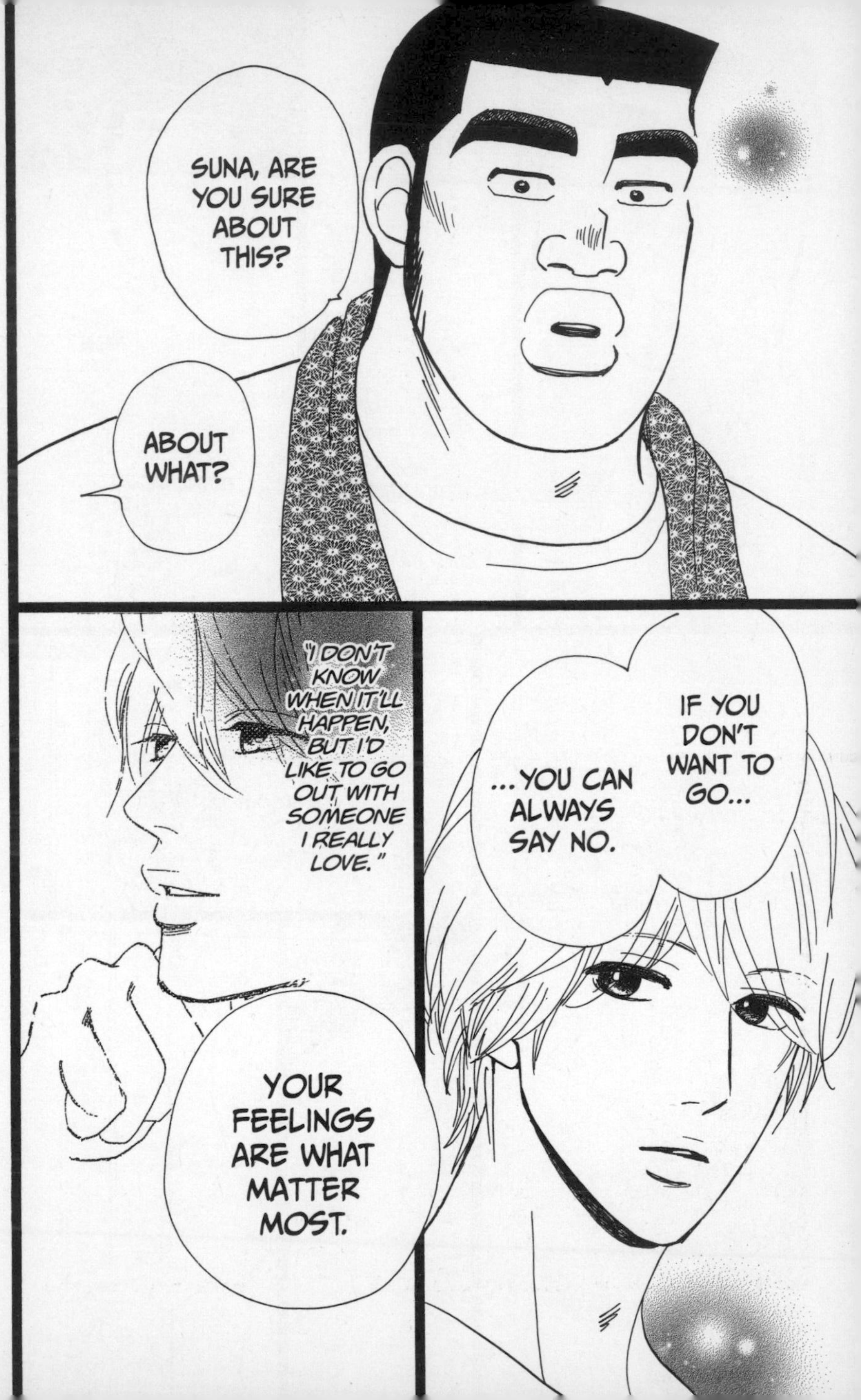
SUNA, ARE YOU SURE ABOUT THIS?
ABOUT WHAT?
IF YOU DON'T WANT TO GO...
...YOU CAN ALWAYS SAY NO.
"I DON'T KNOW WHEN IT'LL HAPPEN, BUT I'D LIKE TO GO OUT WITH SOMEONE I REALLY LOVE."
YOUR FEELINGS ARE WHAT MATTER MOST.

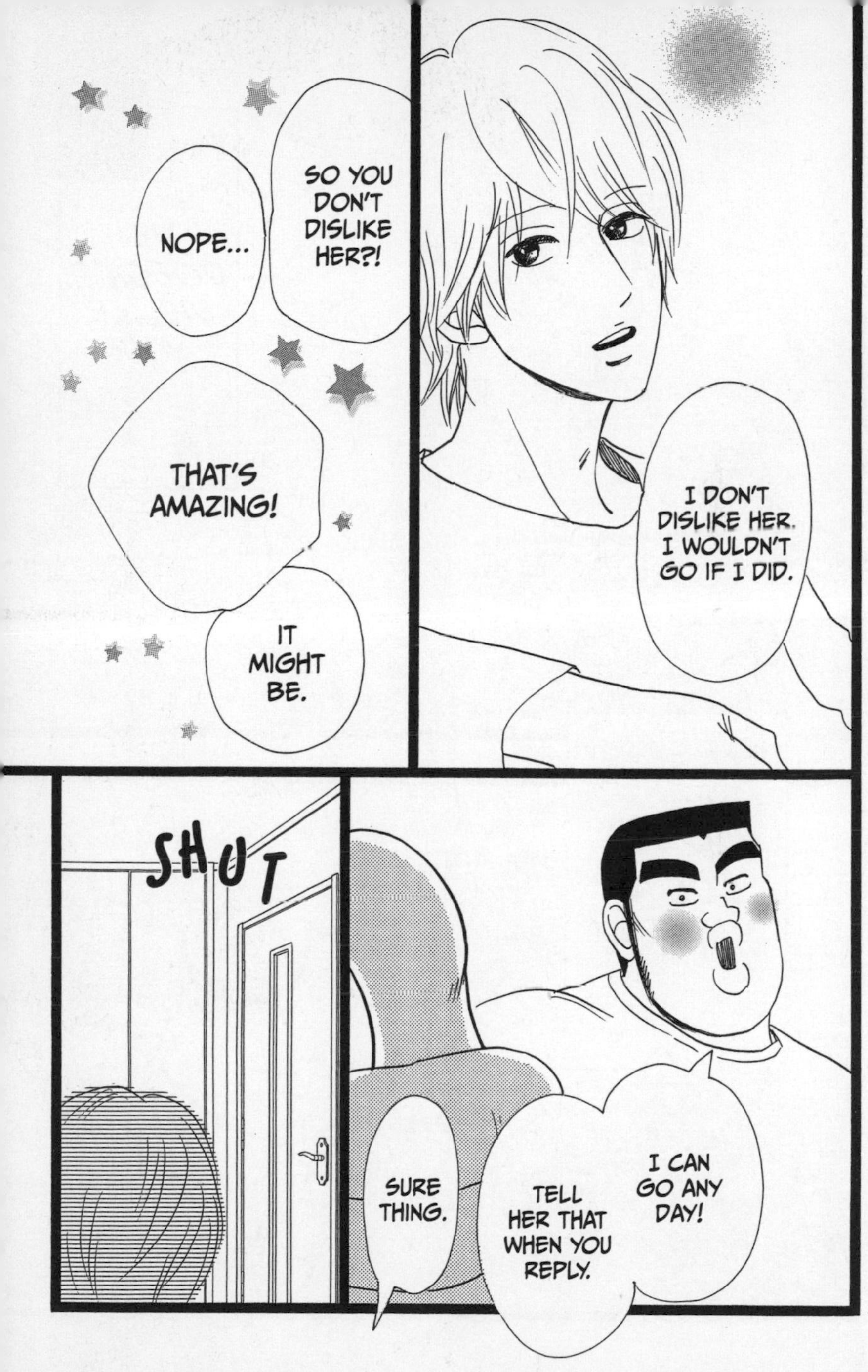
I DON'T DISLIKE HER. I WOULDN'T GO IF I DID.
SO YOU DON'T DISLIKE HER?!
NOPE...
THAT'S AMAZING!
IT MIGHT BE.
I CAN GO ANY DAY!
TELL HER THAT WHEN YOU REPLY.
SURE THING.
SHUT

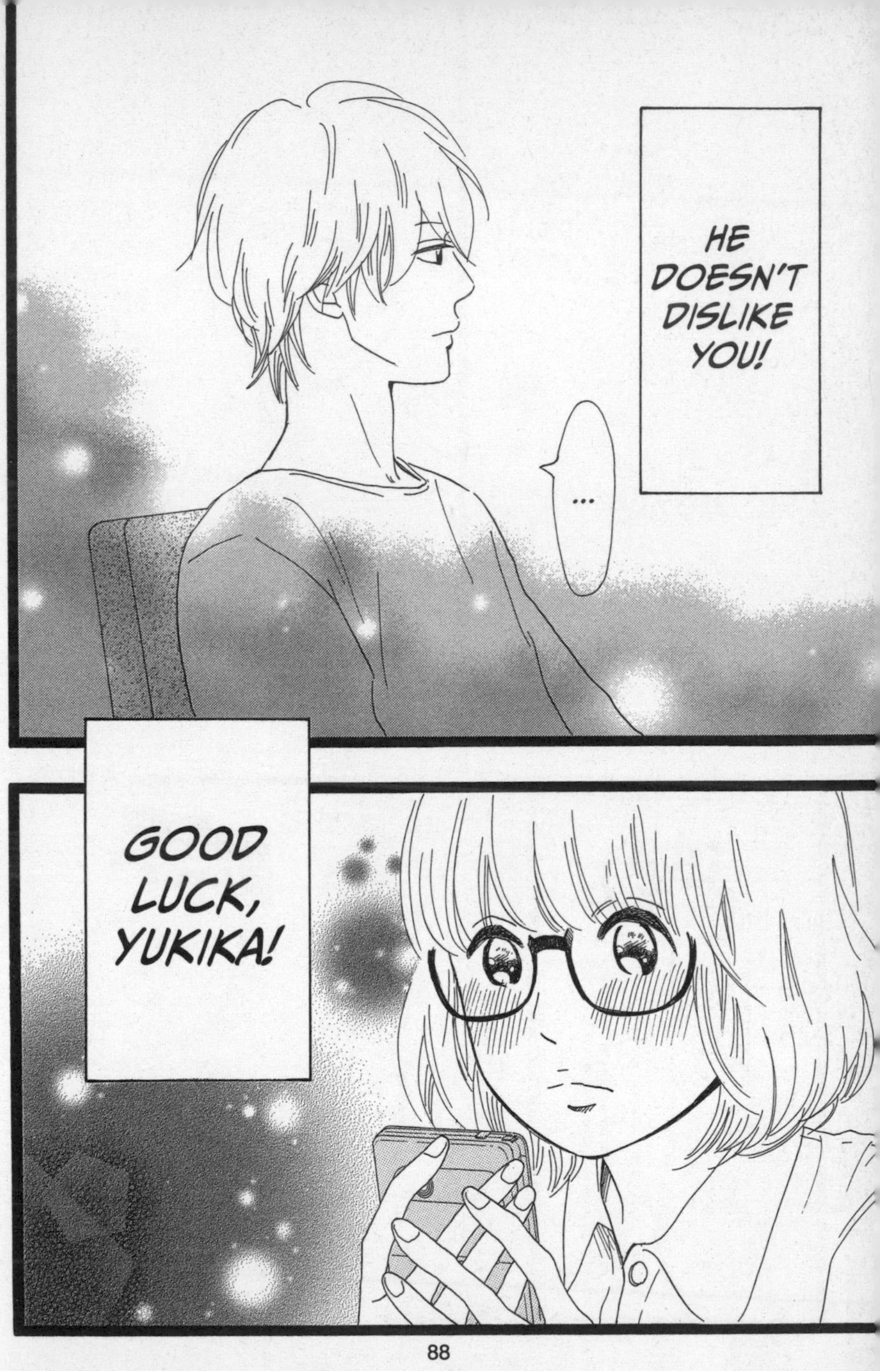
HE DOESN'T DISLIKE YOU!
...
GOOD LUCK, YUKIKA!

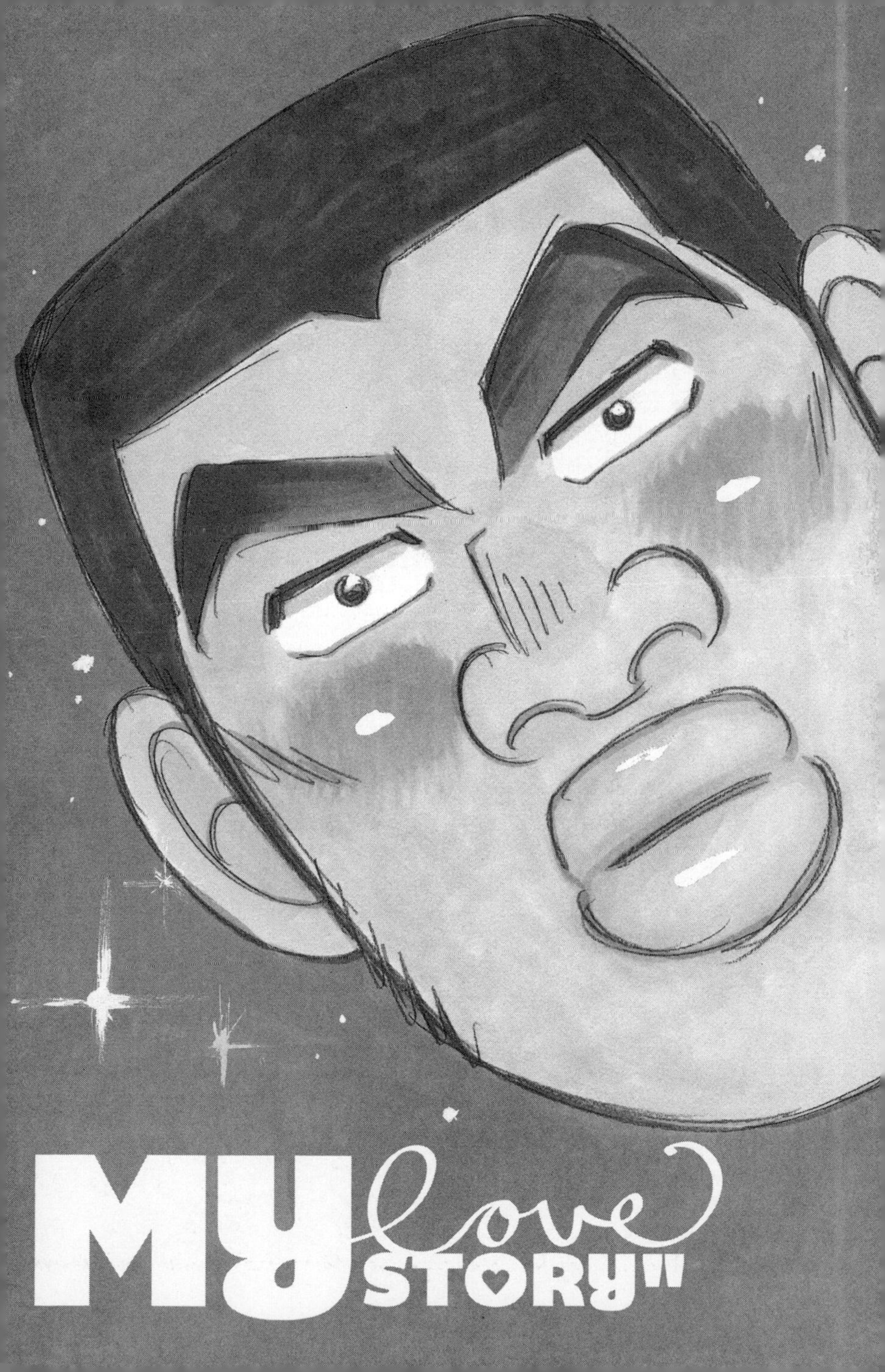
MY love STORY!!

Hello! I always have so much fun writing this story.

I'm sure some of you already know this, but *My Love Story!!* is being made into an anime! Not that long ago (or maybe it was a while ago...) I got to talk to the anime staff. I'm convinced they're going to do a fantastic job, so I'm really looking forward to it!
I usually go to sleep around 9 p.m., but if the anime airs later at night, I'll do my best to wake up and watch it! Or maybe I'll be too excited to sleep in the first place!
I hope you'll all watch and support the anime, and that you'll keep supporting the manga. Kawahara out!

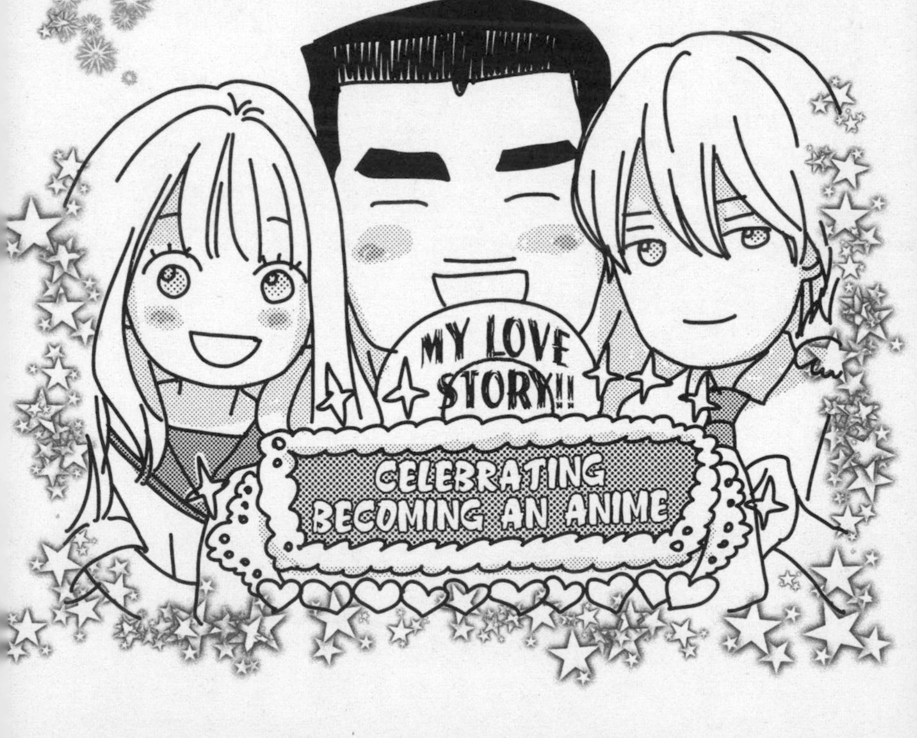
MY LOVE STORY!!
CELEBRATING BECOMING AN ANIME

Yamato,
Thank you very much for the other day.
You and Takeo gave me the courage to ask Sunakawa out.
Thanks so much for listening to me.

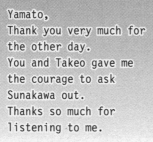

SCROLLING

CLICK
CLICK
CLICK

I'm shopping downtown, but I don't know what kind of clothes to buy. If you're free at all, could you help me out?

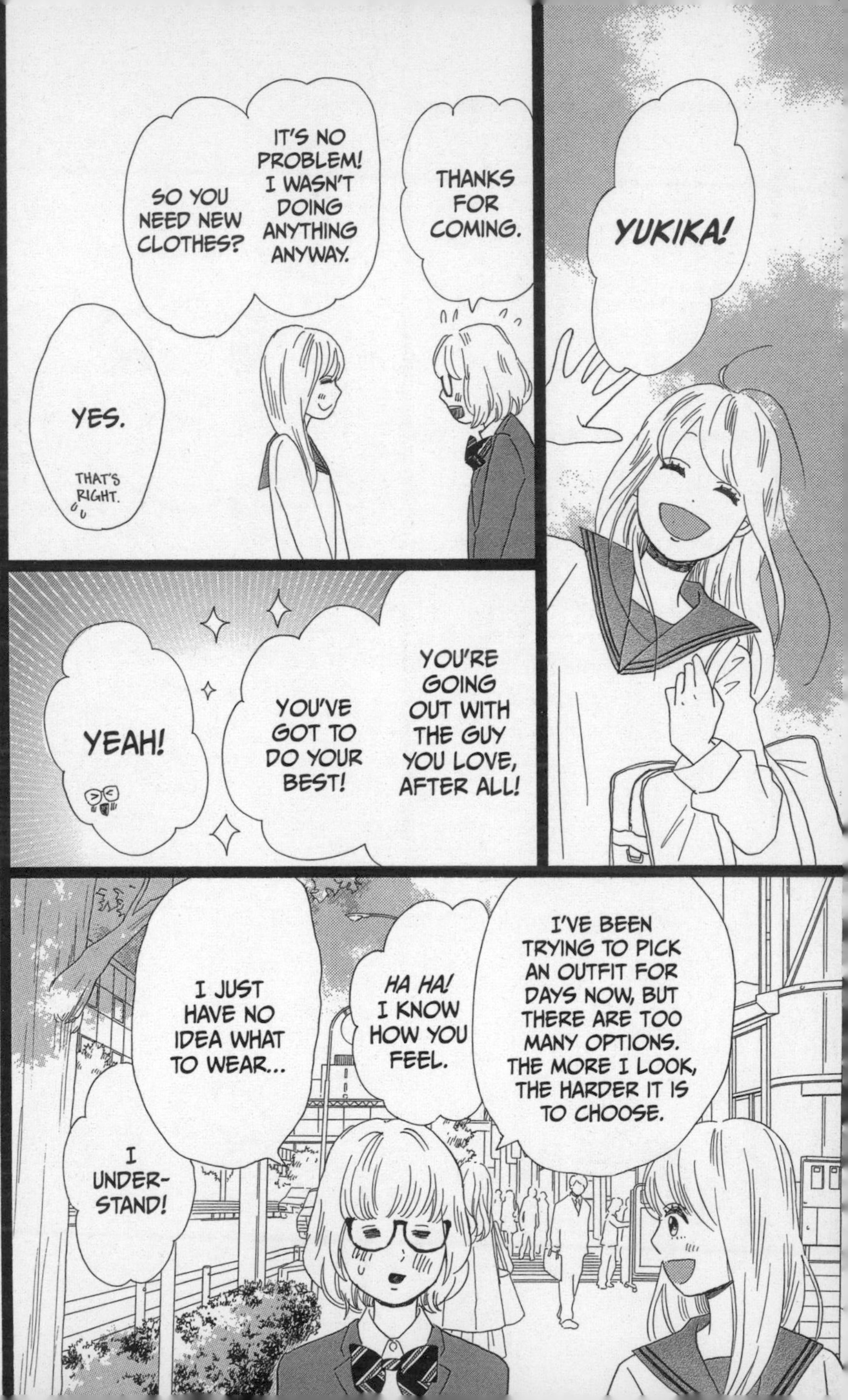
YUKIKA!
THANKS FOR COMING.
IT'S NO PROBLEM! I WASN'T DOING ANYTHING ANYWAY.
SO YOU NEED NEW CLOTHES?
YES.
THAT'S RIGHT.
YOU'RE GOING OUT WITH THE GUY YOU LOVE, AFTER ALL!
YOU'VE GOT TO DO YOUR BEST!
YEAH!
I'VE BEEN TRYING TO PICK AN OUTFIT FOR DAYS NOW, BUT THERE ARE TOO MANY OPTIONS. THE MORE I LOOK, THE HARDER IT IS TO CHOOSE.
HA HA! I KNOW HOW YOU FEEL.
I JUST HAVE NO IDEA WHAT TO WEAR...
I UNDERSTAND!

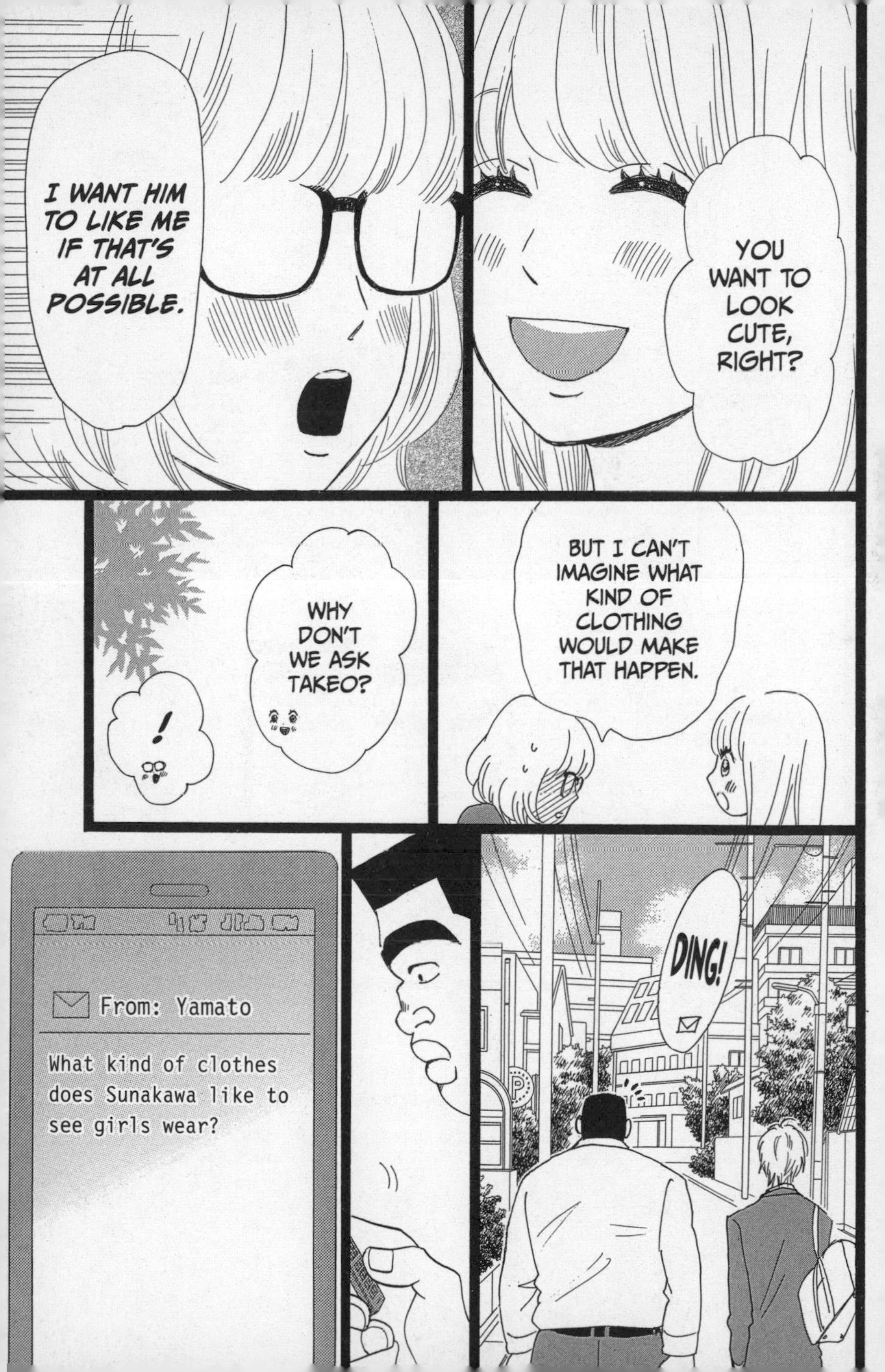
YOU WANT TO LOOK CUTE, RIGHT?
I WANT HIM TO LIKE ME IF THAT'S AT ALL POSSIBLE.
BUT I CAN'T IMAGINE WHAT KIND OF CLOTHING WOULD MAKE THAT HAPPEN.
WHY DON'T WE ASK TAKEO?
!
DING!
From: Yamato
What kind of clothes does Sunakawa like to see girls wear?

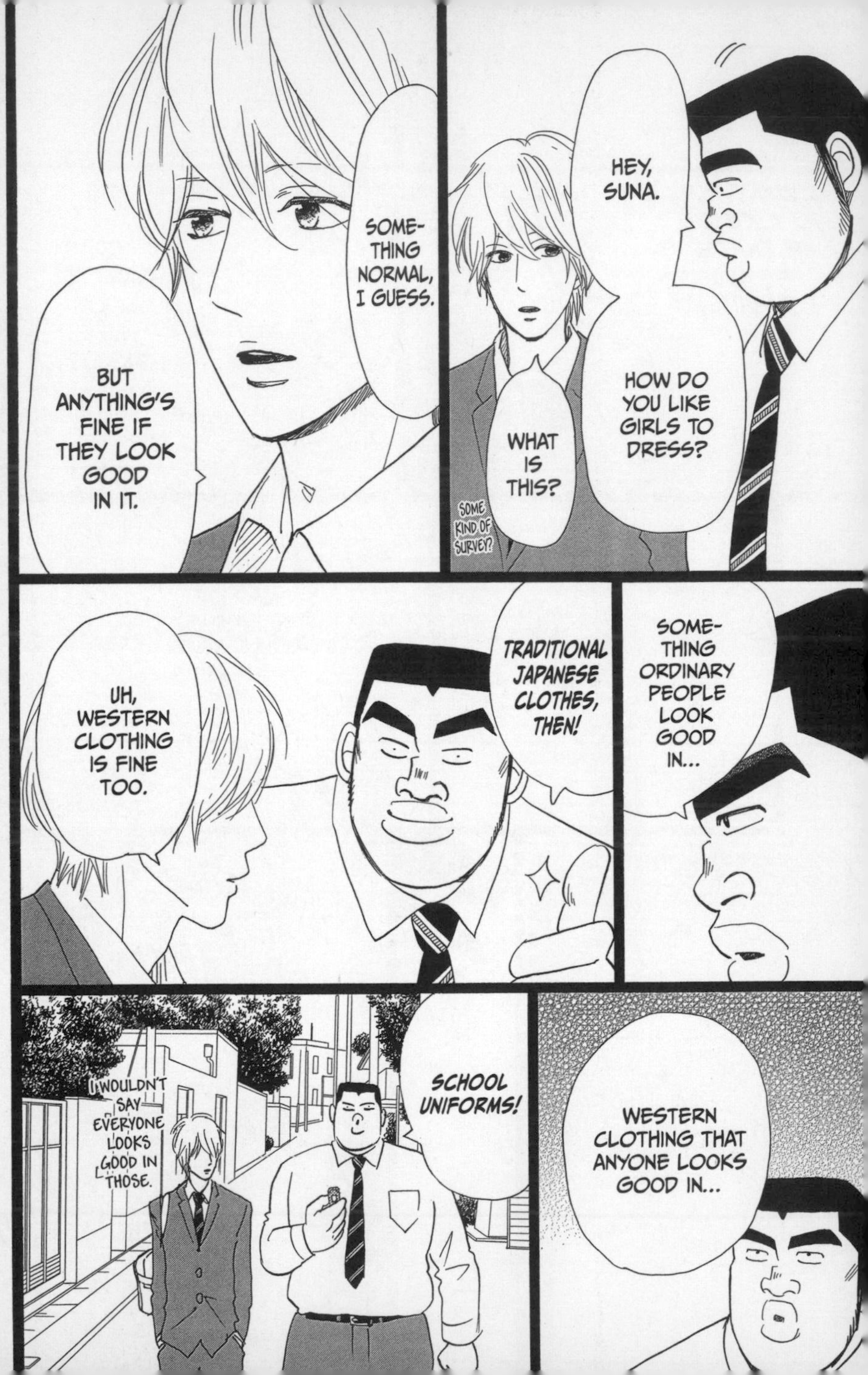
HEY, SUNA.
HOW DO YOU LIKE GIRLS TO DRESS?
WHAT IS THIS?
SOME KIND OF SURVEY?
SOME-THING NORMAL, I GUESS.
BUT ANYTHING'S FINE IF THEY LOOK GOOD IN IT.
SOME-THING ORDINARY PEOPLE LOOK GOOD IN...
TRADITIONAL JAPANESE CLOTHES, THEN!
UH, WESTERN CLOTHING IS FINE TOO.
WESTERN CLOTHING THAT ANYONE LOOKS GOOD IN...
SCHOOL UNIFORMS!
I WOULDN'T SAY EVERYONE LOOKS GOOD IN THOSE.

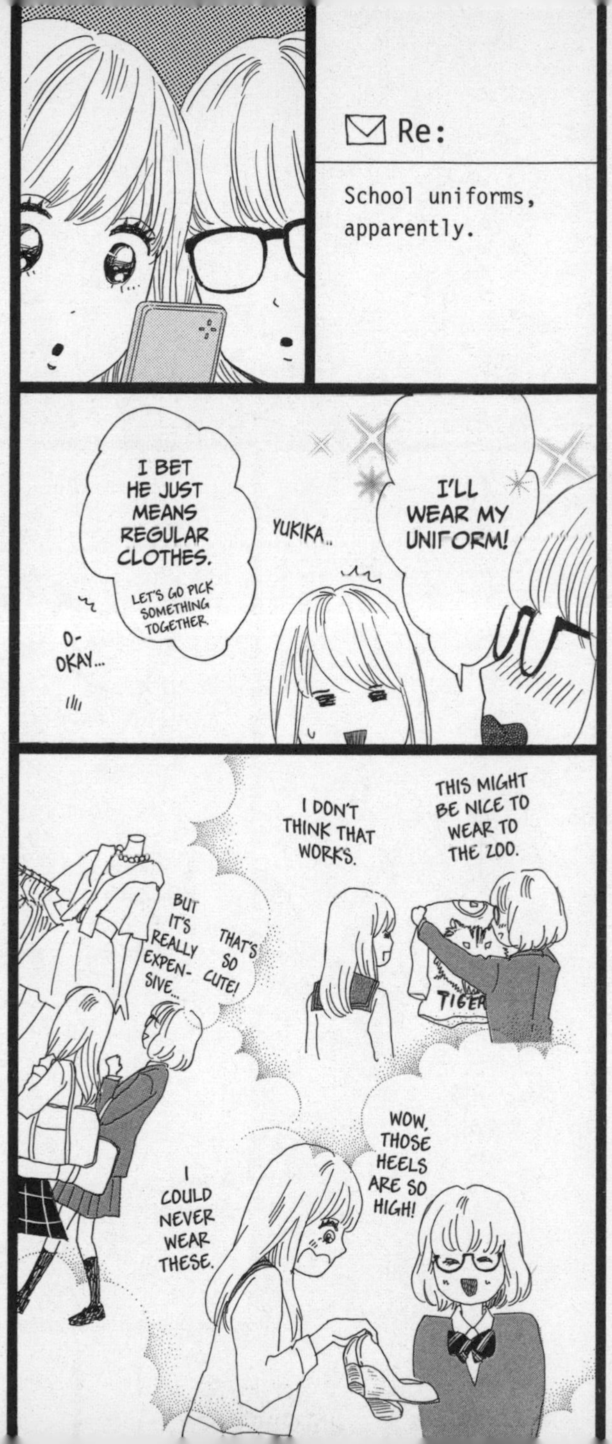
Re:
School uniforms, apparently.
I'LL WEAR MY UNIFORM!
YUKIKA..
I BET HE JUST MEANS REGULAR CLOTHES.
LET'S GO PICK SOMETHING TOGETHER.
O-OKAY...
THIS MIGHT BE NICE TO WEAR TO THE ZOO.
I DON'T THINK THAT WORKS.
TIGER
THAT'S SO CUTE!
BUT IT'S REALLY EXPEN-SIVE...
WOW, THOSE HEELS ARE SO HIGH!
I COULD NEVER WEAR THESE.

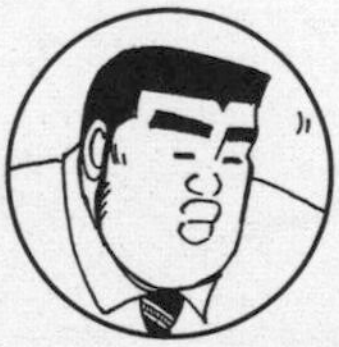

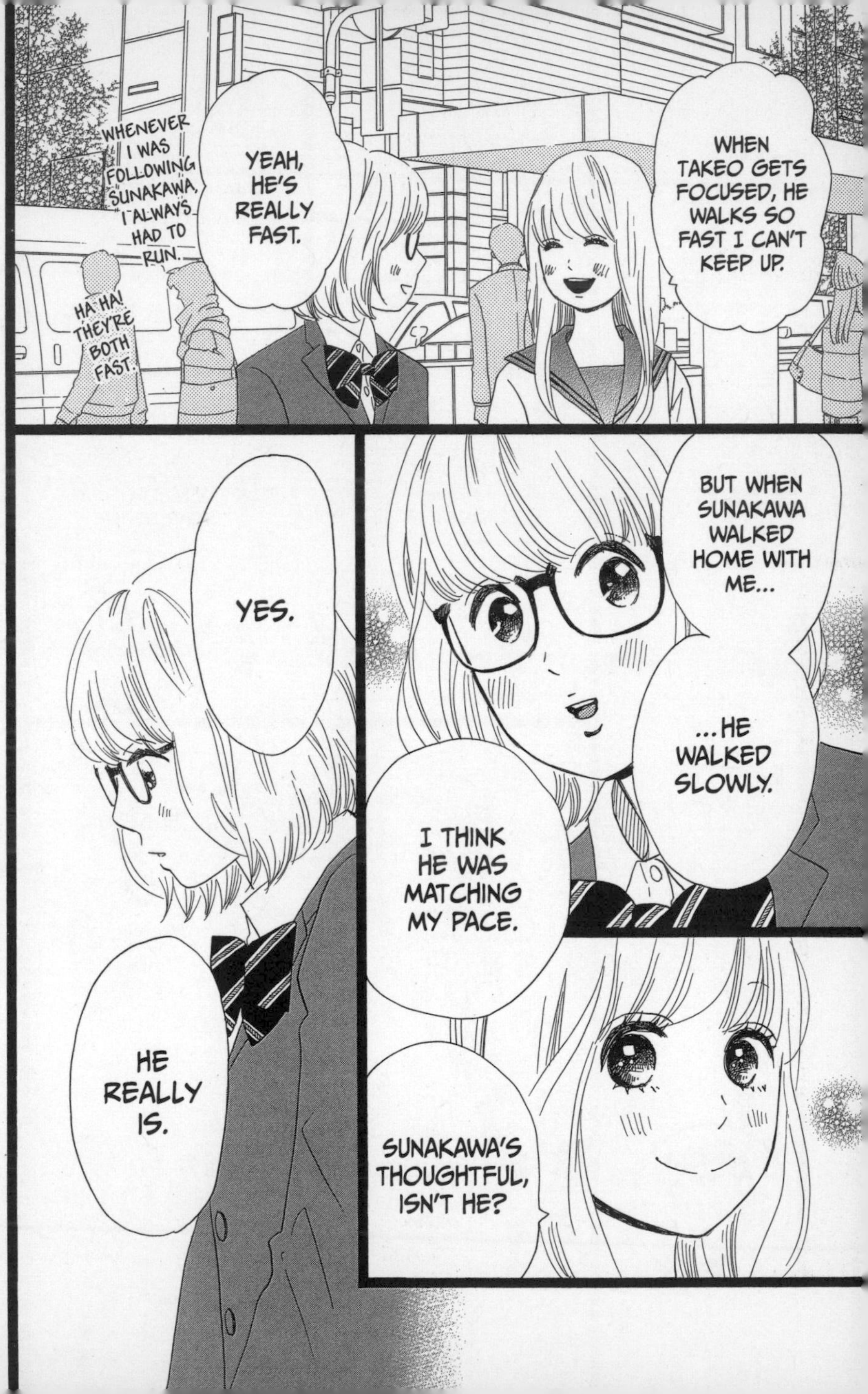
WHEN TAKEO GETS FOCUSED, HE WALKS SO FAST I CAN'T KEEP UP.
YEAH, HE'S REALLY FAST.
WHENEVER I WAS FOLLOWING SUNAKAWA, I ALWAYS HAD TO RUN.
HA HA! THEY'RE BOTH FAST.
BUT WHEN SUNAKAWA WALKED HOME WITH ME...
...HE WALKED SLOWLY.
I THINK HE WAS MATCHING MY PACE.
SUNAKAWA'S THOUGHTFUL, ISN'T HE?
YES.
HE REALLY IS.

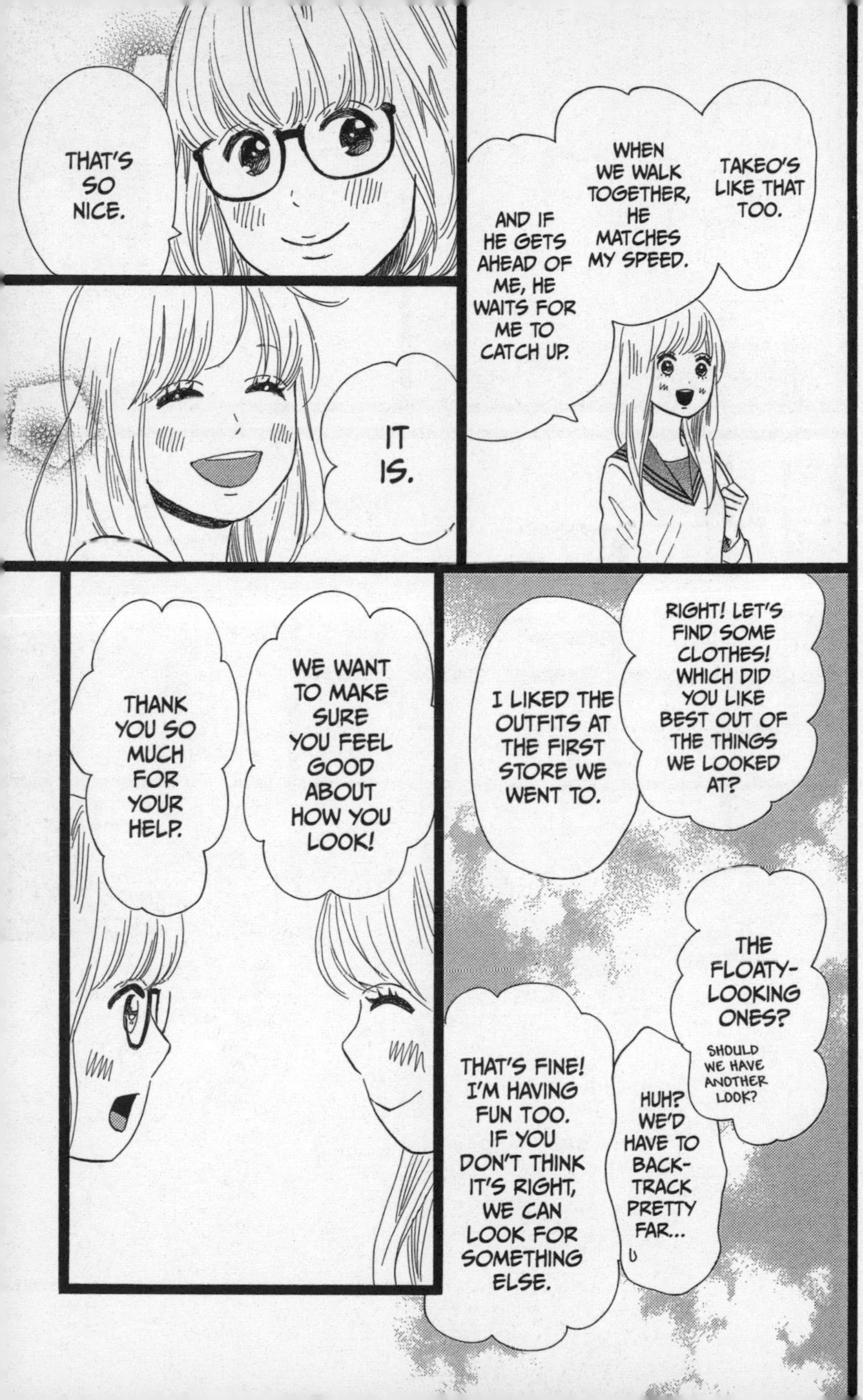
TAKEO'S LIKE THAT TOO.
WHEN WE WALK TOGETHER, HE MATCHES MY SPEED.
AND IF HE GETS AHEAD OF ME, HE WAITS FOR ME TO CATCH UP.
THAT'S SO NICE.
IT IS.
RIGHT! LET'S FIND SOME CLOTHES! WHICH DID YOU LIKE BEST OUT OF THE THINGS WE LOOKED AT?
I LIKED THE OUTFITS AT THE FIRST STORE WE WENT TO.
THE FLOATY-LOOKING ONES?
SHOULD WE HAVE ANOTHER LOOK?
HUH? WE'D HAVE TO BACK-TRACK PRETTY FAR...
THAT'S FINE! I'M HAVING FUN TOO. IF YOU DON'T THINK IT'S RIGHT, WE CAN LOOK FOR SOMETHING ELSE.
WE WANT TO MAKE SURE YOU FEEL GOOD ABOUT HOW YOU LOOK!
THANK YOU SO MUCH FOR YOUR HELP.

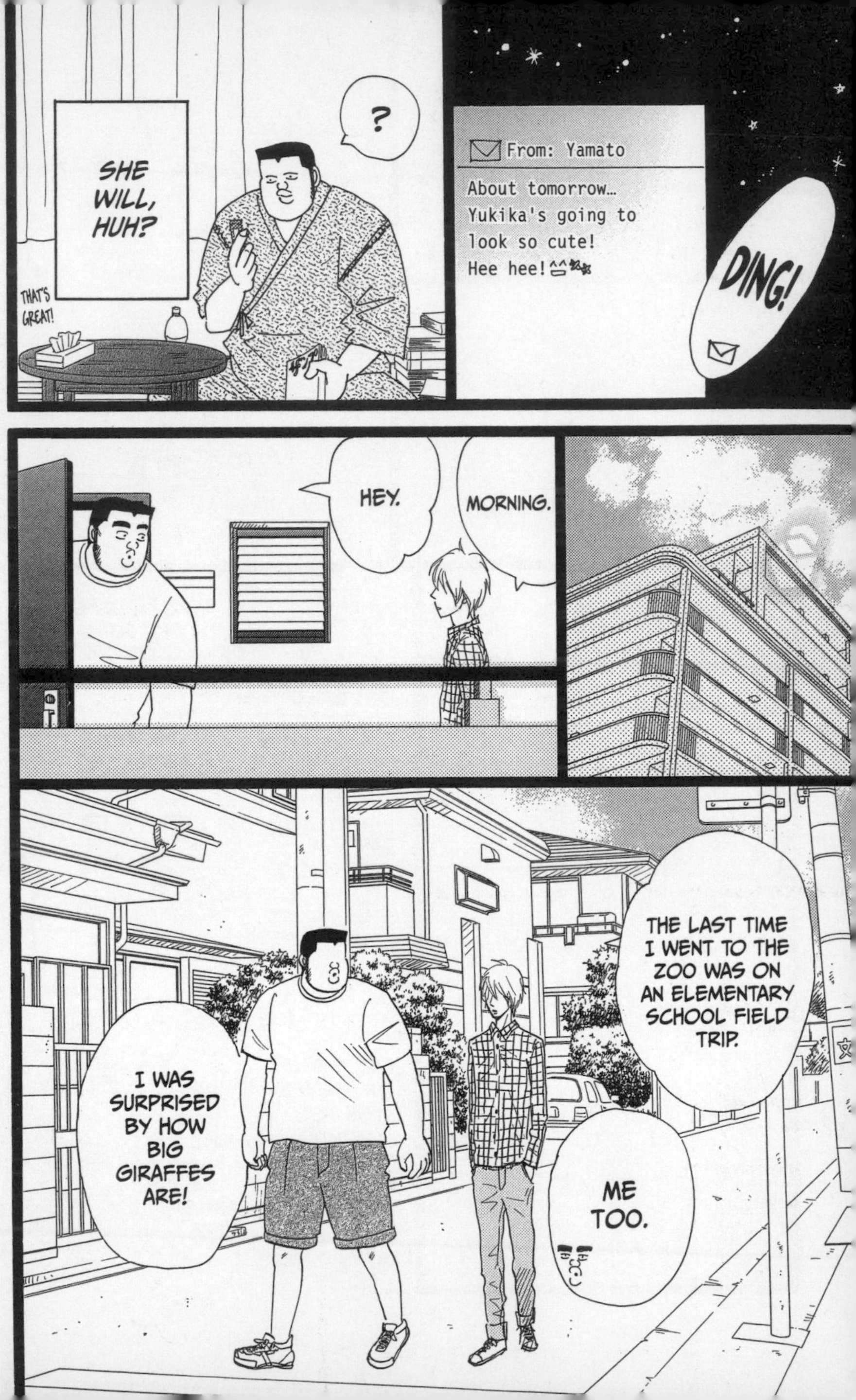
DING!
From: Yamato
About tomorrow…
Yukika's going to look so cute!
Hee hee!
?
SHE WILL, HUH?
THAT'S GREAT!
MORNING.
HEY.
THE LAST TIME I WENT TO THE ZOO WAS ON AN ELEMENTARY SCHOOL FIELD TRIP.
ME TOO.
I WAS SURPRISED BY HOW BIG GIRAFFES ARE!

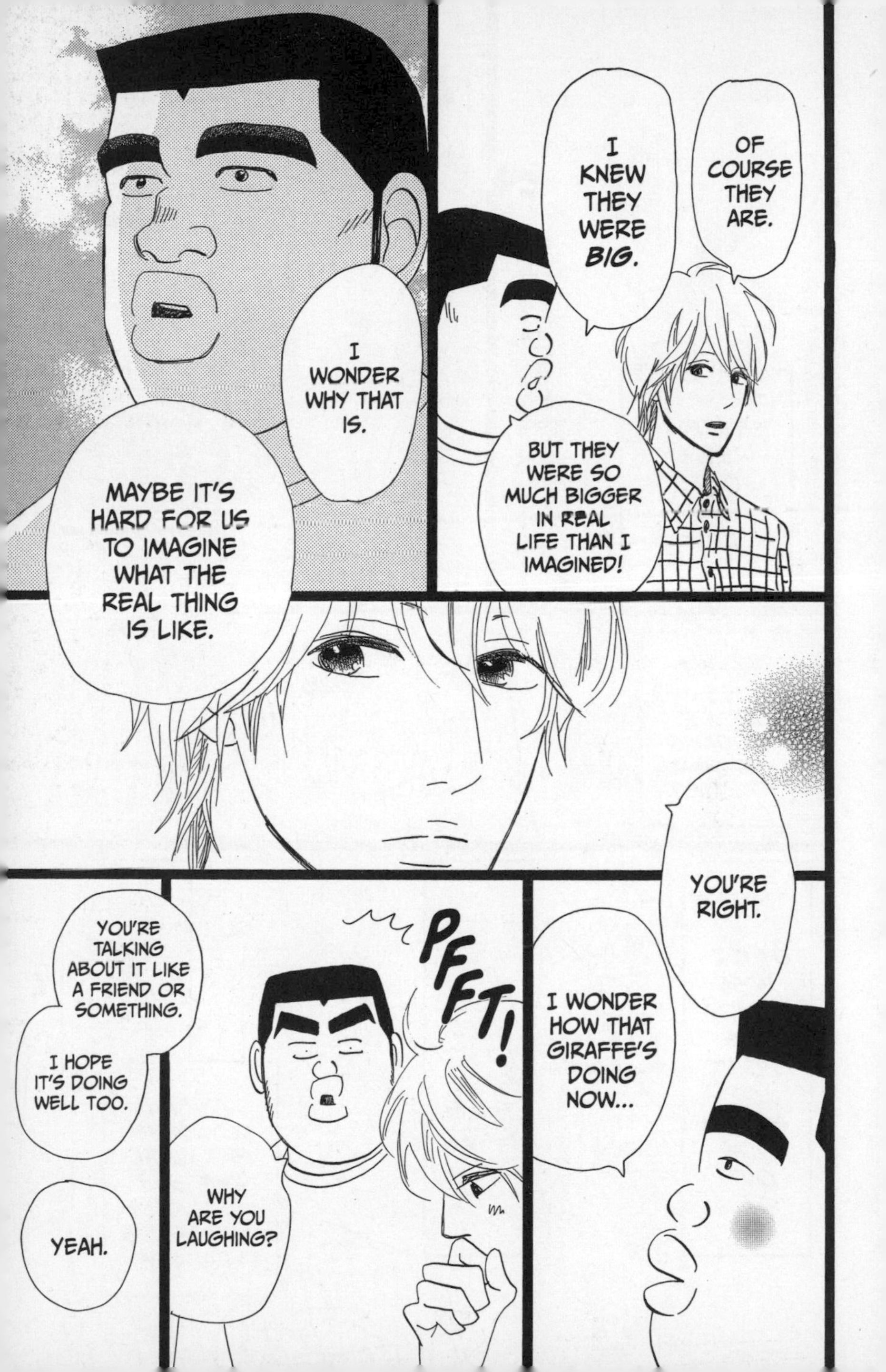
OF COURSE THEY ARE.
I KNEW THEY WERE *BIG*.
BUT THEY WERE SO MUCH BIGGER IN REAL LIFE THAN I IMAGINED!
I WONDER WHY THAT IS.
MAYBE IT'S HARD FOR US TO IMAGINE WHAT THE REAL THING IS LIKE.
YOU'RE RIGHT.
I WONDER HOW THAT GIRAFFE'S DOING NOW...
PFFT!
WHY ARE YOU LAUGHING?
YOU'RE TALKING ABOUT IT LIKE A FRIEND OR SOMETHING.
I HOPE IT'S DOING WELL TOO.
YEAH.

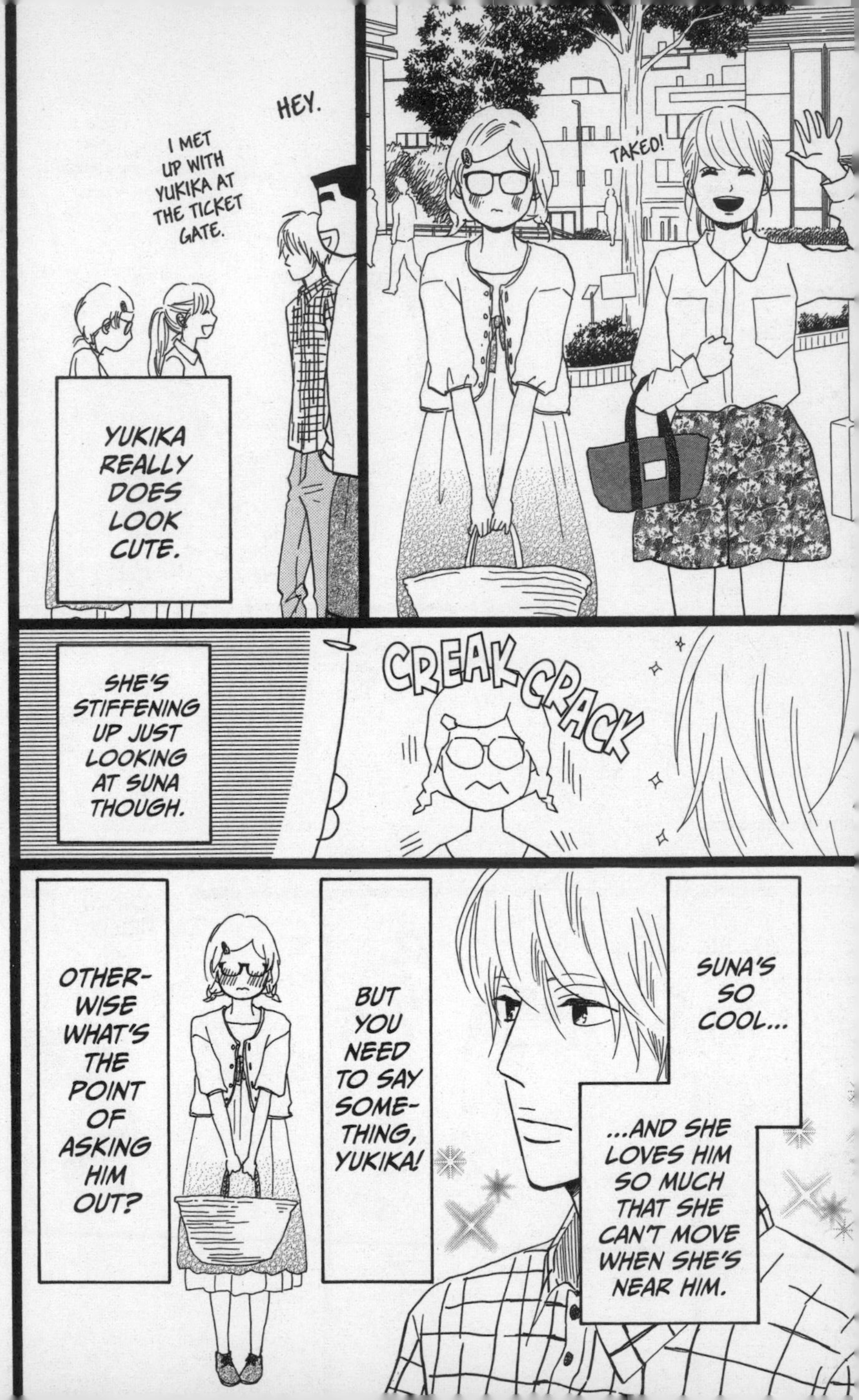
TAKEO!
HEY.
I MET UP WITH YUKIKA AT THE TICKET GATE.
YUKIKA REALLY DOES LOOK CUTE.
CREAK CRACK
SHE'S STIFFENING UP JUST LOOKING AT SUNA THOUGH.
SUNA'S SO COOL...
...AND SHE LOVES HIM SO MUCH THAT SHE CAN'T MOVE WHEN SHE'S NEAR HIM.
BUT YOU NEED TO SAY SOMETHING, YUKIKA!
OTHERWISE WHAT'S THE POINT OF ASKING HIM OUT?

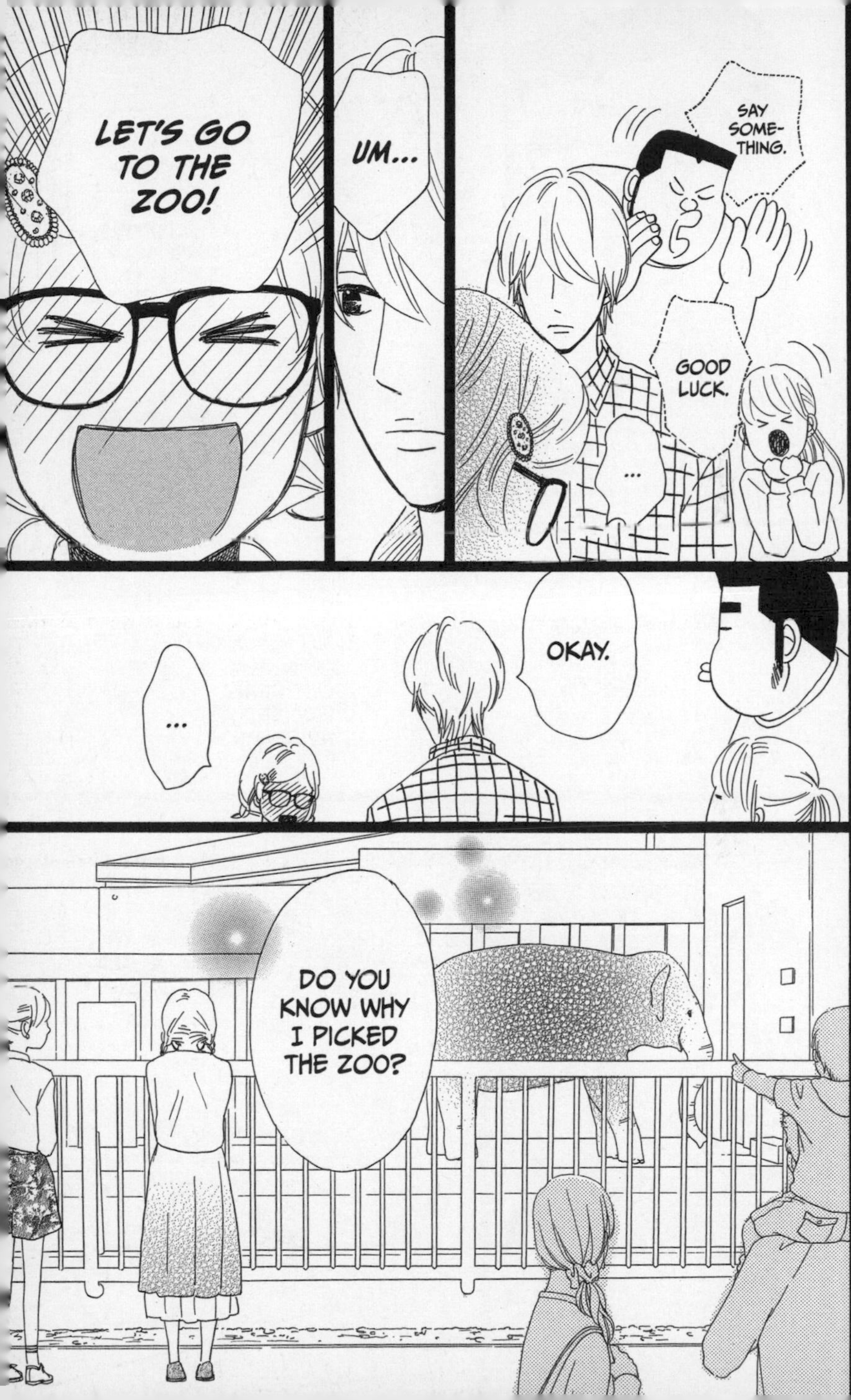
SAY SOME-THING.
GOOD LUCK.
...
UM...
LET'S GO TO THE ZOO!
OKAY.
...
DO YOU KNOW WHY I PICKED THE ZOO?

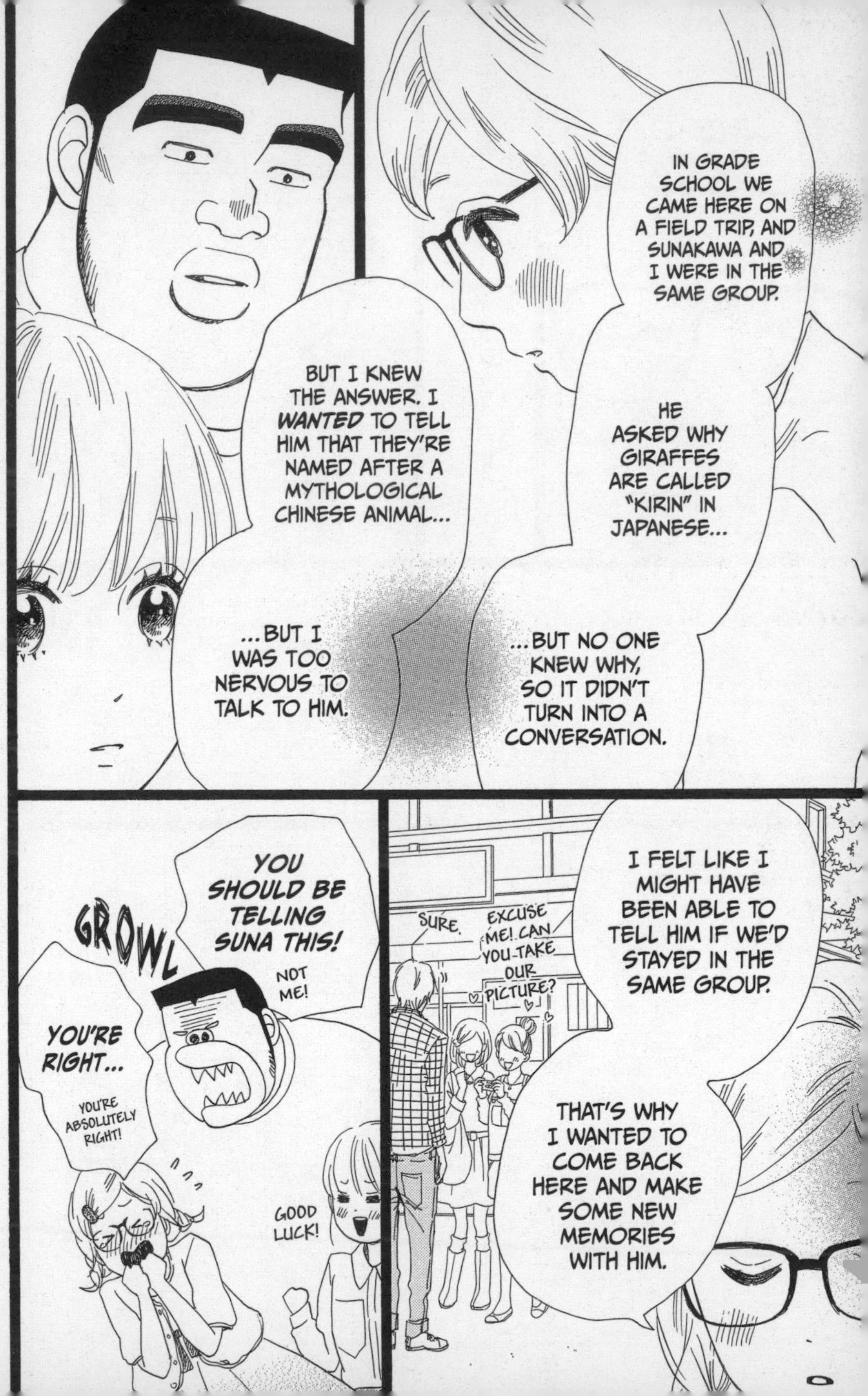
IN GRADE SCHOOL WE CAME HERE ON A FIELD TRIP, AND SUNAKAWA AND I WERE IN THE SAME GROUP.
HE ASKED WHY GIRAFFES ARE CALLED "KIRIN" IN JAPANESE...
...BUT NO ONE KNEW WHY, SO IT DIDN'T TURN INTO A CONVERSATION.
BUT I KNEW THE ANSWER. I *WANTED* TO TELL HIM THAT THEY'RE NAMED AFTER A MYTHOLOGICAL CHINESE ANIMAL...
...BUT I WAS TOO NERVOUS TO TALK TO HIM.
I FELT LIKE I MIGHT HAVE BEEN ABLE TO TELL HIM IF WE'D STAYED IN THE SAME GROUP.
THAT'S WHY I WANTED TO COME BACK HERE AND MAKE SOME NEW MEMORIES WITH HIM.
EXCUSE ME! CAN YOU TAKE OUR PICTURE?
SURE.
YOU SHOULD BE TELLING SUNA THIS!
NOT ME!
GROWL
YOU'RE RIGHT...
YOU'RE ABSOLUTELY RIGHT!
GOOD LUCK!

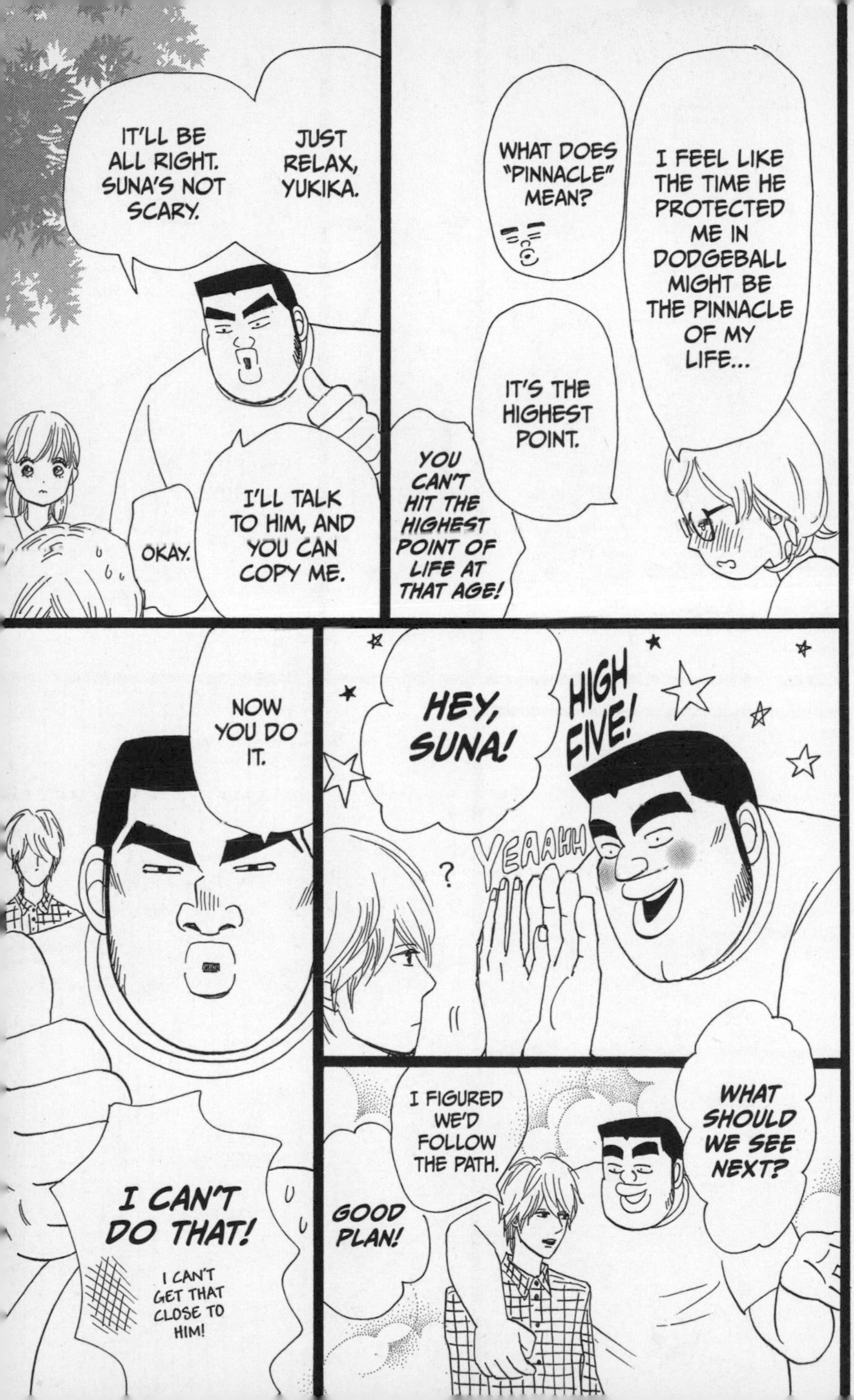
I FEEL LIKE THE TIME HE PROTECTED ME IN DODGEBALL MIGHT BE THE PINNACLE OF MY LIFE...
WHAT DOES "PINNACLE" MEAN?
IT'S THE HIGHEST POINT.
YOU CAN'T HIT THE HIGHEST POINT OF LIFE AT THAT AGE!
JUST RELAX, YUKIKA.
IT'LL BE ALL RIGHT. SUNA'S NOT SCARY.
I'LL TALK TO HIM, AND YOU CAN COPY ME.
OKAY.
HEY, SUNA!
HIGH FIVE!
YEAAHH
?
WHAT SHOULD WE SEE NEXT?
I FIGURED WE'D FOLLOW THE PATH.
GOOD PLAN!
NOW YOU DO IT.
I CAN'T DO THAT!
I CAN'T GET THAT CLOSE TO HIM!

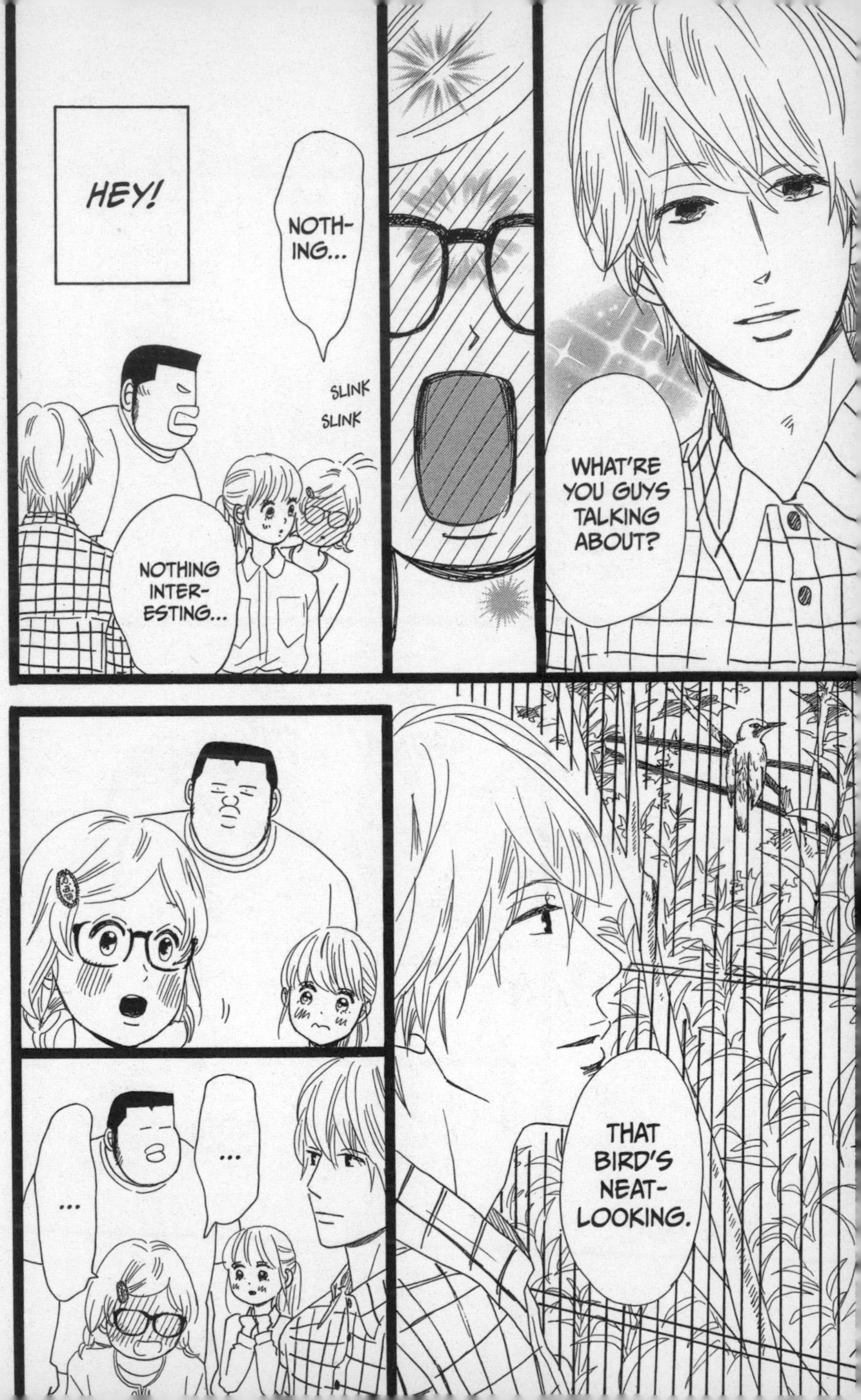
WHAT'RE YOU GUYS TALKING ABOUT?
NOTHING...
SLINK
SLINK
NOTHING INTERESTING...
HEY!
THAT BIRD'S NEAT-LOOKING.
...
...

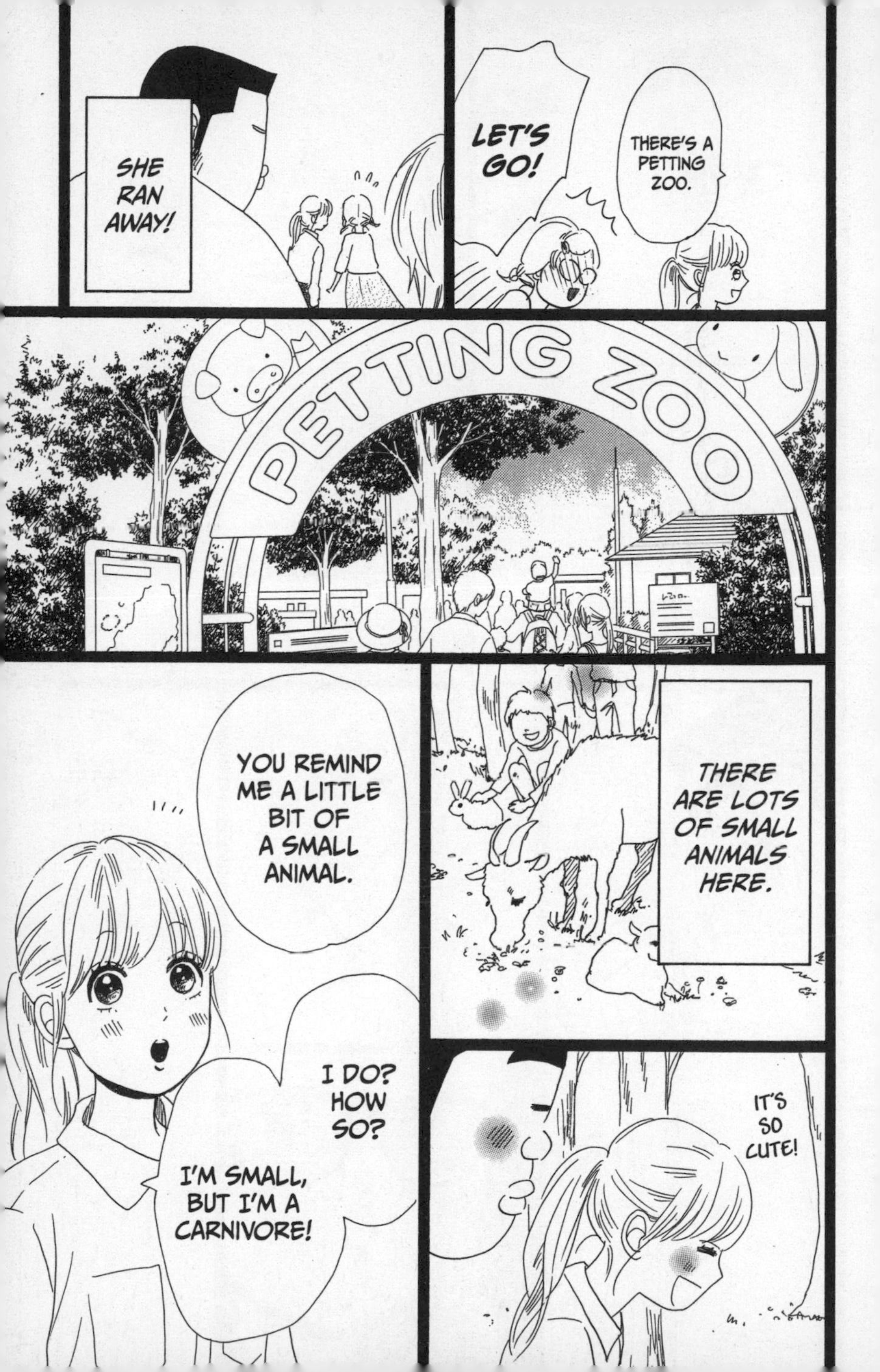
THERE'S A PETTING ZOO.
LET'S GO!
SHE RAN AWAY!
PETTING ZOO
THERE ARE LOTS OF SMALL ANIMALS HERE.
IT'S SO CUTE!
YOU REMIND ME A LITTLE BIT OF A SMALL ANIMAL.
I DO? HOW SO?
I'M SMALL, BUT I'M A CARNIVORE!

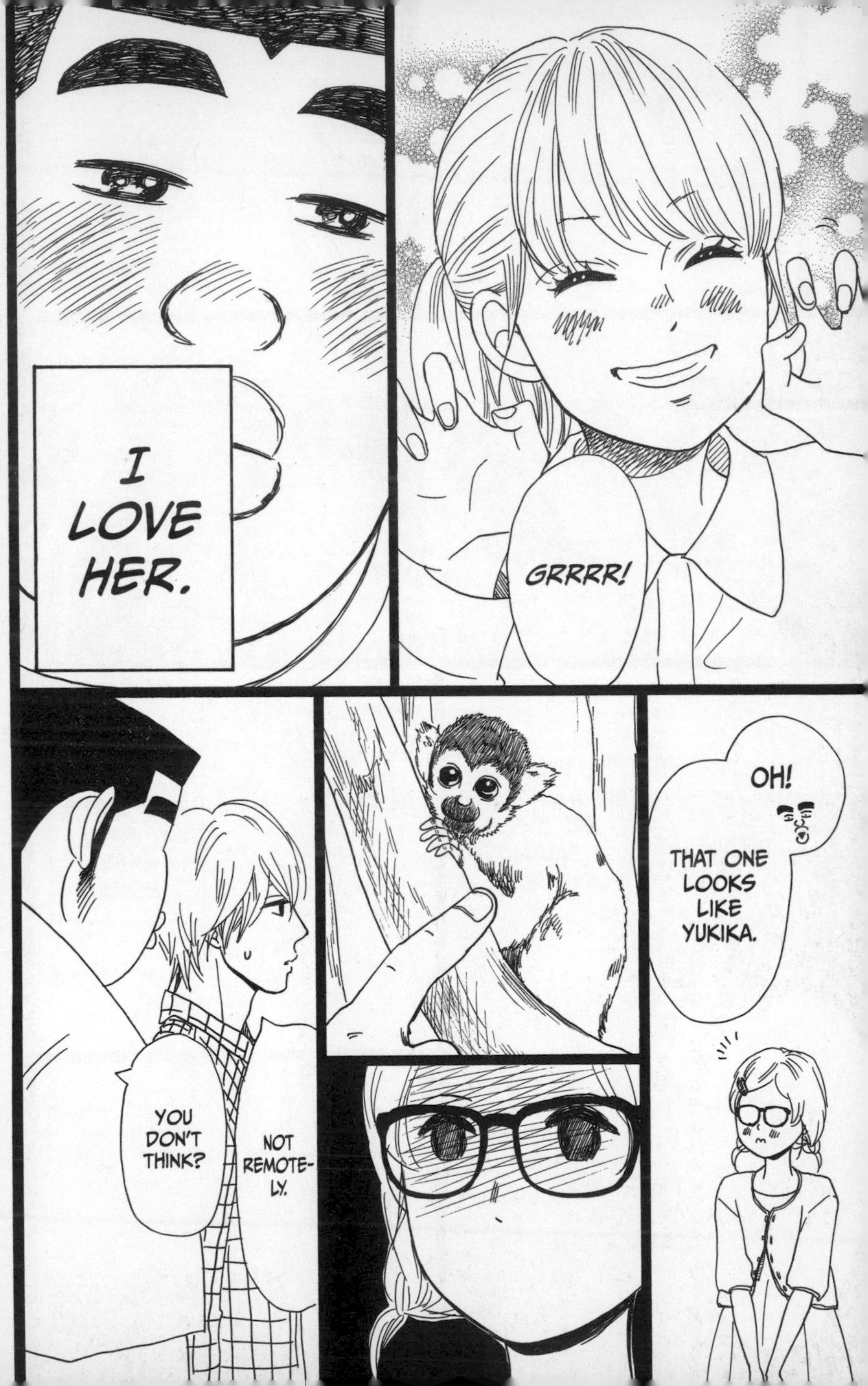
GRRRR!
I LOVE HER.
OH!
THAT ONE LOOKS LIKE YUKIKA.
YOU DON'T THINK?
NOT REMOTE-LY.

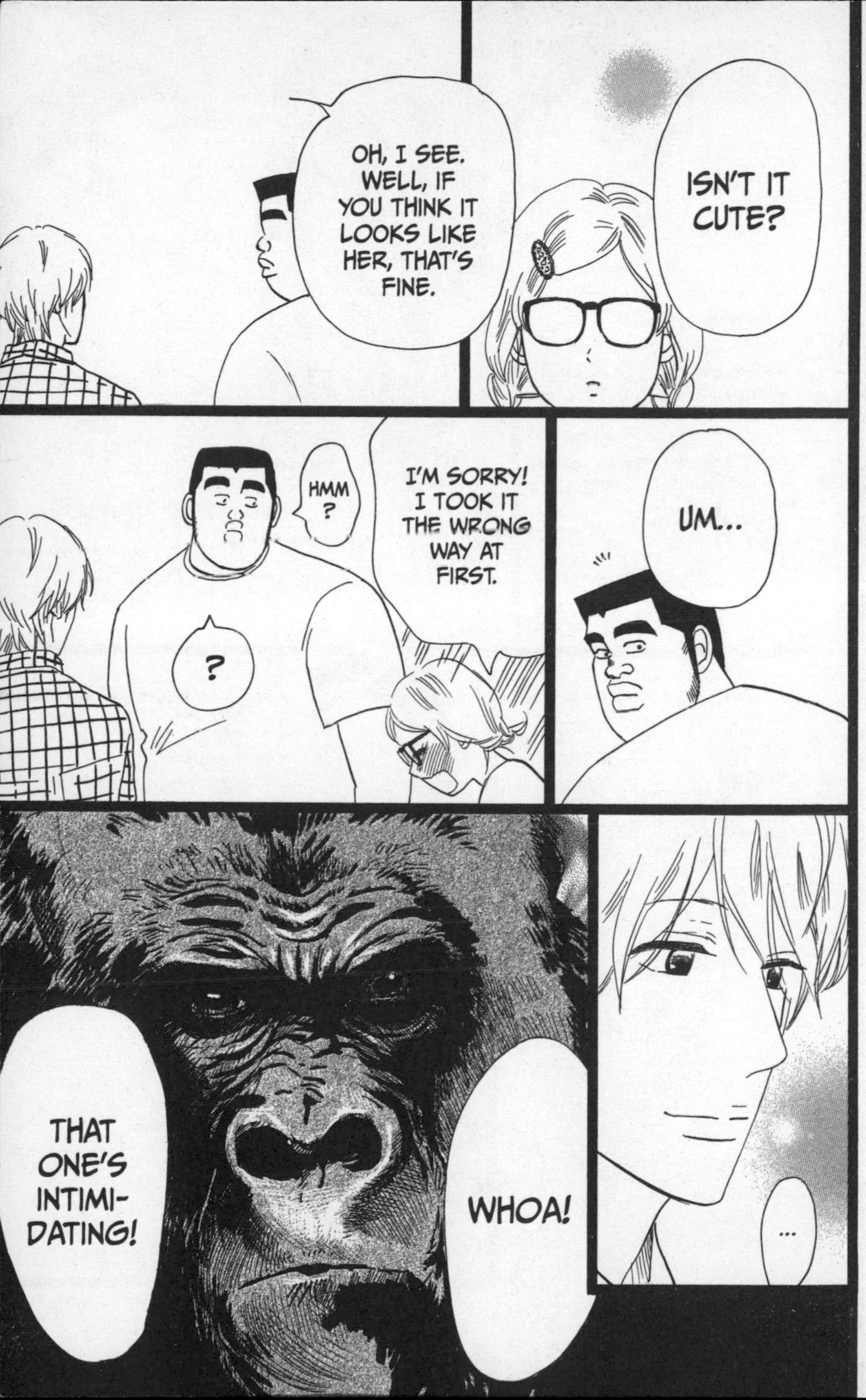
ISN'T IT CUTE?
OH, I SEE. WELL, IF YOU THINK IT LOOKS LIKE HER, THAT'S FINE.
UM...
I'M SORRY! I TOOK IT THE WRONG WAY AT FIRST.
HMM?
?
...
WHOA!
THAT ONE'S INTIMI-DATING!

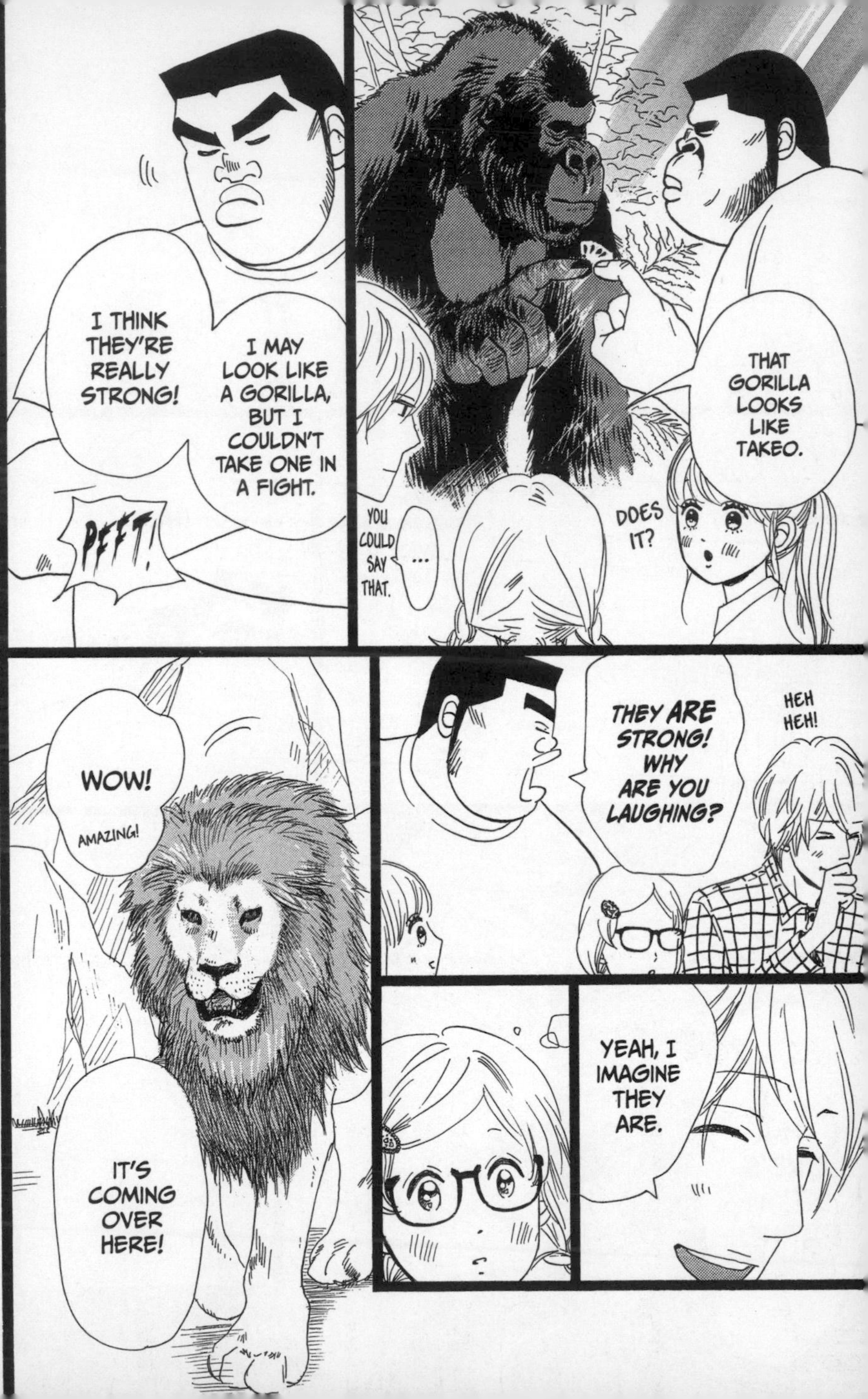
THAT GORILLA LOOKS LIKE TAKEO.
DOES IT?
YOU COULD SAY THAT.
...
I MAY LOOK LIKE A GORILLA, BUT I COULDN'T TAKE ONE IN A FIGHT.
I THINK THEY'RE REALLY STRONG!
PFFT!
HEH HEH!
THEY ARE STRONG! WHY ARE YOU LAUGHING?
YEAH, I IMAGINE THEY ARE.
WOW!
AMAZING!
IT'S COMING OVER HERE!

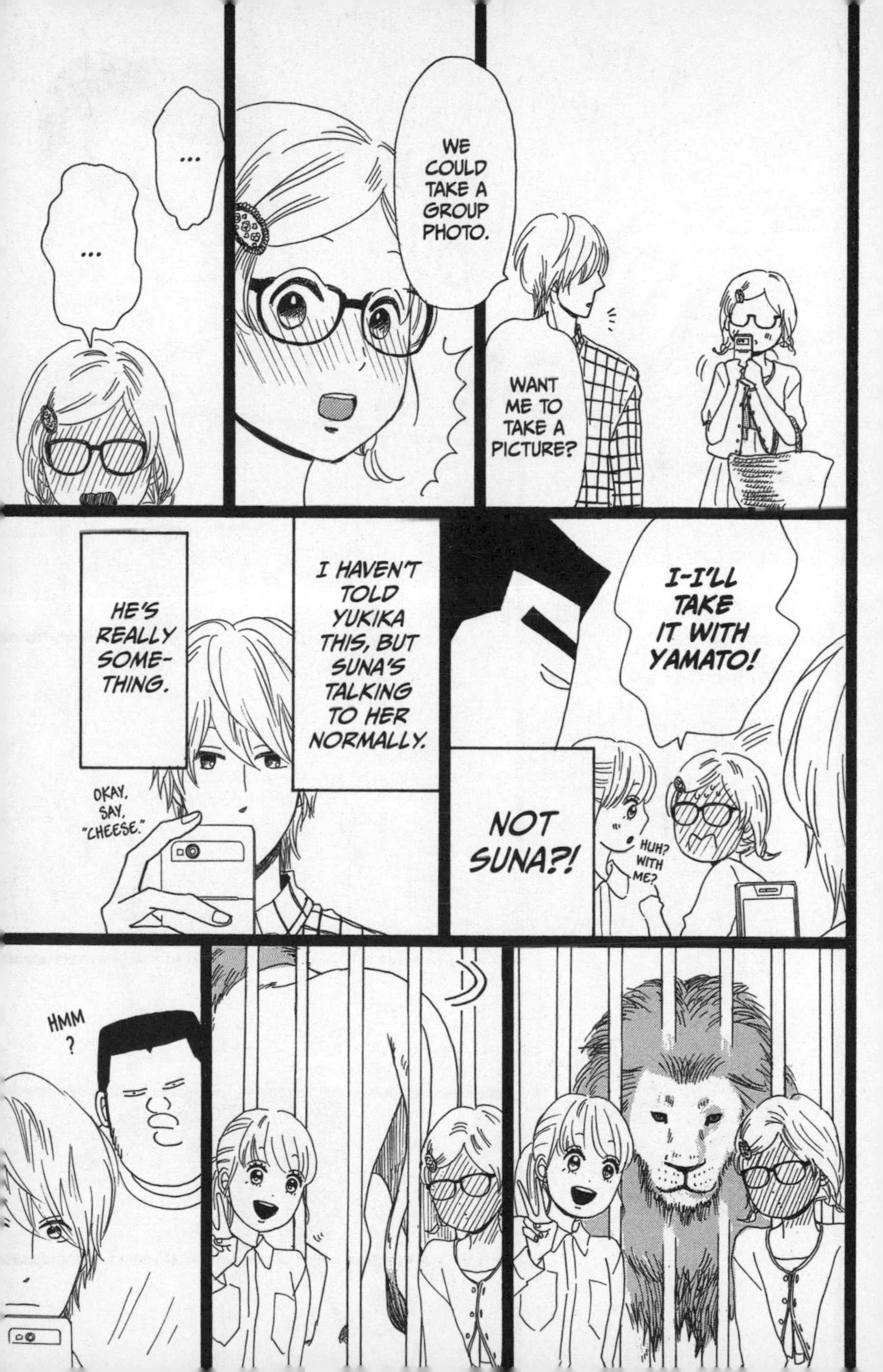
WE COULD TAKE A GROUP PHOTO.
WANT ME TO TAKE A PICTURE?
...
...
I-I'LL TAKE IT WITH YAMATO!
NOT SUNA?!
HUH? WITH ME?
I HAVEN'T TOLD YUKIKA THIS, BUT SUNA'S TALKING TO HER NORMALLY.
HE'S REALLY SOME-THING.
OKAY, SAY, "CHEESE."
HMM ?

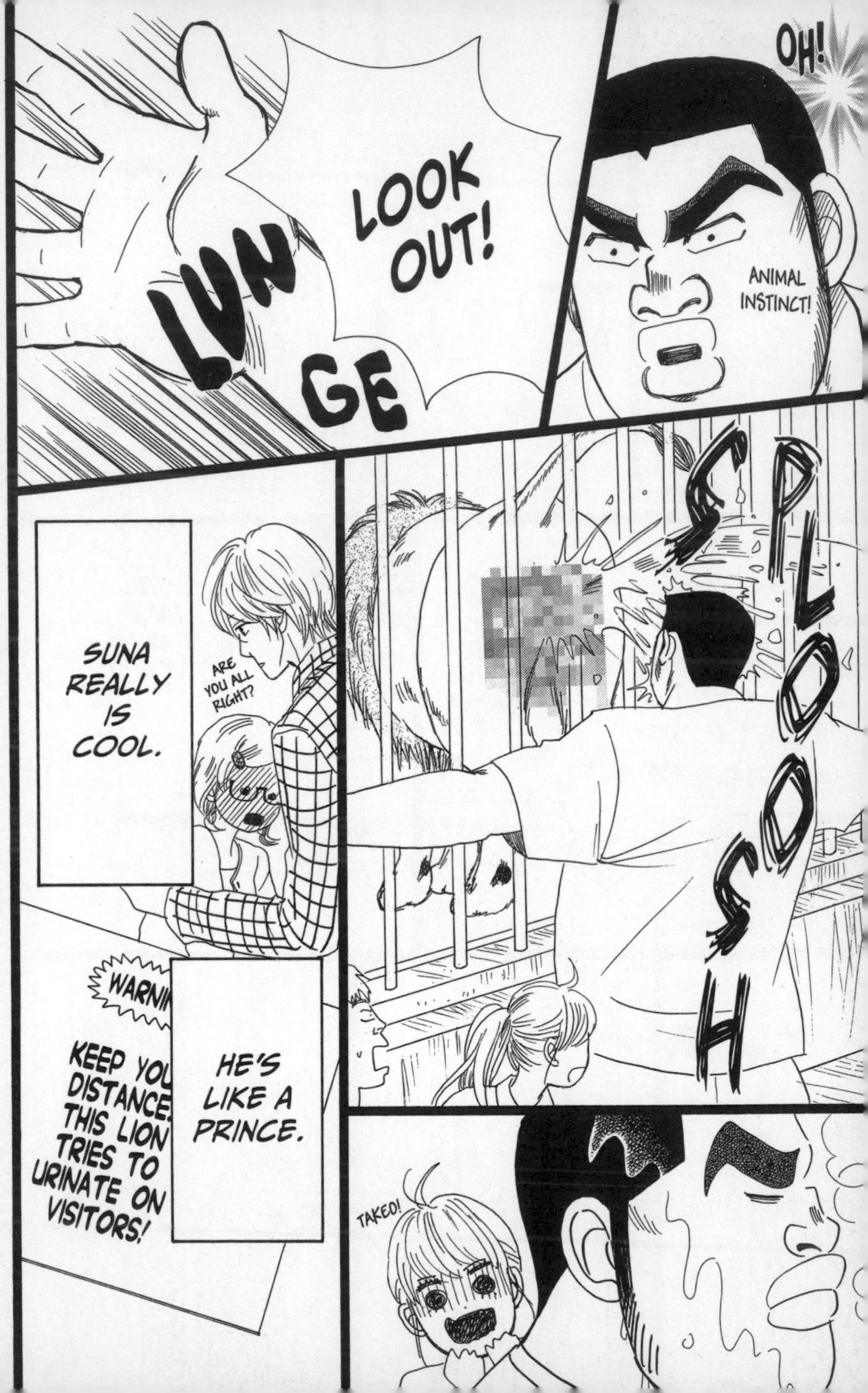
OH!
ANIMAL INSTINCT!
LOOK OUT!
LUNGE
SPLOOSH
TAKED!
SUNA REALLY IS COOL.
ARE YOU ALL RIGHT?
HE'S LIKE A PRINCE.
WARNIN
KEEP YOU DISTANCE. THIS LION TRIES TO URINATE ON VISITORS!

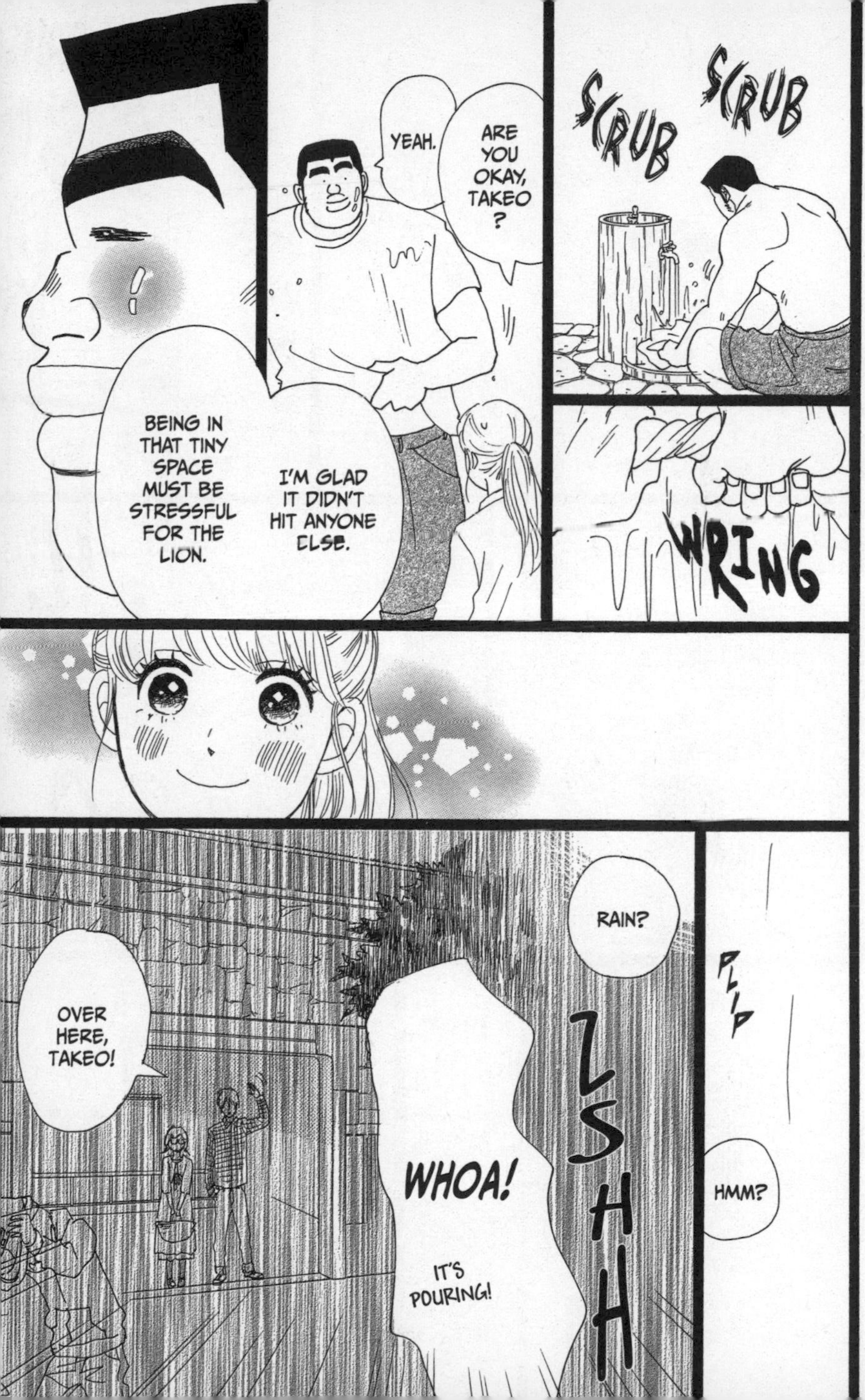
SCRUB SCRUB
WRING
ARE YOU OKAY, TAKEO?
YEAH.
I'M GLAD IT DIDN'T HIT ANYONE ELSE.
BEING IN THAT TINY SPACE MUST BE STRESSFUL FOR THE LION.
RAIN?
PLIP
HMM?
ZSHH
WHOA!
IT'S POURING!
OVER HERE, TAKEO!

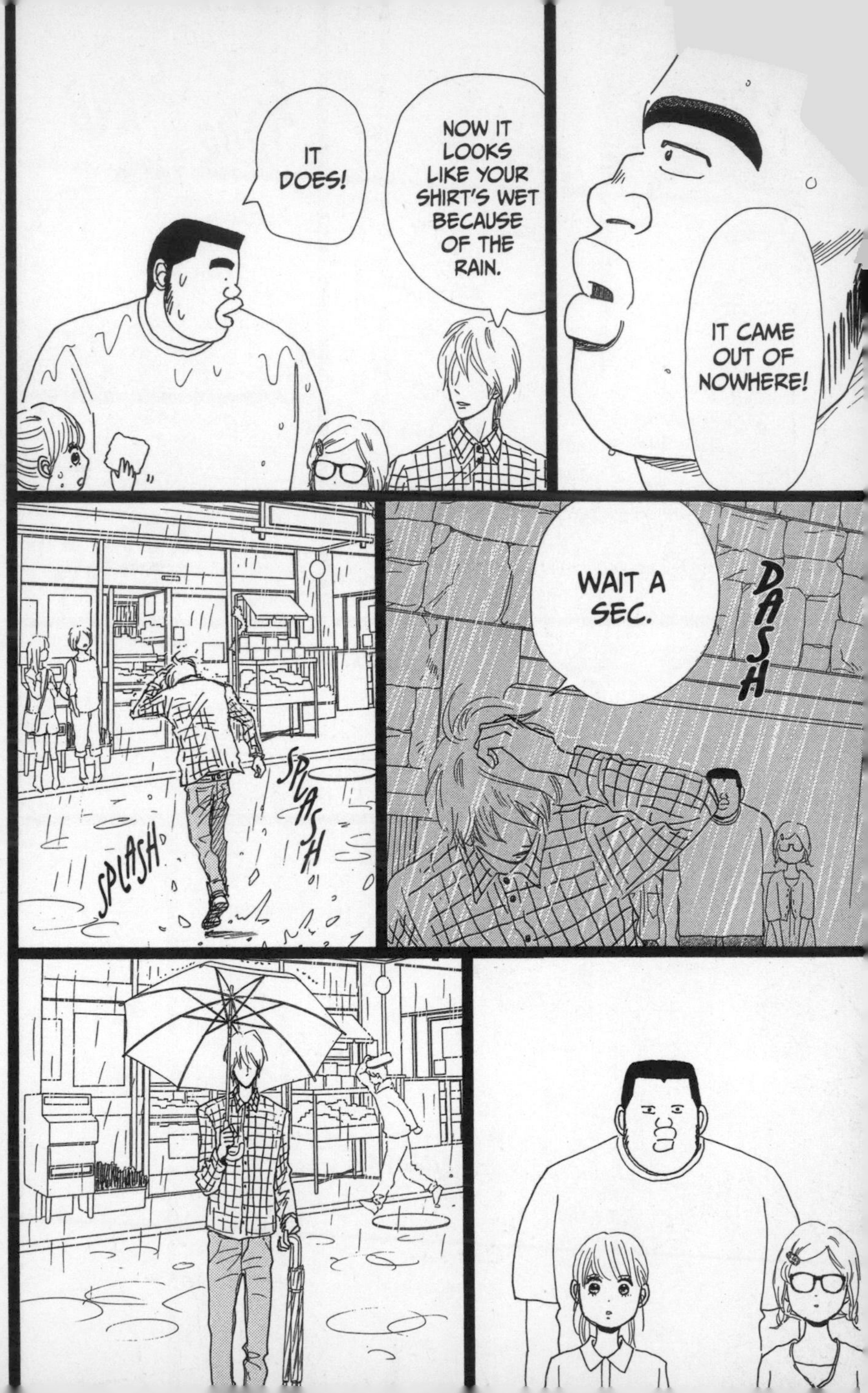
IT CAME OUT OF NOWHERE!
NOW IT LOOKS LIKE YOUR SHIRT'S WET BECAUSE OF THE RAIN.
IT DOES!
WAIT A SEC.
DASH
SPLASH
SPLASH

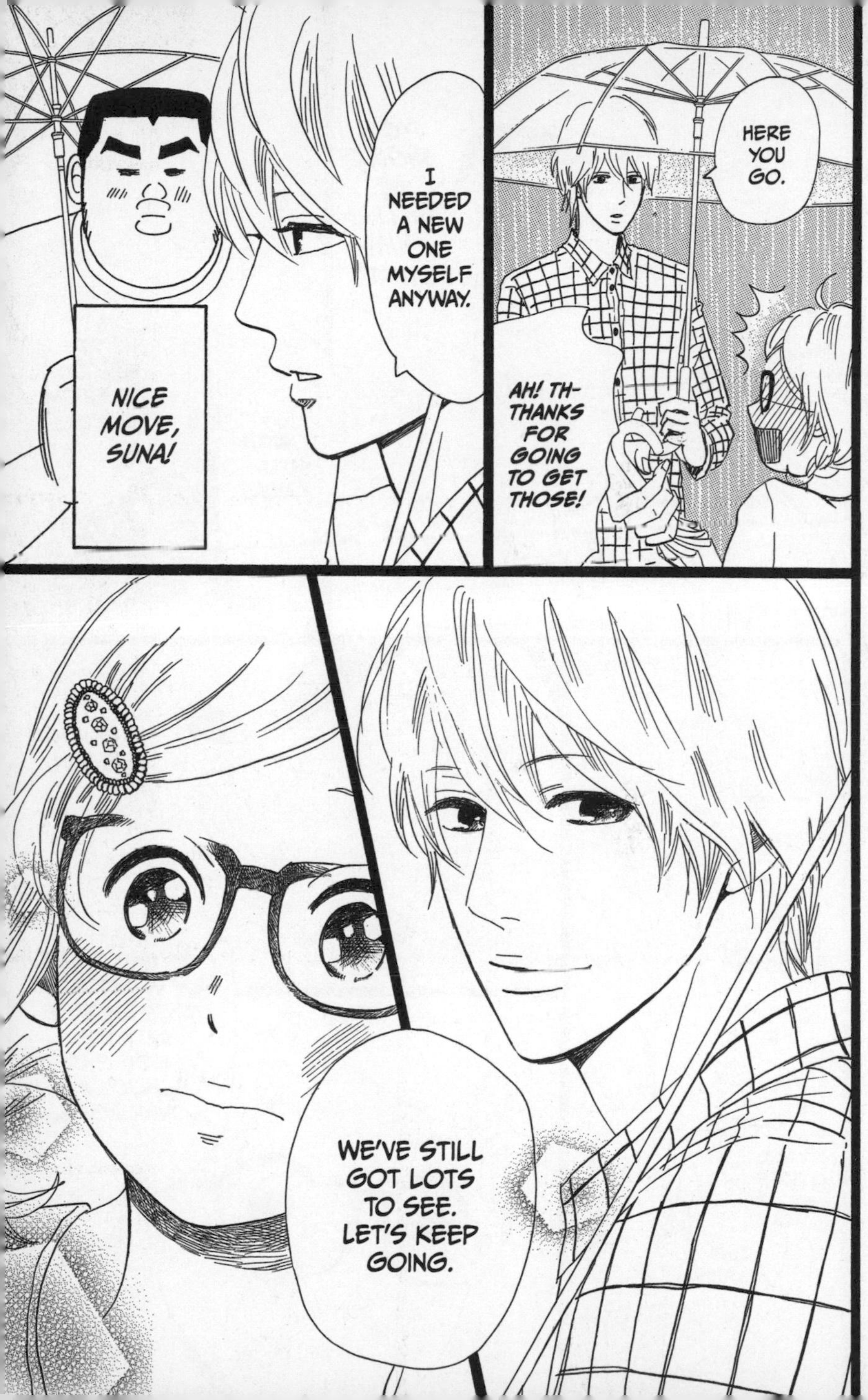
HERE YOU GO.
AH! TH-THANKS FOR GOING TO GET THOSE!
I NEEDED A NEW ONE MYSELF ANYWAY.
NICE MOVE, SUNA!
WE'VE STILL GOT LOTS TO SEE. LET'S KEEP GOING.

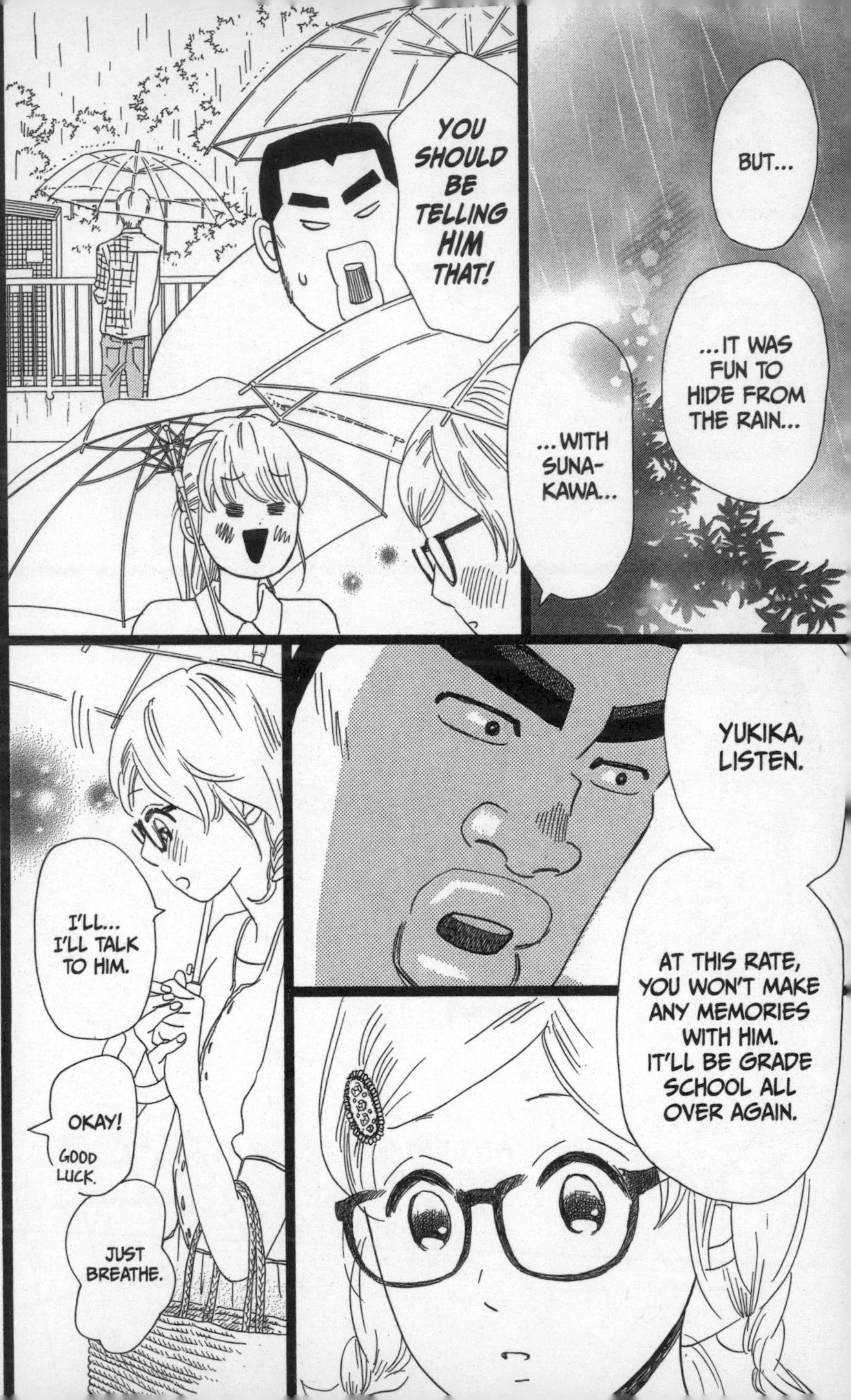
BUT...
...IT WAS FUN TO HIDE FROM THE RAIN...
...WITH SUNA-KAWA...
YOU SHOULD BE TELLING HIM THAT!
YUKIKA, LISTEN.
AT THIS RATE, YOU WON'T MAKE ANY MEMORIES WITH HIM. IT'LL BE GRADE SCHOOL ALL OVER AGAIN.
I'LL... I'LL TALK TO HIM.
OKAY!
GOOD LUCK.
JUST BREATHE.

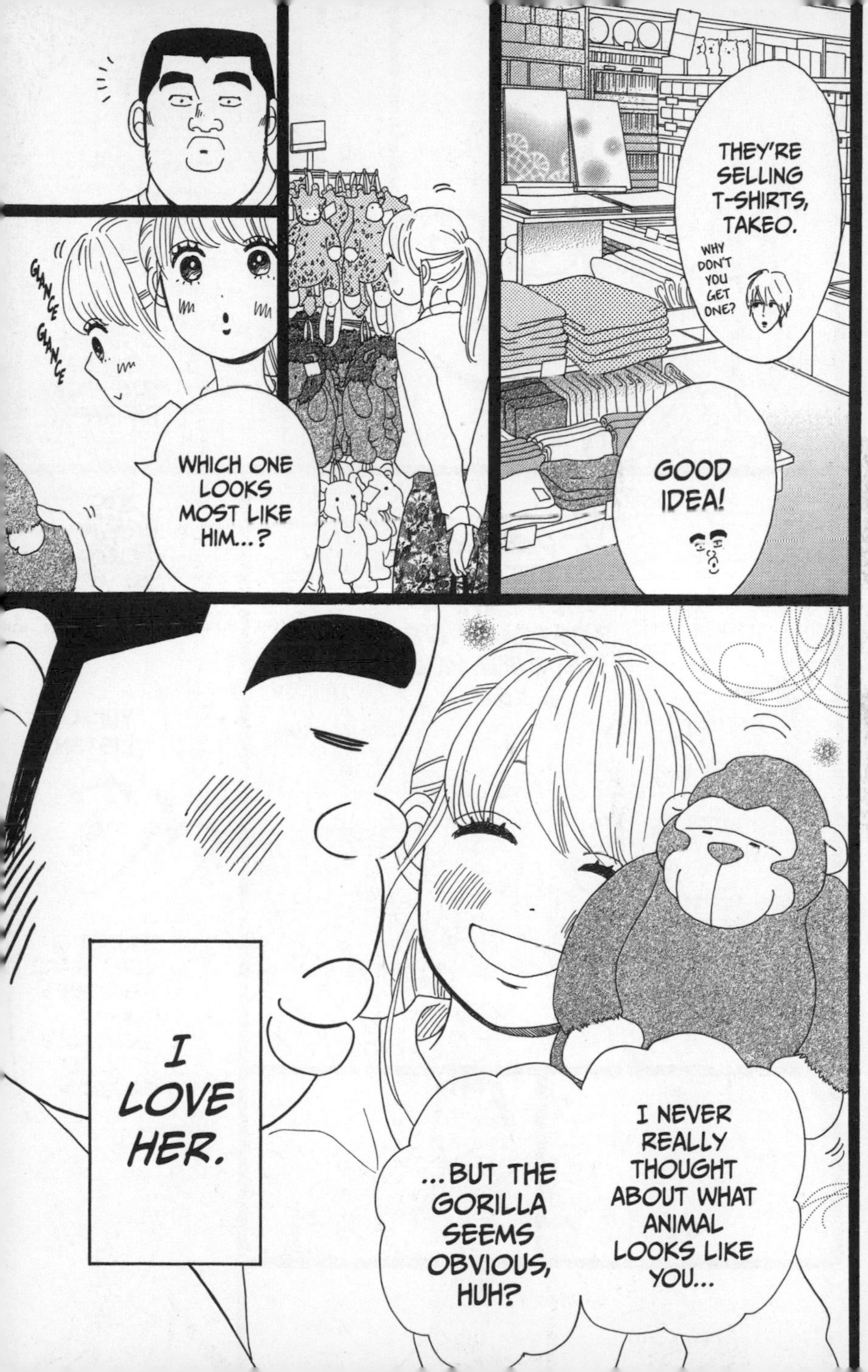
THEY'RE SELLING T-SHIRTS, TAKEO.
WHY DON'T YOU GET ONE?
GOOD IDEA!
GLANCE GLANCE
WHICH ONE LOOKS MOST LIKE HIM...?
I NEVER REALLY THOUGHT ABOUT WHAT ANIMAL LOOKS LIKE YOU...
...BUT THE GORILLA SEEMS OBVIOUS, HUH?
I LOVE HER.

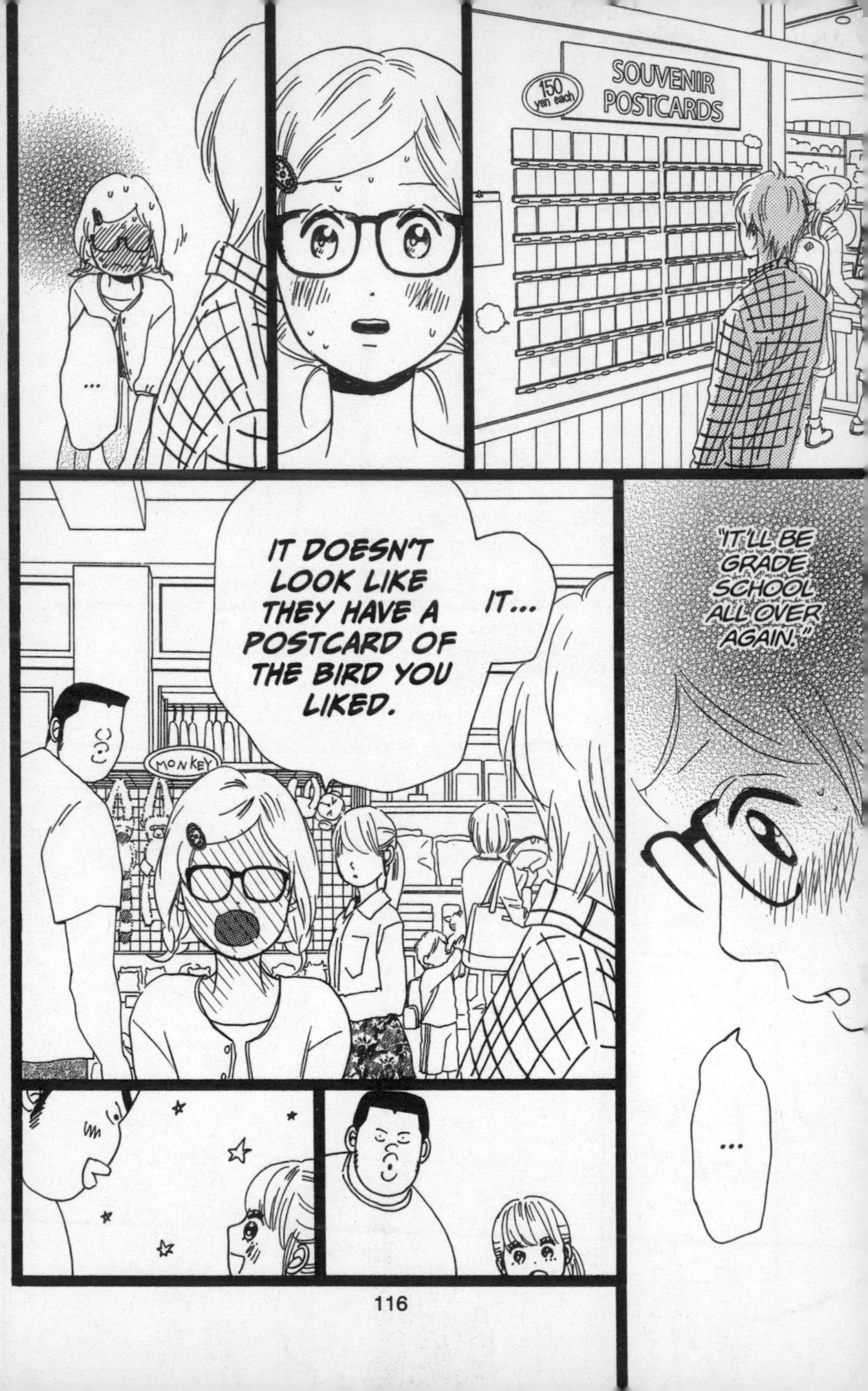
SOUVENIR POSTCARDS
150 yen each
...
"IT'LL BE GRADE SCHOOL ALL OVER AGAIN."
...
IT...
IT DOESN'T LOOK LIKE THEY HAVE A POSTCARD OF THE BIRD YOU LIKED.
MONKEY

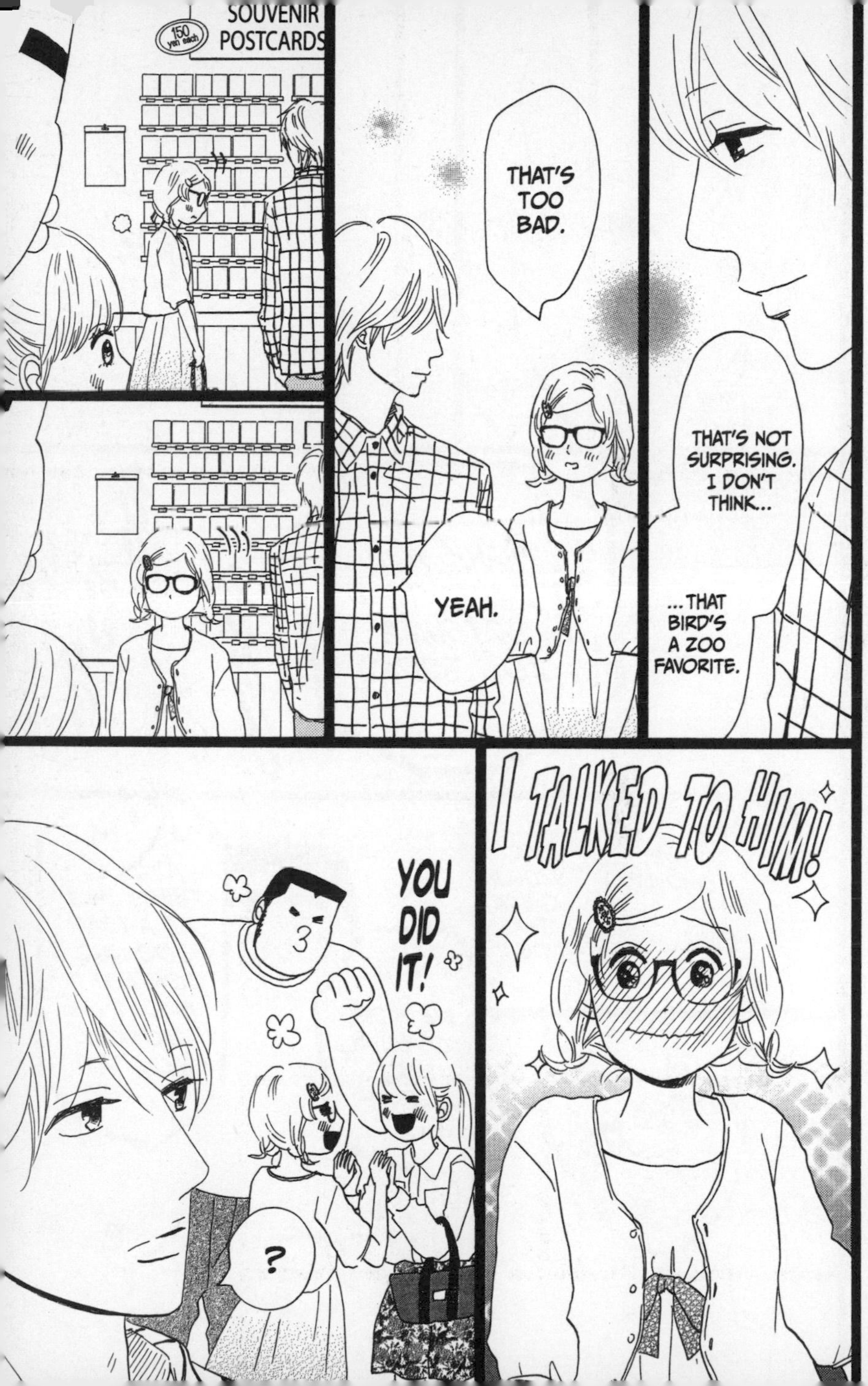
THAT'S NOT SURPRISING. I DON'T THINK...
...THAT BIRD'S A ZOO FAVORITE.
THAT'S TOO BAD.
YEAH.
SOUVENIR POSTCARDS
150 yen each
I TALKED TO HIM!
YOU DID IT!
?

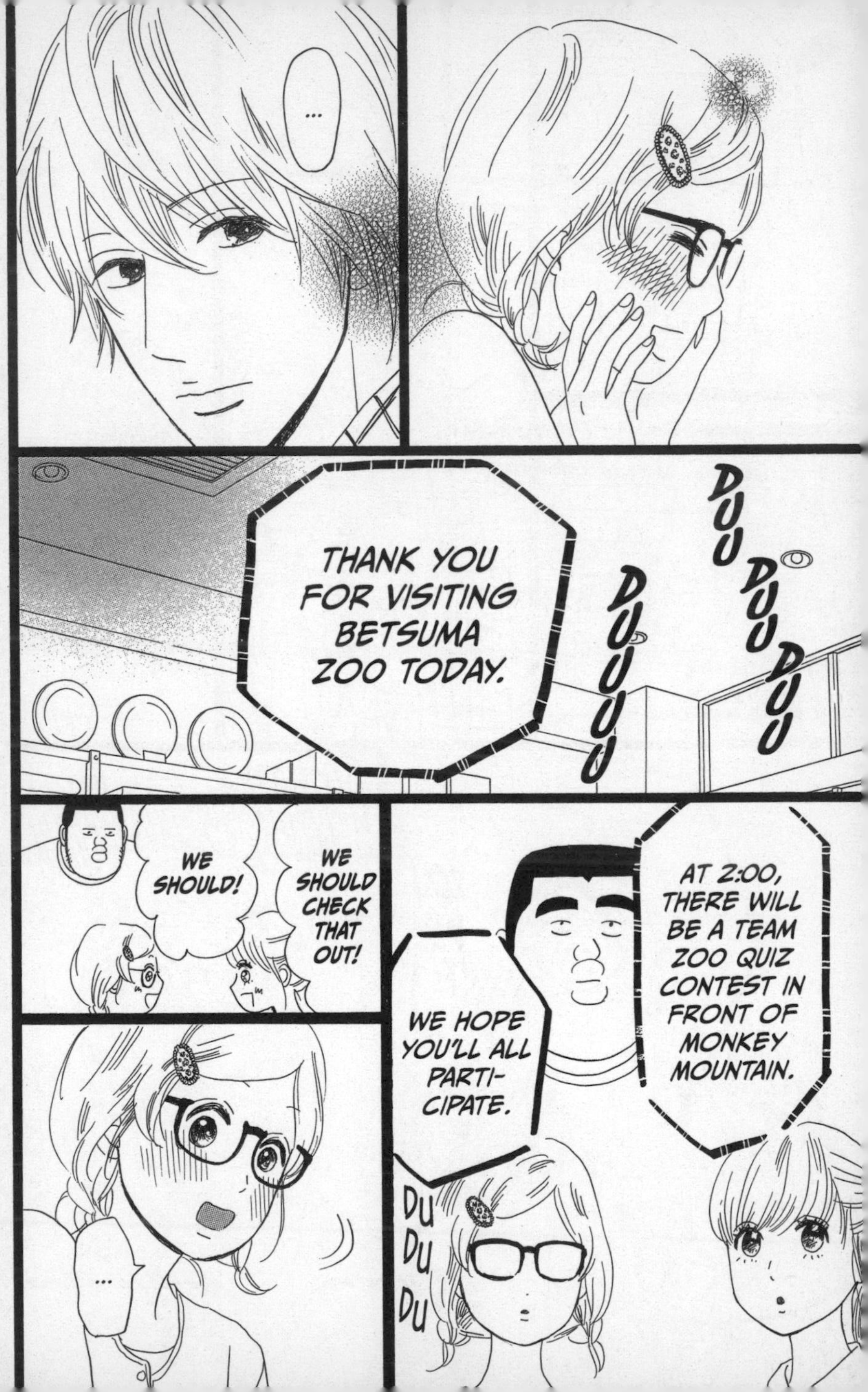
...
DUU DUU DUU
DUUUUU
THANK YOU FOR VISITING BETSUMA ZOO TODAY.
AT 2:00, THERE WILL BE A TEAM ZOO QUIZ CONTEST IN FRONT OF MONKEY MOUNTAIN.
WE HOPE YOU'LL ALL PARTI-CIPATE.
DU DU DU DU
WE SHOULD CHECK THAT OUT!
WE SHOULD!
...

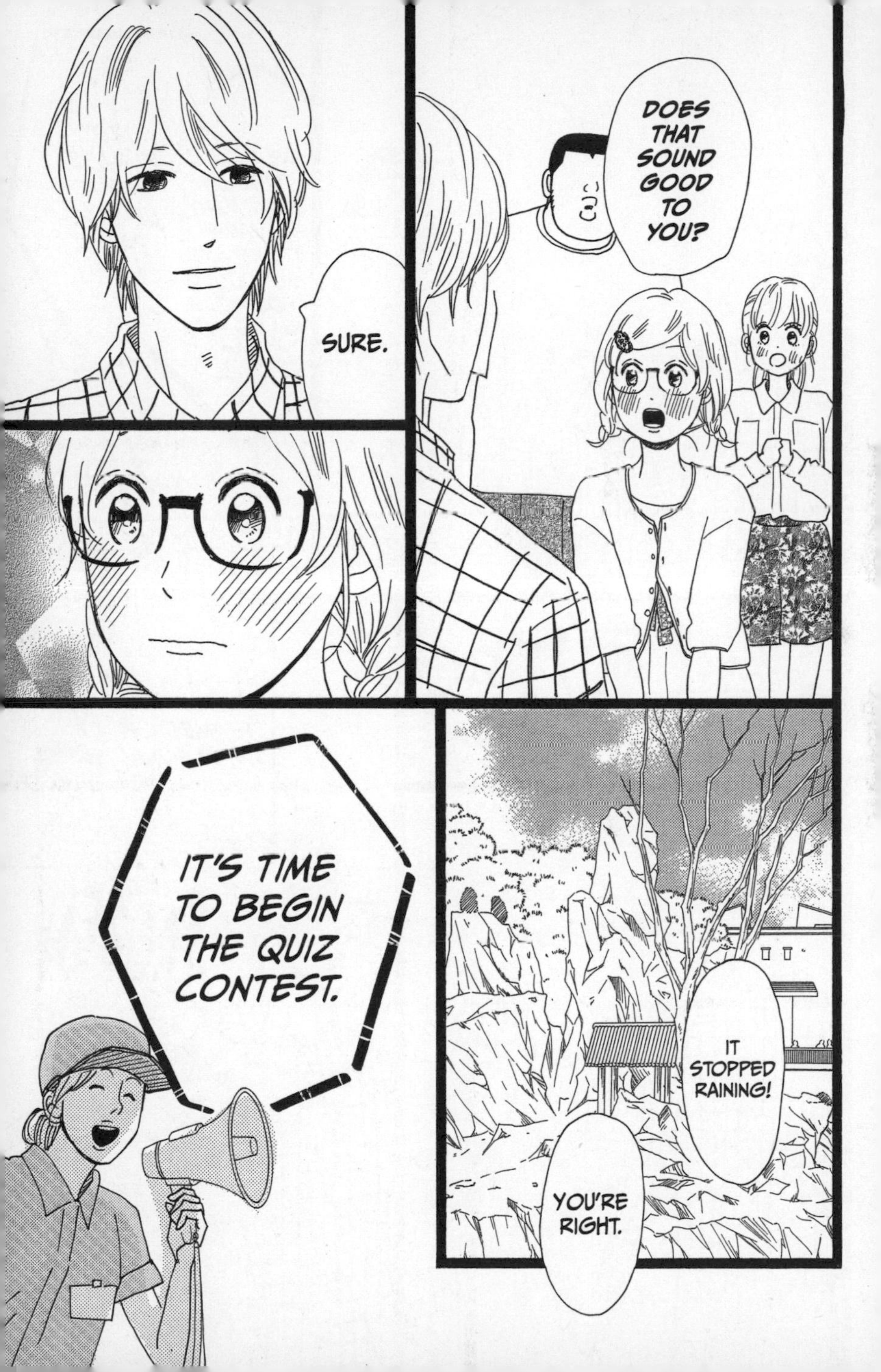
DOES THAT SOUND GOOD TO YOU?
SURE.
IT STOPPED RAINING!
YOU'RE RIGHT.
IT'S TIME TO BEGIN THE QUIZ CONTEST.

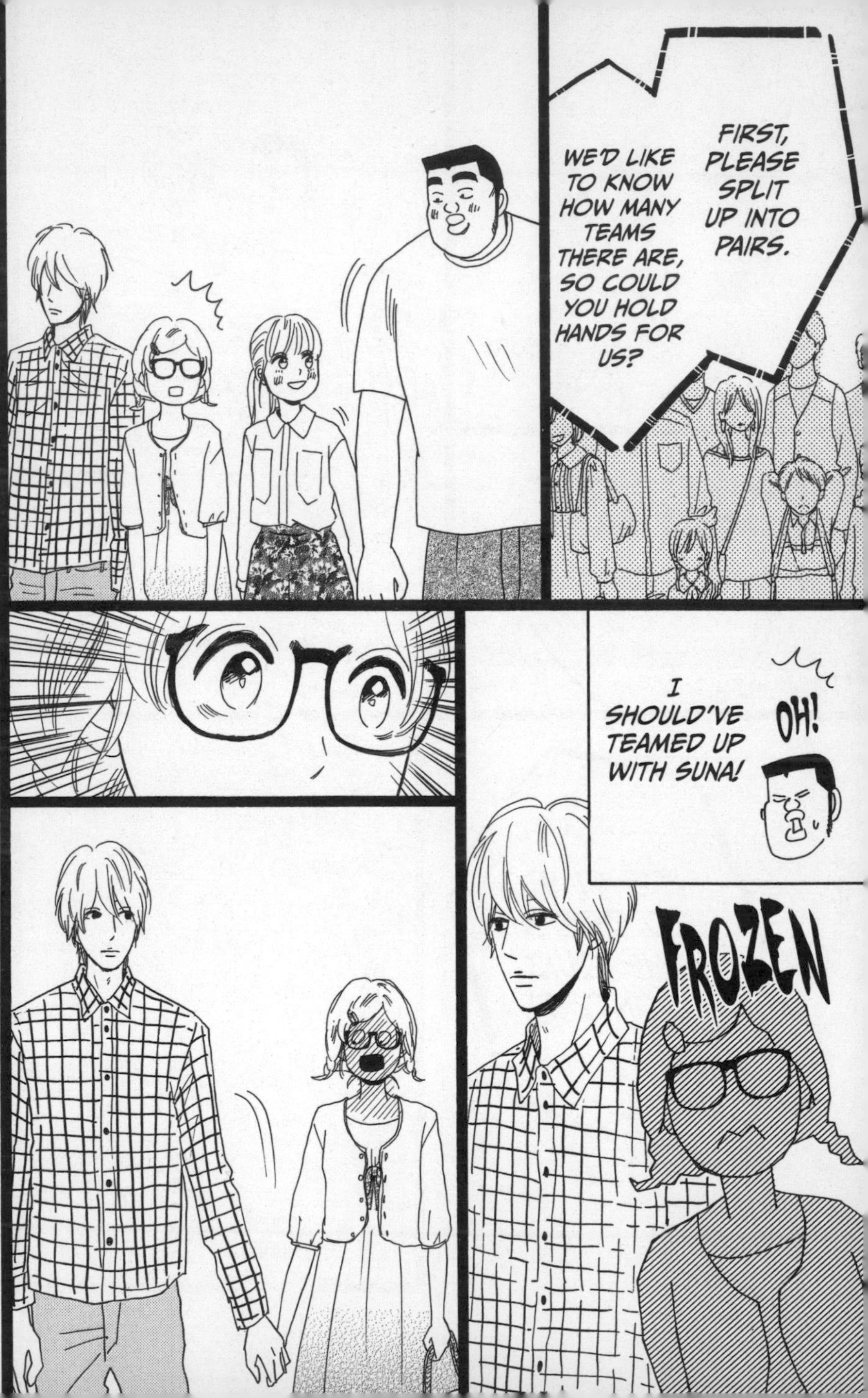
FIRST, PLEASE SPLIT UP INTO PAIRS.
WE'D LIKE TO KNOW HOW MANY TEAMS THERE ARE, SO COULD YOU HOLD HANDS FOR US?
OH!
I SHOULD'VE TEAMED UP WITH SUNA!
FROZEN

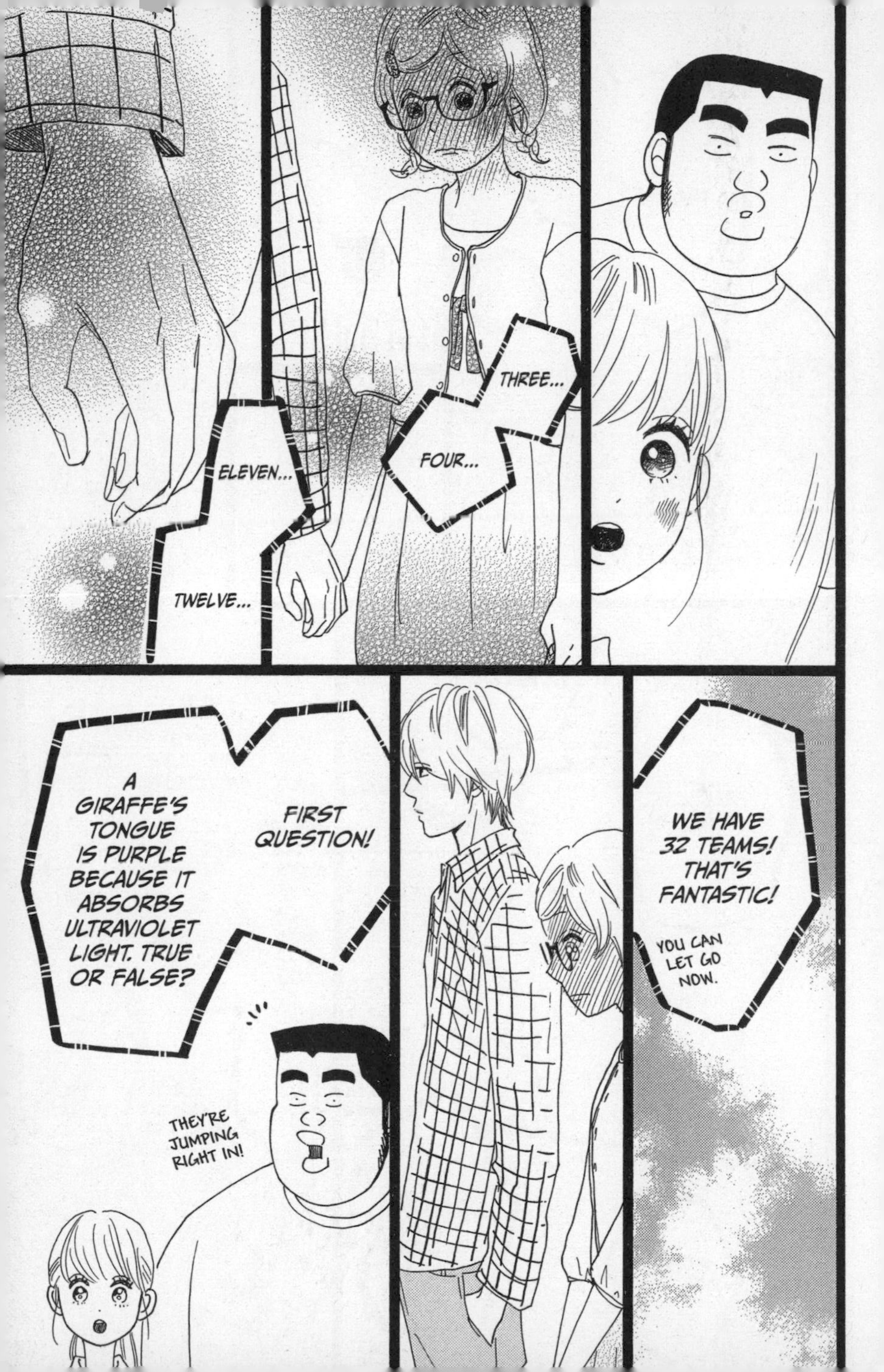
THREE... FOUR...
ELEVEN... TWELVE...
WE HAVE 32 TEAMS! THAT'S FANTASTIC!
YOU CAN LET GO NOW.
FIRST QUESTION!
A GIRAFFE'S TONGUE IS PURPLE BECAUSE IT ABSORBS ULTRAVIOLET LIGHT. TRUE OR FALSE?
THEY'RE JUMPING RIGHT IN!

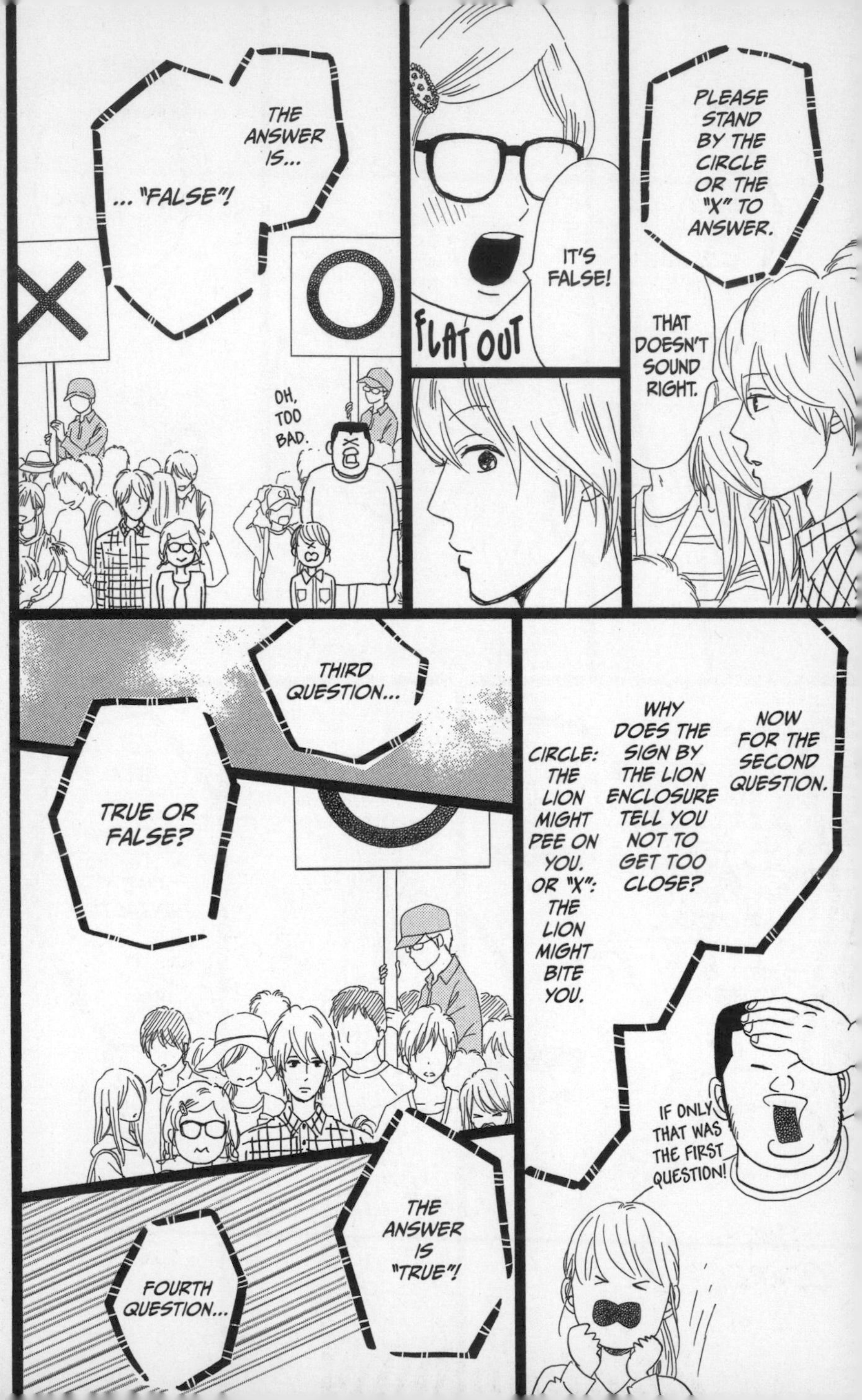
PLEASE STAND BY THE CIRCLE OR THE "X" TO ANSWER.
THAT DOESN'T SOUND RIGHT.
IT'S FALSE!
FLAT OUT
THE ANSWER IS...
... "FALSE"!
OH, TOO BAD.
NOW FOR THE SECOND QUESTION.
WHY DOES THE SIGN BY THE LION ENCLOSURE TELL YOU NOT TO GET TOO CLOSE?
CIRCLE: THE LION MIGHT PEE ON YOU. OR "X": THE LION MIGHT BITE YOU.
IF ONLY THAT WAS THE FIRST QUESTION!
THIRD QUESTION...
TRUE OR FALSE?
THE ANSWER IS "TRUE"!
FOURTH QUESTION...

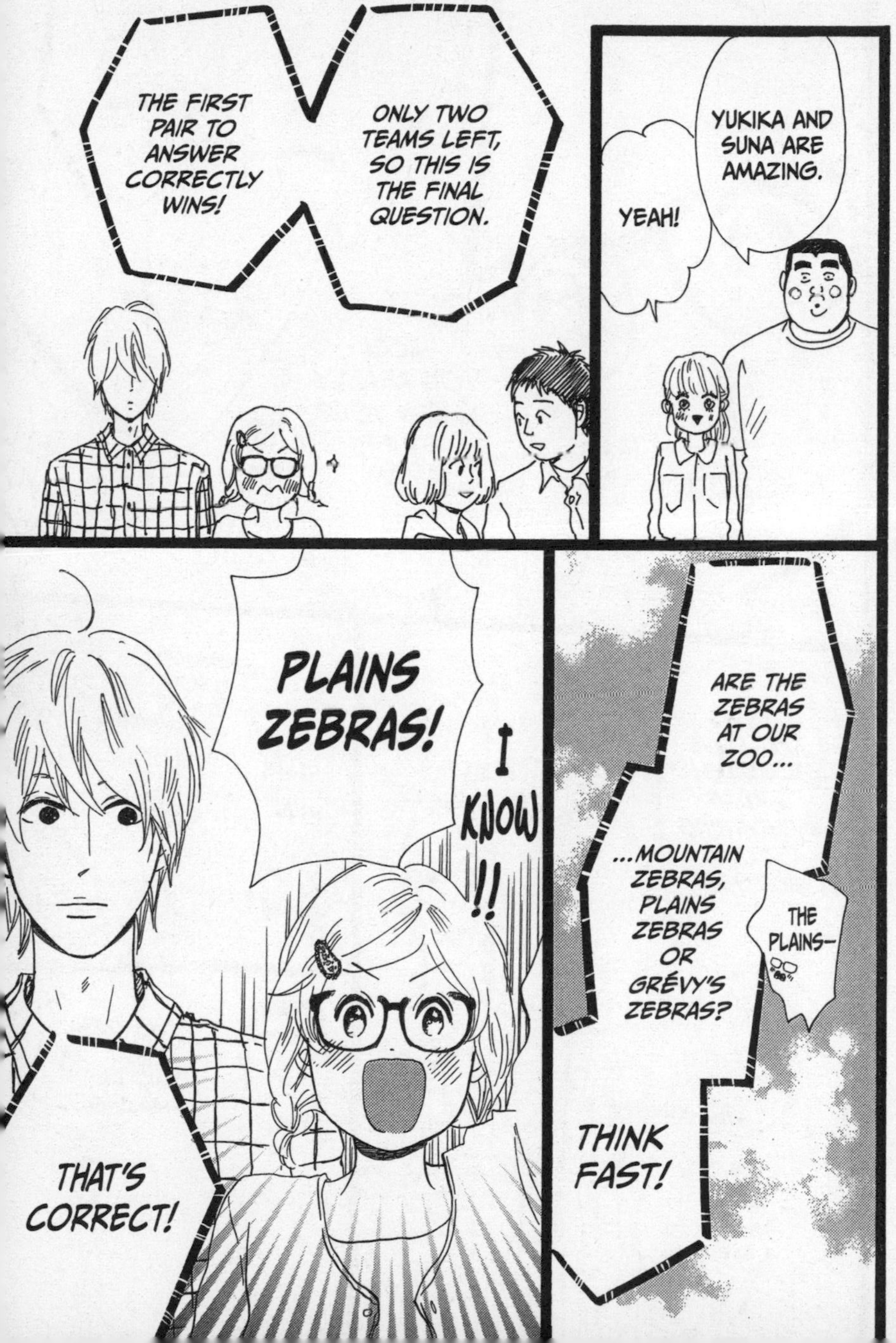
YUKIKA AND SUNA ARE AMAZING.
YEAH!
ONLY TWO TEAMS LEFT, SO THIS IS THE FINAL QUESTION.
THE FIRST PAIR TO ANSWER CORRECTLY WINS!
ARE THE ZEBRAS AT OUR ZOO...
...MOUNTAIN ZEBRAS, PLAINS ZEBRAS OR GRÉVY'S ZEBRAS?
THE PLAINS—
THINK FAST!
I KNOW!!
PLAINS ZEBRAS!
THAT'S CORRECT!

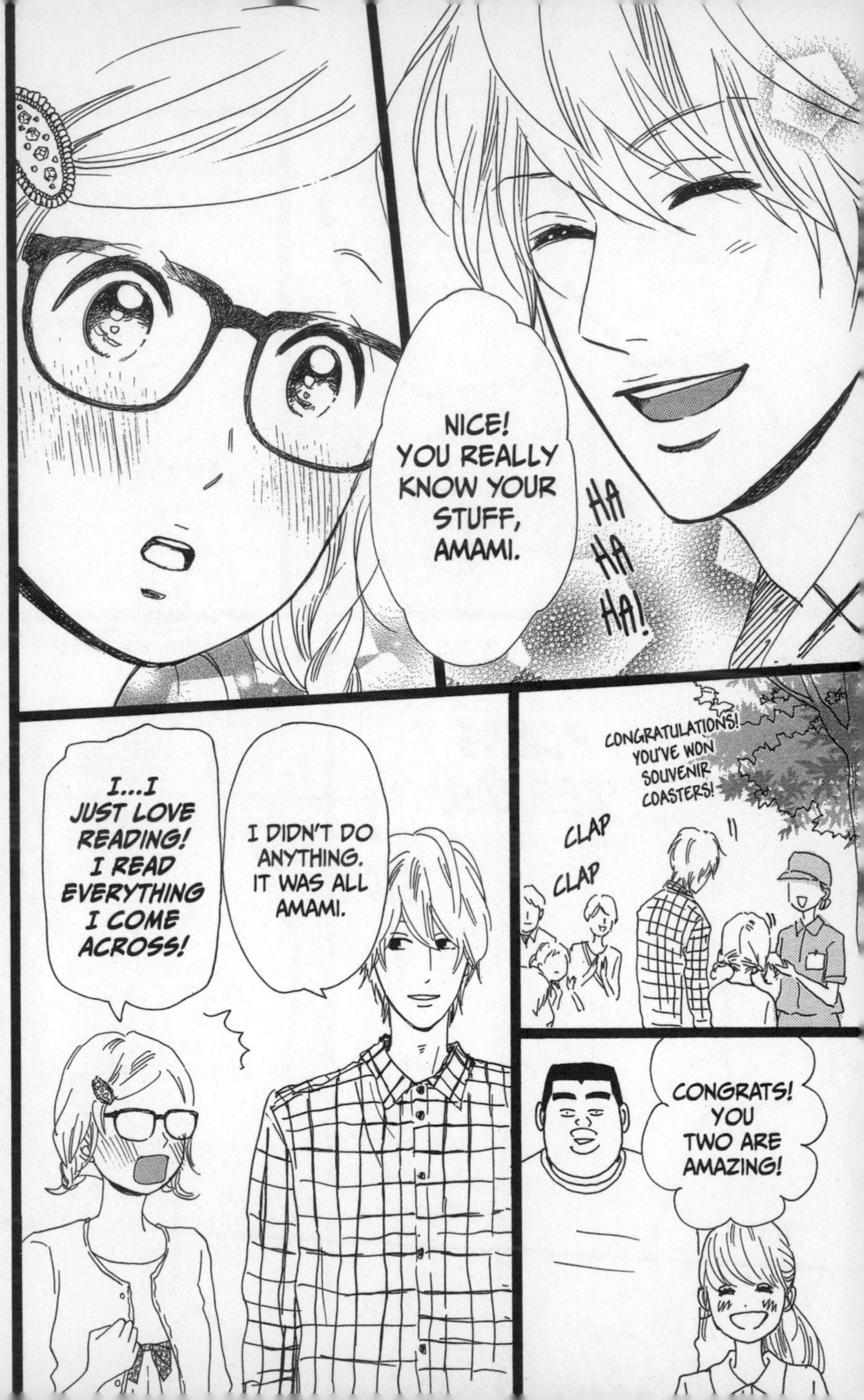
NICE! YOU REALLY KNOW YOUR STUFF, AMAMI.
HA HA HA!
CONGRATULATIONS! YOU'VE WON SOUVENIR COASTERS!
CLAP
CLAP
CONGRATS! YOU TWO ARE AMAZING!
I DIDN'T DO ANYTHING. IT WAS ALL AMAMI.
I...I JUST LOVE READING! I READ EVERYTHING I COME ACROSS!

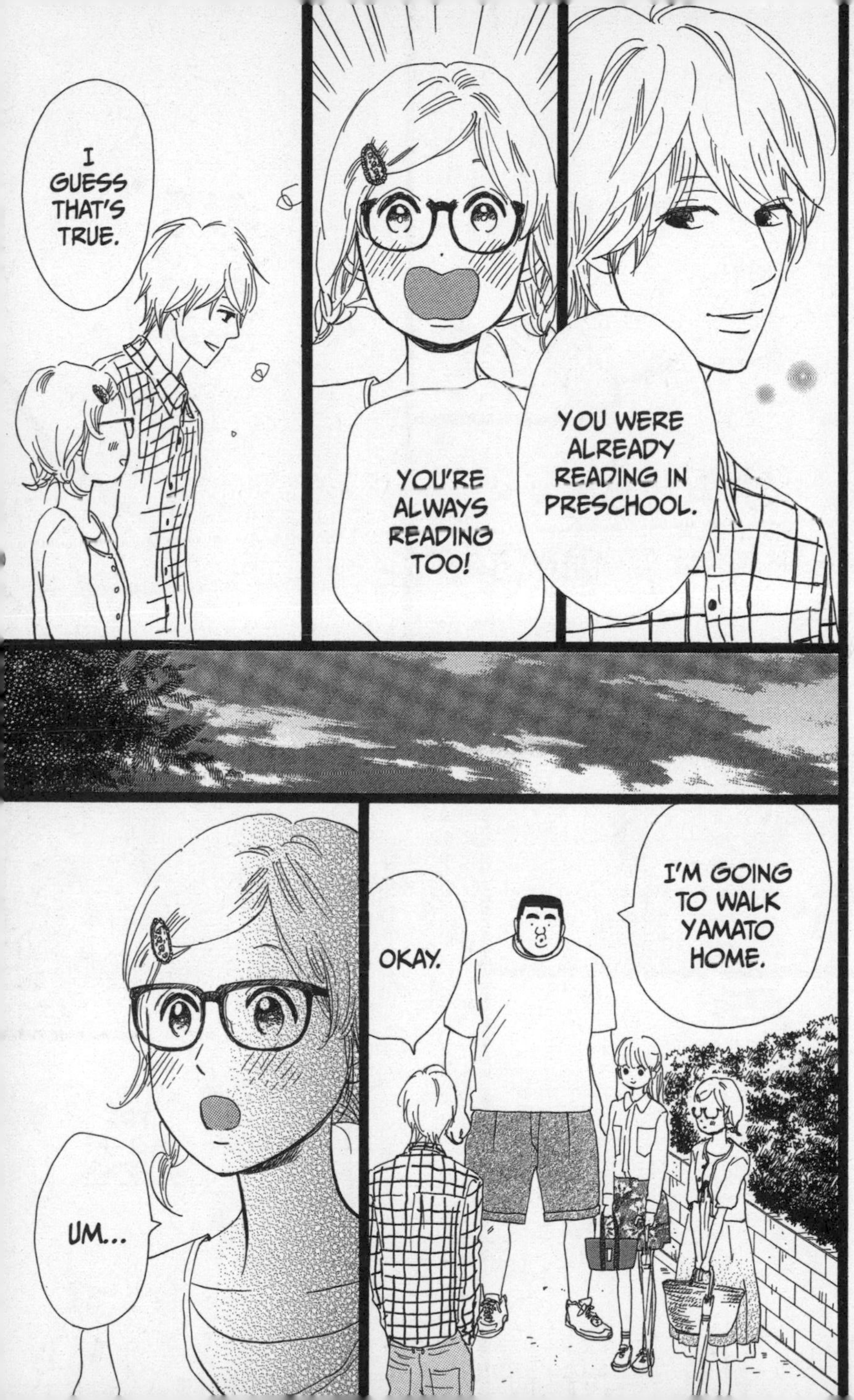
YOU WERE ALREADY READING IN PRESCHOOL.
YOU'RE ALWAYS READING TOO!
I GUESS THAT'S TRUE.
I'M GOING TO WALK YAMATO HOME.
OKAY.
UM...

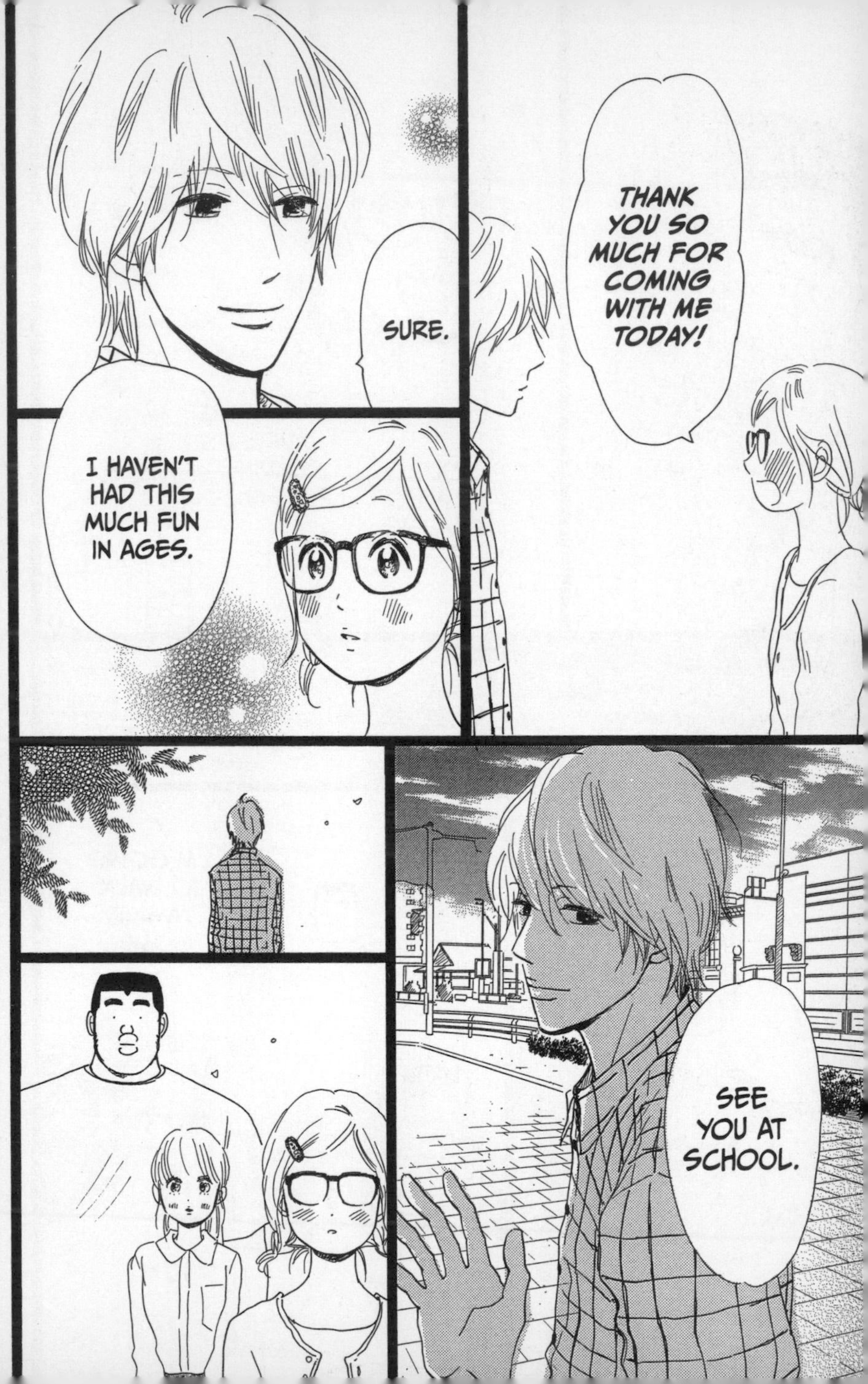
THANK YOU SO MUCH FOR COMING WITH ME TODAY!
SURE.
I HAVEN'T HAD THIS MUCH FUN IN AGES.
SEE YOU AT SCHOOL.

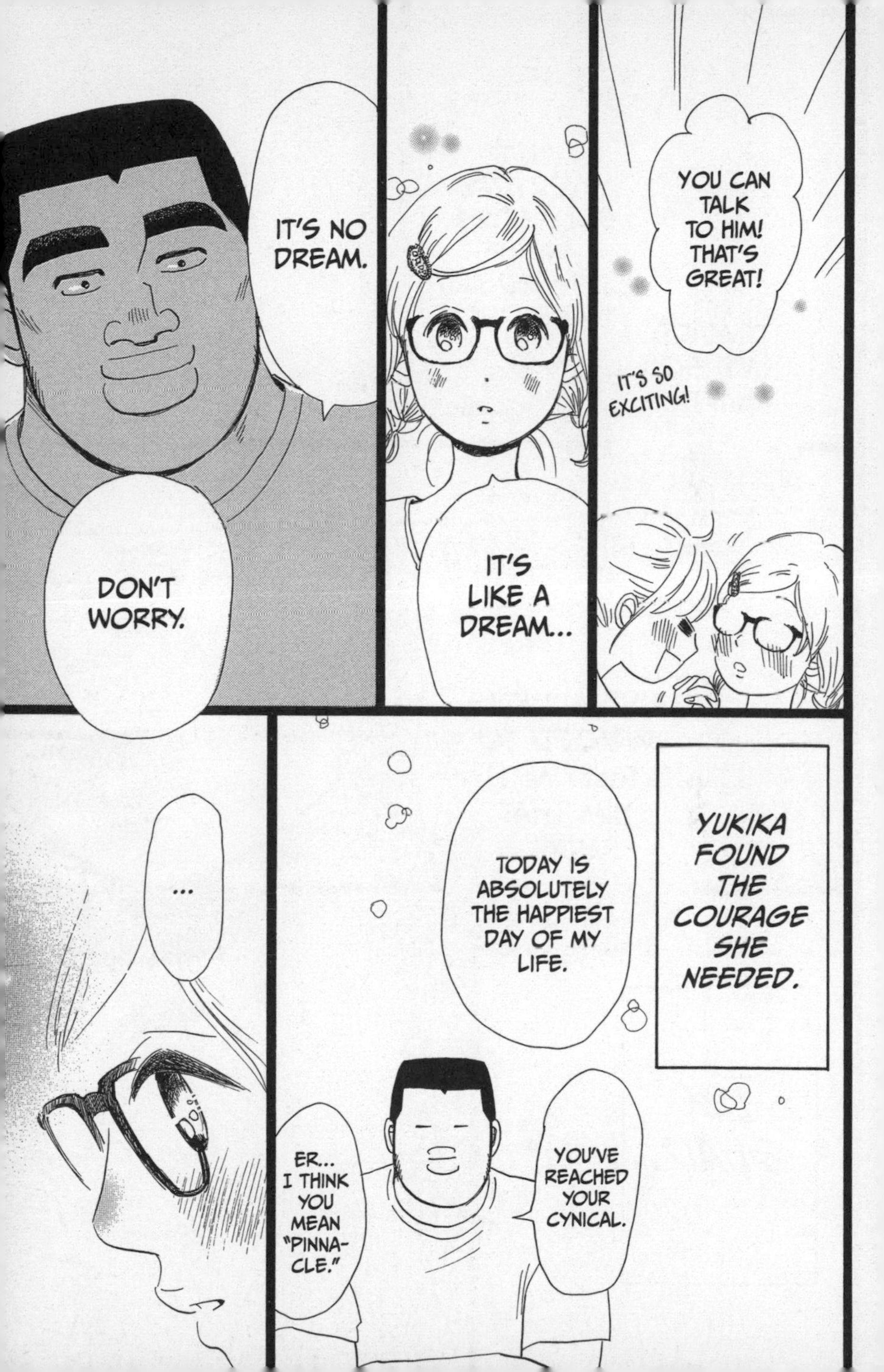
YOU CAN TALK TO HIM! THAT'S GREAT!
IT'S SO EXCITING!
IT'S LIKE A DREAM...
IT'S NO DREAM.
DON'T WORRY.
YUKIKA FOUND THE COURAGE SHE NEEDED.
TODAY IS ABSOLUTELY THE HAPPIEST DAY OF MY LIFE.
YOU'VE REACHED YOUR CYNICAL.
ER... I THINK YOU MEAN "PINNACLE."
...

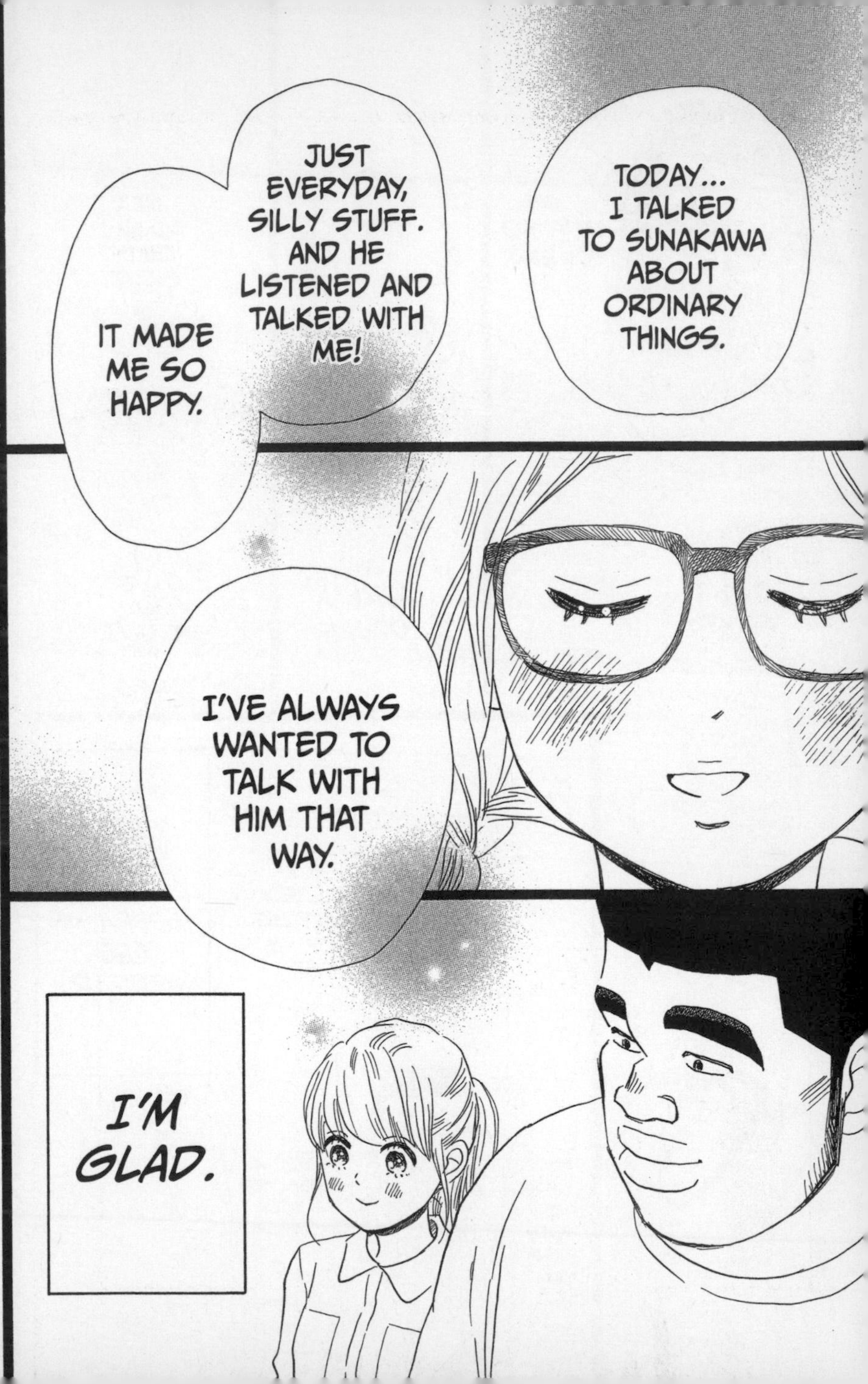
TODAY... I TALKED TO SUNAKAWA ABOUT ORDINARY THINGS.
JUST EVERYDAY, SILLY STUFF. AND HE LISTENED AND TALKED WITH ME!
IT MADE ME SO HAPPY.
I'VE ALWAYS WANTED TO TALK WITH HIM THAT WAY.
I'M GLAD.

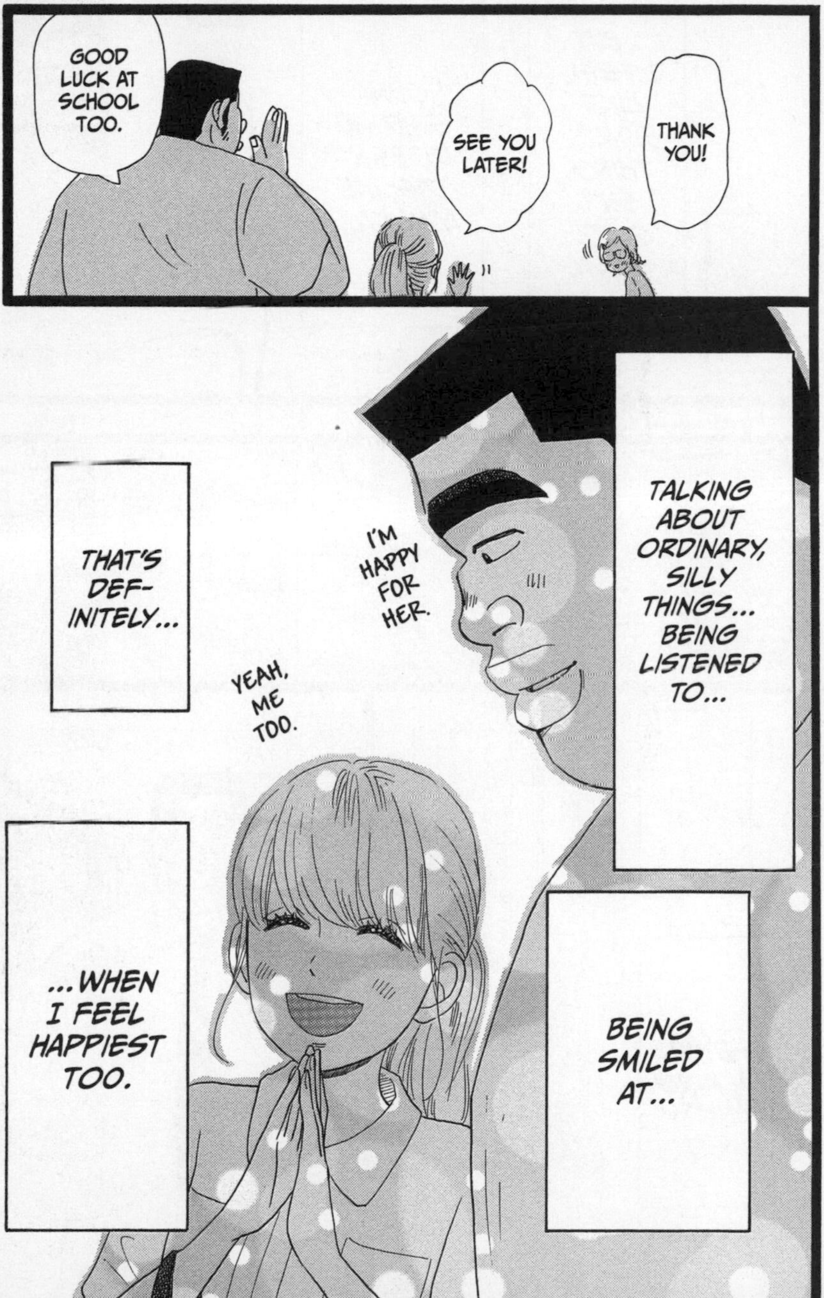
THANK YOU!
SEE YOU LATER!
GOOD LUCK AT SCHOOL TOO.
TALKING ABOUT ORDINARY, SILLY THINGS... BEING LISTENED TO...
I'M HAPPY FOR HER.
YEAH, ME TOO.
BEING SMILED AT...
THAT'S DEF-INITELY...
...WHEN I FEEL HAPPIEST TOO.

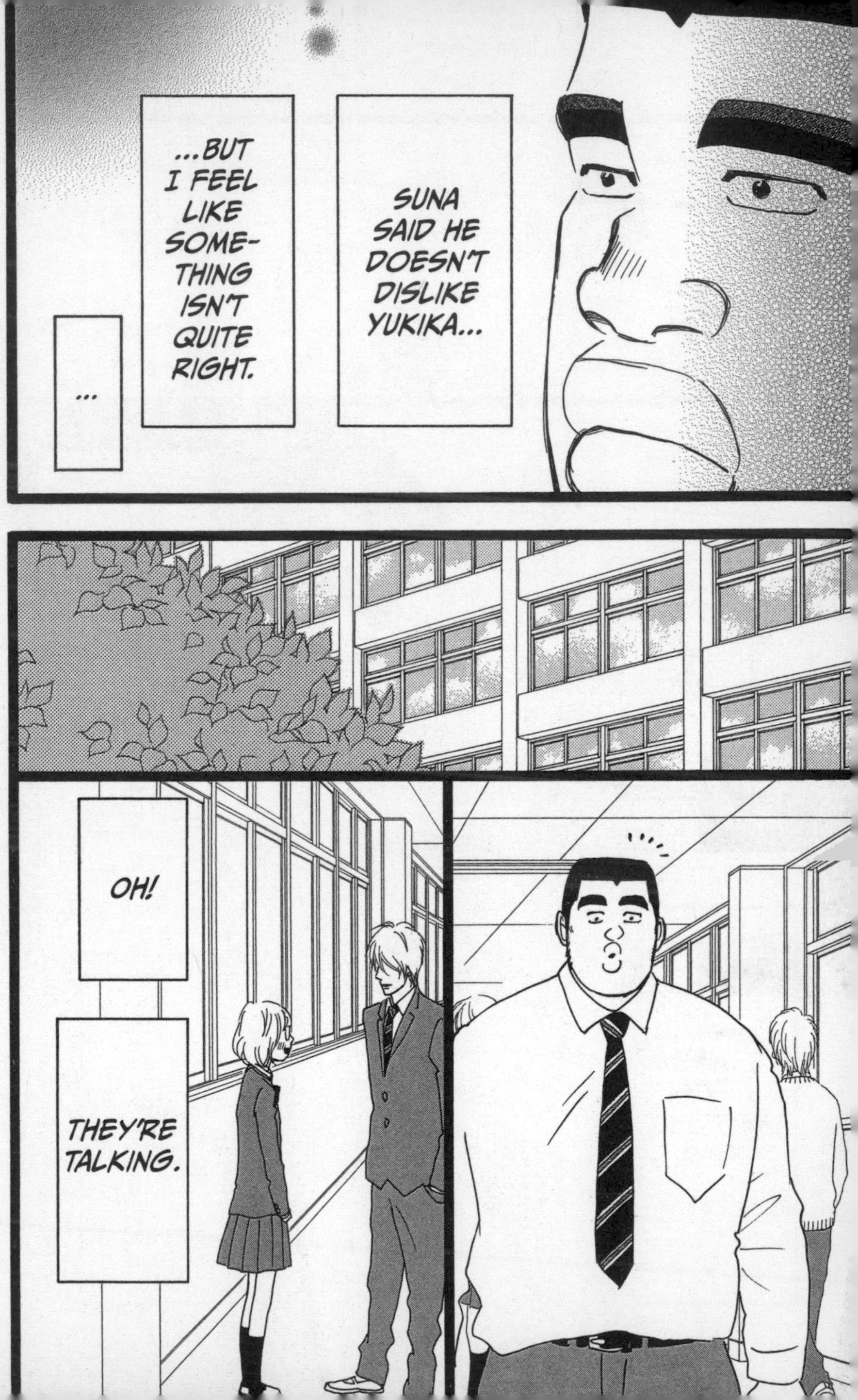
SUNA SAID HE DOESN'T DISLIKE YUKIKA...
...BUT I FEEL LIKE SOME-THING ISN'T QUITE RIGHT.
...
OH!
THEY'RE TALKING.

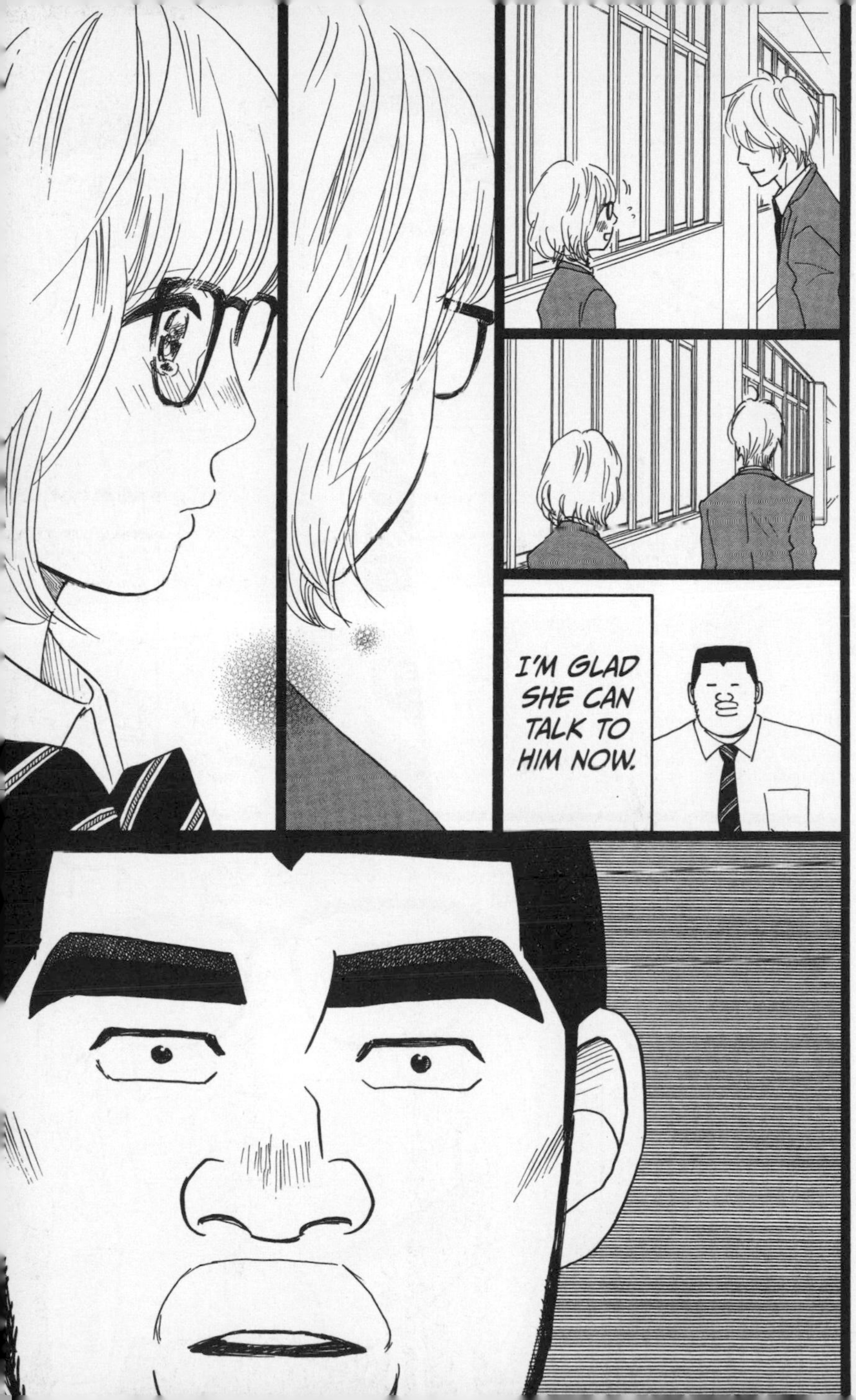
I'M GLAD SHE CAN TALK TO HIM NOW.

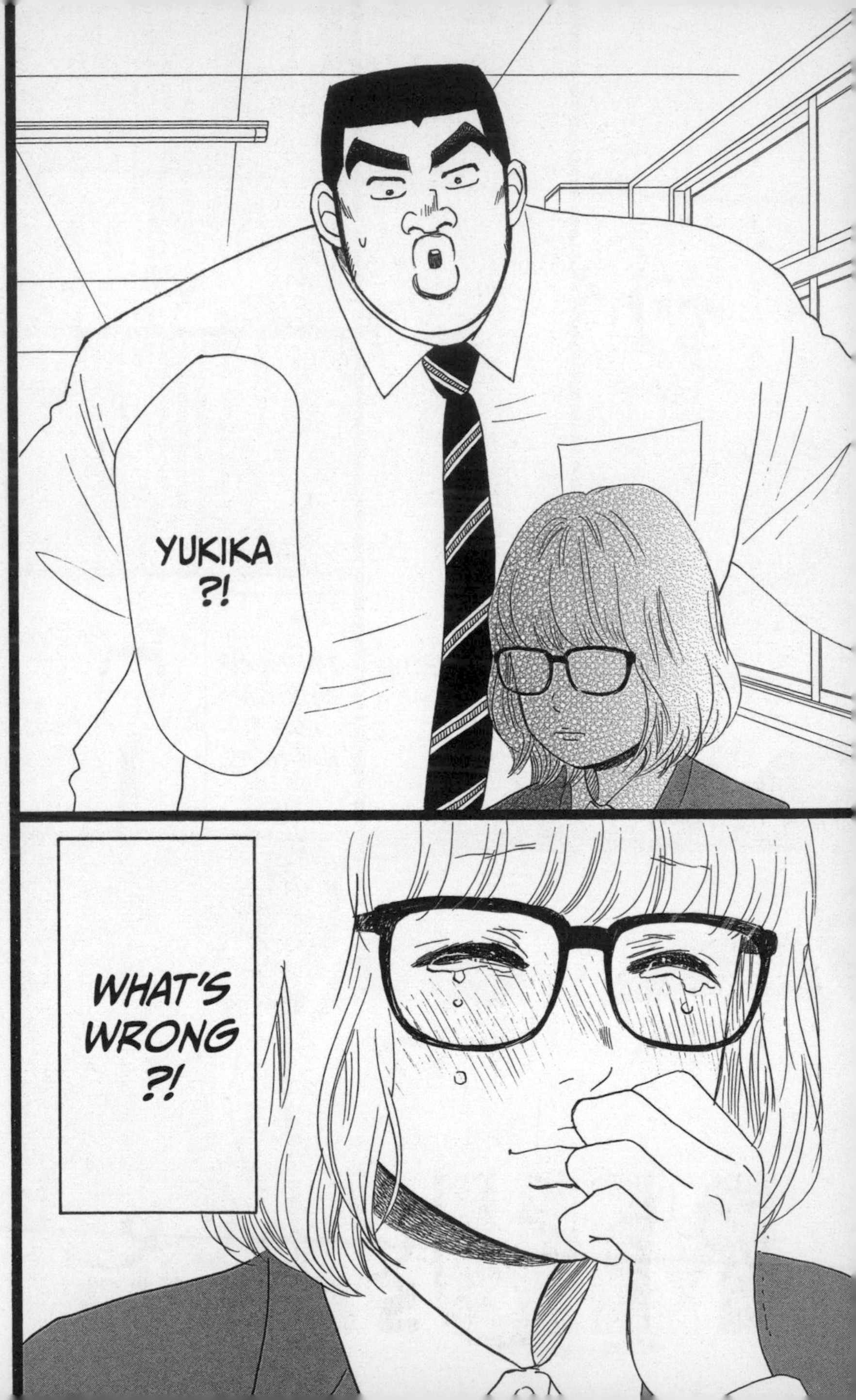
YUKIKA ?!
WHAT'S WRONG ?!

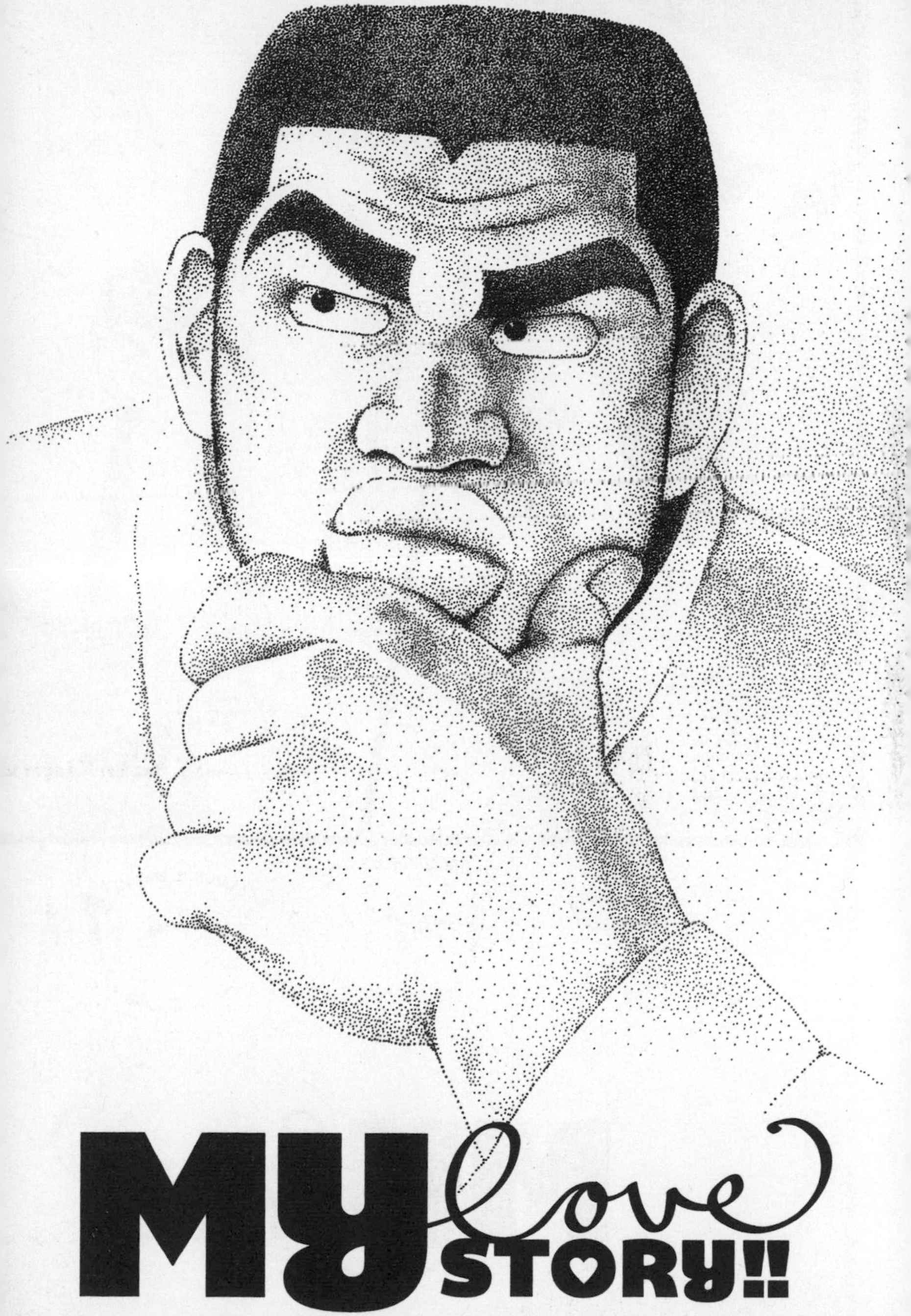
MY love STORY!!

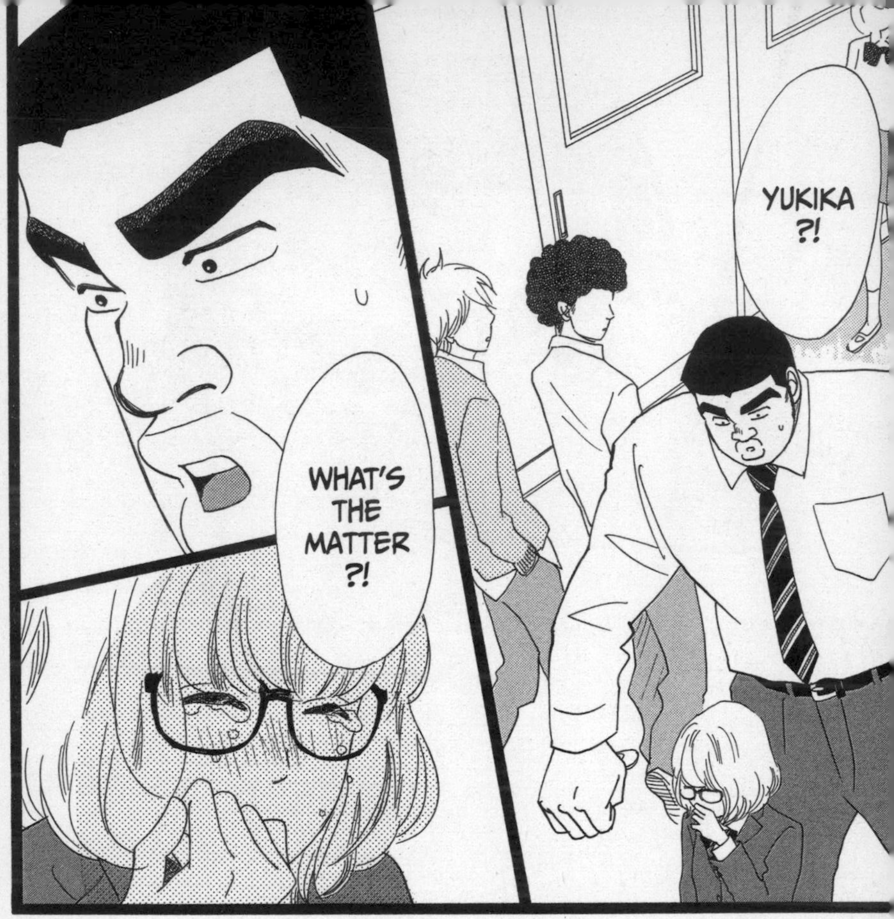
YUKIKA ?!
WHAT'S THE MATTER ?!

MY love STORY!!

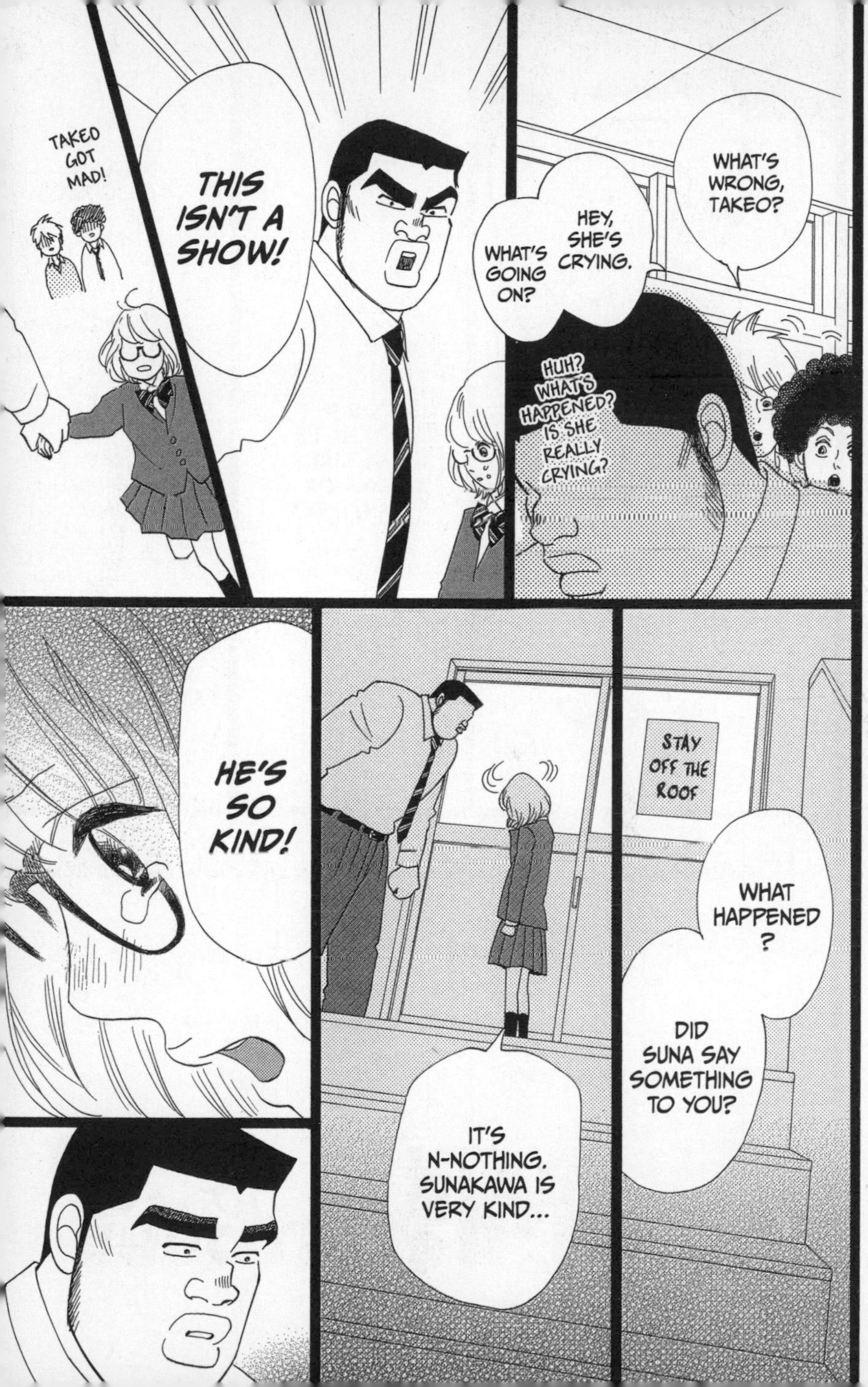
WHAT'S WRONG, TAKEO?
HEY, SHE'S CRYING.
WHAT'S GOING ON?
HUH? WHAT'S HAPPENED? IS SHE REALLY CRYING?
THIS ISN'T A SHOW!
TAKEO GOT MAD!
STAY OFF THE ROOF
WHAT HAPPENED?
DID SUNA SAY SOMETHING TO YOU?
IT'S N-NOTHING. SUNAKAWA IS VERY KIND...
HE'S SO KIND!

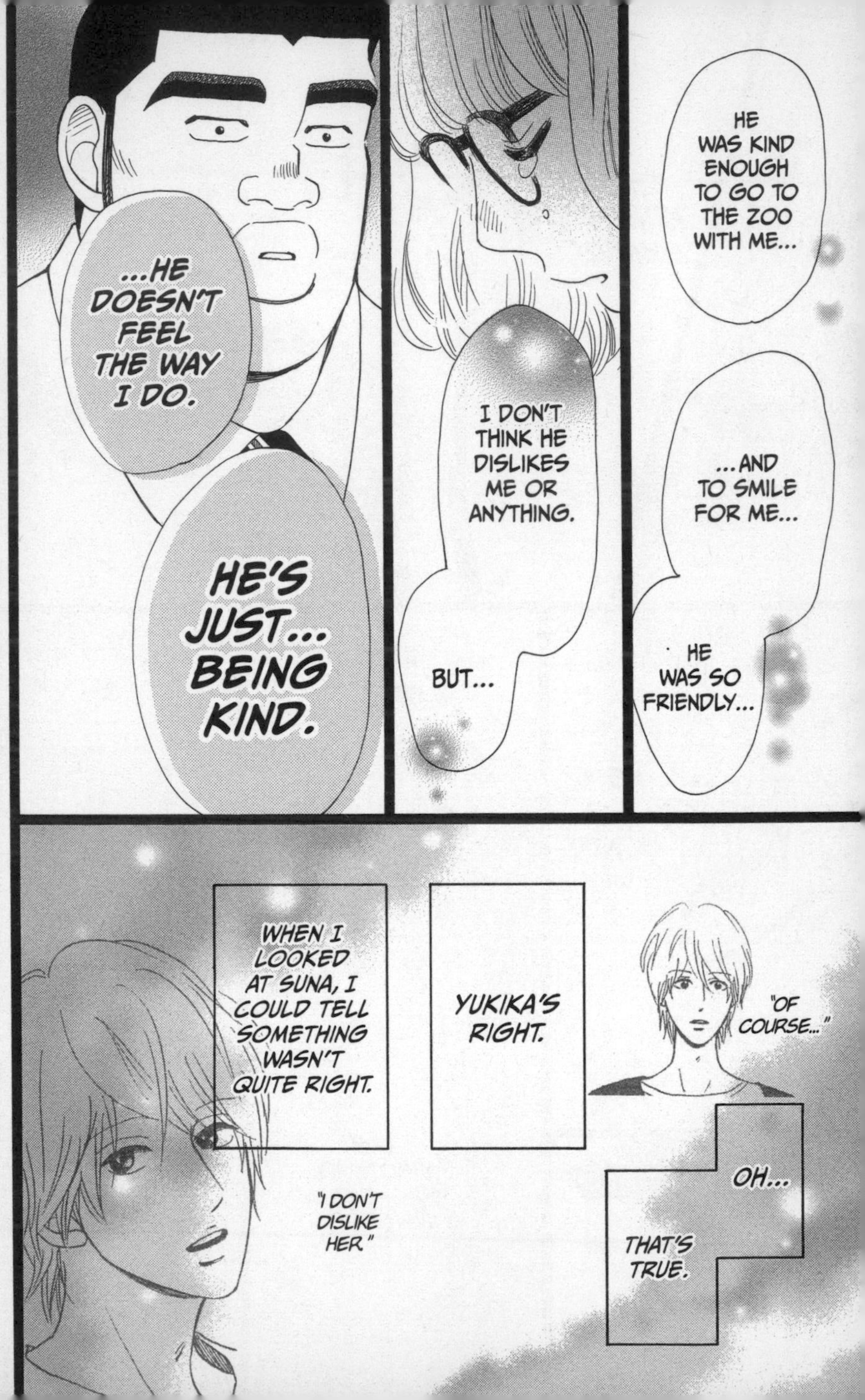
HE WAS KIND ENOUGH TO GO TO THE ZOO WITH ME...
...AND TO SMILE FOR ME...
HE WAS SO FRIENDLY...
I DON'T THINK HE DISLIKES ME OR ANYTHING.
BUT...
...HE DOESN'T FEEL THE WAY I DO.
HE'S JUST... BEING KIND.
"OF COURSE..."
OH...
THAT'S TRUE.
YUKIKA'S RIGHT.
WHEN I LOOKED AT SUNA, I COULD TELL SOMETHING WASN'T QUITE RIGHT.
"I DON'T DISLIKE HER."

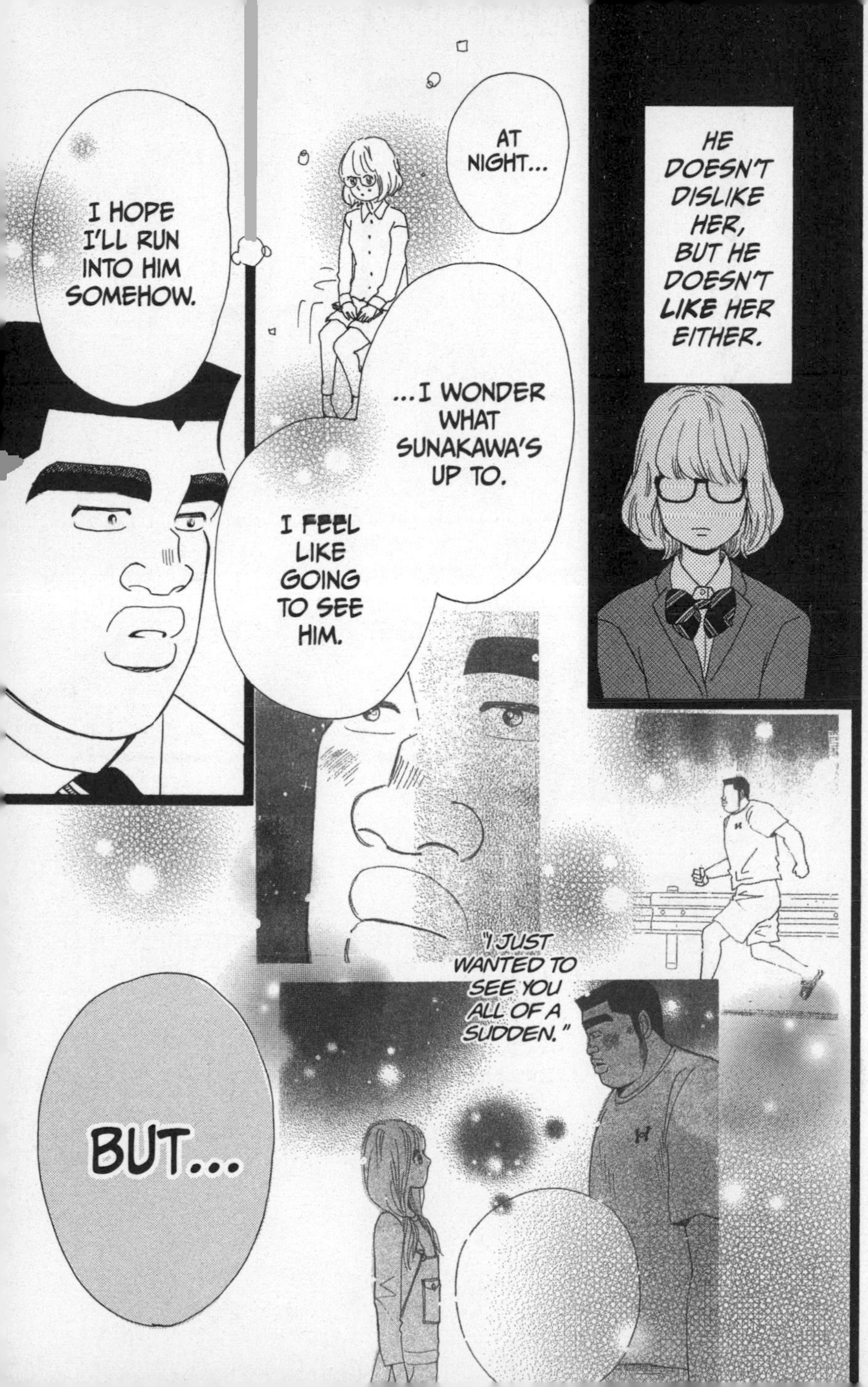
HE DOESN'T DISLIKE HER, BUT HE DOESN'T LIKE HER EITHER.
AT NIGHT...
...I WONDER WHAT SUNAKAWA'S UP TO.
I FEEL LIKE GOING TO SEE HIM.
I HOPE I'LL RUN INTO HIM SOMEHOW.
"I JUST WANTED TO SEE YOU ALL OF A SUDDEN."
BUT...

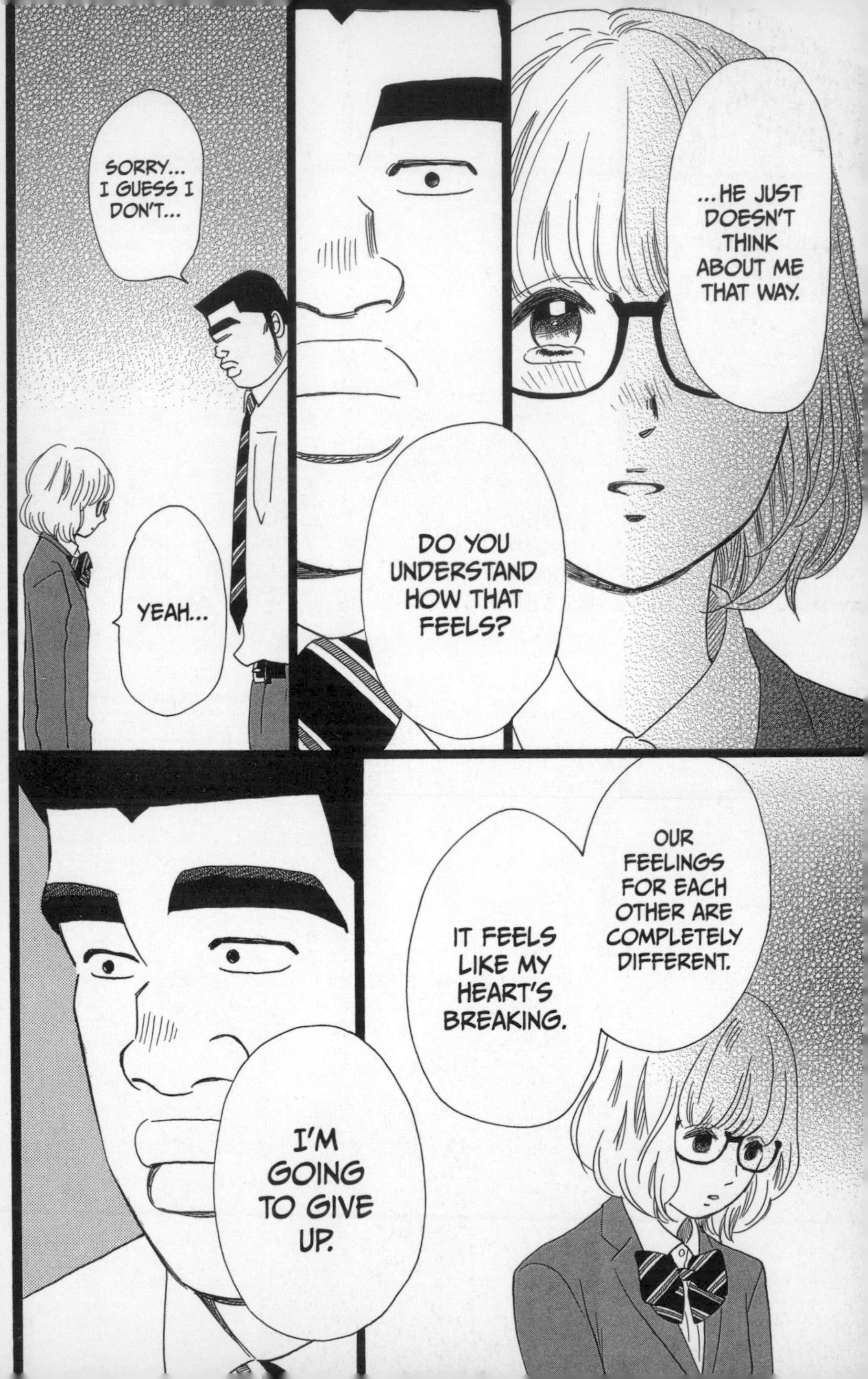
...HE JUST DOESN'T THINK ABOUT ME THAT WAY.
DO YOU UNDERSTAND HOW THAT FEELS?
SORRY... I GUESS I DON'T...
YEAH...
OUR FEELINGS FOR EACH OTHER ARE COMPLETELY DIFFERENT.
IT FEELS LIKE MY HEART'S BREAKING.
I'M GOING TO GIVE UP.

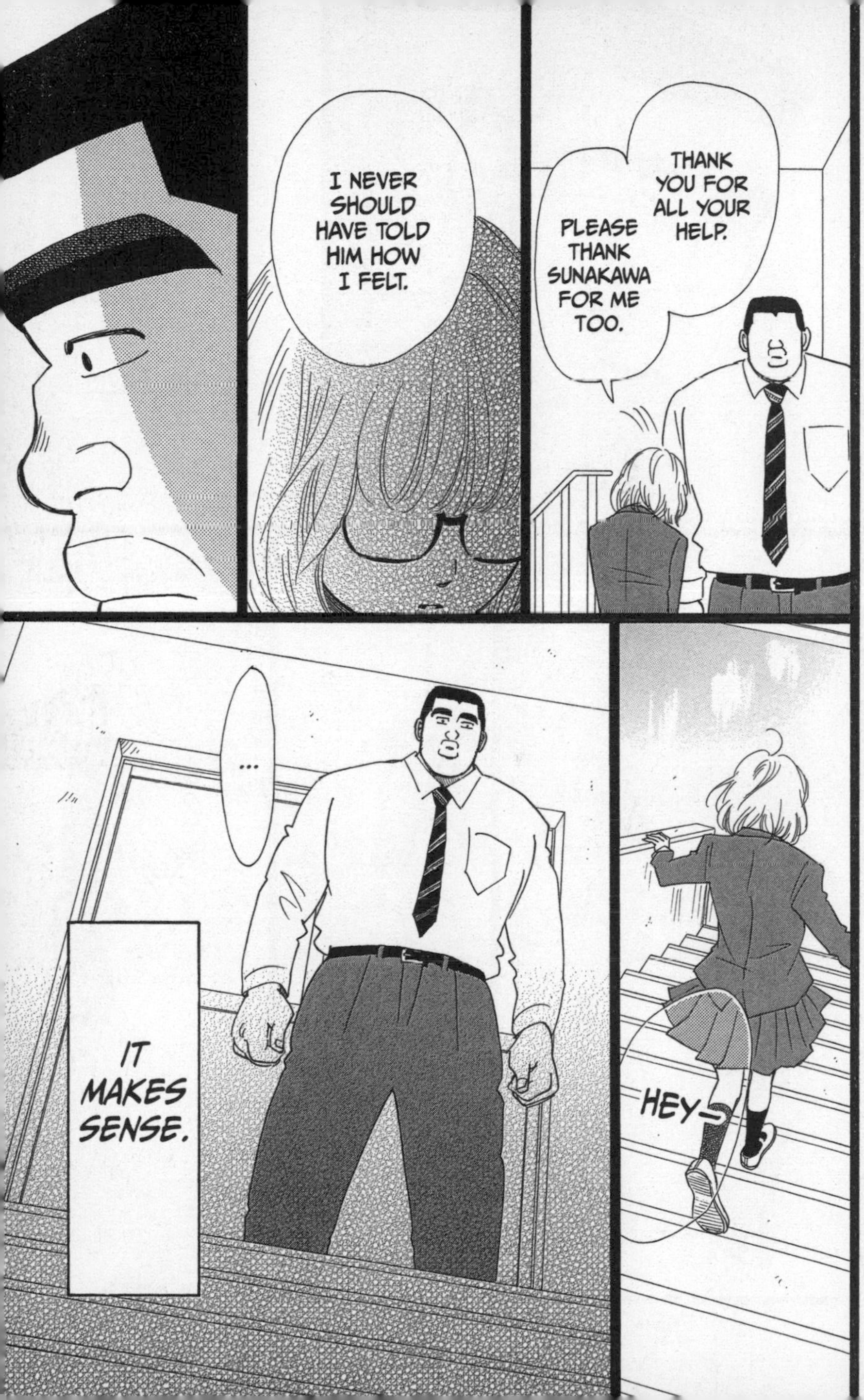
THANK YOU FOR ALL YOUR HELP.
PLEASE THANK SUNAKAWA FOR ME TOO.
I NEVER SHOULD HAVE TOLD HIM HOW I FELT.
HEY—
...
IT MAKES SENSE.

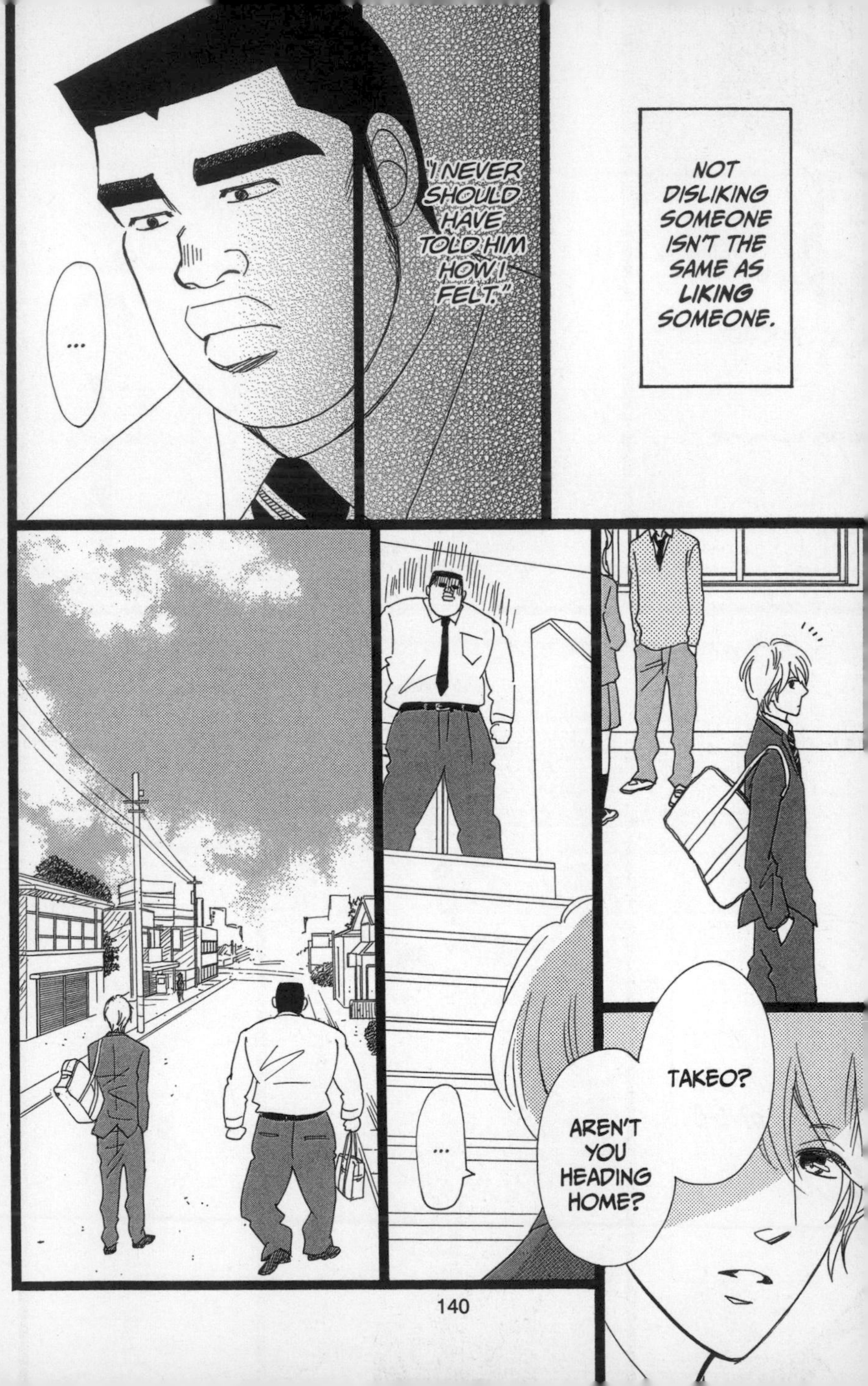
NOT DISLIKING SOMEONE ISN'T THE SAME AS LIKING SOMEONE.
"I NEVER SHOULD HAVE TOLD HIM HOW I FELT."
...
TAKEO?
AREN'T YOU HEADING HOME?
...

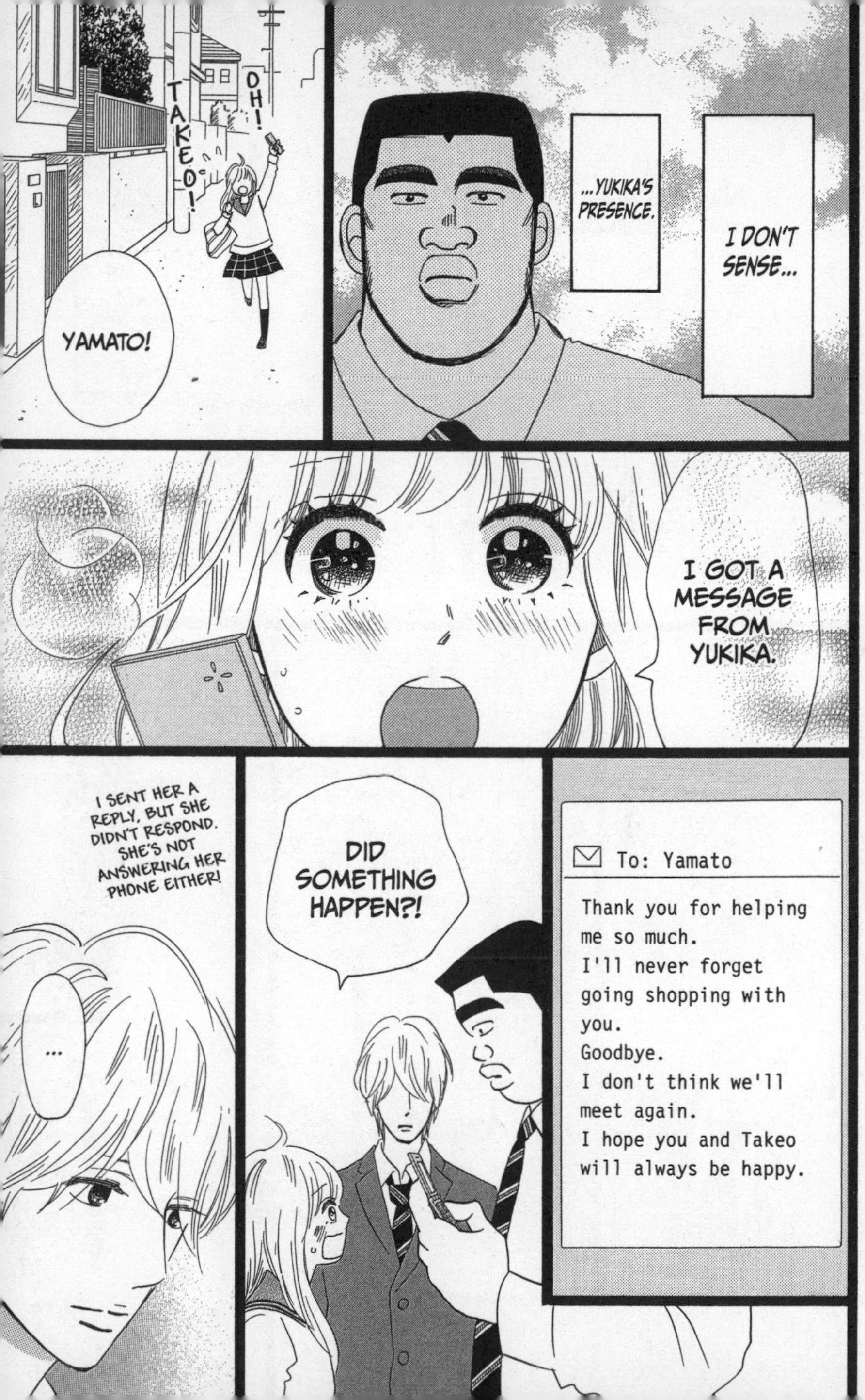
I DON'T SENSE...
...YUKIKA'S PRESENCE.
OH!
TAKEO!
YAMATO!
I GOT A MESSAGE FROM YUKIKA.
To: Yamato
Thank you for helping me so much.
I'll never forget going shopping with you.
Goodbye.
I don't think we'll meet again.
I hope you and Takeo will always be happy.
DID SOMETHING HAPPEN?!
I SENT HER A REPLY, BUT SHE DIDN'T RESPOND. SHE'S NOT ANSWERING HER PHONE EITHER!
...

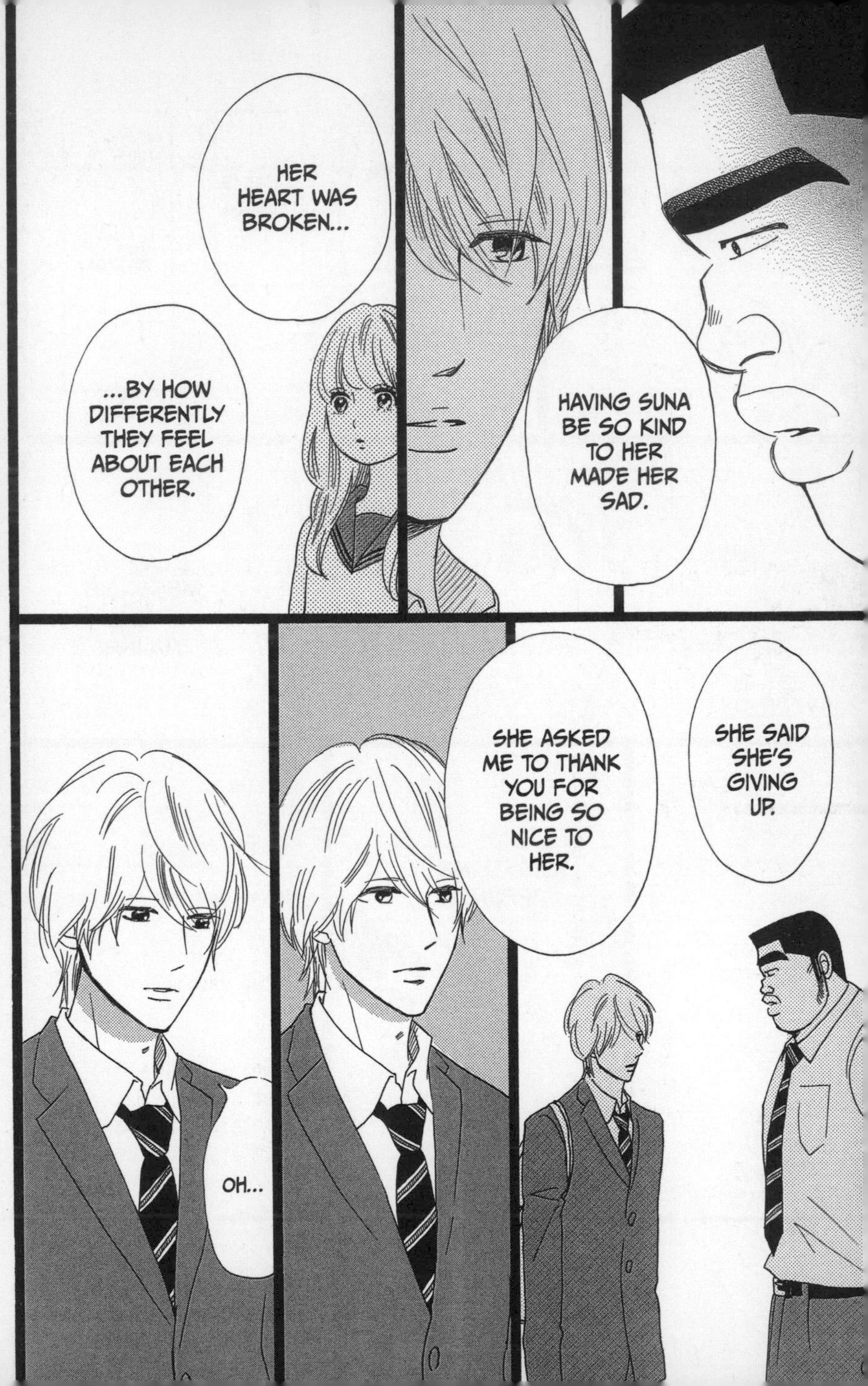
HAVING SUNA BE SO KIND TO HER MADE HER SAD.
HER HEART WAS BROKEN...
...BY HOW DIFFERENTLY THEY FEEL ABOUT EACH OTHER.
SHE SAID SHE'S GIVING UP.
SHE ASKED ME TO THANK YOU FOR BEING SO NICE TO HER.
OH...

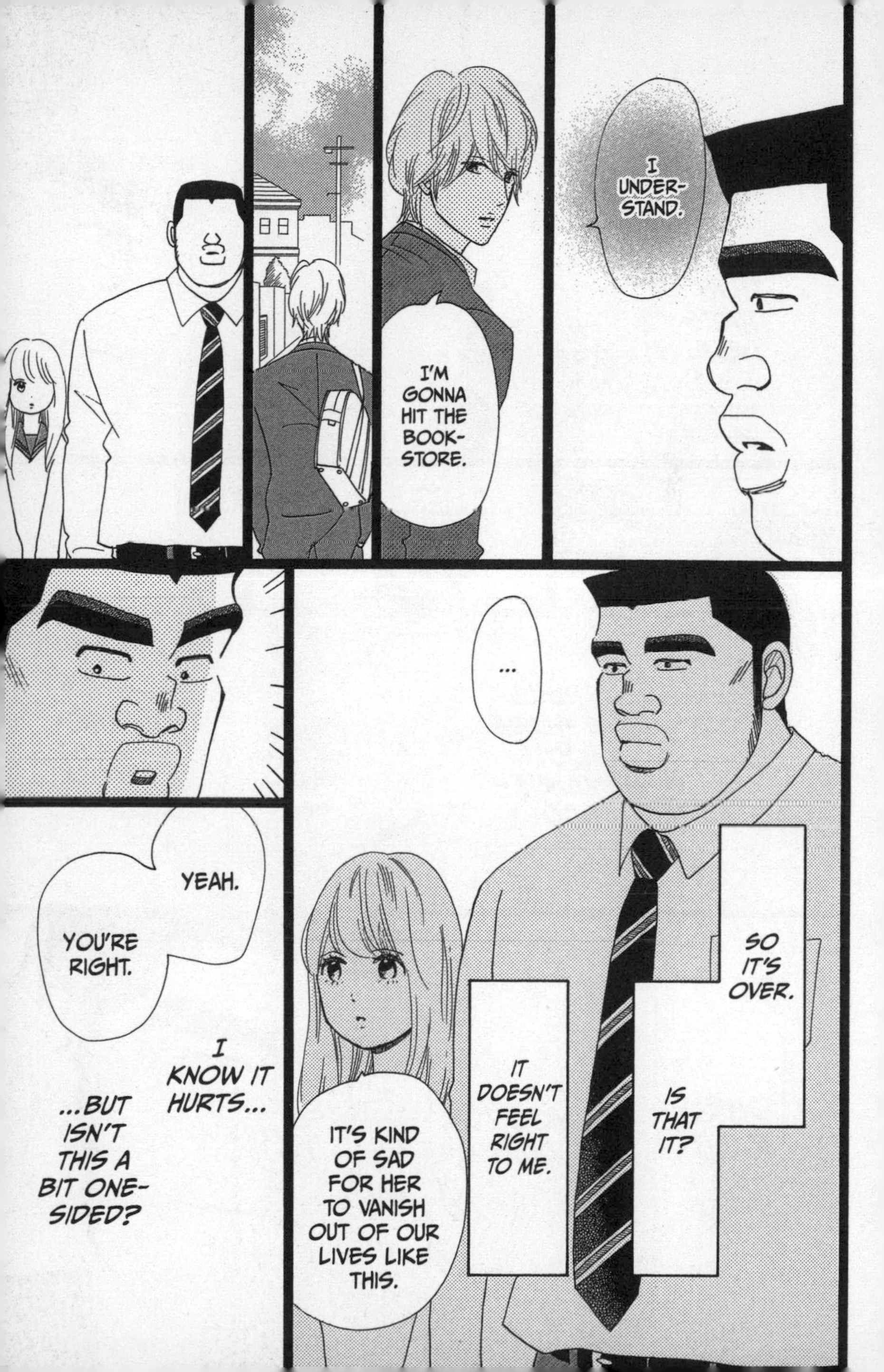
I UNDER-STAND.
I'M GONNA HIT THE BOOK-STORE.
...
SO IT'S OVER.
IS THAT IT?
IT DOESN'T FEEL RIGHT TO ME.
IT'S KIND OF SAD FOR HER TO VANISH OUT OF OUR LIVES LIKE THIS.
YEAH.
YOU'RE RIGHT.
I KNOW IT HURTS...
...BUT ISN'T THIS A BIT ONE-SIDED?

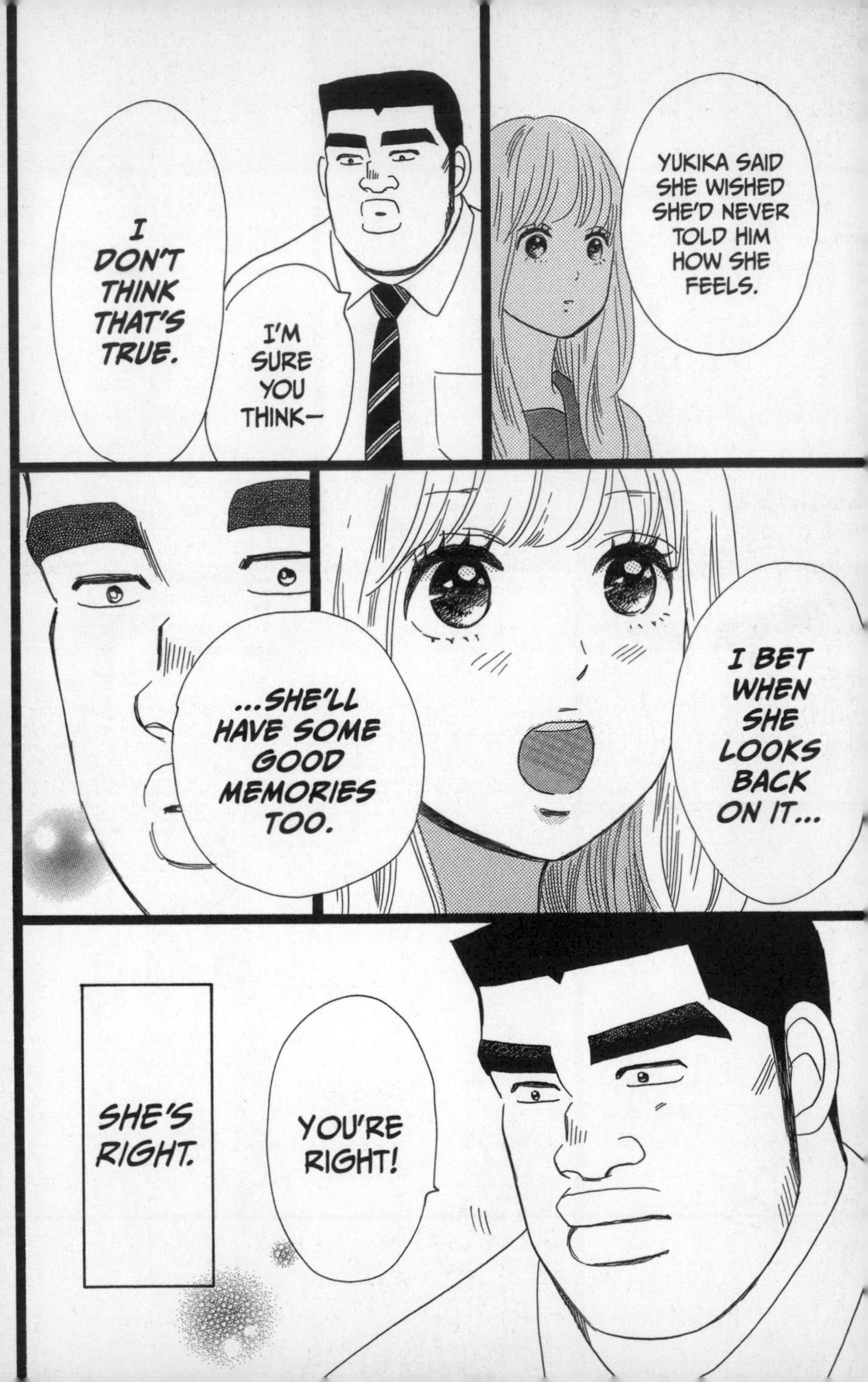
YUKIKA SAID SHE WISHED SHE'D NEVER TOLD HIM HOW SHE FEELS.
I'M SURE YOU THINK—
I DON'T THINK THAT'S TRUE.
I BET WHEN SHE LOOKS BACK ON IT...
...SHE'LL HAVE SOME GOOD MEMORIES TOO.
YOU'RE RIGHT!
SHE'S RIGHT.

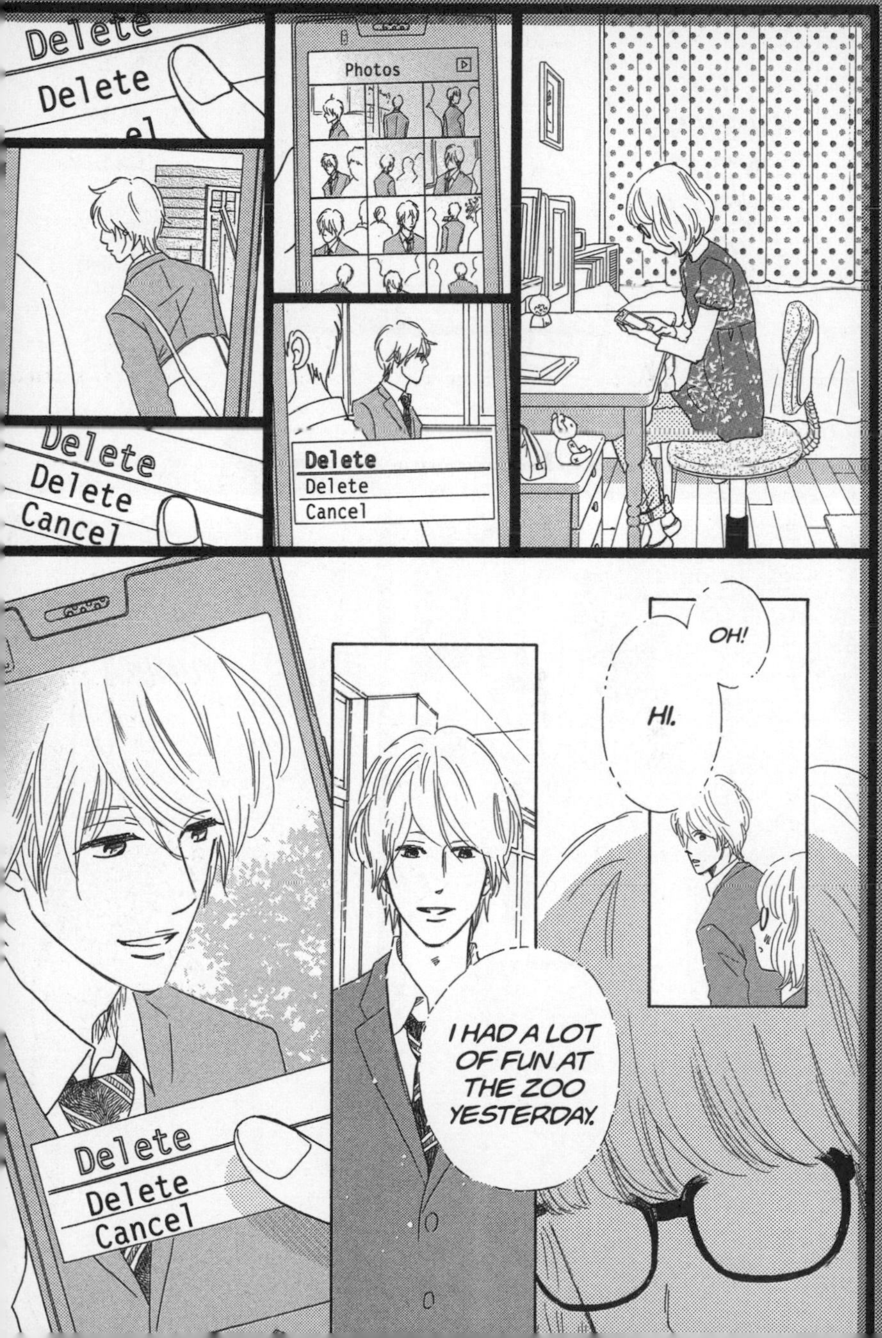
Photos
Delete
Delete
Cancel
Delete
Delete
Delete
Delete
Cancel
OH!
HI.
I HAD A LOT OF FUN AT THE ZOO YESTERDAY.
Delete
Delete
Cancel

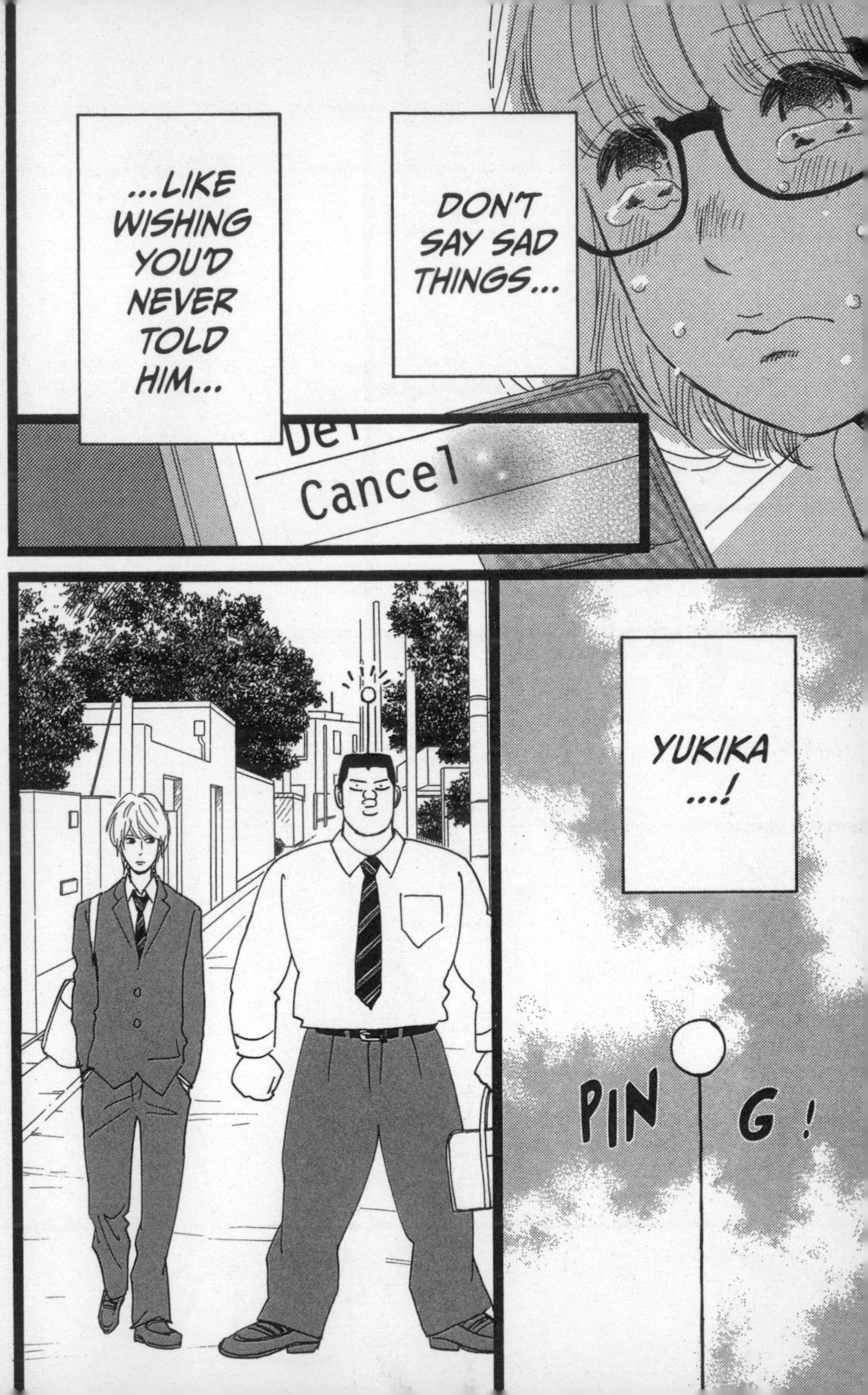
DON'T SAY SAD THINGS...
...LIKE WISHING YOU'D NEVER TOLD HIM...
Cancel
YUKIKA ...!
PING!

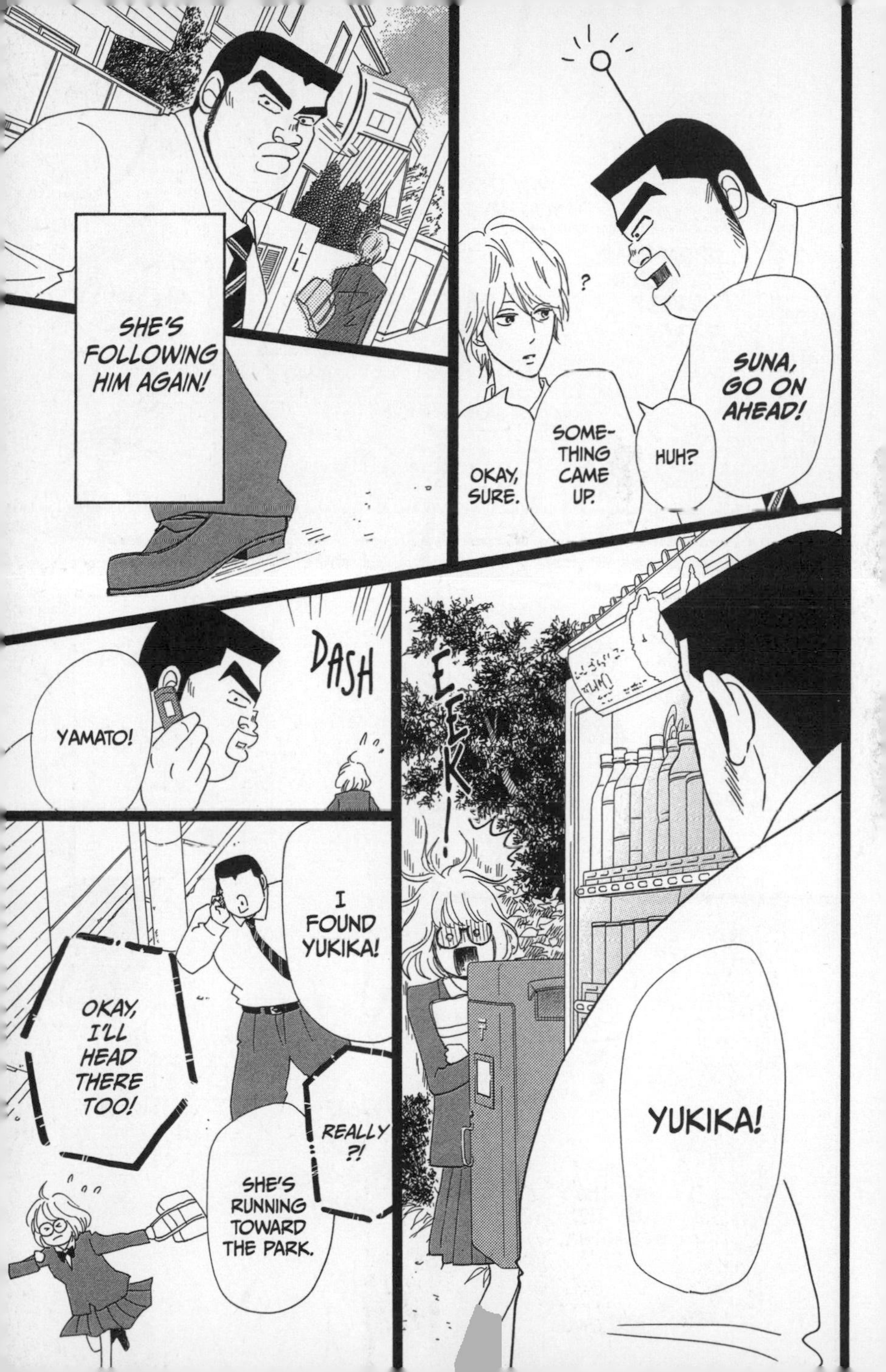
SUNA, GO ON AHEAD!
HUH?
SOME-THING CAME UP.
OKAY, SURE.
SHE'S FOLLOWING HIM AGAIN!
YUKIKA!
EEK!
DASH
YAMATO!
I FOUND YUKIKA!
REALLY?!
SHE'S RUNNING TOWARD THE PARK.
OKAY, I'LL HEAD THERE TOO!

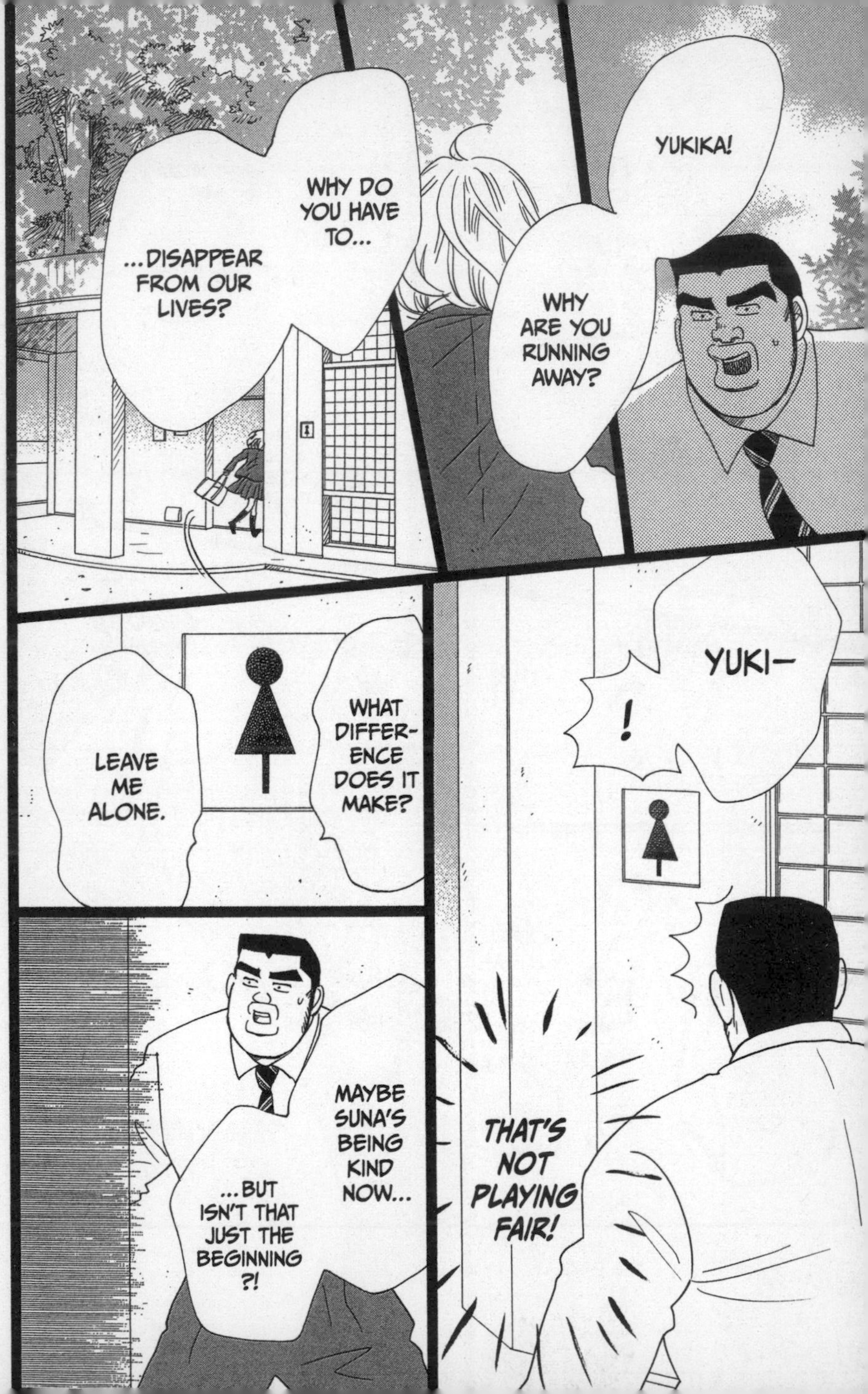
YUKIKA!
WHY ARE YOU RUNNING AWAY?
WHY DO YOU HAVE TO...
...DISAPPEAR FROM OUR LIVES?
YUKI—
!
THAT'S NOT PLAYING FAIR!
WHAT DIFFERENCE DOES IT MAKE?
LEAVE ME ALONE.
MAYBE SUNA'S BEING KIND NOW...
...BUT ISN'T THAT JUST THE BEGINNING?!

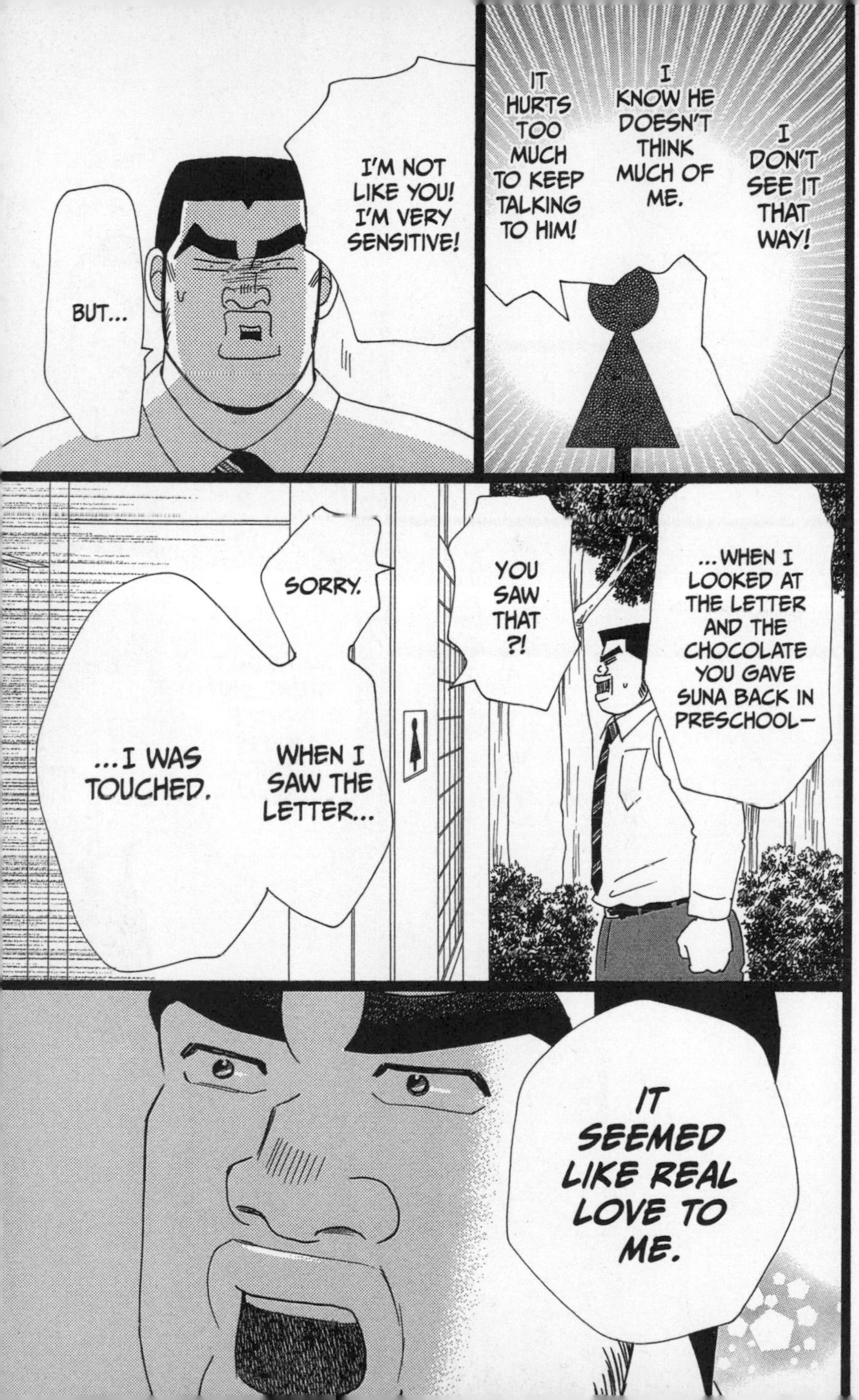
I DON'T SEE IT THAT WAY!
I KNOW HE DOESN'T THINK MUCH OF ME.
IT HURTS TOO MUCH TO KEEP TALKING TO HIM!
I'M NOT LIKE YOU! I'M VERY SENSITIVE!
BUT...
...WHEN I LOOKED AT THE LETTER AND THE CHOCOLATE YOU GAVE SUNA BACK IN PRESCHOOL—
YOU SAW THAT?!
SORRY.
WHEN I SAW THE LETTER...
...I WAS TOUCHED.
IT SEEMED LIKE REAL LOVE TO ME.

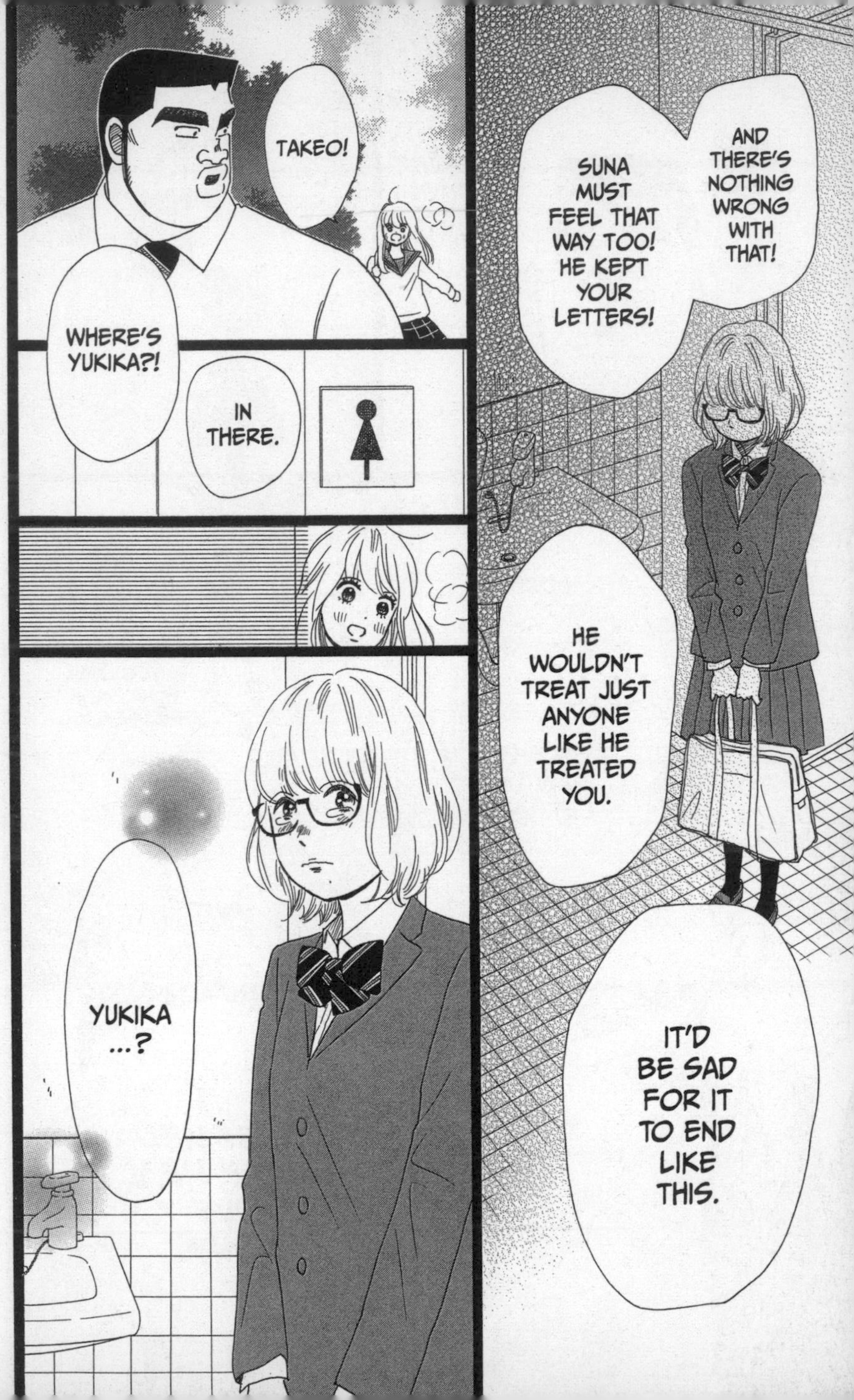
AND THERE'S NOTHING WRONG WITH THAT!
SUNA MUST FEEL THAT WAY TOO! HE KEPT YOUR LETTERS!
HE WOULDN'T TREAT JUST ANYONE LIKE HE TREATED YOU.
IT'D BE SAD FOR IT TO END LIKE THIS.
TAKEO!
WHERE'S YUKIKA?!
IN THERE.
YUKIKA ...?

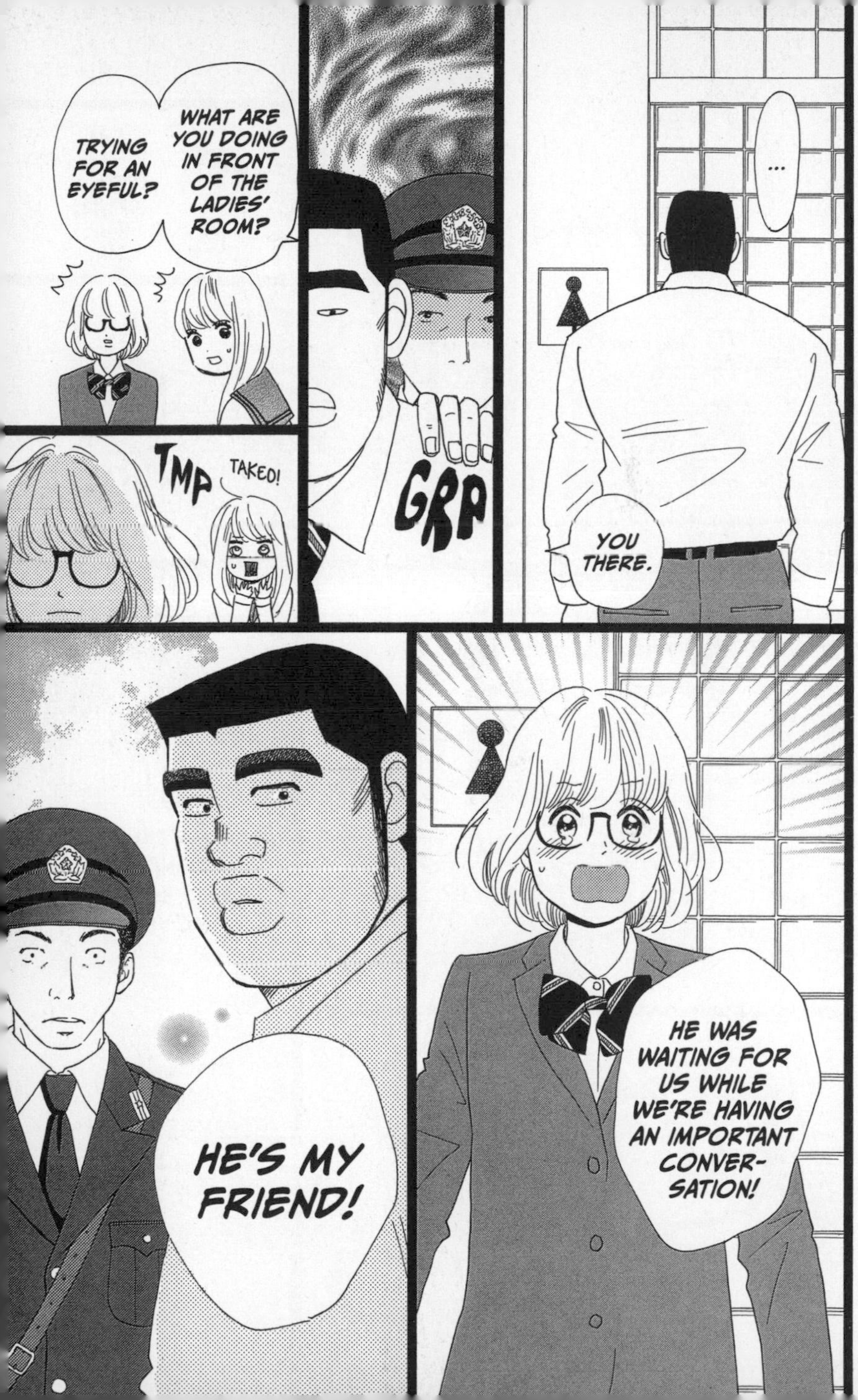
...
YOU THERE.
GRP
WHAT ARE YOU DOING IN FRONT OF THE LADIES' ROOM?
TRYING FOR AN EYEFUL?
TAKEO!
TMP
HE WAS WAITING FOR US WHILE WE'RE HAVING AN IMPORTANT CONVER-SATION!
HE'S MY FRIEND!

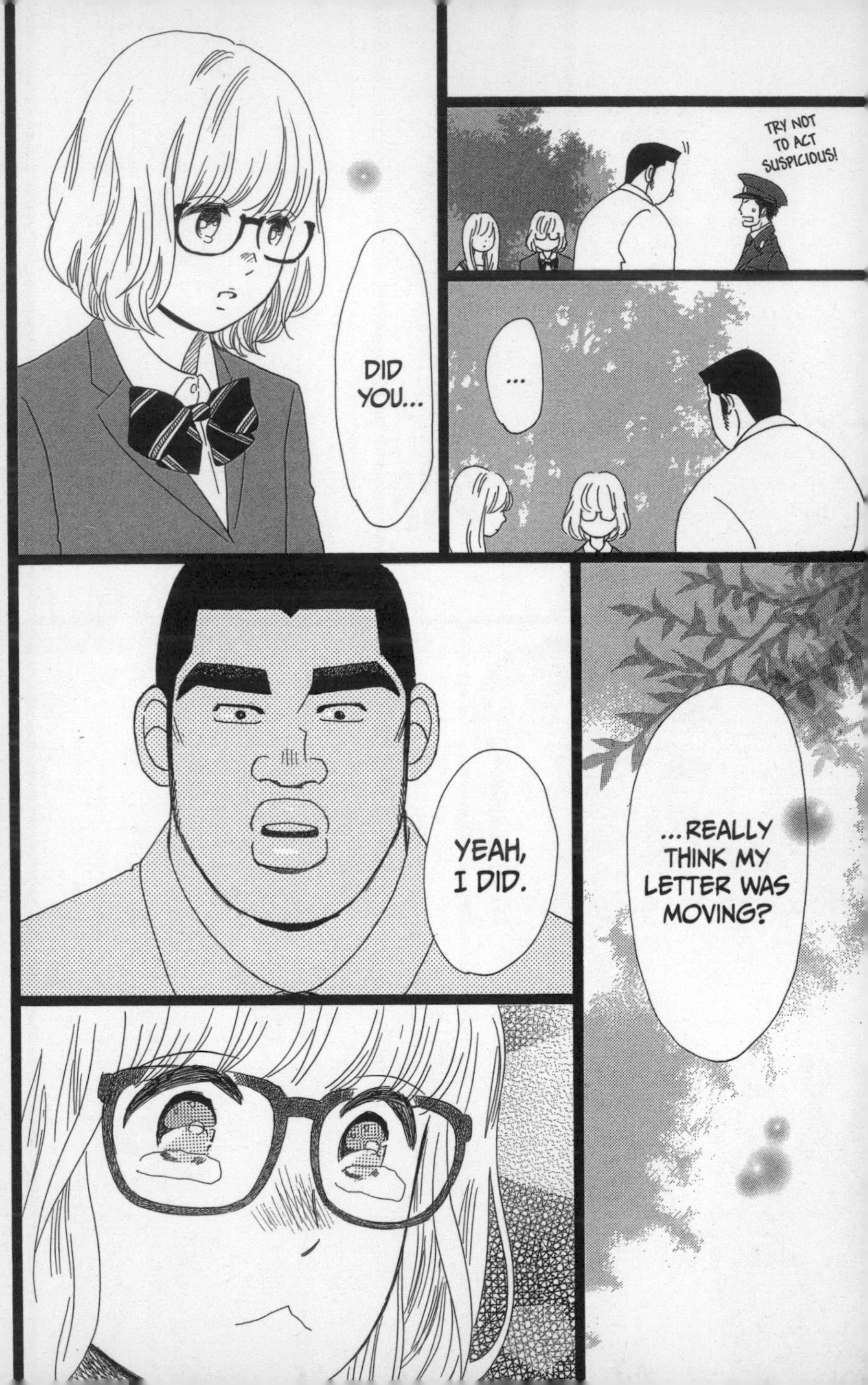
TRY NOT TO ACT SUSPICIOUS!
...
DID YOU...
...REALLY THINK MY LETTER WAS MOVING?
YEAH, I DID.

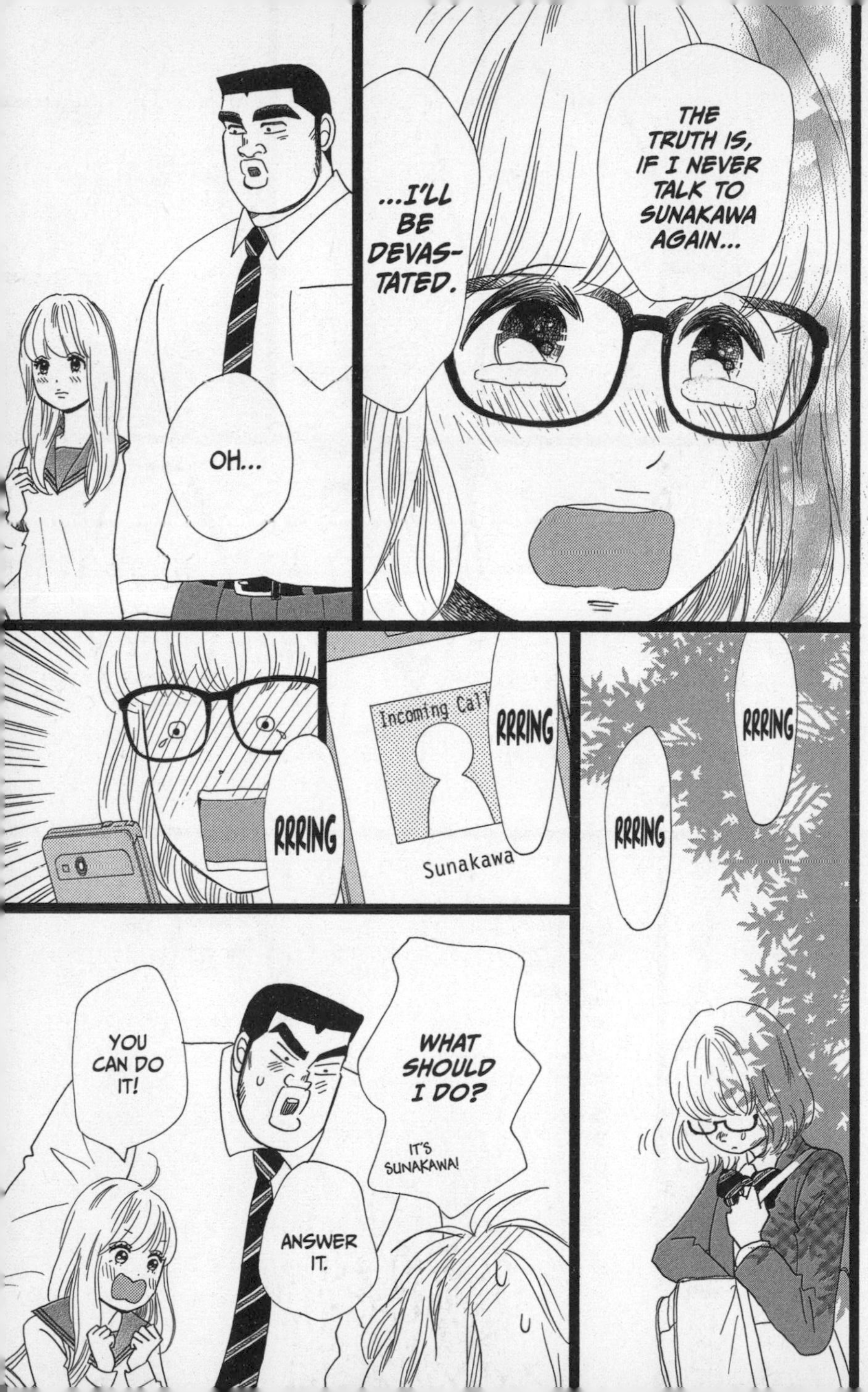
THE TRUTH IS, IF I NEVER TALK TO SUNAKAWA AGAIN...
...I'LL BE DEVAS-TATED.
OH...
RRRING
RRRING
Incoming Cal
RRRING
Sunakawa
RRRING
WHAT SHOULD I DO?
IT'S SUNAKAWA!
YOU CAN DO IT!
ANSWER IT.

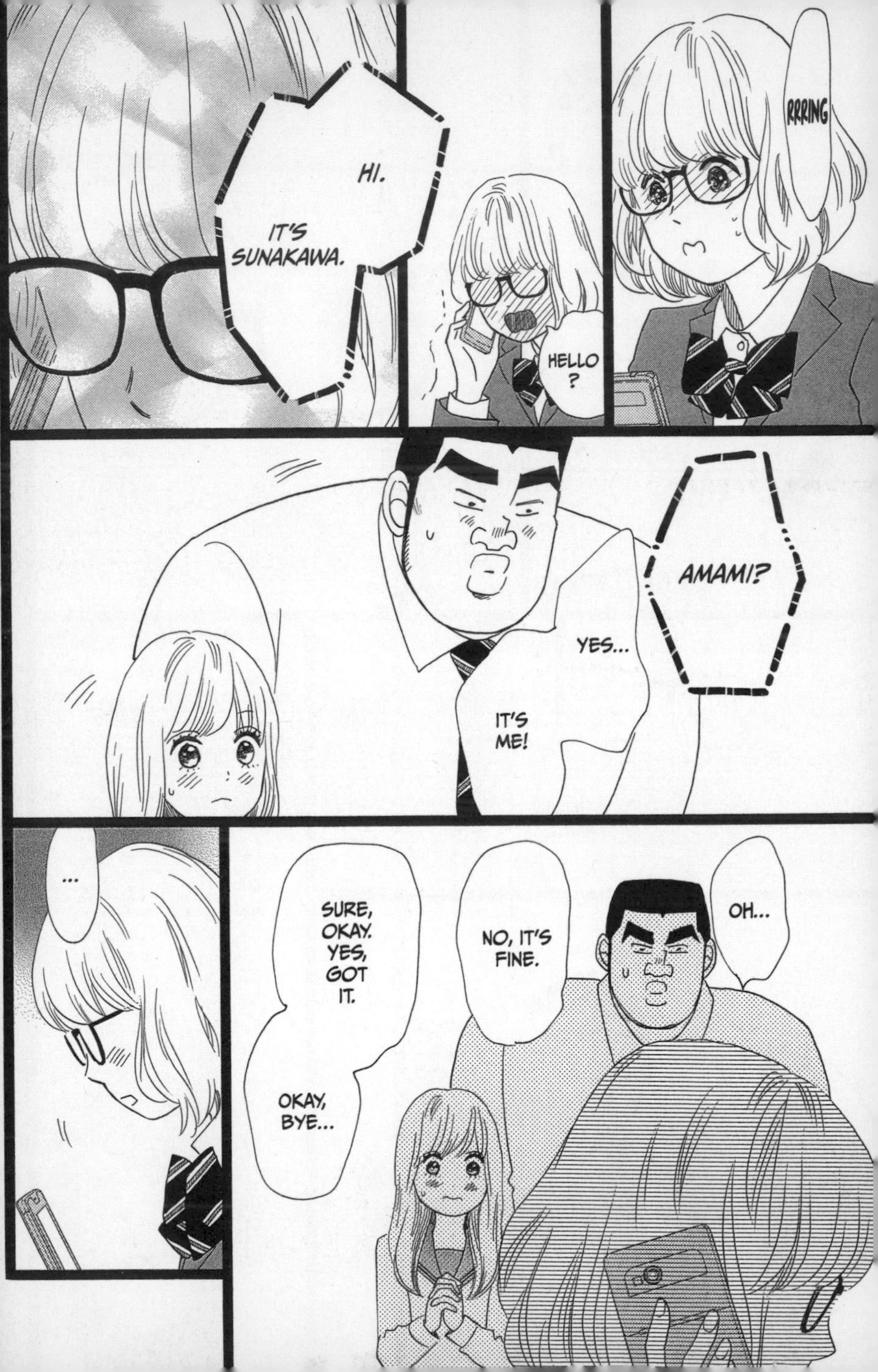
RRRING
HELLO?
HI.
IT'S SUNAKAWA.
AMAMI?
YES...
IT'S ME!
OH...
NO, IT'S FINE.
SURE, OKAY. YES, GOT IT.
OKAY, BYE...
...

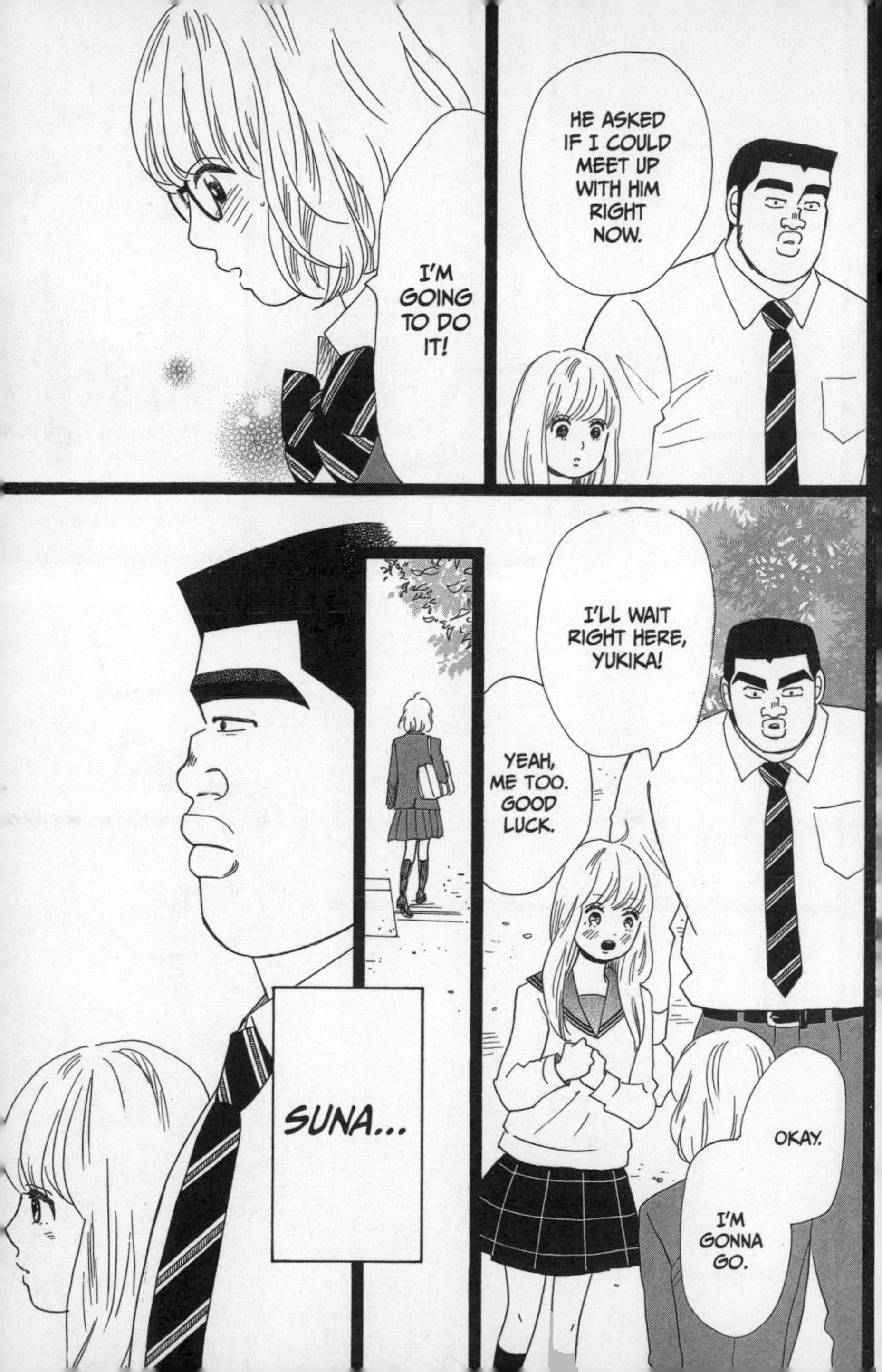
HE ASKED IF I COULD MEET UP WITH HIM RIGHT NOW.
I'M GOING TO DO IT!
OKAY.
I'M GONNA GO.
I'LL WAIT RIGHT HERE, YUKIKA!
YEAH, ME TOO. GOOD LUCK.
SUNA...

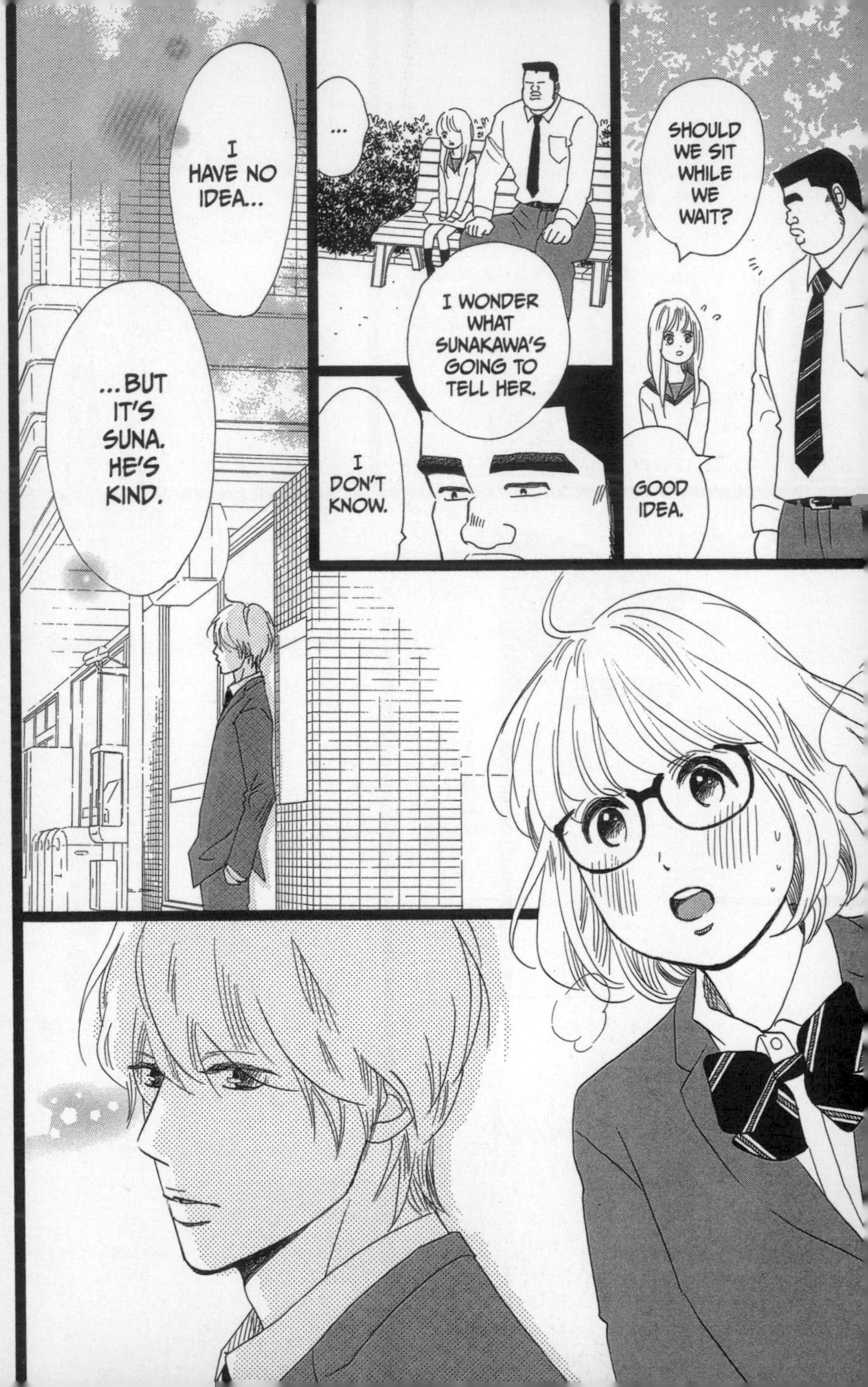
SHOULD WE SIT WHILE WE WAIT?
GOOD IDEA.
...
I WONDER WHAT SUNAKAWA'S GOING TO TELL HER.
I DON'T KNOW.
I HAVE NO IDEA...
...BUT IT'S SUNA. HE'S KIND.

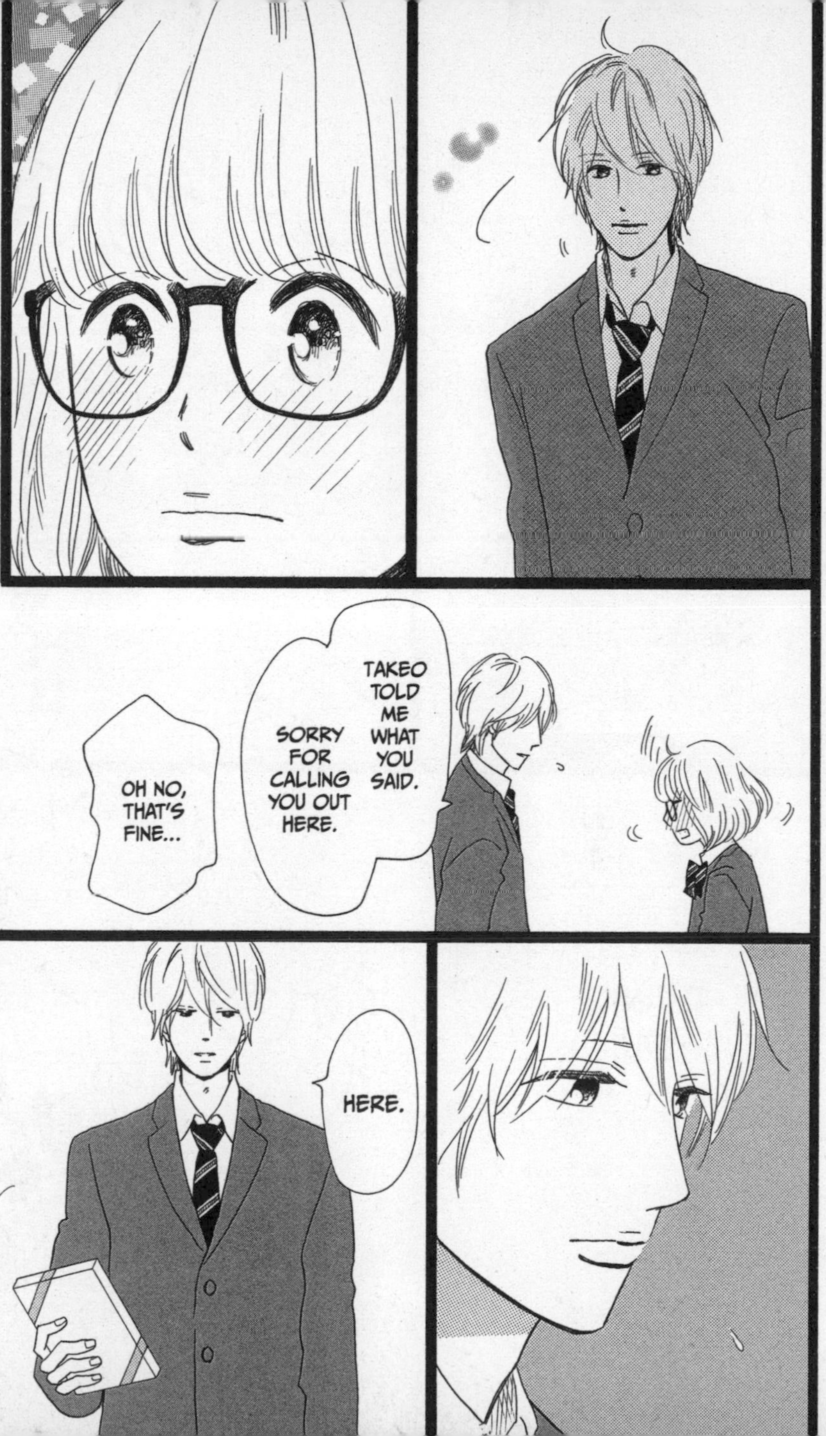
TAKEO TOLD ME WHAT YOU SAID.
SORRY FOR CALLING YOU OUT HERE.
OH NO, THAT'S FINE...
HERE.

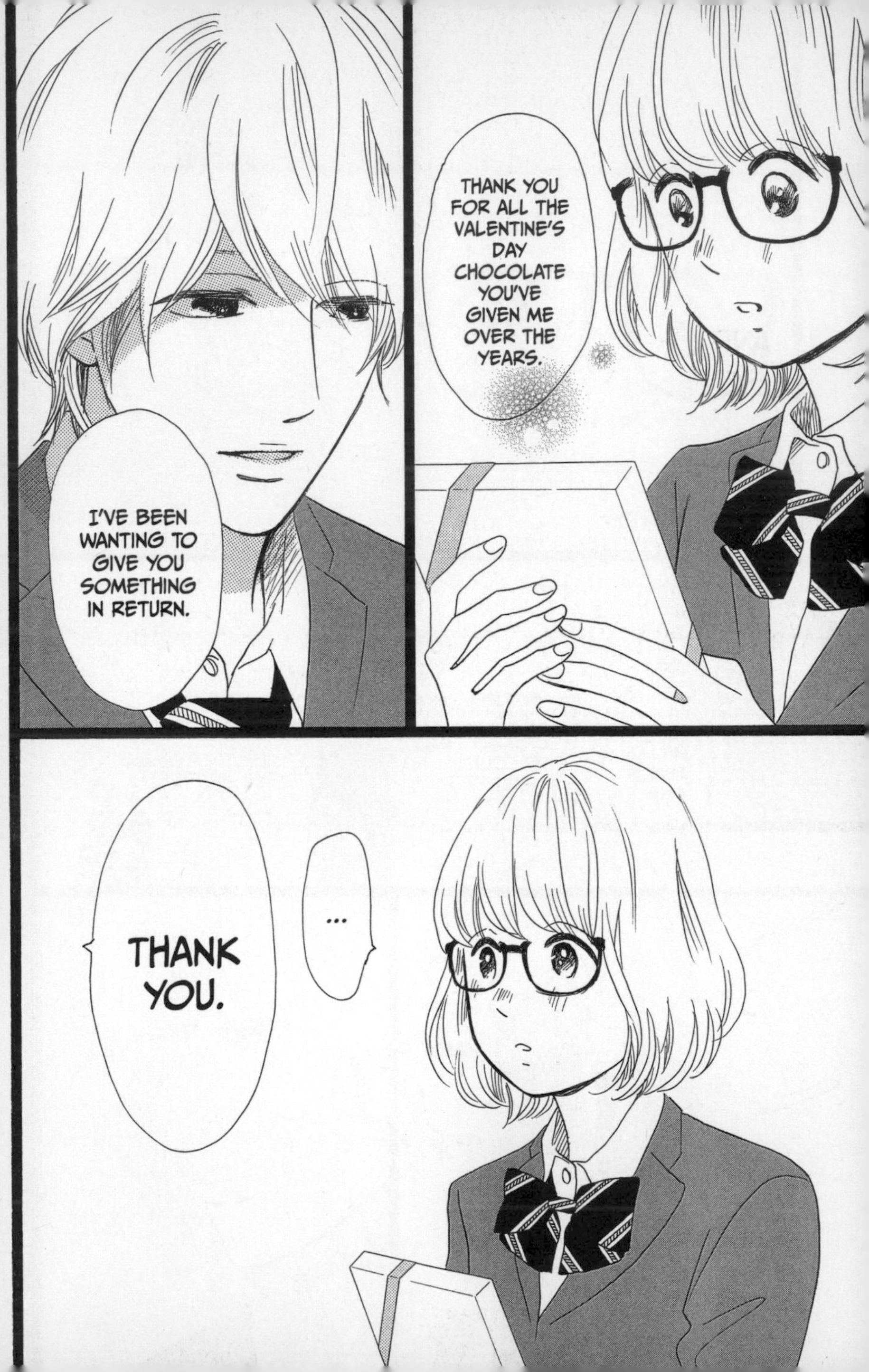
THANK YOU FOR ALL THE VALENTINE'S DAY CHOCOLATE YOU'VE GIVEN ME OVER THE YEARS.
I'VE BEEN WANTING TO GIVE YOU SOMETHING IN RETURN.
...
THANK YOU.

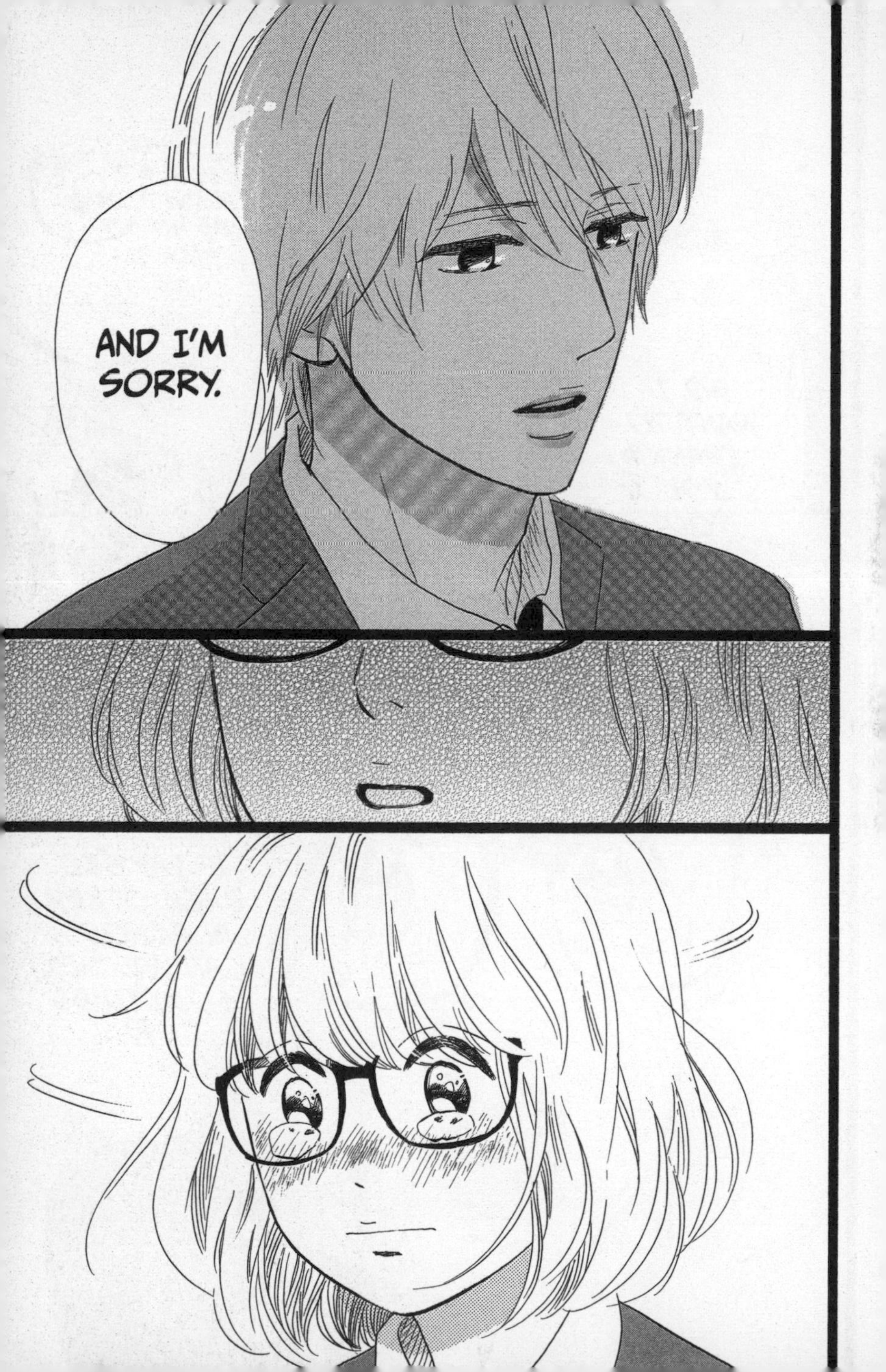
AND I'M SORRY.

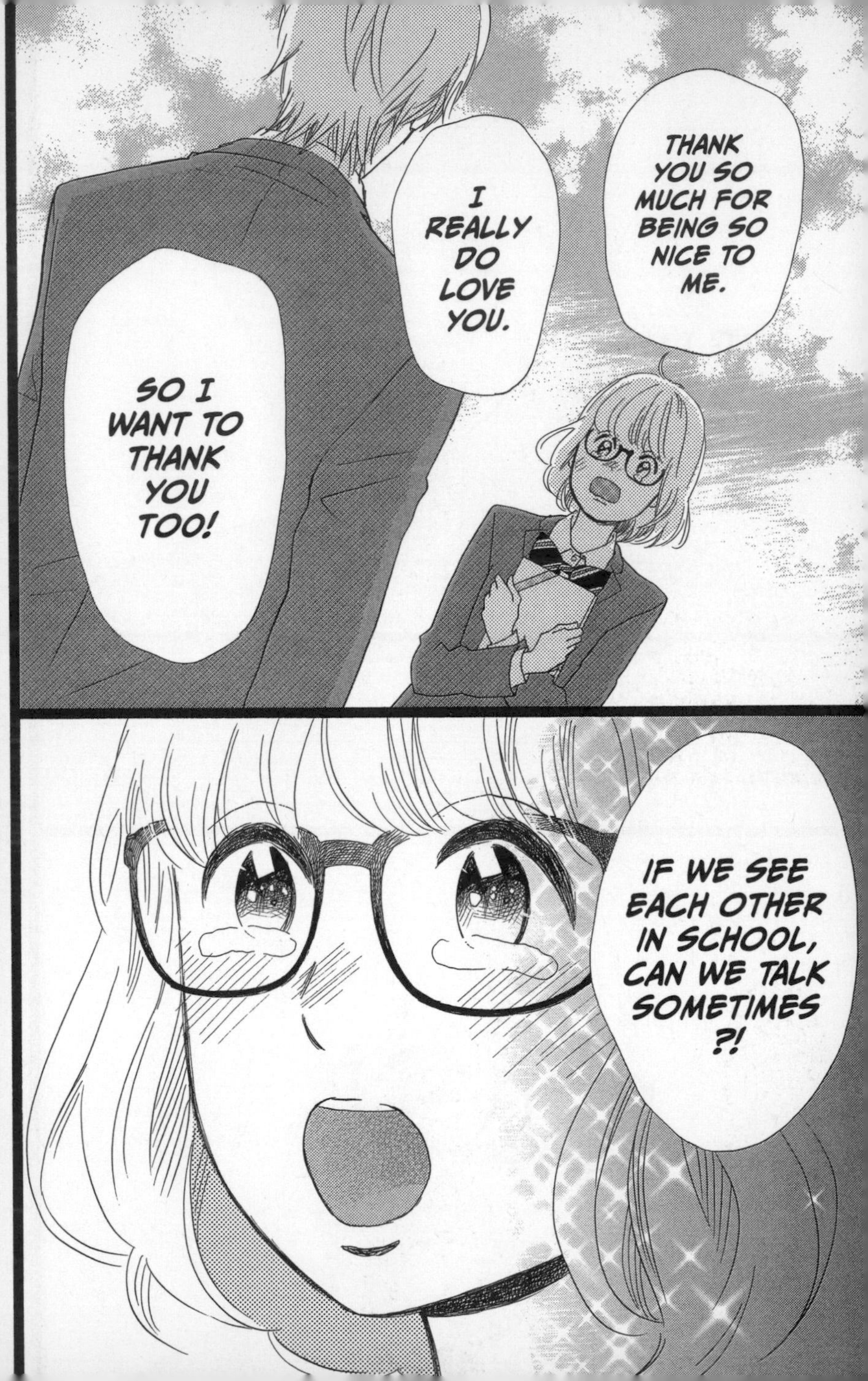
THANK YOU SO MUCH FOR BEING SO NICE TO ME.
I REALLY DO LOVE YOU.
SO I WANT TO THANK YOU TOO!
IF WE SEE EACH OTHER IN SCHOOL, CAN WE TALK SOMETIMES?!

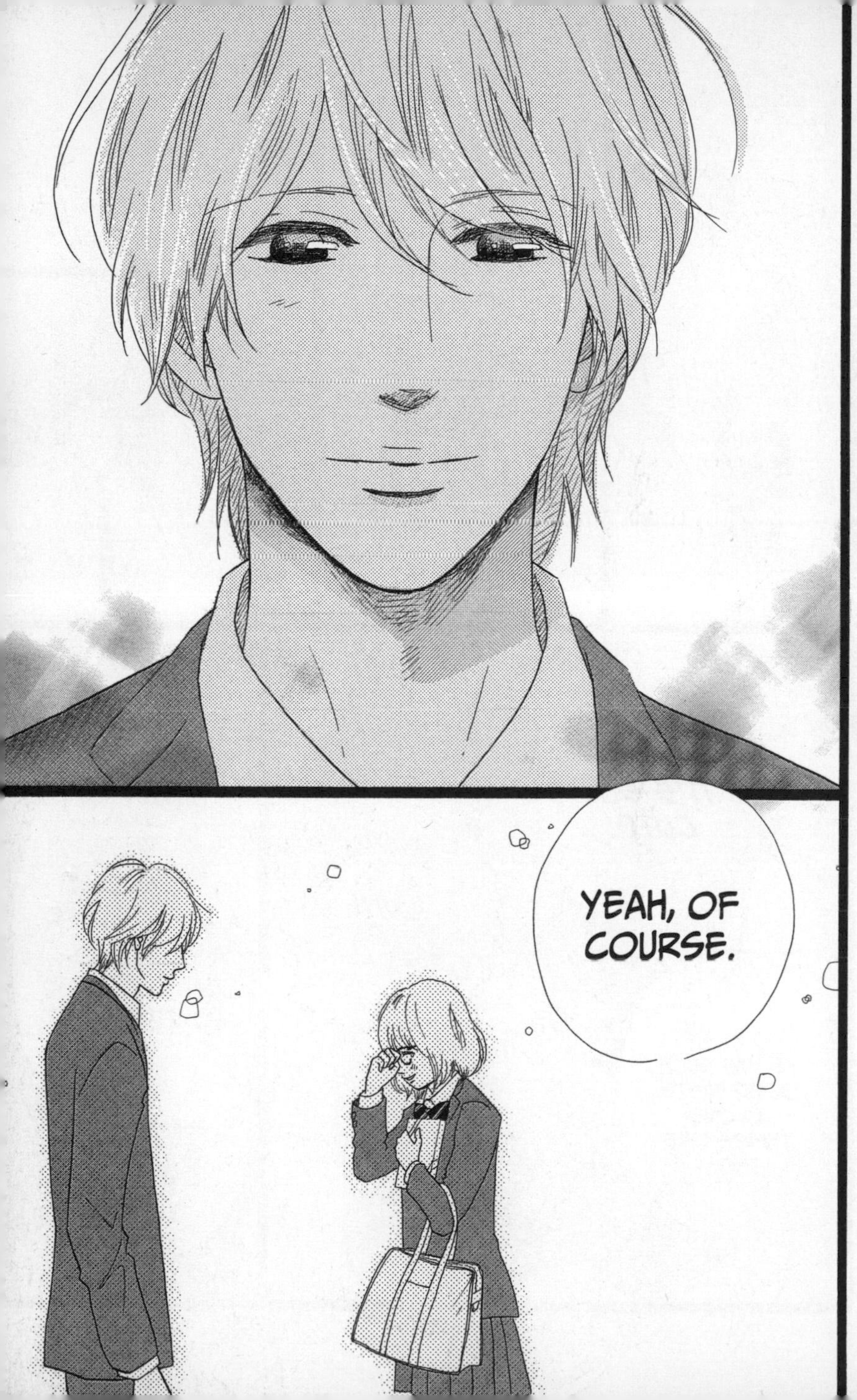
YEAH, OF COURSE.

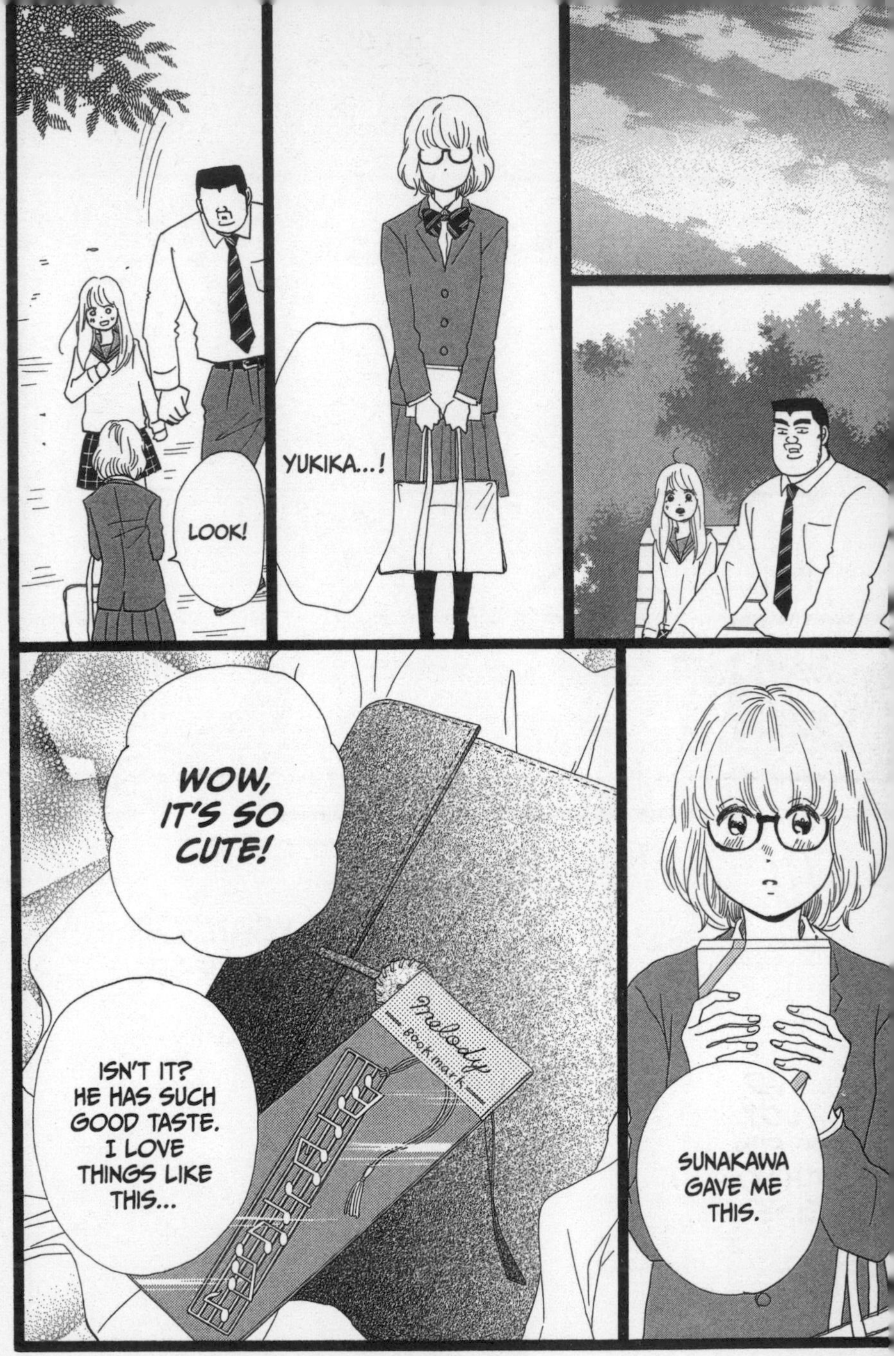
YUKIKA...!
LOOK!
SUNAKAWA GAVE ME THIS.
WOW, IT'S SO CUTE!
melody
bookmark
ISN'T IT? HE HAS SUCH GOOD TASTE. I LOVE THINGS LIKE THIS...

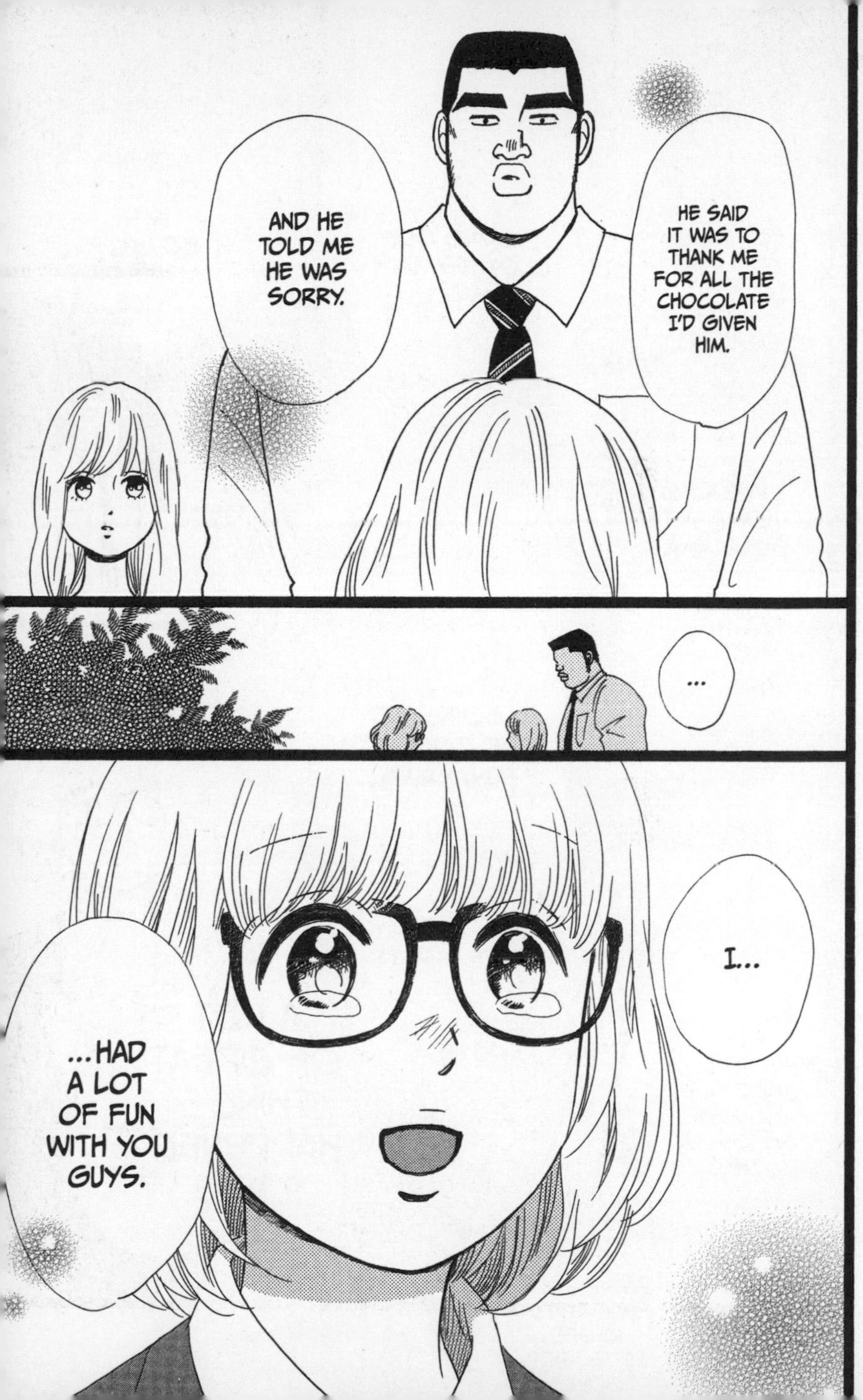
HE SAID IT WAS TO THANK ME FOR ALL THE CHOCOLATE I'D GIVEN HIM.
AND HE TOLD ME HE WAS SORRY.
...
I...
...HAD A LOT OF FUN WITH YOU GUYS.

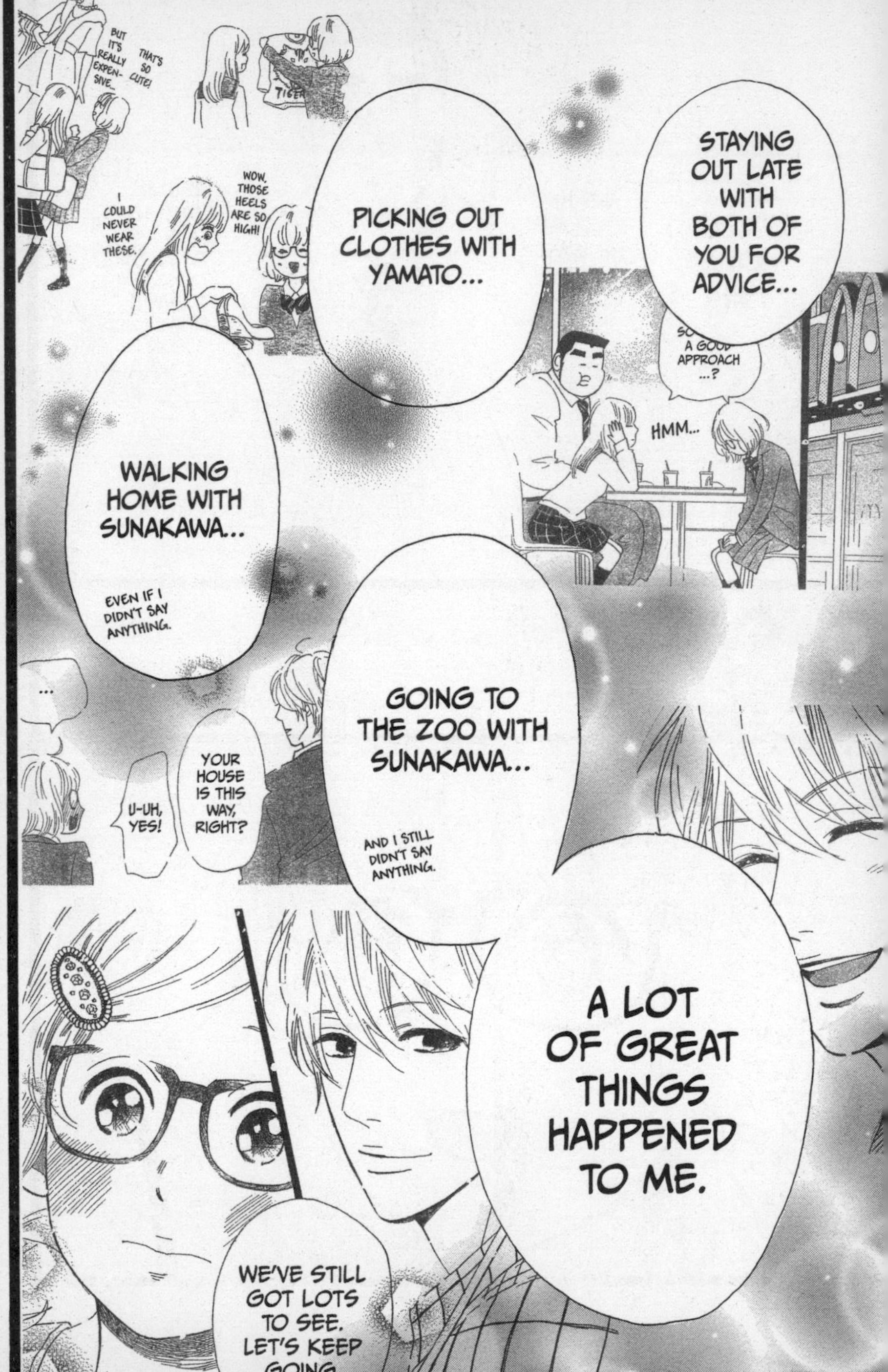
STAYING OUT LATE WITH BOTH OF YOU FOR ADVICE...
SO A GOOD APPROACH ...?
HMM...
PICKING OUT CLOTHES WITH YAMATO...
THAT'S SO CUTE!
BUT IT'S REALLY EXPEN-SIVE...
TIGER
WOW, THOSE HEELS ARE SO HIGH!
I COULD NEVER WEAR THESE.
WALKING HOME WITH SUNAKAWA...
EVEN IF I DIDN'T SAY ANYTHING.
GOING TO THE ZOO WITH SUNAKAWA...
AND I STILL DIDN'T SAY ANYTHING.
YOUR HOUSE IS THIS WAY, RIGHT?
U-UH, YES!
...
A LOT OF GREAT THINGS HAPPENED TO ME.
WE'VE STILL GOT LOTS TO SEE. LET'S KEEP GOING.

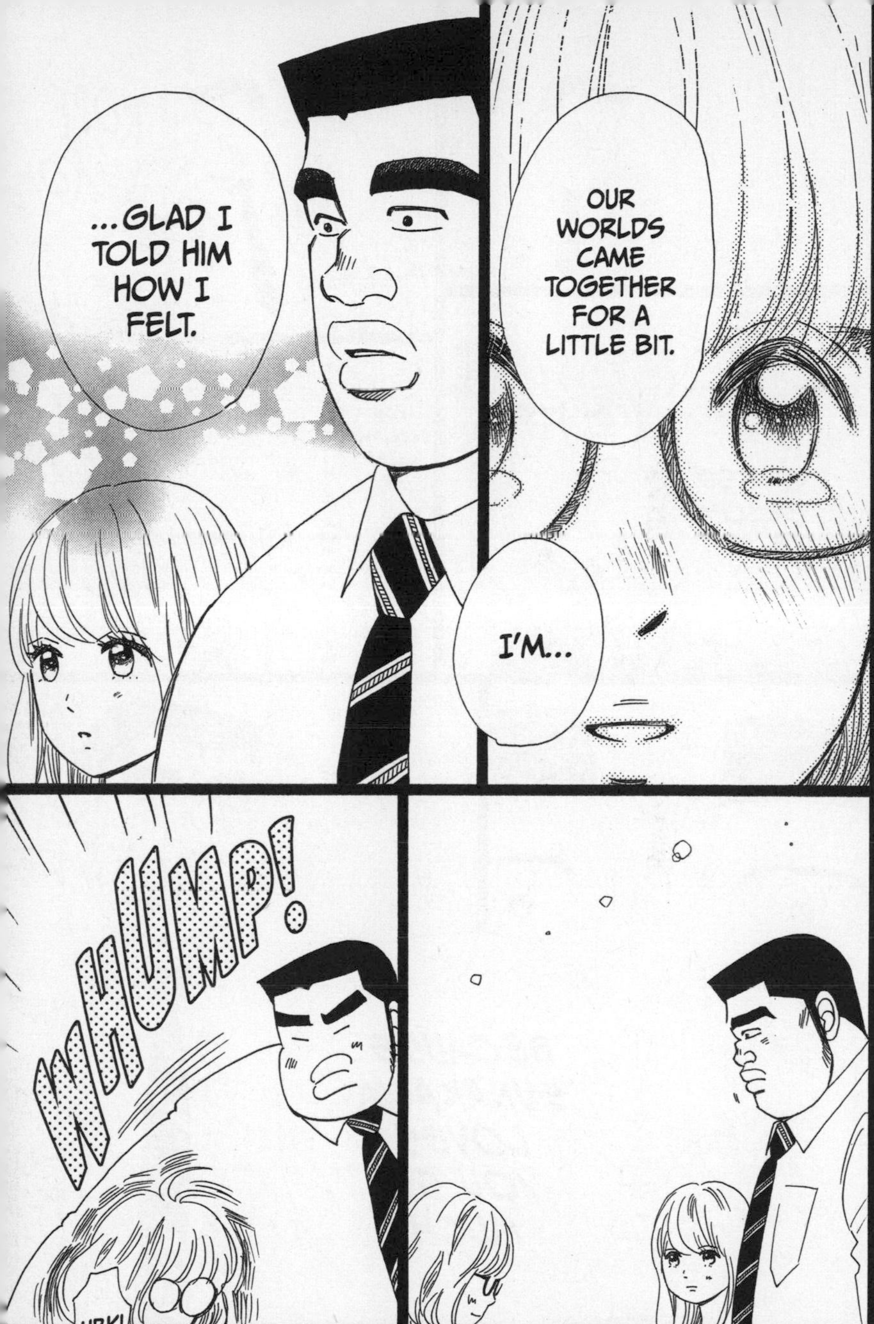
OUR WORLDS CAME TOGETHER FOR A LITTLE BIT.
I'M...
...GLAD I TOLD HIM HOW I FELT.
WHUMP!
URK!

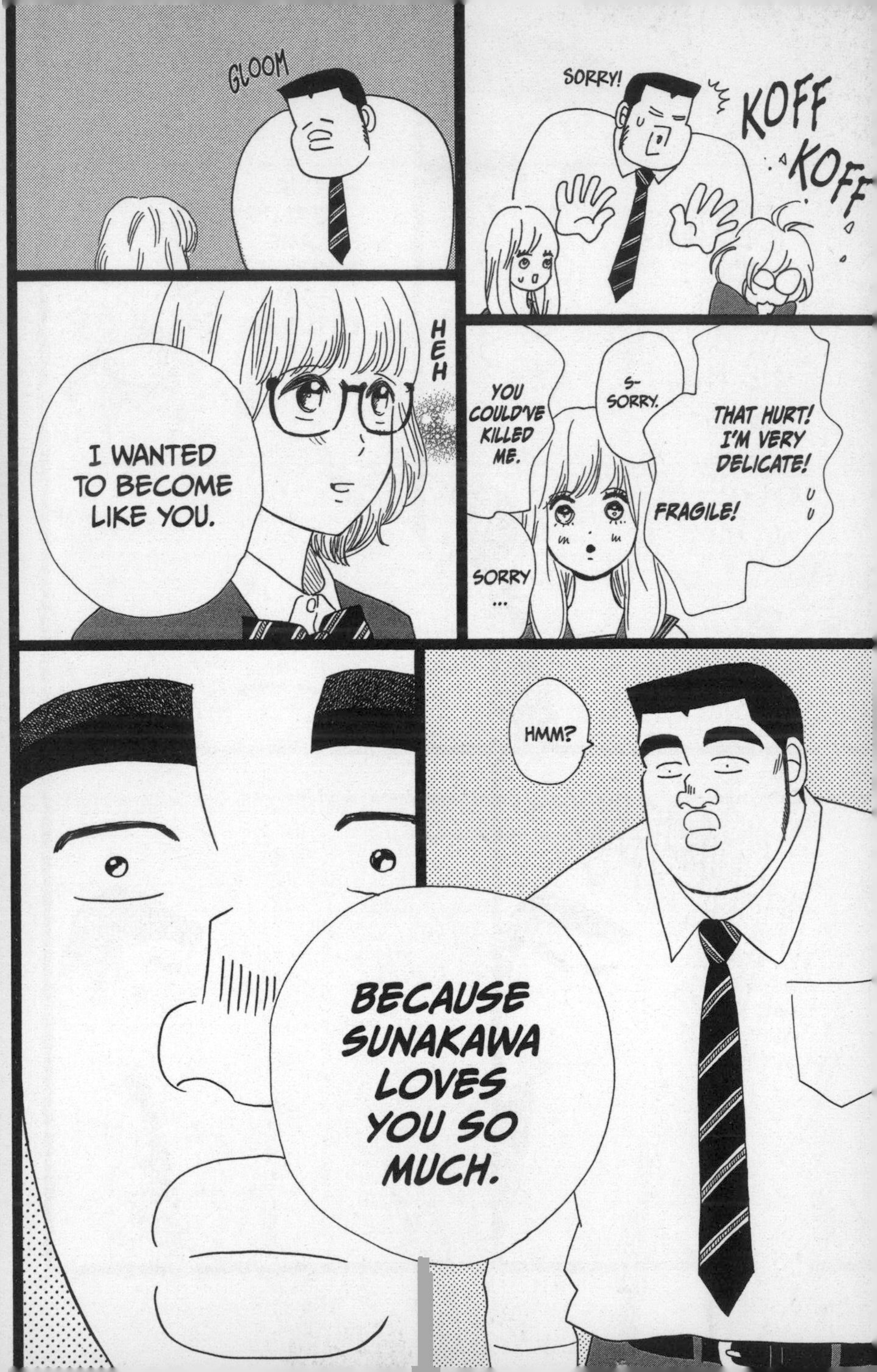
SORRY!
KOFF KOFF
GLOOM
THAT HURT! I'M VERY DELICATE!
FRAGILE!
S-SORRY.
YOU COULD'VE KILLED ME.
SORRY ...
HEH
I WANTED TO BECOME LIKE YOU.
HMM?
BECAUSE SUNAKAWA LOVES YOU SO MUCH.

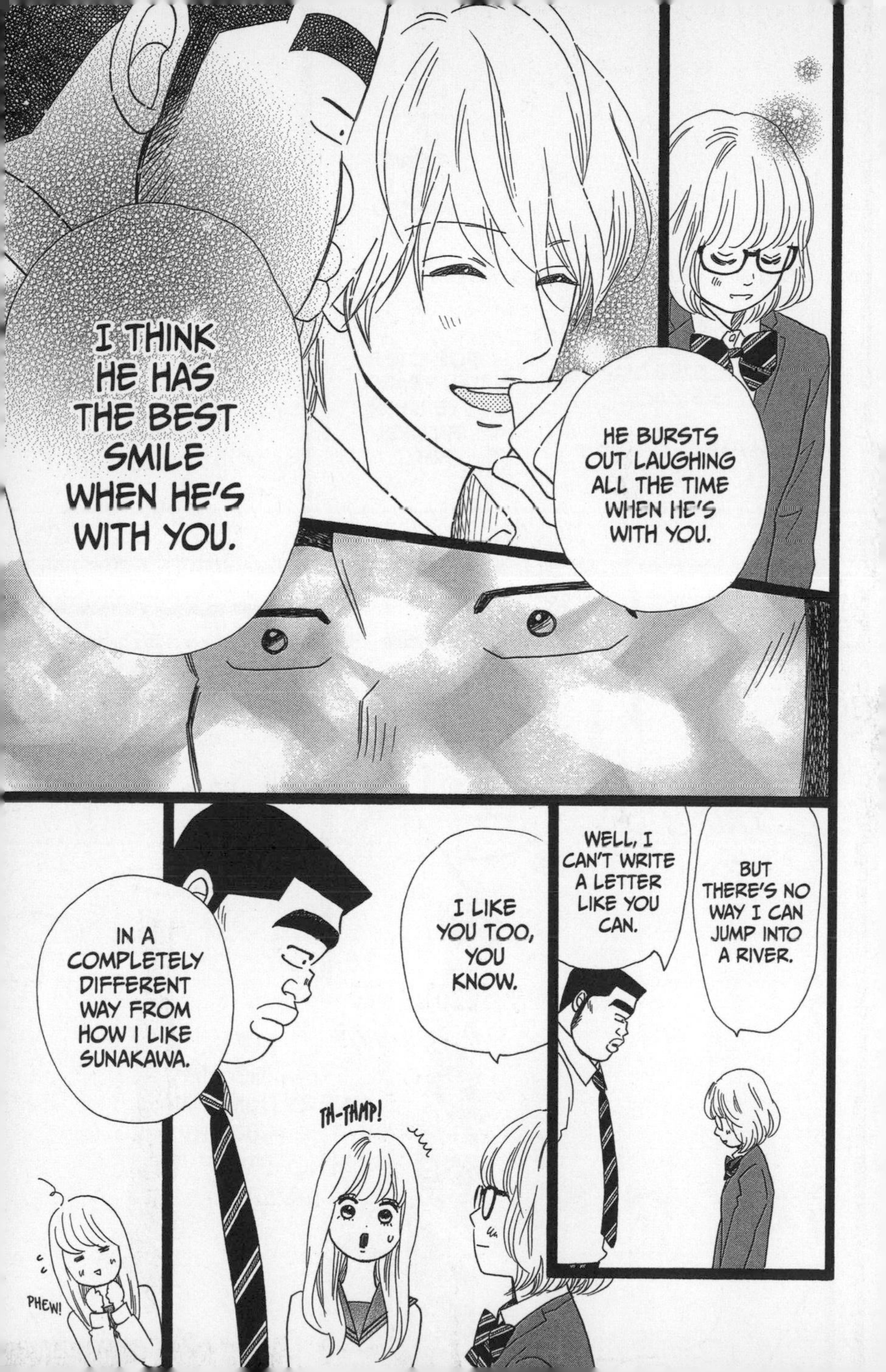
HE BURSTS OUT LAUGHING ALL THE TIME WHEN HE'S WITH YOU.
I THINK HE HAS THE BEST SMILE WHEN HE'S WITH YOU.
BUT THERE'S NO WAY I CAN JUMP INTO A RIVER.
WELL, I CAN'T WRITE A LETTER LIKE YOU CAN.
I LIKE YOU TOO, YOU KNOW.
IN A COMPLETELY DIFFERENT WAY FROM HOW I LIKE SUNAKAWA.
TH-THMP!
PHEW!

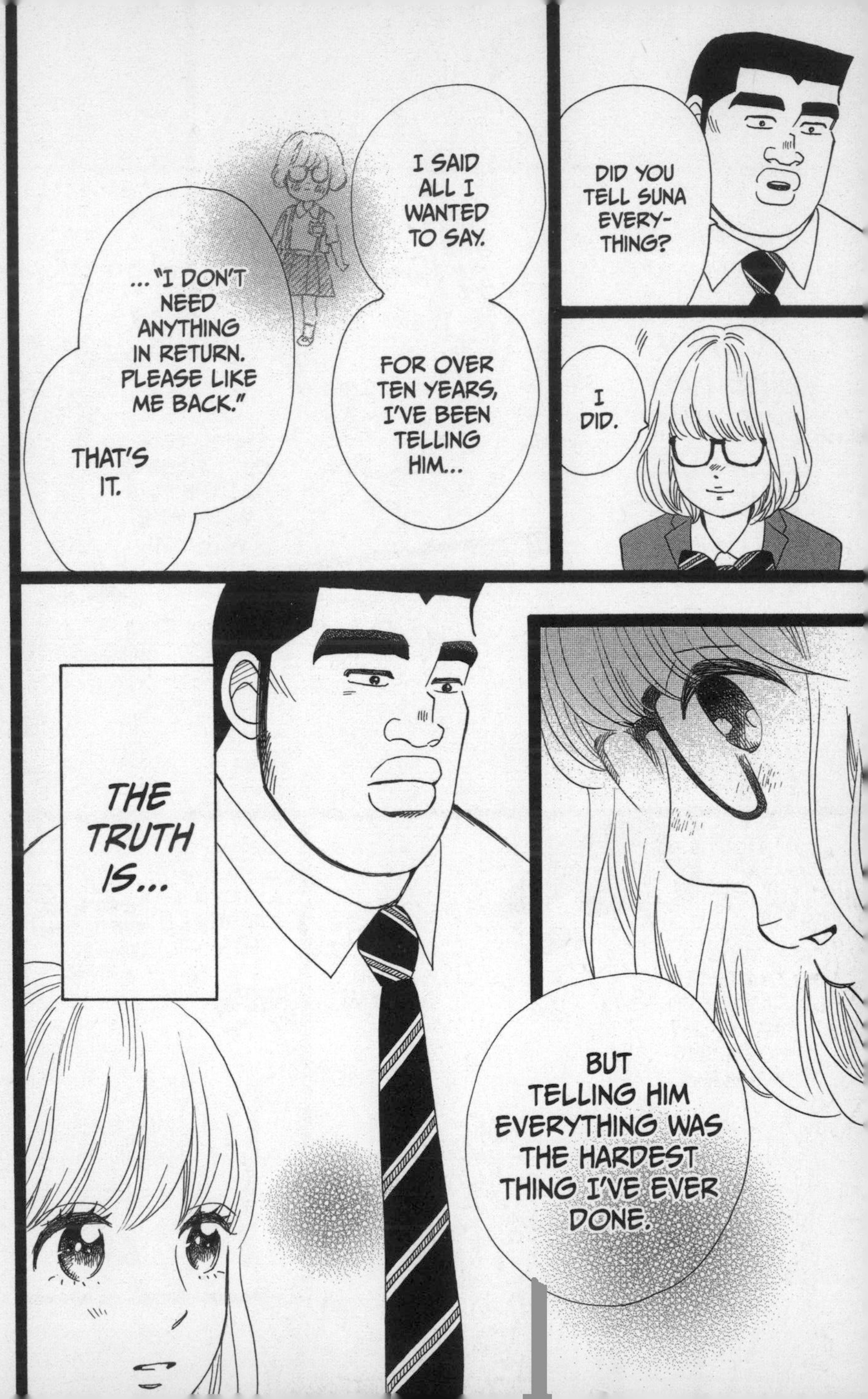
DID YOU TELL SUNA EVERYTHING?
I DID.
I SAID ALL I WANTED TO SAY.
FOR OVER TEN YEARS, I'VE BEEN TELLING HIM...
..."I DON'T NEED ANYTHING IN RETURN. PLEASE LIKE ME BACK."
THAT'S IT.
BUT TELLING HIM EVERYTHING WAS THE HARDEST THING I'VE EVER DONE.
THE TRUTH IS...

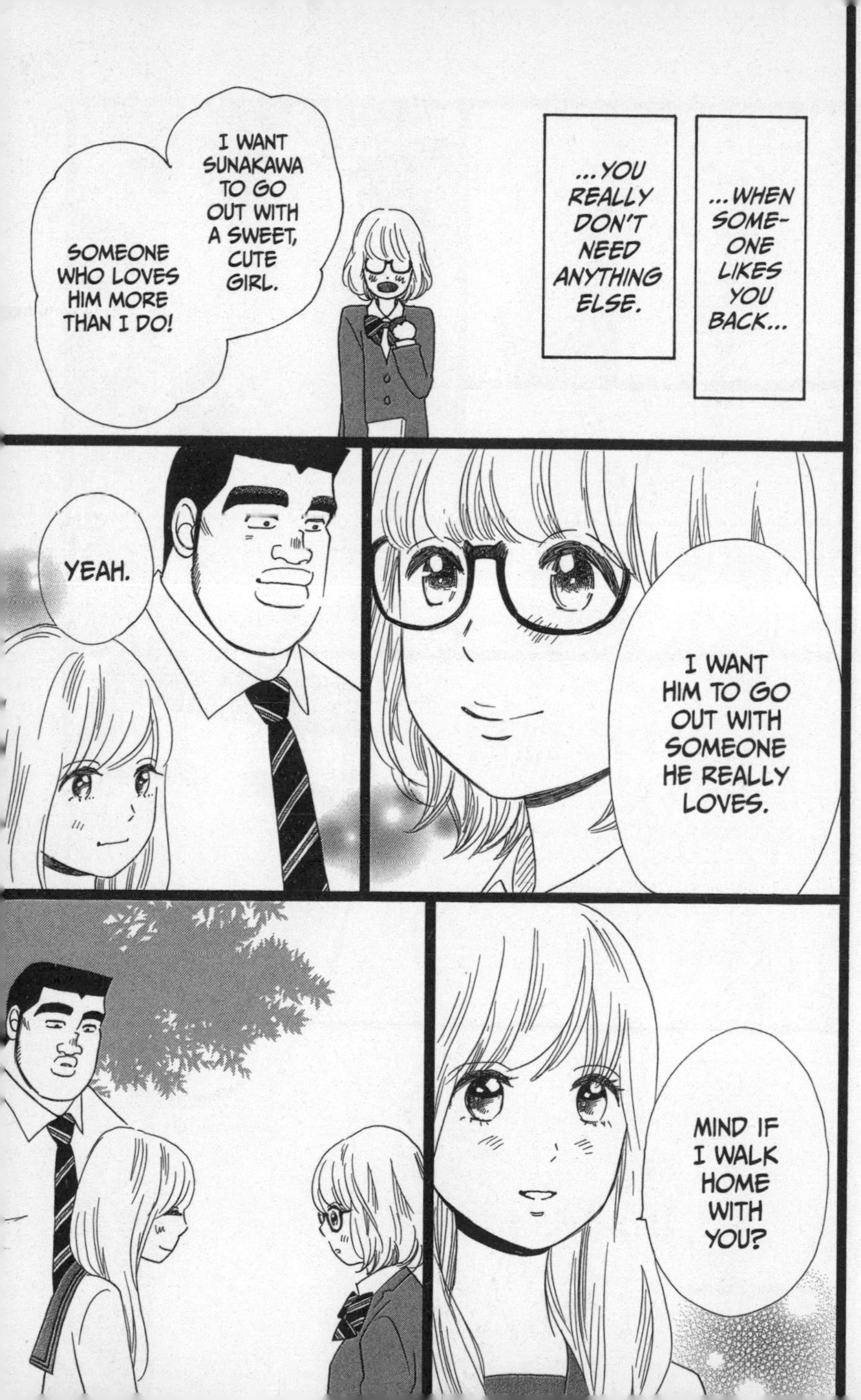
...WHEN SOMEONE LIKES YOU BACK...
...YOU REALLY DON'T NEED ANYTHING ELSE.
I WANT SUNAKAWA TO GO OUT WITH A SWEET, CUTE GIRL.
SOMEONE WHO LOVES HIM MORE THAN I DO!
I WANT HIM TO GO OUT WITH SOMEONE HE REALLY LOVES.
YEAH.
MIND IF I WALK HOME WITH YOU?

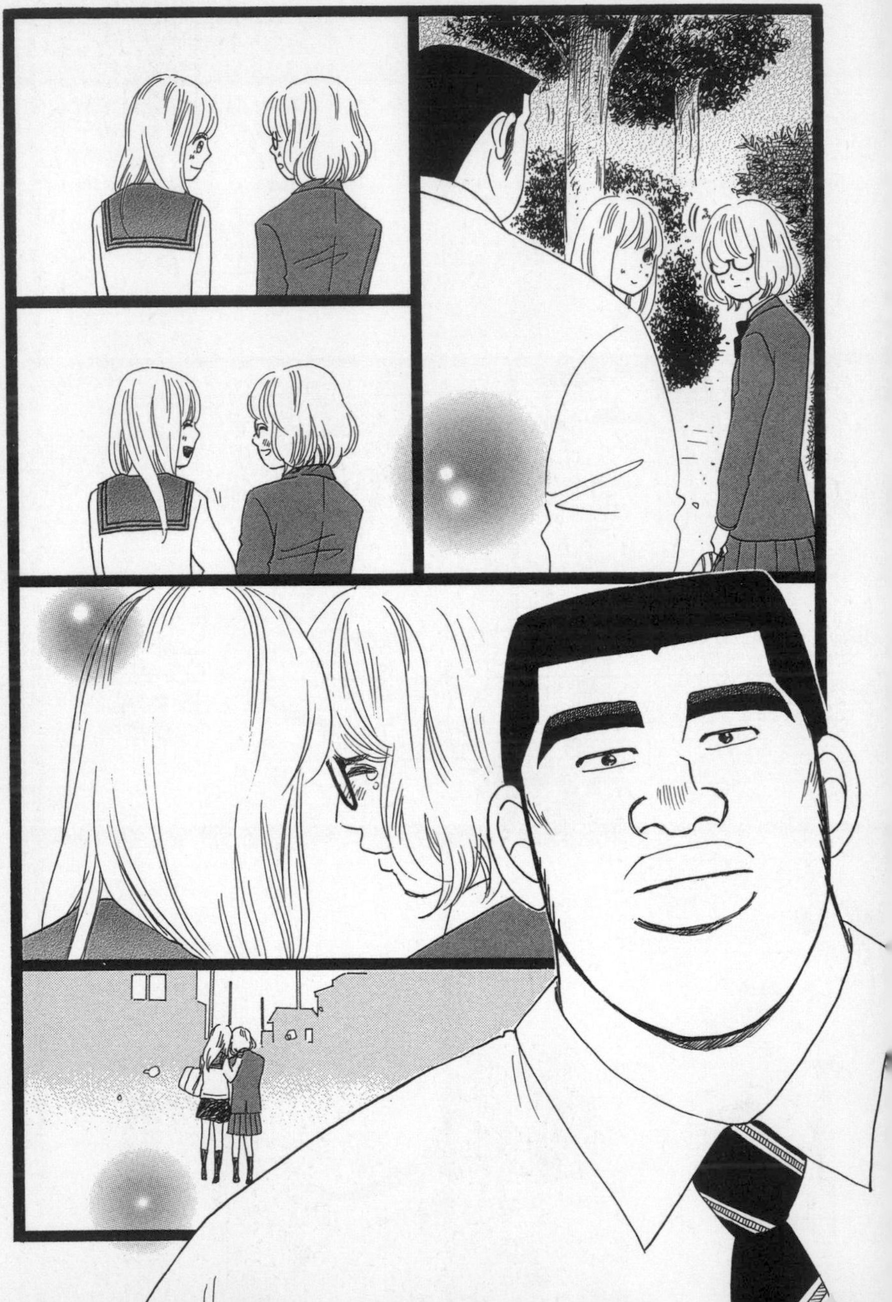

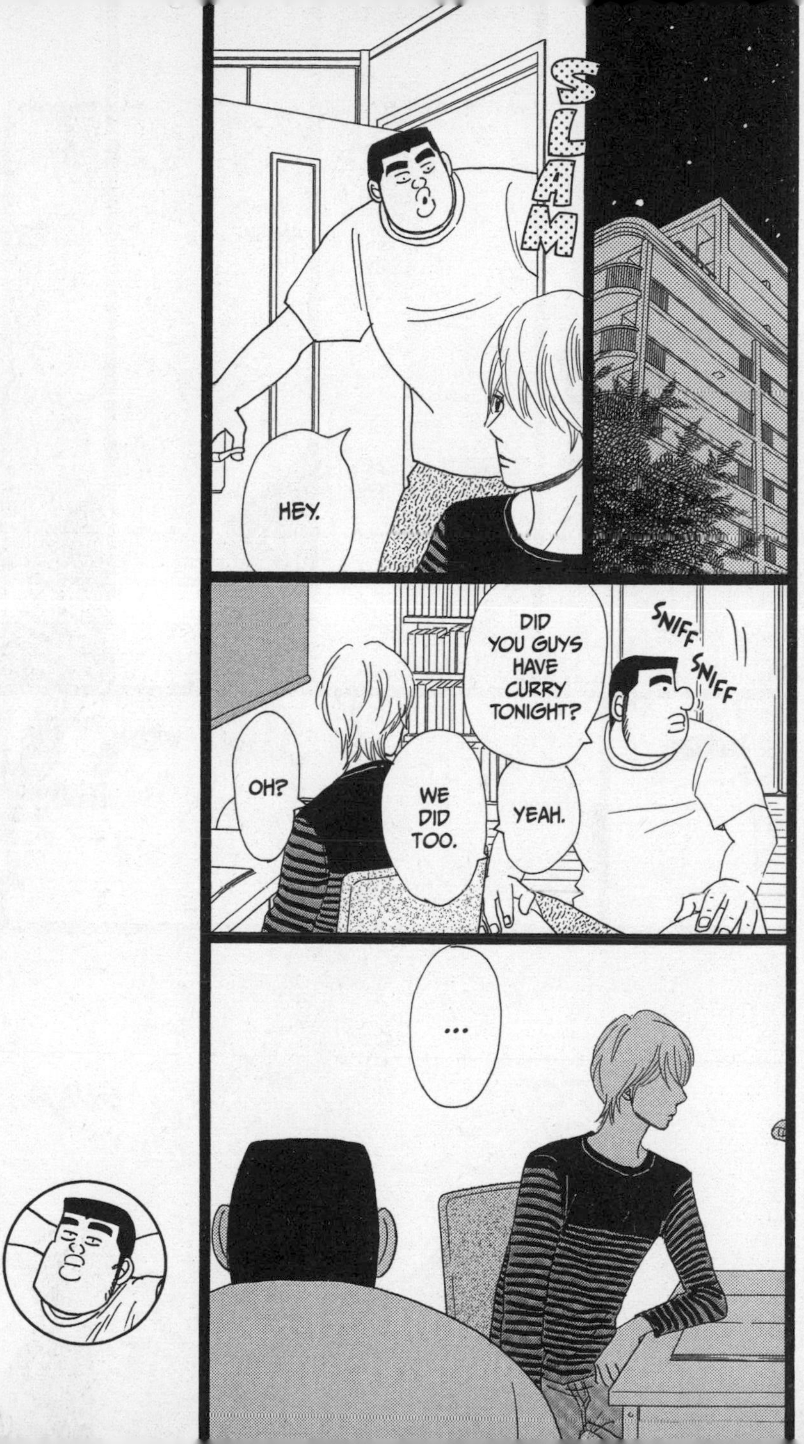
SLAM
HEY.
SNIFF SNIFF
DID YOU GUYS HAVE CURRY TONIGHT?
YEAH.
WE DID TOO.
OH?
...

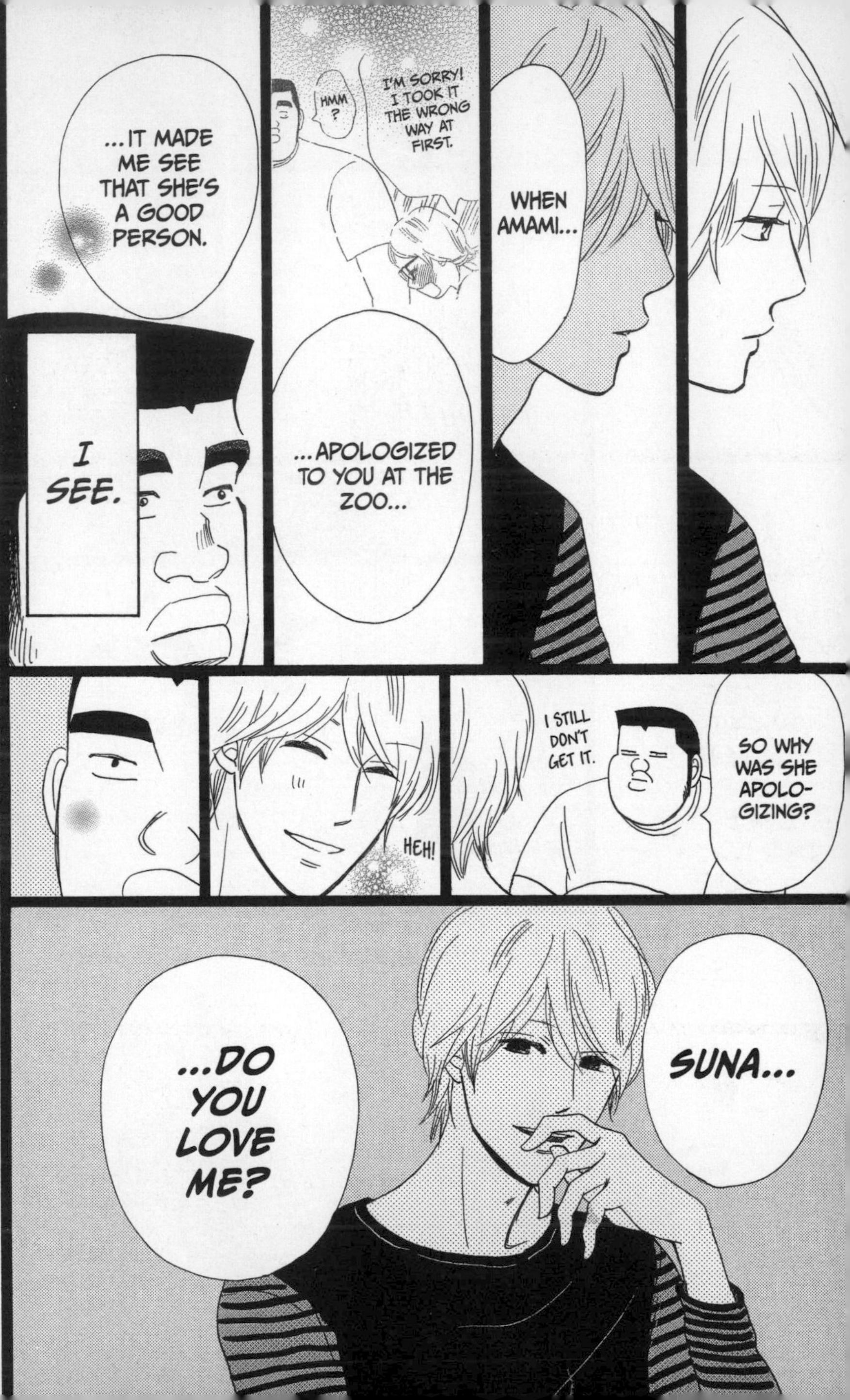
WHEN AMAMI...
I'M SORRY! I TOOK IT THE WRONG WAY AT FIRST.
HMM ?
...APOLOGIZED TO YOU AT THE ZOO...
...IT MADE ME SEE THAT SHE'S A GOOD PERSON.
I SEE.
SO WHY WAS SHE APOLOGIZING?
I STILL DON'T GET IT.
HEH!
SUNA...
...DO YOU LOVE ME?

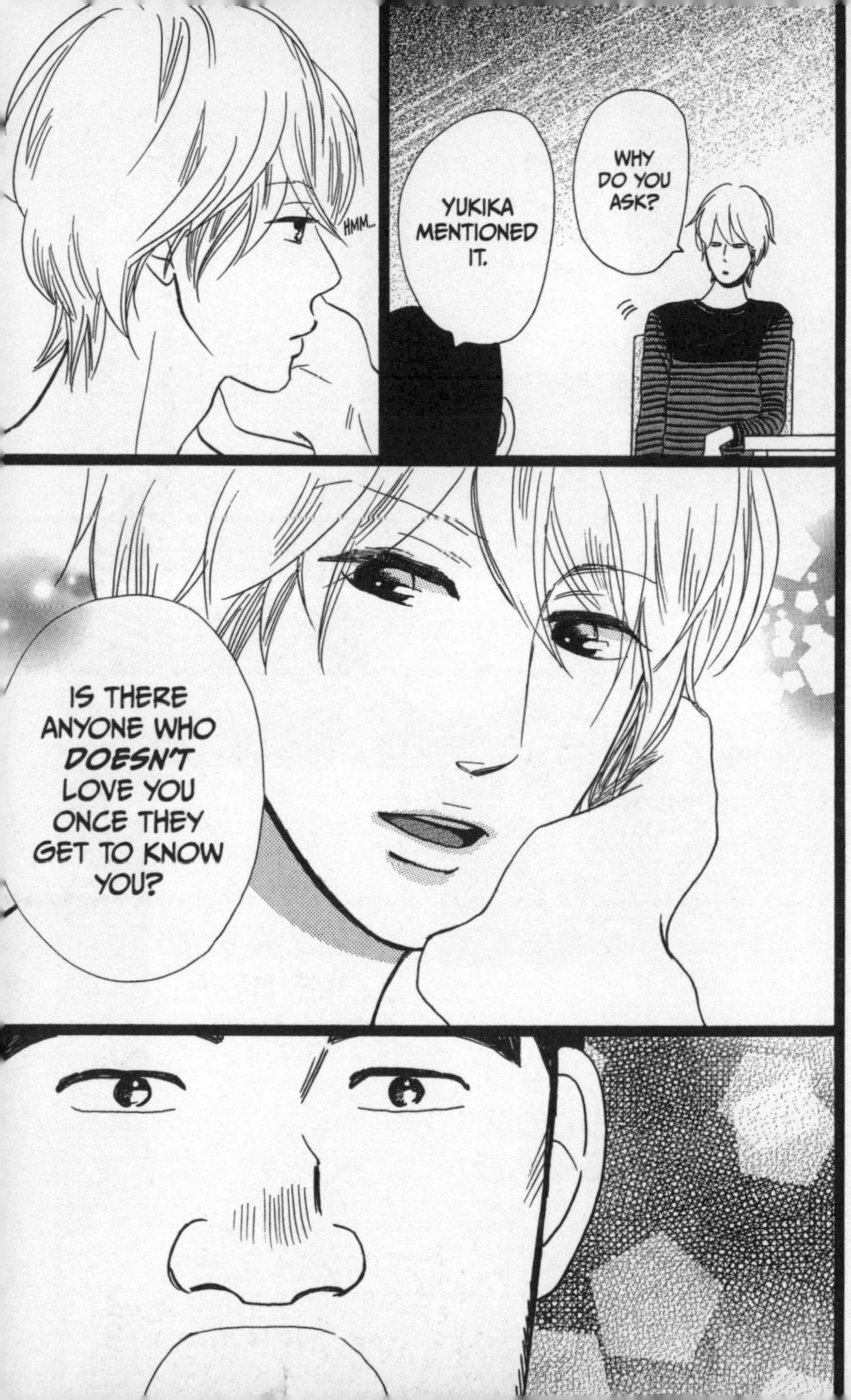
WHY DO YOU ASK?
YUKIKA MENTIONED IT.
HMM...
IS THERE ANYONE WHO *DOESN'T* LOVE YOU ONCE THEY GET TO KNOW YOU?

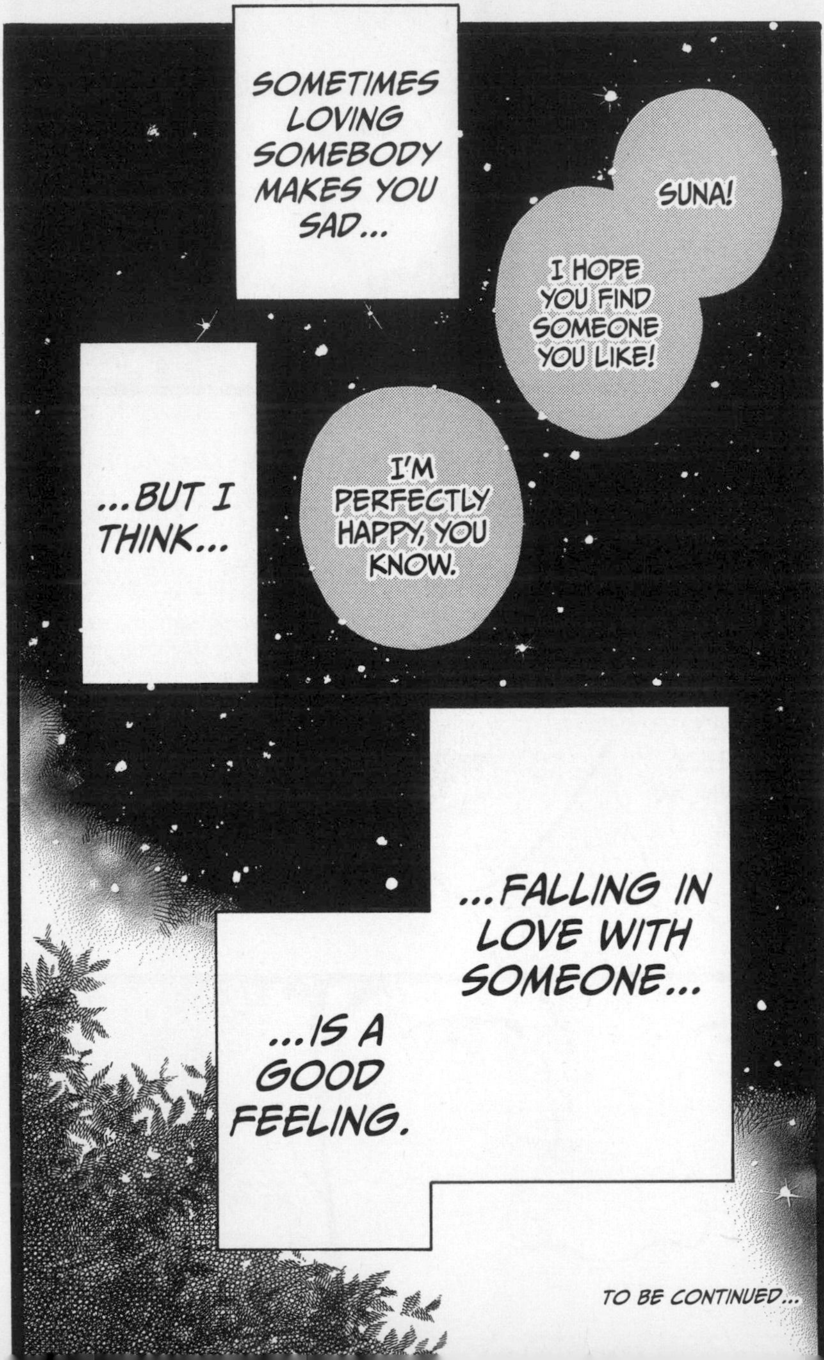
SOMETIMES LOVING SOMEBODY MAKES YOU SAD...
SUNA!
I HOPE YOU FIND SOMEONE YOU LIKE!
I'M PERFECTLY HAPPY, YOU KNOW.
...BUT I THINK...
...FALLING IN LOVE WITH SOMEONE...
...IS A GOOD FEELING.
TO BE CONTINUED...

My Love Story!! has reached volume 7! \(^-^)/ I'm so happy! \(^-^)/ I don't discuss anything beforehand with Aruko when I make comments here and in the magazine, so I think it's amusing when she and I talk about completely different things. I'm looking forward to what she'll write this time!

— Kazune Kawahara

ARUKO is from Ishikawa Prefecture in Japan and was born on July 26 (a Leo!). She made her manga debut with *Ame Nochi Hare* (Clear After the Rain). Her other works include *Yasuko to Kenji*, and her hobbies include laughing and getting lost.

KAZUNE KAWAHARA is from Hokkaido Prefecture in Japan and was born on March 11 (a Pisces!). She made her manga debut at age 18 with *Kare no Ichiban Sukina Hito* (His Most Favorite Person). Her best-selling shojo manga series *High School Debut* is available in North America from VIZ Media. Her hobby is interior redecorating.

Before I realized it, summer was over. How strange. Surprisingly, I had a lot of things to do this summer, and I had a lot of fun.

Whether I was having fun, focused on work or doing nothing, it felt like summer only after it was gone.

— Aruko

MY LOVE STORY!!

Volume 7
Shojo Beat Edition

Story by KAZUNE KAWAHARA
Art by ARUKO

English Adaptation ♡ Ysabet Reinhardt MacFarlane
Translation ♡ JN Productions
Touch-up Art & Lettering ♡ Mark McMurray
Design ♡ Fawn Lau
Editor ♡ Amy Yu

ORE MONOGATARI!!
© 2011 by Kazune Kawahara, Aruko
All rights reserved.
First published in Japan in 2011 by SHUEISHA Inc., Tokyo
English translation rights arranged by SHUEISHA Inc.

The stories, characters and incidents mentioned in
this publication are entirely fictional.

Printed in the U.S.A.

Published by VIZ Media, LLC
P.O. Box 77010
San Francisco, CA 94107

10 9 8 7 6 5 4 3 2 1
First printing, January 2016

www.viz.com

www.shojobeat.com

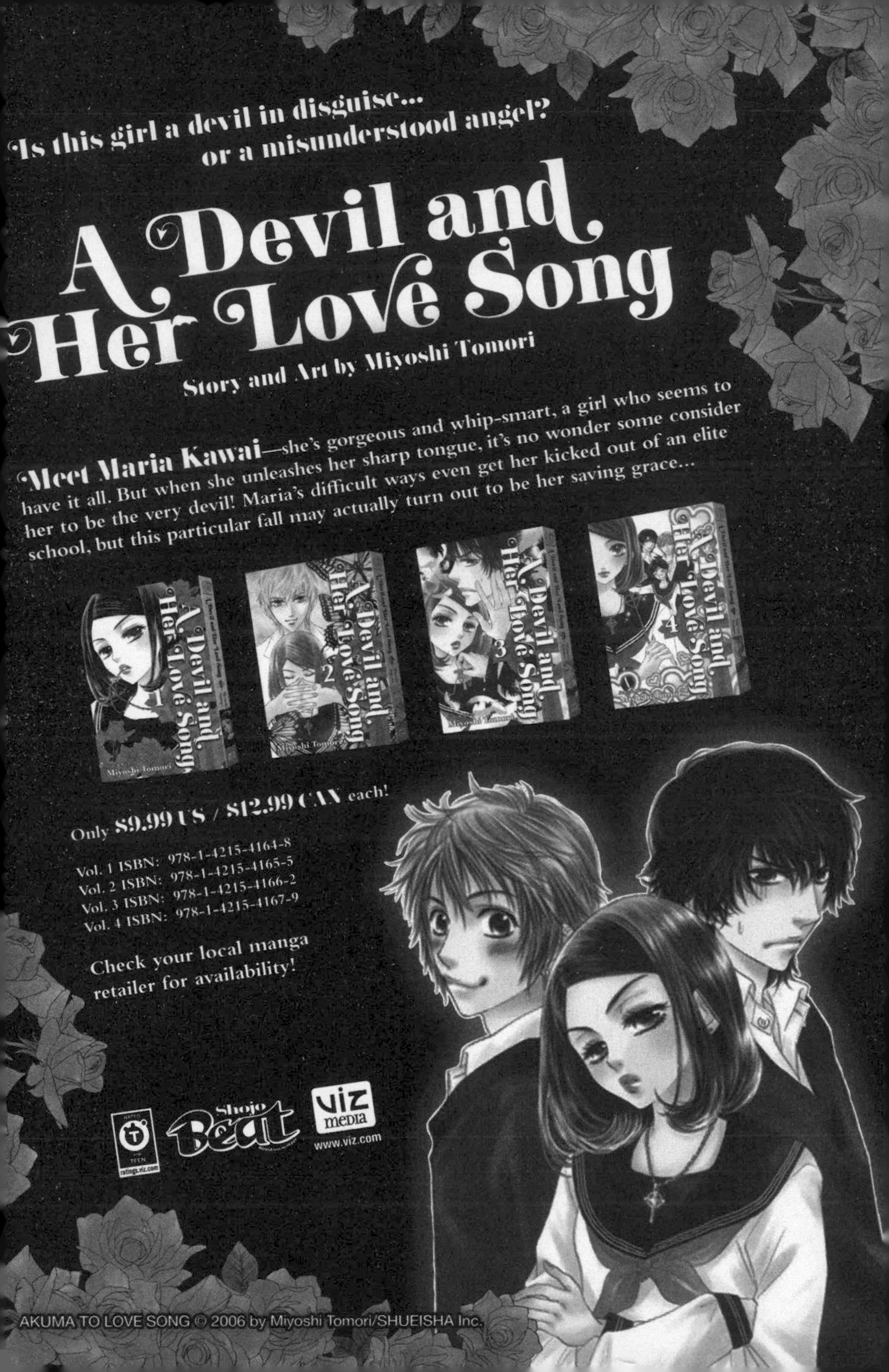
Is this girl a devil in disguise...
or a misunderstood angel?
A Devil and Her Love Song
Story and Art by Miyoshi Tomori
Meet Maria Kawai—she's gorgeous and whip-smart, a girl who seems to have it all. But when she unleashes her sharp tongue, it's no wonder some consider her to be the very devil! Maria's difficult ways even get her kicked out of an elite school, but this particular fall may actually turn out to be her saving grace...
A Devil and Her Love Song 1 Miyoshi Tomori
A Devil and Her Love Song 2 Miyoshi Tomori
A Devil and Her Love Song 3 Miyoshi Tomori
A Devil and Her Love Song 4
Only $9.99 US / $12.99 CAN each!
Vol. 1 ISBN: 978-1-4215-4164-8
Vol. 2 ISBN: 978-1-4215-4165-5
Vol. 3 ISBN: 978-1-4215-4166-2
Vol. 4 ISBN: 978-1-4215-4167-9
Check your local manga retailer for availability!
T TEEN
ratings.viz.com
Shojo Beat
VIZ media
www.viz.com
AKUMA TO LOVE SONG © 2006 by Miyoshi Tomori/SHUEISHA Inc.

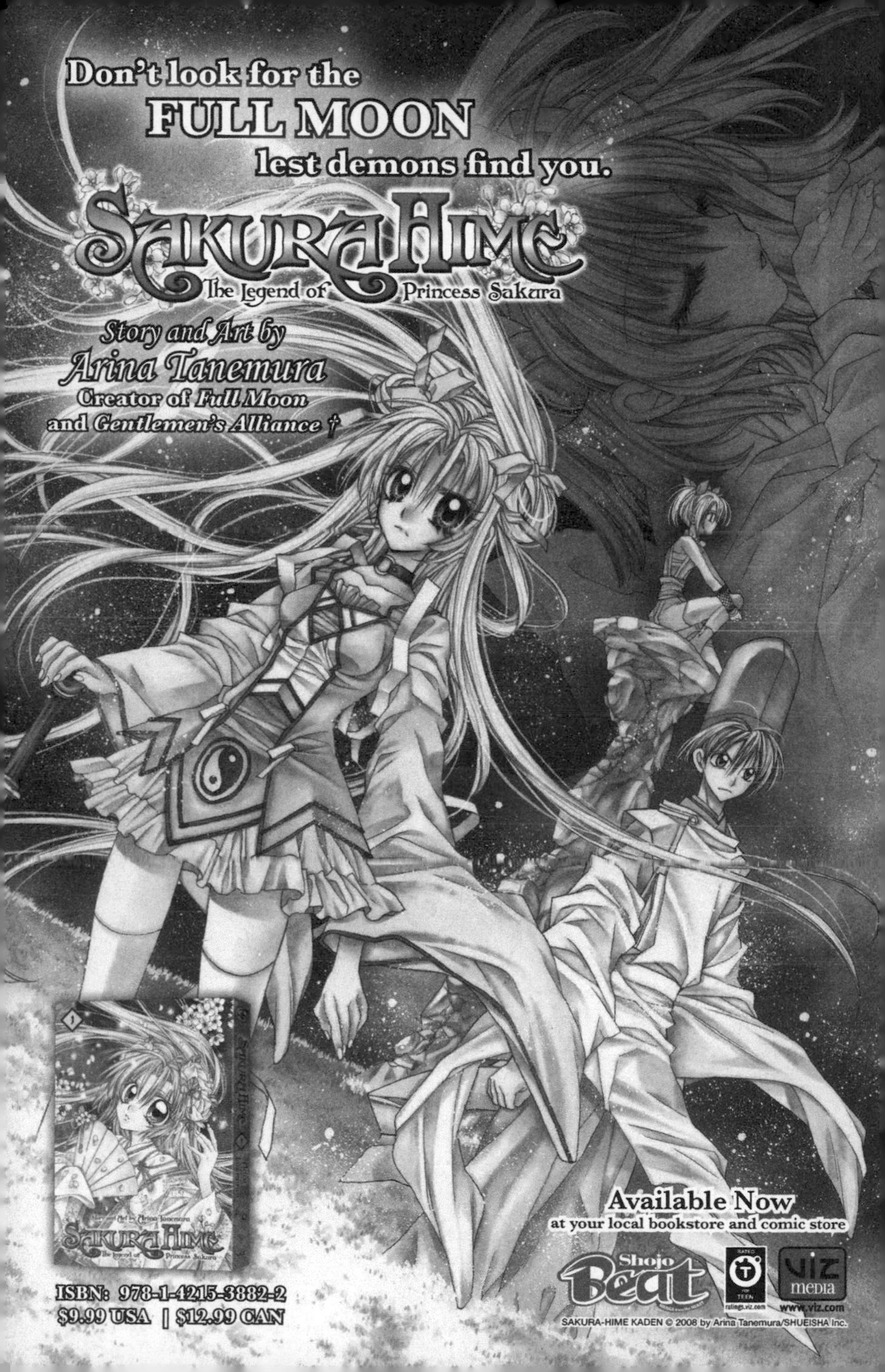

Don't look for the
FULL MOON
lest demons find you.
SAKURA HIME
The Legend of Princess Sakura
Story and Art by
Arina Tanemura
Creator of Full Moon
and Gentlemen's Alliance †
ISBN: 978-1-4215-3882-2
$9.99 USA | $12.99 CAN
Available Now
at your local bookstore and comic store
Shojo Beat
RATED T FOR TEEN
ratings.viz.com
VIZ media
www.viz.com
SAKURA-HIME KADEN © 2008 by Arina Tanemura/SHUEISHA Inc.

You may be reading the **wrong way!!**

IT'S TRUE: In keeping with the original Japanese comic format, this book reads from right to left—so action, sound effects, and word balloons are completely reversed. This preserves the orientation of the original artwork—plus, it's fun! Check out the diagram shown here to get the hang of things, and then turn to the other side of the book to get started!

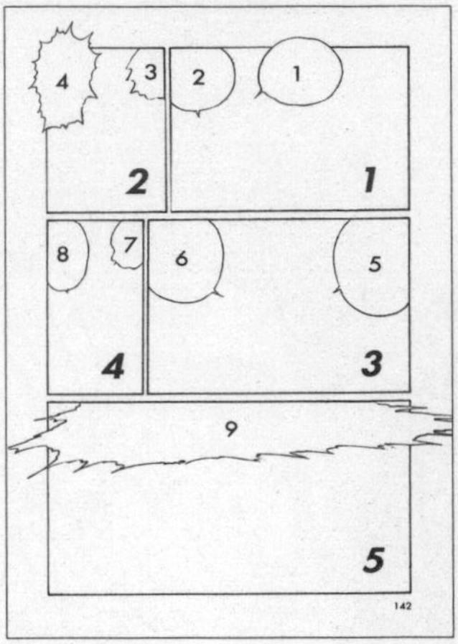
1
2
3
4
1
2
5
6
7
8
3
4
9
5
142

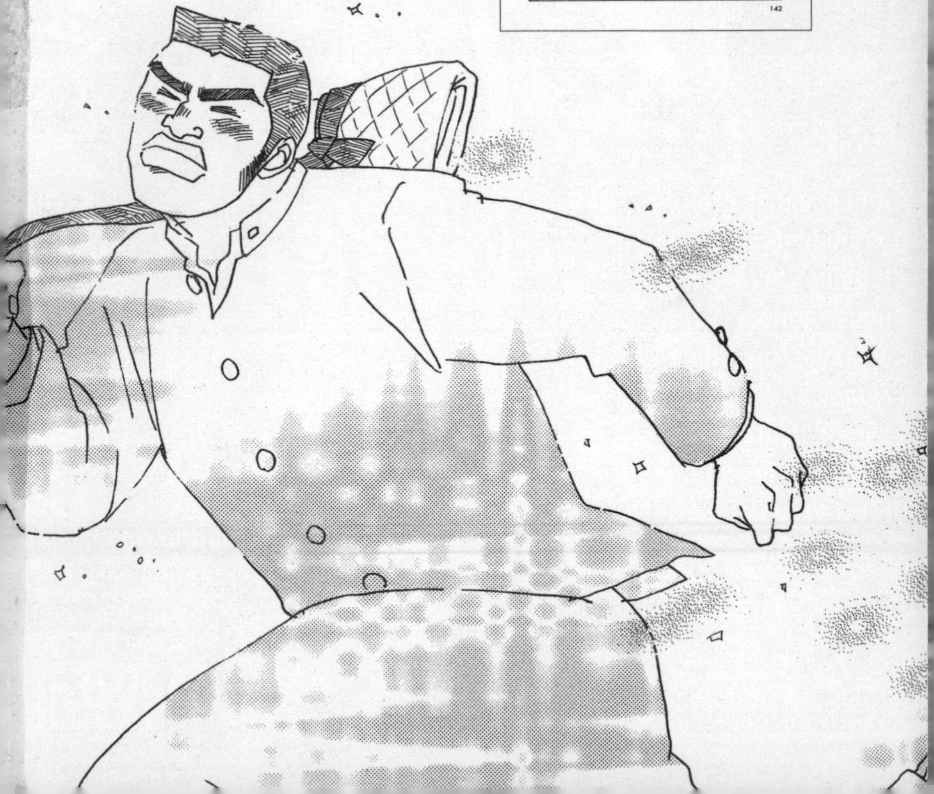